QUALITATIVE COMMUNICATION RESEARCH METHODS

CURRENT COMMUNICATION
AN ADVANCED TEXT SERIES

Series Editor

Jesse G. Delia   *University of Illinois*

CURRENT COMMUNICATION is a series of advanced texts spanning the full range of the communication curriculum and including all the core ideas of the field. Each volume in the series is a substantive, lucidly written book appropriate for use in advanced undergraduate and beginning graduate level courses. All the volumes survey current theories and concepts, research and critical literatures, and scholarly methods, but each does this within a distinctive and original framework that makes the material accessible to students while enhancing and shaping understanding of its area for professionals.

QUALITATIVE COMMUNICATION RESEARCH METHODS

THOMAS R. LINDLOF

Current Communication: An Advanced Text Series   Volume 3

SAGE Publications
International Educational and Professional Publisher
Thousand Oaks   London   New Delhi

For Tim Meyer

For information address:

SAGE Publications, Inc.
2455 Teller Road
Thousand Oaks, California 91320

SAGE Publications Ltd.
6 Bonhill Street
London EC2A 4PU
United Kingdom

SAGE Publications India Pvt. Ltd.
M-32 Market
Greater Kailash I
New Delhi 110 048 India

Printed in the United States of America

Library of Congress Cataloging-in-Publication Data

Lindlof, Thomas R.
   Qualitative communication research methods / Thomas R. Lindlof.
      p.   cm. — (Current communication ; v. 3)
   Includes bibliographical references and index.
   ISBN 0-8039-3517-X (cloth). — ISBN 0-8039-3518-8 (pbk.)
   1. Communication—Research—Methodology.   I. Title. II. Series.
   P91.3.L56   1994
   302.2'072—dc20   94-26079

95 96 97 98 99   10 9 8 7 6 5 4 3 2 1

Sage Production Editor: Astrid Virding

Contents

Preface

Among the many changes in the study of communication since the early 1980s, few have been more striking than the turn to new methods of inquiry—especially those that engage the processes, contexts, and meanings of communication. The best-known name for these methods is *qualitative research*. Others that are used include *ethnography, field study, naturalistic study,* and *case study*. What they have in common is *lived experience* as a subject of systematic study: how people understand who they are, socially and culturally, through their actions, their discourses, and the perceptions they develop of themselves and each other.

Qualitative approaches try to bring us close to the performances and practices of communication. The qualitative inquirer seeks somehow to get inside this action. The research "instrument" is the human investigator, who reflexively becomes part of both the action and the ensuing description. The "human subject" is the other, whom we respect and from whom we learn much. The "data" are texts, which change over time as the researcher's interests, knowledge, and abilities change. The "products" are typically full of voices, stories, events, interpretations, hypotheses, and claims.

Even in these brief remarks, it is clear that the very notions of "inside" and "outside" are artifacts of a way of scientific thinking that separates experience from knowing. This duality does not fit well with the work of the qualitative inquirer, who lives the ethnographic life by relating social intimacy to analytic distance over a period of time. Experiencing and knowing join together in complex, often surprising ways.

This volume is meant primarily for readers who already have a working knowledge of communication theory, concepts, and processes, and of the scientific method. It is meant both for readers who want to become practitioners and for those who want to become more effective users and critics of communication scholarship.

The "qualitative research" of this book concerns the empirical study of communication from an interpretive, or cultural-hermeneutical, perspective. Some related research traditions that are *not* covered here include rhetorical (or textual) criticism, critical theorizing, and structural approaches to conversation analysis. These types of inquiry can sometimes offer useful frames for conceptualizing a field study and elucidating its consequences, but their operational procedures are intended for uses other than apprehending the cultural or social meanings in situated communicative action.

In this book I undertake several tasks. Most important, the volume is intended to serve as a guide to doing qualitative research of communication. Chapters 3 through 8 take the reader through the stages, techniques, and challenges of fieldwork in roughly the order they are encountered in a typical project. Because current research practice is wide-ranging, I provide an array of options for carrying out a study. I do not try to narrow this diversity in order to fit any single vision of what qualitative inquiry should be. This approach should enable readers to make choices of method that align most productively with their specific research problems.

Presenting the intellectual issues that animate the practice of qualitative inquiry is also a central goal. In the first chapter, the reader will find an account of some of the recent history of communication's engagement with different epistemologies and methodologies. Also in that chapter, the reader will learn what is distinctive about the subjects that qualitative communication researchers study: the performances and practices of communication. Chapter 2 gives an overview of the interpretive paradigm in the human sciences and some of the research programs that have influenced qualitative communication study. Other chapters treat some of the conceptual, ethical, and political issues that often affect the conduct of research. These discussions focus on the field situations in which these issues often arise.

It is not easy to think through the possibilities of a procedure without having already experienced it in some way. In a text such as this one, the goal of helping the reader learn to think through such possibilities can be achieved most readily through the inclusion of many relevant examples of research practice. Some of these examples come from my own experience in media studies, but most are drawn from published work in several areas of communication research: interpersonal, mass, organizational, small group, and so on. These examples are not intended to be definitive of research practice. Rather, they have been chosen to represent the variety of research subjects, techniques, and styles that prevails in recent communication scholarship.

A number of people have given their time and expertise toward completion of this book. Deserving special acknowledgment are those who read drafts of chapters and provided detailed comments: Debra Grodin, Chris Foreman, John F. Clark, and James Lull. James A. Anderson gave the manuscript a final, thorough reading, which resulted in many positive changes. Kerry Kind, Joel Kailing, and John F. Clark provided bibliographic and source-finding services. I am also grateful for comments from graduate students in two classes in qualitative communication research—at the University of Kentucky and the University of Montana (thanks to Martha J. Einerson)—who read and used several of the chapters; these were very helpful "field tests."

James A. Anderson, Thomas Benson, and James Lull offered fine critiques of the project when it was being proposed. Douglas A. Boyd, dean of the College of Communications and Information Studies at the University of Kentucky, gave me encouragement and sound advice all along the way, and provided support for my research and writing. Ann West, former communication editor at Sage Publications, stayed in touch regularly and exhibited remarkable patience when the going got tough. Sophy Craze, current communication editor at Sage, effectively managed the final stage of editing, and Astrid Virding saw the book through the production process and into print.

I want to thank my wife, Joanne, for putting up with the beast for the first 14 months of our marriage. She lifted my spirits often, and made it possible for me to finish.

Finally, I dedicate the book to Timothy P. Meyer. It was through my discussions with Tim and his pioneering work that I first encountered qualitative inquiry as a graduate student and began to apply it to my interests in communication. He is a gifted scholar and teacher, my mentor, and a generous friend.

THOMAS R. LINDLOF

1

Introduction to
Qualitative Communication Studies

In Their Own Words, Through Their Own Actions

The people of Wheaton, Kentucky, and surrounding countryside pick up their mail, buy their stamps, and send off their parcels at the Wheaton post office. But much more goes on there than just post office business. When something surprising, unusual, or important happens around Wheaton, discussion of it usually surfaces there. Joel's last three weeks of observation took place while rumors were flying around town about a Satanic cult in the area. A lot of high school students were convinced that some young person in the county was about to be murdered by this group, and many of the adults thought it was more than just a hoax. Almost every person who came to the post office had something to say about the story. Often the conversation would continue without pause as one participant left and another came in.

At one point, two of the regular patrons were talking about this "stuff" when Bill arrived. Without telling him what they were talking about, they asked him what he knew. Bill responded, "They didn't find a thing," and proceeded to tell them about all the police, the sheriff, and the K-9s who had been searching around the railroad in front of his house the

1

previous evening. They were looking for evidence of the cult, but had found none. On a previous night, however, some Satanic paraphernalia had allegedly been discovered in a railroad underpass just outside Wheaton.

In his final visits to the post office, Joel didn't hear whether or not the alleged find was confirmed; in fact, the Satanic cult speculations tailed off altogether. For a while, post office conversation returned to the usual concerns—the weather, tobacco farming, and the national news. Then one day a woman came in and announced that a member of her family had returned from fighting one of the forest fires that were raging that fall, and a discussion ensued about marijuana growers being the ones who set the fires.

The state had just enacted sweeping reform of its public school system, and a massive tax increase had been legislated to pay for it. Excitement and expectations were running high. Educators recognized that the new reforms would be watched closely, both by those inside the state who had staked their political capital to them and by those outside the state who hailed them as a model. It was now up to the educational establishment to make the reforms work, and nowhere was this felt more keenly than at the college of education at the state's leading research university.

Recently, Monica had been hired by the college of education to improve its public relations. She saw this situation as an opportunity to study how the college "tells its story" of research and training activities to external constituencies and to the public. She began to scrutinize as data the normal flow of information that passed through her work life. Fund-raising materials, video features, bulletins, pamphlets, press releases, and newsletters became pieces for making sense of an organizational puzzle. Increasingly, however, Monica found the meetings and other events she attended to be personally unsettling. She was there as a publicity writer, but she was also there seeking to understand the actions of people who tried, sometimes failed, and occasionally succeeded in ambivalent roles.

One such scene of cross-purposes was found in the college's relationship with the media. For example, the university's public relations officials seemed to define "news" as whatever is timely, or can be made to appear timely. They often complained that they didn't hear about stories "in time to do anything about them." A preference also seemed to exist for stories in the form of announcements or media events, the splashier the better. At a small gala hosted by the college, one PR official said to a college faculty member, "Now *this* is worth more than all those little stories you keep sending us." On another occasion, a faculty member spoke ruefully about the way she viewed the typical coverage of college events: "You have to wait until the provost or the president of the university shows up, and then they'll get the credit, as usual. You never hear about the people who really do the work." And later, the education reporter for the local newspaper told Monica that one problem with writing stories about the college was that educators often use excessive "inside jargon," which he thought muddied issues rather than clarified them.

Though she found the people she worked with in the college to be remarkable achievers, and though she concluded in her report that educators and the mass media could work together more effectively if they understood each other's missions better, at the end of the study Monica found it hard not to be a little saddened by it all.

These are glimpses of qualitative communication researchers at work. Joel and Monica were in fact graduate students learning the craft of ethnography, and their stories reveal much about how research problems begin and develop, what researchers think is significant, and how researchers become part of the process of investigation.[1]

Both Joel and Monica came to see something of interest in their own immediate surroundings as amenable to systematic study. Joel resided with his family in Wheaton, and noticed that most of the community's citizens participated in informal, ritualized interactions at a public site, the local post office. His previous experiences—living in villages overseas and in American cities and towns—sensitized him to many of these performances. In other words, his familiarity with similar scenes enabled him to understand rather rapidly what was happening in the post office. Yet it was his analytic interests and abilities—being able to make the experience topical—that created the detachment he needed to recognize it as a research site and to consider what the postmaster and the local patrons did as evidence of communicative actions and contexts. As the study progressed, initial curiosity and speculation gave way to the development of themes, supported by data, concerning community building, the mediation of news, and the functions of "entertainment" and "being neighborly" in a small town.

Monica had worked as a professional writer before. She knew first-hand the tensions that can exist between creative people and the businesspeople who hire them and monitor and use their work. As it had for Joel, this experiential analogue came easily to her. She recognized, and probably empathized with, certain problems faced by the college's administrators, faculty, and staff. As her qualitative research project began, the routine elements of her job started turning into the stuff of organizational symbolic realities. As the ending of the passage above indicates, this transformation was not without its cost to the researcher. The challenge for Monica, as for Joel and most qualitative inquirers, was to relate productively the stances of participation and detachment for long periods of time.

What of the researchers' choices of methodology? Joel's primary approach to data collection was through what is known as *participant observation*. As the term implies, the researcher using this method becomes a participating member of an existing culture, group, or setting, usually adopting a role that other members recognize as contextually appropriate and nonthreatening to them. By participating in the activities of a group or setting, the researcher gains insight into the constraints, motivations, emotions, and meanings that the members experience. Effective participation—in the sense of being able to act, think, and feel as a true participant would—is thought by many to be prerequisite to making effective observations. Stated a little differently, observing based on minimal participation may fail to advance one toward the kind of knowledge usually sought by qualitative researchers: understanding of the lived experience of human beings.

In practical terms, the depth and quality of participation can vary widely. Even the degree to which the individual is known as a researcher is a matter of great variation. In Joel's case, participant status came from his being a resident (but not a native) of Wheaton, the pastor of a Wheaton church, a post office patron, and a graduate student "hanging around" the post office in order to do a study. Even in the small community of Wheaton, it is unlikely that all the people with whom Joel interacted in the post office were aware of all those levels of his participation, particularly the last one. As will be discussed in Chapter 5, the effects of disclosing one's research identity on the conduct and outcomes of a study are not always clear.

Participant observation is not a single method. If it can be called a method at all, participant observation is a method for self-reflexive learning. It depends for its success on the use of and reflection upon one's emotional responses to other human beings (Gans, 1982). Only by living an experience and then explicating what is significant about the (now past-tense) lived experience can a qualitative researcher bring a report back to a reader.

In addition to a great deal of observing in her daily rounds as a staff member, Monica conducted *interviews* of a kind typically employed in qualitative inquiry. Such interviews go by several names, with slightly different shadings of meaning and practice: *in-depth, unstructured, semistructured, intensive, collaborative*, and *ethnographic*. These interviews resemble conversations between equals. Most of what is said and meant by both interviewer and interviewee emerges jointly in interaction. Although the researcher often wants to cover certain areas going into an interview, relatively little structure is imposed on most of what the respondent says.

In qualitative research, one interviews people to understand their perspectives on a scene, to retrieve experiences from the past, to gain expert insight or information, to obtain descriptions of events or scenes that are normally unavailable for observation, to foster trust, to understand a sensitive or intimate relationship, or to analyze certain kinds of discourse. More specialized forms of interviewing, such as the life history and focus group interviews, are used to fit with particular theoretical schemes and with the nature of the participants selected for study.

It was also vital for Monica to consider *documents* and other *artifacts*, because her study concerned stories about the college of education disseminated by the mass media as well as materials processed inside the organization: announcements, memoranda, policy statements, minutes of meetings, research reports, and so on. The analysis of the artifacts of social life (Webb, Campbell, Schwartz, & Sechrest, 1966) is typically used to support more primary research strategies, such as interviewing or participant observation. In recent years, however, it has been argued that material culture (clothing, architecture, personal memorabilia, and the like) can function as a primary means of symbolic expression, and thus merits foreground treatment (Goodall, 1991). Moreover, visual media— for example, photographs, film, or video shot by the researcher, or by group members at the researcher's request—are sometimes used to document behavior, or to capture members' perspectives.

The techniques of participant observation, interviewing, document analysis, and visual-media recording, among others to be examined in this book, permit the sort of flexibility essential to qualitative work. It is the researcher, however, who decides how and when to engage phenomena within the field of action. Qualitative inquiry is personal, involved inquiry. If we hope to understand how people choose to express themselves in everyday life, we must come to terms with our own reasons for studying them.

These remarks about what are only snapshots of Monica's and Joel's time "in the field" convey a sense of the questions that animate this kind of inquiry: What is going on here? What is the communicative action that is being performed? How do they do it? How does it change over time? How do they evaluate what they do? What does it mean to them? How do they interpret what it means to others? How do *we* interpret and document how they act, what they tell us about what they know, and how they justify their actions? What is the relation of us to them, of self to other?

For the qualitative researcher, humans infuse their own actions, and the other actions and worlds to which they have access, with meanings. Meanings are not mere accessories to behaviors. Rather, it is the fact that we reflect on our completed actions, and imagine possible future actions, that makes what we do meaningful. In a world without meaning we would not make choices, because the concept of choice would not be available to us. The scope of choice available to us as social agents is influenced but not limited by genetic, biological, and material conditions (Anderson, 1991). We use cultural rules and resources to create communicative strategies in social interaction. This work of constructing the self through social communication is patterned in any culture, but it also exhibits innovation caused by changes in the environment and the ability of humans to symbolize their own behaviors at different levels of abstraction. These assumptions unite an often bewildering variety of research styles under the banner of qualitative inquiry. They are assumptions that articulate especially well with communication's interests in symbolic action, mutuality of perspective and knowledge, and intention.

Of Soft and Hard Science:
A Brief Historical Tour

This book is predicated on the belief that qualitative inquiry can undertake the task set by James Carey in 1975:

> To seize upon the interpretations people place on existence and to systematize them so they are more readily available to us. This is a process of making large claims from small matters: studying particular rituals, poems, plays, conversations, songs, dances, theories, and myths and gingerly reaching out to the full relations within a culture or a total way of life. (p. 190)

As I now write, 19 years after Carey's article appeared, the long dominance of social scientific communication research by objectivist (or empiricist, rationalist, positivist) science (Bochner, 1985) has been breached. Communication scholars do not as frequently proclaim their goal to be "the prediction and control of phenomena made possible by explanatory theories" (Craig, 1989, p. 107). The methodologies that support the program of objectivist science—especially the use of variable-analytic designs and probability statistics—no longer constitute the only means for doing credible research.[2] Certainly quantitative modes of research, and theories of communication behavior based on causal explanation, are alive and well. Their value is accepted by the great majority of communication scholars. However, there is a growing sense that disciplinewide agreement about the goals and epistemology of a communication science may not be achievable. Communication research now accommodates many different styles of inquiry, living side by side. Some accept this situation reluctantly, some welcome it, and some resist it.

This change occurred largely through the persuasiveness of argument. That is, the pluralism we now see came about by a process of debate by members of the communication discipline, along with the publication of some compelling "experiments" in the use of qualitative methods. Numerous forums organized during the 1980s were instrumental in shaping the new possibilities in communication (e.g., Benson, 1985; Dervin, Grossberg, O'Keefe, & Wartella, 1989; "Ferment in the Field," 1983). These shifts of purpose and practice are not at all unique to communication. In fact, they mirror (or, more often, follow) similar changes in other fields. Scholars looked outside the behaviorist tradition of American communication science for fresh inspiration: to sociology for its symbolic interactionist and phenomenological practice; to literary theory for new ideas about the relationship of readers and texts; to feminist and political theory for alternative explanations of power, agency, and social structure; to cultural studies for ways to integrate theory and method in the study of cultural communication.

Although communication's aspirations to full-fledged disciplinary status may not be helped by these trends, a good argument can be made that a coherent vision has been lacking all along (Peters, 1986). Disciplinary status may even be undesirable if it means that we have to sacrifice a diversity of ways to appreciate communicative phenomena (Bochner & Eisenberg, 1985; Pearce, 1985). In this book, however, I have chosen to characterize communication as a *discipline,* because that term references an understanding of communication phenomena shared by most of the works and authors cited and discussed herein: as practices and performances for constituting the world (Deetz, 1992a).

Because qualitative inquiry has not earned its place among the major communication research approaches by producing key advancements in knowledge, its legitimacy is still questioned. This skepticism has lost some of its edge and energy since the time of Carey's essay, but the schism on crucial research issues is still enacted in classrooms and scholarly convention meeting rooms, and sometimes in the articles published in communication journals. Thus it deserves to be heard and examined as a largely unwritten, but still potent, folklore.

Until recently in the history of the communication discipline, empirical qualitative studies were consigned to the margins of research activity and graduate training (Delia, 1987, pp. 69-73). This is not to say that no qualitative studies were done before the late 1970s, or that a qualitative emphasis was not evident in some types of inquiry. Indeed, Wartella (1987) traces some important, albeit neglected, field studies of children and media (mostly comic books, radio, and movies) from the first half of this century. Nearly all of those studies, however, were conducted by sociologists and social psychologists, rather than by self-identified communication scholars. In 1984, Anderson's survey (cited in Anderson, 1987) of ethnographies in the communication journal literature yielded only 16 examples over the prior five years. Even if one includes work that appears in books and in the journals of other social scientific disciplines, or under other descriptors besides ethnography, it is still true that until recently most qualitative communication research was done by a persistent few.

The outlook shared by most communication scientists until about 15 years ago was rather uncompromising. This view held that qualitative research was a patently "soft" brand of social science, if indeed it was science at all. Among scientists there are few judgments more damning, or dismissive, than calling a work soft, and softness was found *everywhere* in the qualitative endeavor.

What does *soft science* mean? In technical terms, it describes research that uses measurement instruments that are not precise enough to discriminate the things of interest, usually in order to assign numerical values to them. It describes studies that report only selected excerpts of data, not all of the data. It refers to research reports that fail to describe the study methods in such clear and exacting detail that others can replicate the work. It describes studies that lack such standards of rigor as controls for random effects and other threats to internal validity, representative human samples, and ways of falsifying hypotheses. How can we accept a study's conclusions, the skeptic would ask, if plausible explanations cannot be ruled out? Studies that tell us about only one setting or group of people, at one point in time, are often called soft science. Such studies, it is argued, do not contribute to the development and testing of causal statements that are generalizable beyond local, idiosyncratic contexts.

These criticisms are directed at efforts that fail the tests of prediction and control, whereas qualitative inquirers strive to *understand* their objects of interest. Here, an explanation of the constitutive meanings of a phenomenon is sought. How an event occurs, how it functions in social contexts, and what it means to participants are all issues addressed from a cultural-hermeneutical, or interpretive, perspective. Understanding does not entail or require knowledge of how to predict or control a phenomenon. (I will return to the subject of the perspective of understanding in Chapter 2.)

But there is more to the charge of softness than technical matters. There are the attitudes and actions of the researcher to consider as well. Qualitative researchers appear to undertake the very suspect course of seriously studying the sentiments of their human subjects. Rather than treating people's utterances about themselves and their world as inaccurate accounts of social reality, or as outcomes determined by environmental forces, or as manifestations of cognitive processes, the qualitative researcher listens carefully to the utterances. The researcher moves about in the lives of certain people, and subjects and researcher become familiar to each other: they as something more (knowing, authentic) than human subjects, and he or she as possibly something less (exalted, authoritative) than a researcher. The people under study become known to the researcher through their social histories, their personal selves, and the stories they tell. The researcher responds visibly to these people, and the people respond to the researcher's response, and it all goes into the data record. Thus social intimacy is a basis for entering a domain of cultural or interpersonal experience. Later, social distance permits the researcher to interpret its forms and meanings.

Many of the topics of qualitative inquiry—derived from the scenes of organizations, subcultures, families, groups, and individuals—have also connoted a nonscientific softness. These topics are often part of the researcher's world, selected as much for their relevance to the researcher personally as for officially sanctioned communication theory. Some topics, such as gender inequity, are chosen because they represent problems in the politics of communication. Other topics attract attention because of their striking cultural character. For example, the topic of some people's jointly constructing their own scenarios based on *Star Trek* characters (Jenkins, 1988) may be judged trivial (or soft) because, among other reasons, it concerns an esoteric activity engaged in by a small number of people outside what are considered to be important human pursuits. Such cultural performances might be judged irrelevant to the development of universal propositions about media effects. Questions about the fitness of topics add to the notoriety of doing qualitative research.

To sum up, until recently, the work produced by practitioners of qualitative social science was burdened by a reputation of softness. It seemed too imprecise, value laden, and particularistic to be of much use in generating general or causal explanations of communication behavior. This portrait may seem a bit overdrawn now, but only because (a) it is in print; (b) it is portrayed as a limited-player game in which one of the players exercised the power to label others and make it stick, at least temporarily; and (c) it is part of a past that many present-day qualitative researchers either never experienced or have revised in their memories and accounts. The difference between then and now is *not* the absence of labels or an alleged schism. Some communication scholars still contest their values along roughly similar lines (e.g., Bostrom & Donohew, 1992; Fitzpatrick, 1993; Rosengren, 1993). Rather, the difference is twofold.

First, the communication research community as a whole has more understanding of the purposes and methods of interpretive, cultural, and critical approaches. Many communication scientists now acknowledge that inquiries based in the contingencies of meaning can produce insights about the human condition. And qualitative methods are more suitable than quantitative methods for addressing certain questions about culture, interpretation, and power. For these purposes, the "soft" aspects of qualitative inquiry—especially its relational style of fieldwork, its inductive mode of analysis, and its resistance to closure—may be seen as strong attributes indeed.

Second, qualitative scholars can now explain what they mean by thorough, adequate, and meaningful research in an affirmative tenor— even if they do so in many different voices. As is the case anywhere, one needs to have access to the resources of communication to be able to say anything, much less be heard. Otherwise, particular arguments will be excluded—or will be "spoken for" by others. This empowerment occurred during the 1980s, as the qualitative study of communication grew into a thriving area of some visibility and accomplishment. The number of published articles and papers presented at conferences clearly rose during that decade. Journals were established that incorporated a focus on qualitative, naturalistic, and cultural studies (e.g., *Critical Studies in*

Mass Communication, Research on Language and Social Interaction, Cultural Studies). Many of the older journals began to display broader perspectives in their editorial policies and editorial boards. Several academic book publishers actively sought and published cultural/critical communication works. Many bibliographies, reviews, and anthologies bolstered the view that a "critical mass" of theory, methodological arguments, and exemplar studies useful to qualitative communication studies had developed (e.g., Anderson, 1987; Arneson & Weber, n.d.; Herndon & Kreps, 1993; Jensen & Jankowski, 1991; Lemish & Lemish, 1982; Lindlof, 1987b, 1991; Lull, 1990; Pauly, 1991; Philipsen & Carbaugh, 1986).

Out of this period, several subfields in communication developed bodies of empirical work grounded in interpretive or cultural perspectives. A few of these can be discussed briefly here. In *mass communication*, audience ethnography attained prominence mainly as a result of two different events: the recognition by critical theorists of the limits of purely textual and political-economic analysis and the dissatisfaction of many American communication researchers with the limits of empiricist models of audience research. Both communities found their own paths to the discovery of qualitative inquiry: critical theorists through what is called cultural studies (heavily influenced by semiotic and poststructuralist theories), and American mass communication researchers through social phenomenology and other interpretive social science approaches (this is a simplistic account, because both communities borrowed from each other's ideas). Yet the rapid development of audience ethnography has produced insights into the social uses and rules of media, the interpretation of meanings in mainstream media texts, and how specialized or subcultural forms of mediated communication develop (Anderson & Meyer, 1988; Lindlof, 1991; Morley, 1992). Similarly, in the area of development communication, ethnography is seen as an approach that can study local realities and needs without imposing the value assumptions of traditional media effects research (Bourgault, 1992).

Another domain of mass communication in which qualitative analysis has made inroads is that of the production of content in media organizations. Participant observation work has examined the social construction of news in the routines of journalists and newsrooms (Lester, 1980; Tuchman, 1991) and the processes of producing entertainment programs (Gitlin, 1983; Mast, 1983; Saferstein, 1991).

Organizational communication researchers turned to interpretive models and philosophies in the early 1980s partly out of frustration with the barrenness of rationalist and functionalist explanations (Putnam &

Pacanowsky, 1983). They learned from their colleagues in management (as well as from popular authors and their own experiences as paid consultants) that organizations can be likened to cultures. That is, an organization does some of the same things a traditionally defined culture does: It initiates members and, sometimes, expels them; it creates and passes along myths and stories, often about the organization's leaders and critical events; it creates information to sustain and orient its activities; and it deals with internal and external threats to its continuance. The studies following from this perspective focus on such subjects as the performative and scripted aspects of organizational roles, the metaphors the organization represents to its members, and the actual practices enacted for creating corporate life (e.g., Goodall, 1991; Kelly, 1985; Pacanowsky & O'Donnell-Trujillo, 1982; Smircich & Calas, 1987).

Another dimension of this field uses critical theory to understand the ways power and domination are exercised in organizations through communication (e.g., Deetz, 1982, 1992b; Deetz & Mumby, 1990; Mumby, 1988; B. C. Taylor, 1990). The symbols and discourses of an organization represent sites of struggle over the interests of management, employees, and external constituencies. Much of this research examines the communicative means of organizational control and the kinds of legitimacy an organization seeks to impose through its control mechanisms.

In *interpersonal communication*, qualitative applications are evident in studies of the rules and situated accomplishments of speech and nonverbal communication. This area owes much, but not all, of its direction to contributions from ethnomethodology (especially the interest in communication rules) and the perspective called the ethnography of communication, pioneered by Dell Hymes (see Chapter 2). The empirical study of routine communication conduct—for example, in sorority rushes (Knuf, 1989-1990), discourse in the *Donahue* television program (Carbaugh, 1988b), and nursing home adjustment (Sigman, 1986)— forms the basis for positing cultural codes and rituals and theorizing about the kinds of sense making those codes and rituals represent. The analysis of performances, such as nonverbal gestures (Ray, 1987) or adult male talk (Philipsen, 1975), can also lend insight into how a community's understandings and relationships are communicatively constructed.

Other kinds of interpersonal research focus on the concepts that underlie such forms of social life as family and friendship (e.g., Jorgenson, 1989; Katriel & Philipsen, 1981; Rawlins, 1983, 1989). In most of these studies, the self is conceptualized as relational and cultural in nature, rather than as a self-sufficient ego. Interest centers on the ways in which people describe their relational bonds, and the dilemmas and difficulties they encounter.

Communicative Performances and Practices

Our understanding of qualitative inquiry begins with what it seeks to investigate, interpret, and describe. For sociologists, the social collectivity—its organization, functions, and change processes—is the object of interest. Anthropologists have traditionally studied the global diversity of forms of human life. For communication inquirers, the fields of study are the performances and practices of human communication. In communicating, humans signify to each other what they mean by using physical signs that mediate time and space. In order for a person to construct a sign, or to make sense of one, he or she must know its social use value in the specific situation, and in the culture generally. Whether the sign is designed to achieve congruency or to control, there is always a concern with the meanings it produces. It follows, then, that communicating is virtually indistinguishable from the making of meanings in all their contexts.

Communicative practices and performances—of competence, belief, knowledge, and valuation—constitute the textures of our everyday life experiences and the way we act on our interests. Through them we enact the meanings of our relationships in dyads, families, groups, organizations, institutions, and technologies. Virtually any act of communication can be studied as a kind of performance, which can in turn be viewed as a skillful variation on a practice. Even the behavioral effects of a message—a time-honored problem of communication science—can be reinscribed in terms of communicative performance and practice. An example may help to distinguish these different ways of conceptualizing communication.

Consider an experimental study of how young children behave following exposure to a television program that contains acts of violence. Such a study might be done at a day-care center, for a more naturalistic dimension. The construction of hypotheses logically precedes the execution of this study, and informs both the assignment of values to behaviors and the subsequent analyses. Because sex is probably a salient factor, the researcher would want to code the behaviors of boys and girls separately. For the experimentalist, a boy in the treatment group who hits a stand-up doll after viewing television violence may be exhibiting a "disinhibition" effect (a cued release from normal self-control). Such a conclusion would follow from coding many children's behaviors using a standardized coding system and testing experimental and control group differences of aggression scores against one or more hypotheses. However, it is likely that the explanation of disinhibition guided the experimentalist's thinking from the start, rather than arose from what was interpreted at the scene. In this experimental protocol, the *situated performance* of an act and *what the act means* for a subject are not important. Certainly what the individual boy did in hitting the doll is not of much interest to the experimentalist.

What if a qualitative analyst is present at the experiment, and has the chance to do her own investigation? Probably she would ask a very different set of questions, almost all of which would arise from what she witnesses at the scene. Concerning the boy hitting the doll, she might ask: What was the boy doing before it happened? How did he approach the doll, and how did he follow through in the action? What was his reaction to what he did? Were other children or staff members watching, and what did they do? How did the boy feel as he "smacked it" (*his* term for what he did, as she found out)? What did the boy say and do earlier in the day, as the procedure was being explained to all of the children? The analyst then tries different readings of the "aggressive" act. Was it a bid for attention, or an effort to best another child's slap at the doll, or a mocking of the experiment itself? Was it a "play" act or a "serious" act? As the inquiry proceeds, and other evidence is gathered, the boy's performance begins to make sense.

The child's hitting performance is finally described. Specific social and cultural conditions enable this child to perform a meaningful action, which is then interpreted locally by the boy himself and by others as a completed act. The description includes an analysis of the performance as an event, including what it means to the boy and others, which the researcher organizes into an explanation of the practices of this child-care facility and of the experimental protocol itself—that is, how "behavioral academic research at a public day-care center" is done. The significance of a performance is expanded by the analyst's consideration of many levels of evidence and the part that she played in the action she interprets.

PERFORMANCES

In performing, people engage in symbolic actions with respect to things that are meaningful to them. Not only do utterances and gestures signify unique senses or attitudes for specific occasions, but documents, clothing, and countless other artifacts also enter into the making of communicative action (e.g., Katriel & Farrell, 1991; Lachmann, 1988). In fact, in any situation in which people define a purpose for acting, it is practically impossible *not* to perform. Even silent inattention, pauses, repetitions, or listening can indicate symbolic expression (Basso, 1988). Folklorist Richard Bauman (1986) conceives of performance as "a mode of communication, a way of speaking, the essence of which resides in the assumption of responsibility to an audience for a display of communicative skill, highlighting the way in which communication is carried out, above and beyond its referential content" (p. 3). Although Bauman is interested in oral storytelling, his definition can be applied as well to bodily performance, as in the above example of the "violence experiment." Conquergood (1991) writes:

> Performance-centered research takes as both its subject matter and method the experiencing body situated in time, place, and history. The performance paradigm insists on face-to-face encounters instead of abstractions and reductions. It situates ethnographers within the delicately negotiated and fragile "face-work" that is part of the intricate and nuanced dramaturgy of everyday life. (p. 187)

In their treatment of the concept as it applies to mediated communication, Anderson and Meyer (1988) define performance as "an *improvisation* on the premises of the routines of social action, locally produced and under local control" (p. 140; emphasis added). Said more simply, it is the *carrying out of communicative acts in sensible form* that makes what we do performing. We engage our choices of messaging in different ways and with different effects, according to our skills, passions, cultural knowledge, and the circumstances of the moment.

However, improvising is also engendered from what we think is expected of a certain type of performance. These expectations may be inferred from an actual audience at the event, or from a "generalized other" (Mead, 1934) who is not literally present at the moment of performance. We perform not just for ourselves, but for ourselves in relation to responsive others.

Although the notion of performance might seem to relate only to acts happening in natural settings, this is not the case; it applies also to interviews and other contrived situations. In fact, qualitative techniques often call for the elicitation of specific kinds of interview performances, as will become clear in Chapter 6. Performances constitute essential evidence of how communicating gets done, and with what effects in the immediate scene. Analyses of performances offer insight into the processes of human affiliation, celebration, discord, and deviance, and they are necessary as well to the examination of the practices of communication.

PRACTICES

It is no exaggeration to say that people make sense of who they are and how they get through the day by their knowledge of communicative practices. A practice constitutes *a way of doing things* that is sanctioned by a social collectivity. One becomes practiced in standardizing one's performances in order to bring off situational roles faithfully.

In a sense, then, the coin of a communicative act has two sides. Performances are the personal, unique, emergent, improvised side. Practices are the generic, routinized, socially monitored, and socially enforced side. Both are present in any act of communication.

Let us consider Morley's (1986) study of television viewing in British families as an example of an analysis of practices. Among several conclusions, Morley notes that there are differences in the ways men and women engage in home viewing. Men are more interested in manipulating the channel selector, more proficient at operating the VCR, make most of the videotaping and video rental decisions, and tend to view unbothered by other needs of the household. Women approach viewing with a different set of practices and meanings. They tend to view their favorite programs alone, when men are not around. In their remarks to Morley, women seemed to adopt the men's definitions of their own viewing practices as passive, nonserious, and a waste of time. Morley claims that these viewing practices derive from a general pattern of gender relations in British working-class culture. As a performance, television use was undoubtedly improvised somewhat differently in each instance Morley studied.[3] But it was gendered practices that formed the heart of his analysis. It was not so much how men and women carried out instances of viewing that impressed Morley, as it was the strong patterning of their reported viewing within the construct of gender.

As social actors, we are highly conscious of the quality of our performances, but pay less attention to our communicative practice, which tends to be tacit. Moreover, as Morley's study shows, different social actors may play different parts in a practice and see those parts differently. According to Giddens (1986), decisions about how people use language derive from a "practical consciousness," that is, "from the methods which speakers and agents use in the course of practical action to reach 'interpretations' of what they and others do" (p. 538). The cultural reasoning behind these methods may fade from conscious awareness once they have been successfully learned, or the social actor may learn to account for them in a shorthand manner. A practice has a way of becoming "second nature." It becomes "what everyone knows"— common sense.

When examining the taken-for-granted character of communicative practices, qualitative researchers often theorize about what institutional purposes are served by the acceptance of the practices as natural. Such purposes are sometimes viewed by analysts as subversive of people's true interests. For example, in business settings, the corporate ideology of superior management knowledge may, in the long run, foster worker acquiescence (Alvesson, 1991; Deetz, 1992b). As ideologies are always expressed symbolically, qualitative studies may be needed to document a "false consensus" in the communicative practices of an organization. Potentially, such studies can raise awareness of the political or economic biases of management, and even suggest some ways to reform a system. However, communication scholars continue to debate whether the analyst's primary goal should be the description or the critique of values discerned in communicative practices (Carbaugh, 1991; Fiske, 1991b).

PERFORMANCES AND PRACTICES COMPARED

We should not draw too sharp a distinction between performance and practice. The interdependence of the two has already been asserted: Practices must be performed, and performances are carried out with respect to normative references (practices). A practice represents a criterion for behaving that is upheld by and responsible to an institution, relationship, or ideology. A performance is an exemplar-in-action of that criterion; it is always contingent on circumstances, and prevents a practice from ever being completely stable or final.[4]

Performances concern individual events. Like a narrative, a performance has its invoking conditions, its external movements and internal motivations, and its finalizing moments. Communicative performances are rich with symbolization. The analyst closely studies the content and modes of communicative action, including aspects of emotion, thought, personal bearing, style, and story. Finally, performances are "authored" by individuals. They are geared into others' performances, and are performed before and critiqued by audiences. We need the perspective of the ones doing the performing to know what they do and why they do it. In all, there is creativity in the ways people construct their performances. The actor's interactional skills, use of resources, and sense of timing all go into the making of controlled artworks of communication.

Practices inform us about how the role requirements in a social system are enacted in specific contexts. Practices imply a focus on the routine and the recurring. One analyzes practices as recipes for constructing a certain kind of interpersonal or organizational reality. Therefore, communicative practice is apt to be defined by its structure and its rules, and not so much by message content or style, or by the subtleties of the moment. Practices are "authored" within institutions, in that a practice exists before a particular actor arrives on stage to perform it. They do not change easily over time, but *will* change if a performance can be considered to have solved a problem, created a problem, or opened possibilities for changing practices.

Many of the practices studied by communication analysts seem to be enacted by people in a tacit, even unconscious, manner. How this happens, and why it continues, is an enduring concern to many. However, it usually applies only to the practices in which *we* as social actors engage. The practices of the "other"—the other ethnic group, the other economic class, the other gender—often appear to us as exotic, fascinating, deviant, repugnant, or incomprehensible, mostly because the normative reference of the other's performances is unclear. Certainly both of these are compelling themes for the qualitative inquirer.

Defining Terms

Before venturing further, I should acknowledge that the term *qualitative* is inconsistently defined in communication and the other social sciences, and is often confounded with other terms that share some of its properties. In some cases, the differences are crucial for how we use specific methods and arguments. Therefore, I offer below a clarification of the way *qualitative* and other terms are to be developed in this book, beginning with the cognate terms.[5]

NATURALISTIC INQUIRY

The term *naturalistic inquiry* is often used interchangeably with *naturalism*, which takes cultural description as its primary objective. Naturalism proposes that the indigenous behaviors and meanings of a people can be understood only through a close analysis of "natural" settings (Hammersley & Atkinson, 1983, pp. 6-9). Natural settings are the customary activity arenas for those being studied. According to Denzin (1977), "Naturalism implies a profound respect for the character of the empirical world. It demands that the investigator take his theories and methods to that world" (p. 31).

The naturalist's injunction that social actions be studied in their own contexts does not mean that contrived situations, such as interviews, are avoided. On the contrary, a host of data-gathering techniques is used in the study of social settings, including informant interviews, maps of settings, and artifact analysis. The naturalistic inquirer combines different techniques to compensate for the limitations of each one individually. This practice underscores naturalism's concern with discovering a single objective reality.

However, in their quest for full ecological validity, naturalists sometimes ignore the effects of the research itself (Hammersley & Atkinson, 1983, pp. 10-14). They try to document what is going on "out there," but the "there-ness" also includes their own research presence. For naturalistic and all other kinds of social research, the researcher cannot claim a privileged position separate from the phenomena being studied. It is to the credit of interpretive forms of inquiry that this reflexivity is accepted explicitly. The practice of *reflexive* analysis—accounting for the researcher's own role in social action—sensitizes the researcher to the different orders of reality in a scene (Myerhoff & Ruby, 1982). Guba and Lincoln (1982) note that "naturalistic approaches [should] take full advantage of the not inconsiderable power of the human-as-instrument, providing a more than adequate trade-off for the presumably more 'objective' approach that characterizes rationalistic inquiry" (p. 235).

ETHNOGRAPHY

The term *ethnography* does not imply any single method or type of data analysis, although participant observation is a strategy that nearly all ethnographers employ. Nor do ethnographers disavow the use of quantification. On the contrary, they often use censuses and statistical procedures to analyze patterns or to determine who or what to sample (e.g., Silverman, 1985). Ethnographers also sometimes employ diagnostic tests, personality inventories, and other measurement tools (Pelto & Pelto, 1978). Basically, ethnographers will turn to any method that will help them to achieve the goals of good ethnography.

Ethnography is a matter of the epistemic posture of the researcher, the manner of engagement with the social scene, and the kind of research story that is told. The term itself is explained by it roots, *ethno* (people) and *graphy* (describing). Thus ethnography usually involves a holistic description of cultural membership. As a descriptive enterprise, ethnography is distinguished from ethnology, which is the comparison, explanation, and classification of cultures (Spradley & McCurdy, 1972). By *holistic* I mean that an ethnography traditionally tries to describe *all* relevant aspects of a culture's material existence, social system, and collective beliefs and experiences. "Thickness" of description is a key attribute of ethnography (Geertz, 1973). The more detail that goes into the description, the more multidimensional our understanding, and the more meaning each element of the culture holds for the reader. Meanings are the value-added component of thick description.

With anthropologist Bronislaw Malinowski's visits to the Trobriand islands in the 1920s, ethnography became identified with "living intimately and for a prolonged period of time within a single native community whose language [the researcher] had mastered" (M. L. Wax, 1972, p. 7). Prolonged engagement of the researcher in a culture became not only the norm, but the *sine qua non* of ethnographic fieldwork. Generations of students in anthropology went to far-off locales to undergo the same disciplinary baptism through fieldwork. Like Malinowski before them, ethnographers live inside the life space of the cultural membership ("intimately"). Within that space, the ethnographer must make decisions about the appropriate mix of perspectives through which cultural phenomena are studied. However, such decisions must be made *with* the culture members in some manner, because it is they who admit the ethnographer into their midst and open activities of their group to scrutiny. The documenting of social life and other aspects of culture can be realized only through negotiation with the people being studied.

Finally, in ethnography, process and product are joined closely. Ethnography is textual in the dual sense that (a) writing is a key activity in all phases of field research, and (b) writing "fixes" cultural analysis within the dialectic of field relations worked out between researcher and culture members. It is the second point especially that has raised questions in recent years about the descriptive goal of ethnography (see Chapter 8). What is left in and what is left out, whose point of view is represented, and how the scenes of social life are depicted become very important matters for assessing the value of the ethnographic text (Clifford & Marcus, 1986).

QUALITATIVE RESEARCH

Fundamentally, qualitative researchers seek to preserve the form and content of human behavior and to analyze its qualities, rather than subject it to mathematical or other formal transformations. As Anderson and Meyer (1988) note, "Qualitative research methods are distinguished from quantitative methods in that they do not rest their evidence on the logic of mathematics, the principle of numbers, or the methods of statistical analysis" (p. 247). Actual talk, gesture, and other social action are the raw materials of analysis.

Unlike naturalistic inquiry, qualitative study does not need to be carried out in the habitat of the culture members. For instance, many qualitative studies are based solely on interview data. Unlike ethnography, qualitative study does not always take holistic account of a fully interacting group with an enduring history (Press, 1989b). In fact, studies using qualitative methods often focus on only some partial set of relationships in group life or on one aspect of a scene.

Despite these differences, qualitative research has a great deal in common with both ethnography and naturalistic inquiry. In fact, most scholars and other professionals tend to think of qualitative research as the broader concept. A useful perspective is offered by Lofland (1971), who views qualitative inquiry in terms of the questions it asks:

> What kinds of things are going on here? What are the forms of this phenomenon? What variations do we find in this phenomenon? That is, qualitative analysis is addressed to the task of delineating forms, kinds and types of social phenomena; of documenting in loving detail the things that exist. (p. 13)

These characteristics—a logic of discovery and attention to the diverse forms and details of social life—are shared by nearly all approaches that are interested in human understanding. They converge on issues of how humans articulate and interpret their social and personal interests.

For the purposes of this book, then, qualitative research is understood to be an approach that subsumes most of what goes by the names of ethnography and naturalistic inquiry. It also includes several approaches that go by other names: case study, action research, collaborative research, phenomenological research, field study, and interpretive interactionism, among many others (Tesch, 1990). They are all qualitative, by virtue of the following characteristics:

- They all have theoretical interest in human interpretational processes.
- They all are concerned with the study of socially situated human action and artifacts.
- They all use human investigators as the primary research instruments (and all involve the application of reflexive analysis).
- They all rely primarily on narrative forms for coding data and writing the texts to be presented to audiences.

The qualitative researcher usually begins a study out of a personal and scholarly fascination with a phenomenon, and continues to respect its integrity while carrying out field activities. The researcher turns his or her attention to the forms and functions of the phenomenon as it operates in natural contexts. Yet a qualitative (or ethnographic or naturalistic) approach depends critically on the investigator's interacting with the subjects under study. To the extent possible, this is done on the subjects' turf, under the constraints they bear, and with the same consequences for acting. The researcher can attain an understanding of the subjects only insofar as he or she can participate in the subjects' own scope of interpretation.

Conclusion

If communication is primarily a matter of signifying meanings and purposes, then qualitative inquiry is interested in how signifying occurs and what it means for those who engage in it. This is no simple task, nor is it a lowly one. For too long in the history of communication scholarship, we have focused on what messages refer to, or the effects they have, without examining what messages are or how their articulation creates social realities for speakers and audiences. We have ignored the exquisite timing and skillfulness of the most obvious-seeming acts. We have glossed the cultural and historical variation of events of social participation, and failed to understand the profound ways in which communicating constitutes the rituals, functions, and power arrangements of contemporary life.

Objectivist science and quantitative methods have been insufficient to perform those tasks—not because these modes of inquiry are faulty, but because they advocate views of the world that do not value the study of situated, emergent, and reflexive human phenomena (Deetz, 1992a; Schwandt, 1989). I close this chapter with some brief discussions of the principal distinctions between objectivist and interpretive sciences.

Exact versus hermeneutical solutions. Objectivist science depends on literal meanings of events and processes that can be mathematicized in nonlinguistic propositions about which there can be universal agreement. Such propositions are themselves dependent on "meaning realism," or the notion that meanings always have fixed phenomenal referents. In other words, only those events that all inquirers can examine with respect to given meanings, and are therefore publicly available as "facts," merit scientific standing—which is why introspection and intuition are not generally valued as scientific tools.[6] Exact solutions are made possible by the development of measurement metrics for classes of facts—and their given meanings.

For interpretive science, meanings are an accomplishment of practical human action. Events are not endowed with meaning; rather, the very recognition of an event involves the creation of meaning by some community (C. Taylor, 1977), supported by cultural resources and enacted in readable performances. Such a science is based on the belief that human behavior is strategic, not causal, and is expressed in tactical performances. Moreover, the actor in a communicative performance is capable of entertaining many meanings of an event because of the reflexive character of linguistic discourse. All interpretive science solutions will be indeterminate, partial, and ever changing.

Determinacy versus agency. Objectivist theories propose mechanisms that govern the actions of objects. The world is assumed to be organized mechanistically so that *A* determines in some part the outcome of *B*, regardless of the action of the individual actor or the context of the performance. Control-type explanations predominate in objectivist communication science, and are the basis of the experimental physics upon which this model is founded. As a result, objectivist science's explanations aspire to be *nomothetic* in scope (i.e., explanations that apply to all instances of general types wherever they occur). However, not many human science theories approach this level of generality. The diversity of human cultures is implicitly recognized in the limited scope of theoretical statements.

For interpretive science, meanings arise out of the intentions, practical purposes, and reciprocal perspectives of the social actors. "Intention" is not just an abstraction that a researcher conjures up, or a black box in our theories. Intention can be detected in the goal-directedness of our acts of communication and in the explanations we give (Hawes, 1977). Communicative action is intended behavior. However, just because humans construct plans and try to carry them out does not mean they have free will. Subjective experience is not owned by the individual, but gets formulated only in some dialogical relation to others. We do invent new strategies for living, but only with the genres and materials given us, and subject to the critique of relevant interpretive communities. Certain traditional postulates of objectivist science—such as the idea that communication is an interaction of preexisting senders and receivers—become highly problematic once human agency is conceived as an emergent phenomenon (Stewart, 1991).

Representation versus interpretation. Objectivist science gives us a "representation" not only of the events under study but, more significant, their underlying causal mechanism. Again, the model is mathematics. By mapping a representation system onto some portion of the material world, objectivist science claims an authoritative account. The research text strives to be authorless: to present a picture of human behavior faithful to its own revealed meaning. Its writing standard is highly prescriptive, so that each scientist can claim to be writing "neutrally." The text persuades readers by logic, method, and evidence alone. Only the validity of facts can be contested, not issues of how the facts were constructed.

Interpretive science does not assume that a text contains one meaning for all who encounter it. Semiotics, in particular, has encouraged a view of texts as inherently ambiguous and unstable. The meaning of an interpersonal or technologically mediated text depends on its relationships to other texts, the competencies and interests of its interpreters, and the cultural conditions in which it is produced and read. The notion that meanings are continually constructed lies at the center of interpretive approaches in communication. This argument implies something very important: that *how* we describe the world constitutes *what* we describe. The language used in scientific discourse, then, becomes not just an instrument of description, but the very phenomenon we call science. This denies final authority to any scientific explanation, because the object of explanation becomes meaningful only in a discourse that is always changing, and whose signs refer only to other signs. In the final analysis, qualitative reports are all about perspectives of lived experience. The researcher must decide what kind of author he or she will be, and what sort of story to construct of the "facts" of the case.

Objective knowledge versus ideology. It is generally assumed in objectivist science that theory development, and the application of method, should be free of human values and other contaminating influences. This premise has led to the development of the double-blind experiment and other protocols that prevent the investigator's preferences and assumptions from affecting the conduct of a study. *Scientific objectivity* basically means refusing to let value positions affect the way a study is designed, or the way empirical data are collected or evaluated. Such objectivity is supposed to ensure the development of knowledge untainted by human interests or politics.

Objectivist science's claims to trustworthiness depend on its being able to make an impermeable boundary between its research operations and the world of personal, ethical, and political choices. But the "facts" and applications of method found in scientific study are thoroughly laced with tacit meanings (Feyerabend, 1975; O'Keefe, 1975), and scientists' professional values and practices inevitably affect what is studied and how it is studied, and these are not always logically motivated (e.g., Becker, 1967; Latour & Woolgar, 1986).[7] Moreover, communication science has often served particular power arrangements and public or private policy interests (e.g., Delia, 1987; Rowland, 1983; Schiller, 1969). It is naive to think that the resources devoted to conducting social research do not come without a price, or at least the expectation of certain kinds of solutions.

Interpretive science does not deny the interested nature of its inquiries. As will become clear throughout this book, qualitative research deals at every level with the interests, often competing, of various stakeholders. Qualitative studies often originate in some local conflict or quandary or subversive activity, in which a political issue writ large seems to be at play. The introduction of the study itself may complicate things as the participants begin to see it as creating something of a theatrical stage that will someday eventuate in a full-fledged morality play in front of an audience.

More critically, the practice of science, especially a human science, is itself an ideological act. Qualitative research involves the production of knowledge, not its discovery. From the pragmatist point of view, we are in the business of creating the beliefs from which we can act. As such, we are ideological agents fully enmeshed in the ethical consequences of our claims. We are in the business of creating dangerous knowledge—knowledge that changes people's lives.

What Eagleton (1983) has to say about literary criticism applies with equal force to qualitative research: "It is not a matter of starting from certain theoretical or methodological problems: it is a matter of starting from what we want to *do*, and then seeing which methods and theories will best help us to achieve these ends" (p. 210). We have no choice but to act ideologically in a world where real consequences flow from our decisions. What is really crucial is deciding what we want to do.

Notes

1. Joel Kailing and Monica Ganas conducted their projects as doctoral students in my qualitative communication research seminar. The names of the people and places they studied are replaced with pseudonyms in these passages. I should point out two things about these examples. First, both Joel and Monica started their projects in scenes in which they were already functioning members. This manner of engagement is not the rule in the qualitative research literature, as it bears the risk of the researcher's carrying unexamined presuppositions about behaviors and beliefs into the scene as well as already defined relationships with members that may hinder the execution of research objectives. As we will see later, however, their approach is neither uncommon in the literature nor an inexorable path to invalid conclusions. Indeed, they managed their research roles rather well. Second, my narration of their field experiences represents an editing of parts of their reports with my own talks with them about their reports (in my role as seminar leader), for the pedagogical intent of this book. In a sense, then, I also operated in the dual researcher-member role. One way to resolve a dilemma of this kind is to ask those members who are written about to read and critique the narrative, and perhaps make revisions or amendments. This Joel and Monica did.

2. I would be derelict in this account if I did not also acknowledge the strides made by communication science in the past 15 years. Among them are the development of cognitive theories and constructs for explaining behavior, advances in theoretical integration, greater use of time-series designs, the refinement and validation of key scales and indexes, and the use of powerful multivariate statistics for modeling and analyzing multiple influences.

3. What Morley actually documented were the practices to which the interviewees referred, not how they spoke in the interview context or what the interview context meant (performances).

4. Eisenberg's (1990) concept of "jamming"—moments of transcendently expressive experience with others, with minimal self-disclosure—is an acute example of this point.

5. As one who did not take out liability insurance against readers' claims of being misled about the "real" meaning of these terms, I hasten to add an escape clause. You, the reader, should be prepared, as you visit the literature on your own, to meet a polysemic situation of classic proportions. You will find varied definitions and uses of these concepts that might well contradict or undermine my own. You should make your own judgments about what *naturalistic inquiry, ethnography, qualitative research,* and other terms mean.

6. C. Ellis (1991), however, does advocate the use of systematic sociological introspection for producing accounts of emotional experience.

7. The "discovery" of cold fusion in spring 1989 exemplifies this point on a spectacular scale. We witnessed vanity, secrecy, disciplinary rivalries, institutional rivalries, a "gold rush" to get funding and establish research centers, and global electronic networks that seemingly could not get experimental results disseminated fast enough. Science (including interpretive science) is conducted by people whose interests are unmistakably of this secular world.

2

Sources of the Interpretive Paradigm

Communication as a Human Science

> Only from his actions, his fixed utterances, his effects upon others, can man learn about himself; thus he learns to know himself only by the roundabout way of understanding. What we once were, how we developed and became what we are, we learn from the way in which we acted, the plans which we once adopted, the way in which we made ourselves felt in our vocation, from old dead letters, from judgments on us which were spoken long ago. . . . A study belongs to the human studies only if its object becomes accessible to us through the attitude which is founded on the relation between life, expression, and understanding. (Dilthey, 1944/1974, pp. 16-17)

This chapter considers communication as one of the human sciences, as conceived by the nineteenth-century German philosopher Wilhelm Dilthey. For Dilthey, the human sciences comprise historical studies, social and psychological sciences, moral theory, legal and political studies, and literary criticism. All of these fields share a concern with the humanistic problems of choice, value, and understanding.

It is significant that Dilthey chose to group the social and psychological sciences with literary criticism, rather than with the sciences of physics and chemistry. As Ricoeur (1977) has noted, we begin to unpack the meaningfulness of lived experience by presupposing that it is as purposeful as a written text (even if it does turn out to be contradictory or stubbornly devious). Like a literary text, a social action "constitutes a delineated pattern which has to be interpreted according to its inner connections" (p. 322). Just as one wends through the allusions of many other texts in order to understand *this* text, in the "roundabout way" Dilthey describes, so the researcher understands a person's communicative acts through the motives, thoughts, and feelings of that actor in relations with others.

Learning to use a methodology without being grounded in its epistemology (its theory of knowing) and intellectual traditions is not unlike learning blues guitar while having no idea of who Robert Johnson and John Lee Hooker are, or any idea what distinguishes the styles of Delta, Texas, and Chicago blues. You may be able to pick up some mechanics of chord progressions, but fundamental things will be missing: the genres to play in, the feeling in the music, the limits and freedoms of style. Much the same can be said of not knowing the lineage of qualitative inquiry. In this chapter we examine the interpretive paradigm and how it has been applied in communication research, before turning to the exposition of method that begins with Chapter 3. We engage this endeavor by touring several varieties of interpretive inquiry that developed their own philosophies and empirical programs in the twentieth century. These varieties—ethnomethodology, symbolic interactionism, ethnography of communication, and cultural studies—have been adapted to the study of communicative performance and practice. This presentation does not pretend to be comprehensive, but it should make the learning of chord progressions, later in this book, more fluent and meaningful.

The Interpretive Paradigm

PARADIGMS

In recent years, the concept of *paradigm* has become a popular element in discussions of how scientific knowledge is produced as well as how scientific practices change. As defined by Thomas Kuhn in his influential work *The Structure of Scientific Revolutions* (1970), paradigms are "universally recognized scientific achievements that for a time provide model problems and solutions to a community of practitioners" (p. viii). A paradigm offers a framework for what Kuhn calls "normal science": an accepted set of theories, methods, and ways of defining data in a domain. A paradigm becomes dominant in a discipline because of its ability to account for empirical reality, and also because of its fecundity of problems to be solved. During a period of normal science, practitioners are preoccupied with solving the empirical problems that arise from the explanatory framework of their discipline's dominant paradigm.

It is important to note that paradigms are incommensurable. That is, the assumptions and explanations of two or more paradigms within a given discipline are so different that they cannot be compared by means of an independent value system. Thus adherence to one paradigm forecloses the possibility of the acceptance of a competing one. This is not a problem as long as one paradigm reigns as the dominant one for all, or nearly all, members of the scientific community. Only in times of crisis, when facts appear that challenge the dominant theory, will conflict over basic matters of epistemology surface in the community. Science may then become "revolutionary." At that point, basic assumptions are questioned, unusual methodologies flourish, and argument over the fundamental ideas of the discipline (and even over the status of the discipline itself) becomes intense. Out of such revolutionary periods, which may last for decades, will often emerge new dominant paradigms. The revolutionary turnover of paradigms does not produce an accurate or complete representation of nature; it does produce a "better science" that explains the available data more satisfactorily, and usually more inventively.

Kuhn has been criticized for viewing science as a less than rational enterprise, and for ambiguities in the paradigm concept (see Bernstein, 1978, pp. 84-106). However, his explanation has been so persuasive to most observers of science (see, e.g., Naughton, 1982) that parts of it can be applied to communication, which of course lays claim to a scientific mission.

One stands on shaky ground, however, in arguing that any communication theory or perspective has come remotely close to paradigmatic status, as it is understood in the physical sciences. If anything, communication may have achieved the Leninist ideal of a permanent revolutionary state. Communication has been described variously as being preparadigmatic, quasi-paradigmatic, and multiparadigmatic (see the chapters in Dervin et al., 1989). Indeed, in most discussions, *paradigm* has come to mean simply a coherent set of assumptive beliefs, theoretic propositions, constructs, modes of inference, and domains of subject matter. We speak, for example, of a cognitive paradigm, a functionalist paradigm, and an interpretive paradigm. Each of these is a program of inquiry that does not negate the others or threaten their survival in the academy. Clearly, all of this departs from the original senses of *paradigm* and *normal science.*

Whether or not it is a true paradigm, we need to understand interpretive inquiry as a coherent way of studying communication. This is an important goal, because the current coexistence of perspectives has resulted in only slight relief from debates about what counts as a legitimate explanation. Many still believe that objectivist science is communication's de facto "normal" science, even as a great deal of empirical activity occurs in other quarters. And many qualitative researchers themselves are not sure that they want their work to be characterized as "scientific." So, with apologies to Kuhn, I will first outline some basic notions about interpretive inquiry, before turning to the separate research traditions.

VERSTEHEN (UNDERSTANDING)

All research paradigms proceed from certain *axioms,* or "first principles" that must be accepted as true if one is to work at all within a paradigm. For interpretivists, it is axiomatic that one needs to see a social situation from the point of view of the actors in order to understand what is happening in that situation. The paradigm governing the use of qualitative methods, the interpretive paradigm, takes *understanding* as its principal topic and as the wellspring of its methodology. Dilthey calls this way of gaining an empathic insight into others' attitudes *Verstehen.*

The origins of *Verstehen* reach back to the eighteenth century, a time when the effects of Cartesian rationalism on intellectual discourse were being felt. Philosopher Giovanni Battista Vico's New Science proposed that a proper understanding of human nature and artifacts requires an inductive, historical study of cultural forms. Vico was one of the first to see a basic disjuncture between the aims of the natural sciences and those of the human sciences. In *The Critique of Pure Reason,* Immanuel Kant (1929) maintains that our perception of the world is mediated by conceptual categories. These categories provide the presuppositional framework by which knowledge and questions about empirical reality develop.

Verstehen developed mostly as a reaction to efforts to apply Enlightenment rationalist philosophy and positivist science to the study of human behavior, argued most forcefully by John Stuart Mill and Auguste Comte. At that time, there was confidence that universal principles could be derived through the study of how human beings respond behaviorally to their environments. These principles would specify the psychobiological elements and mechanisms that determine the complicated particularities of human life. The rapid movement during the late nineteenth century of positivist science into areas that had been the preserve of the humanities caused significant alarm in the academy. It bred a "preparadigmatic" phase of competition among explanations of social behavior (Martindale, 1968, pp. 310-311).

Hermeneutics

By the early twentieth century, the concept of *Verstehen*, and debates about its use in science, formed the basis for a science of social phenomenology (see the discussion of Schutz below) and other ways of doing interpretive research. These alternatives were conceived as concepts and methods in opposition to those of positivist science. In hermeneutics, which originally concerned itself with interpreting ancient scripture, the work of Dilthey, F. D. E. Schleiermacher, and, much later, Hans Gadamer formalized the techniques and broadened the scope of textual study (Palmer, 1969). The hermeneutical method involves interpreting the meaning of a text through continual reference to its context (Ricoeur, 1977). The method can be applied to any situation in which one wants to "recover" historical meaning. Recalling the discussion at the start of this chapter, we can analyze a communicative act much as we would a literary text. Thus hermeneutics has proven useful for interpretive anthropologists and for those involved in cultural studies.

Weber

Max Weber was responsible for grounding sociological theory in meaningful social action and for suggesting the methodological uses of *Verstehen* (Morris, 1977; Winch, 1958). By arguing that subjective motives direct human conduct, Weber tried to rid *Verstehen* of its mystical quality and put it on a scientific footing (see Weber, 1968). In his view, the formation of institutions, authority, and policy results from the sharing of motives in interaction. A sustained study of motivated conduct should lead to the discovery of *ideal types* of subjective orientation by hypothetical actors in a given type of action. Contrary to many interpretivist thinkers, however, Weber continued to believe that science should seek value-free, causal explanations of conduct. As we will see, Alfred Schutz extended Weber's ideas about *Verstehen* by elaborating the concepts of motive, the coordination of social action, and the natural attitude.

Husserl

Edmund Husserl had perhaps the greatest impact on the development of a science of interpretation. Though Husserl is not directly associated with the concept of *Verstehen*, his belief that *intentionality* and *consciousness* should be central concerns of any scientific investigation allies him with others similarly interested in subjective experience.

Husserl's philosophy of *phenomenology* sought to define the "essence" of the objects of our perceptions (see Husserl, 1931; Kockelmans, 1967). He argued that human consciousness orders the ways by which we apprehend the physical nature of the world. Human consciousness is a fundamentally intentional activity, in the sense that intentions are always directed toward objects. In other words, consciousness is always a consciousness *of something*. Objects are defined in terms of the practical intentions we have at hand when we encounter them.

Each of us lives in a world of objects, people, actions, and institutions that is constituted in a characteristically taken-for-granted fashion. This *Lebenswelt*, or life world, is the unique world of being for all human beings. Though arbitrary and transient when analyzed historically, the life world is typically experienced as timeless and natural. This sense of naturalness about the way we perceive our world Husserl called the "natural attitude."

The scientific problem of the life world is how it gets to be that way: how it acquires the aspect of naturalness. The method Husserl developed to address this problem was that of *epoche* (or transcendental reduction). In order to understand the essence of things, the phenomenologist "brackets" the structures and appearances of the life world. This is an effort to make strange what seems normal and natural so that one can characterize its essential features. Through a series of bracketing exercises, the phenomenologist can achieve an understanding of how common objects of perception are meaningfully constituted. As Anderson (1987) has written, Husserl's *epoche* "is a purified form of scientific induction" (p. 239). In effect, it permits one to begin a systematic and intensive study of how intentional activity is able to form meanings. One engages in phenomenological analysis to develop fundamental principles of sense making in everyday life.

This brief look at Husserl's phenomenology hardly does justice to the subtlety of his philosophy. Yet the kinds of inquiry we will encounter later in this chapter, especially ethnomethodology, owe a great deal to Husserl's foundational ideas about consciousness.[1]

SCHUTZ AND SOCIAL PHENOMENOLOGY

In many ways, Alfred Schutz represents the synthesis of Weber's and Husserl's efforts to elucidate the subjective basis of social action and the problem of the life world, respectively. But in Schutz's work we find much more than a synthesis. Particularly in his writings on the role of intersubjectivity in communication and social knowledge, Schutz established a conceptual basis for interpretive social science.

Intersubjectivity

In his analysis of the life world, Husserl encountered a basic problem that he never solved: How does a human being learn to construct a life world that can be shared with other human beings? How can there be so much continuity of meaning in people's actions? What Husserl was puzzling over was the problem of *intersubjectivity*.

In *The Phenomenology of the Social World*, Schutz (1967) approaches this problem by claiming that individuals unquestioningly accept that (a) a mundane world exists,[2] and (b) others share our understandings of the essential features of this world. Moreover, Schutz posits that individuals orient to objects and actions by assuming a reciprocity of perspective with other humans. That is, in communicating with others, we operate with this notion: If you were to trade places with me, you would see situations in the same way I do, and vice versa. This presupposition supports a natural attitude of the social world.

In every phenomenological situation—the spatial, temporal, and historical positions that uniquely locate an individual—we possess and apply a *stock of knowledge* that consists of all the facts, beliefs, desires, prejudices, and rules we have learned from personal experience as well as the ready-made knowledge available to us in the world to which we are born. The former kind of knowledge is personal and unique to each of us in the face-to-face interactions we have with others. The latter knowledge comes in preformed *typifications* of experience that are more widely available to all members in a culture. Typified knowledge consists of myths, cultural knowledge, and common sense. Whatever we view as relevant to any current object of our attention shifts according to changes in our biographical situation and our stocks of knowledge at hand.

Given these constitutive features of the social world, intersubjectivity is enacted in the kinds of relationships we enter into with others. In the primary "we-relation," persons occupy a mutual time and place with each other. Actions are geared together with respect to a common system of relevance. In Schutz's phrase, these consociates "grow old together," each person defining him- or herself through the negotiated relationship. We also enact intersubjectivity in our relationships with contemporaries (those who live concurrently with us, but whom we do not know), predecessors (those who lived before us), and successors. These last two modes of relating invoke more typified stocks of knowledge, because they do not involve the same directness of exchange as we-relations. Our knowledge of ourselves changes as we grow into and out of relationships with others. Thus "the intersubjective world is the epistemic context for human action, the significative horizon in terms of which individuals, events, and even things are understood" (Natanson, 1968, p. 221).

Act, Action, and Motive

Schutz embraced Max Weber's concept of action as meaningful behavior, but went on to clarify how it acquires meaningfulness. A starting point is Schutz's (1967) definition of meaning as "a certain way of directing one's gaze at an item of one's own experience. . . . Meaning indicates, therefore, a peculiar attitude on the part of the Ego toward the flow of its own duration" (p. 42). In other words, *only when attention is turned toward the self does experience become meaningful.*

Schutz then distinguished action and act. An action is a project that is in process. An action becomes an act when the individual directs his or her gaze on the action and thus makes it meaningful. To put it another way: "Action is subject-bound, it builds up in temporal development, and its full significance is always on the far side of the actor's intention. The act is a unitary phenomenon which is object-oriented and whose meaning is graspable" (Natanson, 1968, p. 222). The meaning of any action can be grasped only in its completion, or in the projected act (i.e., the goal we imagine for the thing we wish to do).

We gain insight into people's motives for action by engaging them through their acts—primarily, acts of speaking. These motives are of two types: *in-order-to motives* (e.g., "I joined the Army to see the world") and *because motives* (e.g., "I joined the Army because I was unhappy"). The two types of motive can be differentiated in terms of their temporality (Bernstein, 1978, p. 155). In-order-to motives concern projected acts; because motives offer accounts or attributions for past experience.

Schutz's overall analysis of action, act, and motive clarified previously vague notions of action and meaning. In *The Phenomenology of the Social*

World and his other works—most notably the essay "On Multiple Realities" (Schutz, 1962)—he shows how individuals actively construct numerous life worlds that overlap one another. Schutz provides a sophisticated analysis of how we gain access to others' subjectivity, an issue with real significance for methodology.

SUMMARY

The frameworks for interpretive social science were many years in the making, and involved the development of concepts from several branches of the human sciences. In their work, Weber, Husserl, and especially Schutz provided warrants for many of the concepts that later became important, including the *social construction of reality* (e.g., Berger & Luckmann, 1967; Garfinkel, 1967), the *rules of language use* (e.g., Cicourel, 1974), and the *self in social life* (e.g., Goffman, 1959). Their ideas continue to influence nearly all of the human sciences.

Ethnomethodology

PRACTICAL ACCOMPLISHMENTS OF SOCIAL LIFE

In developing phenomenology, Husserl was concerned about its implications for the study of psychology and society. He believed that every empirical science, including sociology, must be based on the firm foundations of an *eidetic science*. An eidetic science of sociology would define the essential objects and relationships of society. Instead of assuming consensual meanings for such constructs as "family" and "organization," an eidetic sociology would go "to the things themselves" and attempt to account for their existence as entities in human discourse. In Husserl's view, without a fundamental understanding of how social life comes to have significance, empirical work would be fruitless.

Husserl did not provide the analysis of intersubjectivity necessary to undertake studies of the social realities that people share. Schutz did clarify how intersubjectivity *should* operate in terms of abstract ontology, but he went no further in probing the actual features and processes of intersubjectivity in their natural contexts.

The empirical program that has come closest to a true eidetic science is *ethnomethodology*. In fact, of the many varieties of phenomenologically based sociology that have appeared, only ethnomethodology has hewed closely to the original purpose and method of bracketing the "mundane" (Heap & Roth, 1973) or the everyday world of social practices.

Ethnomethodology, as a term and as a research program, is the invention of Harold Garfinkel, whose seminal work is *Studies in Ethnomethodology* (1967). In simple terms, ethnomethodology seeks to understand how the taken-for-granted character of everyday life is accomplished. The *methodology* in the term refers not to scientific methodology, but to the methods people use to construct sensible, orderly ways of doing things. Going to class, having a conversation, viewing television—these are coherent activities because they are performed so well, and because we expect (without really having to think about it) that others can also perform their parts. The question that inspires most ethnomethodological research is, How do they do it? The "it," however, is not the activity as such (e.g., television viewing), but *the participants' sense of its objectivity, factuality, and orderliness* (O'Keefe, 1980; Wilson, 1970). Ethnomethodologists are fascinated with how "appearances" are able to sustain participants' complete belief in their reality. Yet, for Garfinkel, there is nothing behind the appearance: The practice of creating a consistent, convincing appearance *is* reality.

TOPIC AND RESOURCE

As a sociological approach, ethnomethodology is a peculiar one. It forsakes the usual theory-building path of developing explanations of human behavior in topical fashion. Conventional social science starts with topics or constructs, such as "family," that are shot through with other commonsense meanings (such as kinship, obligation, trust). These tacit meanings are not explicated in the course of most sociological studies (Atkinson, 1988). Neither is it clear how constructs and their tacit meanings are used as practical means of informing and coordinating behavior.

Ethnomethodology's "topic" is the local construction of meaning through certain interactional practices, mostly conversational (Sacks, 1963). The content of those practices is of little, if any, consequence. What *are* consequential are the situational resources and the sequence of activities used in constructing coherence for a given practice.

The work of Garfinkel and his associates on physical scientists' practices illustrates this difference between topic and resource (see Garfinkel, Lynch, & Livingston, 1981; Lynch, Livingston, & Garfinkel, 1983). Rather than examining the epistemology, logic, or outcomes of scientific work (the presumed "content" of what scientists do), these researchers focused on scientists-doing-science as revealed in sequences of activities in the lab. They found the scientists' technical and occupational languages, especially, to be resources for doing laboratory science. In the view of Garfinkel and his colleagues, work is "self-explicating." That is, the nature of work of any kind is not to be found in the products, proclamations, or expressed ideologies of organizations, but in the observable activities and use of artifacts in the workplace. Ethnomethodological principles have been employed in such settings as classrooms (e.g., Mehan, 1979), computer centers (e.g., Johnson & Kaplan, 1980), and newsrooms (e.g., Tuchman, 1991). Every setting has its own organization of resources and sequence of activities. The focus is on how and when people engage in an activity, not what its functional status might be. A look at some key concepts reveals the interpretive basis of ethnomethodology.

INDEXICALITY AND ACCOUNTS

All social life is enacted in contexts. The practical reasoning in which people engage depends upon their use of situational resources in specific contexts. Expressions that draw upon particular aspects of the local context to establish orderliness, naturalness, and factuality are called *indexical expressions*. The meanings of most, if not all, utterances would be unfathomable if we did not know the contexts in which they were spoken (Dore & McDermott, 1982).

For example, a ribald joke told among coworkers around the grill at a company cookout engages situational resources: the spacing and posture of the actors; the joke teller's gestures and inflections; the nods, chuckles, and comments as the joke is being told. From the ethnomethodological stance, what makes this communicative event "joke telling"? Not a synopsis of the joke. Not even the narrative content of the joke. Rather, we begin to understand joke telling in its indexical expressions: the timing, placement, sequence, and relative emphasis of resources (both conversational and material). The same joke told to one's pastor as one leaves church would have to engage a very different set of contextual resources to achieve any conventional meaning at all. (The competent actor probably wouldn't even attempt it!)

Indexicality involves the artful organization of behavior and other resources of a setting to create a meaningful act. Indexical expressions become the resources for other indexical expressions. As Garfinkel (1967, pp. 1-11) carefully points out, indexical expressions possess rational properties because they are responsible for creating the order in interaction. The rules and norms of social situations are evident in the indexicality of communicative action.

People engaged in action together need to make their practical reasoning somehow "visible" to each other. In some cases, this may mean keeping the reality of the situation clear and explicit to everyone. In other cases, the social situation might mandate keeping one or two participants in the dark about what is happening. According to Garfinkel (1967), "The activities whereby members produce and manage settings of organized everyday affairs are identical with members' procedures for making those settings 'account-able,' . . . [by which I mean] observable-and-reportable, i.e., available to members as situated practices of looking-and-telling" (p. 1). Thus the evidence for social order can be found in people's *accounts* of their activities, which are usually produced verbally.

Most ethnomethodological research consists of close analysis of talk-as-accounts. Ethnomethodologists view talk as the means by which actors construct their shifting, yet "objective," realities (Heritage, 1984). Accounts are practical action. As practical action, accounts frequently economize on (or *gloss*) what they purport to explain or coordinate. In fact, an enormous amount of what we say is purposely vague or incomplete. We rely on others to do a great deal of work to figure out what we mean—or might mean.

The ethnomethodologist may intervene to elicit more detail or justification for the account, which results in more accounts. The quest to define the actor's "background expectancies" (another term for the natural attitude) by generating and interpreting accounts has been criticized as solipsistic—that is, explaining only as a solitary, experiencing self (Mayrl, 1973). This is a mistaken notion: Ethnomethodologists have in fact shunned subjectivity as a concept not useful to their purposes. What ethnomethodologists seek to describe are the concrete methods people use to create and sustain an *intersubjective* reality. Their recent directions have been toward describing sequences of coordinated activity as well as toward linkages of social rules with ideology and larger social structures (Atkinson, 1988).

INFLUENCE IN COMMUNICATION RESEARCH

Ethnomethodology has had a major impact on the communication research agenda. Its most direct application is in the area of *conversation analysis*. This focus derives its methodological and conceptual impetus from the work of Harvey Sacks and his associates (e.g., Sacks, Schegloff, & Jefferson, 1974; Schegloff, 1968), who were fascinated with such features of ordinary talk as the way conversations open, the order in which speaking turns occur, the sequencing of utterances, the repairing of problems, reflexive expressions about the talk, and, in general, the manner in which spontaneous conversation displays the appearance of a polished performance.

In communication, ethnomethodology has contributed to the conception of conversation as an interactional accomplishment. As is evident from the above list of research concerns, the overriding interest in the structure of talk leaves little room for its relational, affective, or cultural aspects. The value of conversation analysis as a way to describe the local construction and organization of interactional coherence has been increasingly recognized in the communication field (Heritage, 1984; Hopper, Koch, & Mandelbaum, 1986; "Sequential Organization," 1989; D. H. Zimmerman, 1988). In terms of method, conversation analysis often relies on transcripts of discourse tape-recorded in naturalistic settings. Unlike discourse analysis, however, conversation analysis admits additional types and levels of contextual detail beyond the transcript itself, and usually results in an interpretive, rather than statistical, analysis (Hopper et al., 1986).

Some ethnomethodological thought, particularly that influenced by the work of Aaron Cicourel (1974, 1980), has emphasized *rules* in social conduct. Following Schutz's ideas rather more closely than Garfinkel's (D. J. O'Keefe, 1980), Cicourel sees the order in everyday interaction as emanating from sets of cognitive rules he calls "interpretive procedures." These rules embody an ongoing schema of the social structure and provide the actor with guidelines concerning the appropriate ways to act in specific situations.

Similarly, rules concepts in communication hold that actors' communicative regularities in situations are the result mostly of the social-cognitive rules they have learned. Rules explanations have been adopted in communication partly because they offer ways to explain both variability (or creativity) and order (or conformity) in interaction. They also fit very well with the idea that communication relies on intersubjective codes of meaning. Probably the most prominent of these explanations in the interpersonal area have been the consensual rules perspective of Cushman and his associates (see, e.g., Cushman, 1977; Cushman & Whiting, 1972), which also draws on symbolic interactionist thought (see below), and the coordinated management of meaning perspective of Pearce and his associates (e.g., Pearce & Cronen, 1980), which is also based on theories of speech acts and cybernetics. A third tradition, deriving from the ethnography of communication (reviewed later in this chapter), investigates the rulelike character of language performance (e.g., Philipsen, 1975; Sigman, 1980). Although a full discussion of communication rules cannot be pursued here, it should be noted that the area continues to struggle over a number of issues, including how intentional and conscious social actors are when they carry out rule-governed behavior, whether or not people can verbalize the rules they "follow," what degree of creativity is involved in rule use, how specific a rule statement should be, and how universally applicable rules are (see Morris & Hopper, 1987; Shimanoff, 1980).

As we will see in later chapters, qualitative methods have been used to study rules in communicative action. Because rules are parsimonious formulations for action, empirical work usually focuses on defining a finite set of such rules for a group or community. However, the extent to which observations, as opposed to accounts, are relied upon seems to depend on how one views some of the problems of rule use listed above. For example, asking people to talk about how they carry out some action is likely to elicit only the most conscious qualities of rule use. The technique does reveal the grounds of justification, or accounts, for why they use a communication rule. Observing permits us more direct access to the indexicality of their actions. It is usually necessary to elicit accounts from those whom we observe, however, if we wish to understand the communicative (rather than just interactional) basis of rule-governed behavior.

Ethnomethodology has persuaded many in communication to adopt a rules perspective, but ethnomethodology itself has not been widely adopted as a way to study rules (see Morris & Hopper, 1987, pp. 14-15). It is probably in the study of mass-media audiences that ethnomethodology's conception of rule as a resource has been applied most explicitly (e.g., James & McCain, 1982; Lull, 1982; Wolf, Meyer, & White, 1982). The interest in those studies is in the ways people use media forms and content to construct relationships.

Symbolic Interactionism

PRAGMATISM

Symbolic interactionism is the study of how the self and the social environment mutually define and shape each other through symbolic communication.[3] Many of the concepts of interactionism originated in the philosophy of pragmatism. Despite a good deal of diversity among the interests and accomplishments of its main exponents (William James, John Dewey, George Herbert Mead, and Charles Sanders Peirce, who coined the term), pragmatism can be summarized in a few propositions. Primary among these is pragmatism's view that meaning is invoked in practical consequences. Thus differences of meaning between two terms (or between two people using the same term) arises out of differences in their usage in concrete situations. The different uses that people have of concepts imply different procedures for anticipating and orienting to the social world. The semiotics developed by Peirce laid the groundwork for the consideration of signification as a social process (Jensen, 1991).

Allied with this view of meaning is pragmatism's rejection of the rationalist belief in an obdurate reality and behaviorist techniques for knowing it. Rather, the pragmatists claimed that reality is indeterminate. In other words, the world that we perceive and act in consists of multiple, emergent realities always in transformation. Such realities are formed through a process of negotiated definitions between self and various societal agents:

> Pragmatists emphasized that action is constituted by, as much as it constitutes, the environment. It is in the course of this mutual constitution that reality opens itself up to the knower. Knowing does not exist for its own sake, but for the sake of doing. Whatever doubts the knower has about the nature of things, he alleviates practically, by manipulating his objects, putting them to different uses, literally forcing these objects to conform to his notion of them, and in the process of doing so establishing—*in situ*—whether a thing in question is what it is thought to be. (Shalin, 1986, p. 11)

This passage captures the particular relationship in pragmatist thought between knowing and experiencing. It is only in action that individuals define the limits of their knowledge. For Dewey (1929/1958) and Mead (1934), the interactional construction of the self was a cornerstone of their social psychologies.

Finally, in disavowing scientific knowledge as an end in itself, pragmatism embraced the analysis and amelioration of social problems. Pragmatists' belief in the mutual constitution of self and society led them to advocate social reforms in labor and education to mediate the destructive effects of industrial capitalism. Pragmatists such as Dewey (1927/1954) were particularly sensitive to the moral imperative of open discourse for fostering democracy. The interest of symbolic interactionists, especially the "Chicago school" of sociology, in studying the ecology of urban communities, ethnic assimilation, and disenfranchised groups reflect its pragmatist legacy (Rock, 1979; Shalin, 1986).

SELF AND SOCIETY

A capsule description of symbolic interactionism, as this must be, still begins with George Herbert Mead, who was "clearly the single most important influence shaping symbolic interactionism, in part because his basic social psychological dictum was most compatible with the thinking of sociologists. That dictum . . . asserted: Begin social psychological analysis with the social process" (Stryker & Statham, 1985, p. 316).

The processes of social communication, according to Mead, give rise to the development of a self in every human being. Society consists of realms of group life premised on cooperative behavior. Through these cooperative interactions, each person ascertains the intentions of others through the use of *significant symbols*: gestures (verbal or nonverbal) that "implicitly arouse in an individual making them the response which they explicitly arouse, or are supposed to arouse, in the individuals to whom they are addressed" (Mead, 1934, p. 47).

Significant symbols are not a mere signaling to another of one's internal state. Rather, the act of engaging in symbolic communication incorporates the anticipated response of the other. In anticipating the other's response (or taking the role of the other), a person momentarily imagines his or her self as it might be seen by the other. In order to perform *role taking*, then, an individual must understand all the roles making up the particular group life. Mead's famous example of the ability of baseball players to execute their positions because of their knowledge of all of the other players' positions is illustrative, at a rudimentary level anyway, of the importance of role taking in cooperative activity.

Social life of any kind depends on continuous adjustments of expectation and response, all connected and informed by the production of messages in face-to-face interaction. In actual practice, such adjustments can be enormously complicated. For example, consider this bit of role taking: "I think you are looking at me strangely because I choose not to wear my convention badge. You are aware that I am aware that you recognize it is fashionable to do so." Levels of role taking can be nested so far within each other, and put into action so rapidly, that the inferences we draw can be very tenuous. The entire work of Erving Goffman (see especially Goffman, 1959, 1967) can be considered an extended consideration of how we learn who we are and what parts to play by the way we perceive others' attitudes toward us.

In Mead's theory, the self in communicative action embodies an expressive component (the "I") and an evaluative component (the "me"). The "I" directs the creative expression of the person, whereas the "me" calls upon the imagined attitudes of others (either general or specific) in order to adjust the "I." The interplay of the two enables a person to engage in the controlled exchange of significant symbols. However, one is not born competent in the use of significant symbols. Neither is one born with a self. A self is not a transcendent ego, but an ego defined in large part by others. Biological and cognitive maturation makes it possible for one to view oneself reflexively. By taking the role of others, including both primary others (such as parents) and generalized others (e.g., educational and religious institutions), one learns to act flexibly in different social situations. The self is therefore a product of participation in social life. Such participation involves manifold expectations of communicative competence on the part of the self. Society in turn reproduces itself in its patterned acculturation of individual selves. But it is in the continuing dialectic between the "I" and the "me," as manifested in face-to-face interaction and in larger-scale organizations (Maines, 1977), that society itself changes.

MEANING IN INTERACTION

The unstated assumption in the discussion so far is that people are able to *understand* each other's motives, thoughts, and emotions. In fact, without the miraculous achievement of understanding, the whole edifice of society-making-selves could not exist. Mead provides a formal description of the intersubjective basis for the prototypical forms of face-to-face interaction. Other contributors to symbolic interactionist thought have elaborated on the role of meaning in social action. W. I. Thomas merits mention for suggesting that an individual *defines a situation* prior to acting. His statement, "If men define situations as real, they are real in their consequences," still stands as an interactionist touchstone (see Thomas & Thomas, 1928).

Herbert Blumer (1969) played a significant role in developing the implications of Mead's social psychology. For Blumer, meaning arises directly from social interaction. In fact, meanings are the only basis people have for acting toward things or other people. People align their actions with respect to meanings held in common with others as well as perceived differences with conflicting groups. The generic form of behavior in group life is the *joint act* (Denzin, 1977), which is produced through a consensual line of action by individuals who share a community of symbols. Joint action is organized by relational and cultural rules of conduct as well as by the civil-legal codes (Denzin, 1969) that define the solidarity of group life. These rules and codes determine acceptable types and ranges of conduct. They are also invested with meaning and authority by group members and can therefore be changed through innovative joint action.

Blumer encourages a direct immersion in group life, via participant observation, as the only way for researchers to understand the meanings of joint action. Despite the more deterministic role theory approach of the "Iowa school" (M. H. Kuhn, 1964; Kurtz, 1984, pp. 40-42), symbolic interactionism is typically associated with close interpretive studies of group or community life. The "documentary" investigations of urban life directed by Robert Park, Ernest Burgess, and others of the sociology department of the University of Chicago in the 1920s and 1930s (Delia, 1987; Kurtz, 1984) characterize this style of inquiry. Those studies combined survey, census, document analysis, and observational techniques to document changes in the human ecology of Chicago neighborhoods and ethnic groups, and in the working lives of marginalized people. Interactionist research has come to be associated with an emergent, inductive style of inquiry. Participant observation, as we will see in Chapter 5, enables the resourceful researcher to explore the "inside" of group life.

A study by Gary Alan Fine (1987) on the social construction of Little League baseball demonstrates the kinds of insights that interactionism can yield. Little League is revealed as consisting of many intersecting realities. It is a structure for learning athletic skills, a microcosm of preadolescent male socialization, a site for the exchange of lore and slang, a context for negotiating mass-mediated imagery of sport, and much more. Fine's research reveals the obligations and difficulties of the boys who play and the men who manage the teams. His presence was obviously required for this sort of study; he in fact describes the culture so well that we can judge for ourselves the adequacy of this adult's account.

INFLUENCE IN COMMUNICATION RESEARCH

Like ethnomethodology, symbolic interactionism has several points of affinity with communication. It is concerned with the role of symbolic expression in processes of social affiliation as well as of conflict. It provides explanations for the relationships among understanding, motive, and message design. Most important for students of communication, symbolic interactionism offers a way inside the meanings inherent in roles and actions (Duncan, 1962; Faules & Alexander, 1978).

Symbolic interactionism has directly influenced the development of the *constructivist* approach to interpersonal communication (e.g., Delia, 1977; Delia & O'Keefe, 1979). Constructivism seeks to explain how persons adjust and adapt their communicative strategies by means of such cognitive assessments as perspective taking. The approach is particularly interested in how cognitive complexity relates to abilities for responding flexibly to different communicative situations. Constructivism has borrowed widely from rhetorical theory, personal construct theory, and cognitive-developmental psychology. It also draws on such concepts from symbolic interactionism as role taking, the definition of the situation, and the emergence of meaning in interaction. Qualitative or naturalistic methods of inquiry have played a small role in empirical studies of constructivism. For the most part, the approach relies on structured coding systems applied to simulated social situations.

Elsewhere in the interpersonal area, interactionism has helped to frame such communication concerns as socialization, social cognition, role and identity management, and relational negotiation. The fact that few communication researchers call their work "symbolic interactionist" does not deny this influence.

Interactionist concepts have also contributed to the interest in looking at organizational communication as a cultural phenomenon. The approach's interpretive debts are quite eclectic, with strong elements of ethnomethodology, narrative theory, and cultural hermeneutics cited in its founding essays (Pacanowsky & O'Donnell-Trujillo, 1982, 1983). However, its emphasis on the performance of organizational myth, ritual, and everyday interaction, as well as the focus on conflict, belies an interactionist influence.

Early symbolic interactionists were involved in studies of motion picture impact and interpretation (see Wartella, 1987), and Blumer (1969) wrote a fine essay on the misdirected nature of media effects research. Some theoretical work has argued that media formats (comprising elements of symbolization, story, and technology) provide important material for audiences' constructions of reality (Altheide & Snow, 1988; Anderson & Meyer, 1988). However, qualitative studies of mass communication only occasionally claim an interactionist perspective (e.g., Frazer & Reid, 1979; Lindlof, 1987a). The rich possibilities of symbolic interactionism for studying the sites and events of popular communication have not yet been adequately explored.

Ethnography of Communication

ORIGINS AND SCOPE

A third tradition leading to qualitative communication inquiry draws inspiration from anthropological and sociolinguistic approaches to language. The *ethnography of communication* (also known as the ethnography of speaking) considers discourse as pivotal to the study of social life.

However, by moving beyond speech phenomena alone, the ethnography of communication lays claim to interests in signifying phenomena of all kinds. Its methods are mostly ethnographic, and its subject matter ranges across the compass of human expression: kinesic (the study of human movement), proxemic (the study of social distance), postural, gestural, and paralinguistic, in addition to the linguistic. This expanded sense of signification can be attributed in large part to Ray Birdwhistell (1970), who developed the study of kinesics in social context, and to Edward T. Hall (1959), who pioneered in the cross-cultural study of proxemics. The theoretical stance characterizing these topical foci has been called *social communicational.* This stance conceives communication as a field of continuous information flow, rather than as exchanges of message units (Sigman, 1984, 1987b). In this view, context comes into play when participants jointly engage in a communication event. Analyses of such events often consist of moment-by-moment interpretations of the multiple channels of information that inform and constrain the "sense" of the action (e.g., Scheflen, 1973). The results are very detailed descriptions of communication codes and their functions.

The greater part of research falling under the ethnography of communication rubric concerns speech performance. Its epistemic grounding derives from several sources, the most prominent of which is the philosophy of Ludwig Wittgenstein. In *Philosophical Investigations* (1953), Wittgenstein asserts that the practice of language can be analyzed only in terms of the logic of "language games." He argues that there are no private rules of meaning in language. The meanings of language emerge only when we know the social rules that govern its usage.

Two streams of empirical study came together to form the ethnography of communication research program: *sociolinguistics* and *folklore.* Sociolinguistics is concerned with the relationship between linguistic forms (especially grammatical rules and vocabularies) and their social uses and meanings. It includes a focus on how people as members of a culture gain competence in the use of linguistic codes and forms. Folklorists study oral and material cultures. Operating somewhere between humanistic (literature and ethnic studies) and scientific (anthropology and linguistics) disciplines, folklore studies involve the collection of examples of *in situ* speech or musical performance in order to develop an understanding of their cultural and historical origins and functions. In contrast to sociolinguistics, which stresses the social practice of language, folklore studies stress the artful performance of feeling and thought in regional, ethnic, or national cultures.

THE ETHNOGRAPHY OF SPEAKING

Dell Hymes named this field and defined its research goal: the field study of the social pragmatics of language. In "The Ethnography of Speaking," Hymes (1962) states, "The ethnography of speaking is concerned with all the situations and uses, the patterns and functions, of speaking as an activity in its own right" (p. 16). Stewart and Philipsen (1984) summarize three main elements of Hymes's "assumptive foundation":

> First, the speaking of a community, like its linguistic code(s), can be described in terms of rule and system. . . . Hymes proposed to examine the structure in speech, saying there was something fundamental to know about both language and culture by studying them in their social use, as constitutive of spoken life.
>
> Second, the functions of speech vary cross culturally. . . . Previously, investigators had inquired into how a given function was performed in a given society, but Hymes proposed the radical insight that, in different speech communities, the very function(s) of speech be made an empirical question.
>
> Third, the speech activity of a community is the primary focus of inquiry in studies of speech behavior. . . . Hymes proposed that investigators of speaking first identify a social community and then ascertain the codes, patterns, and functions which could be observed in that context. This shifted focus from code to community and the speech which occurred within, and in part defined, that community. (pp. 195-196)

In the 1960s, Hymes focused on the *speech event* as a way to understand how interpretive activity in a speech community is ordered. Because the functions of speech events cannot be assumed, but only understood through local enactments in the community, ethnographic investigation was mandated. The events themselves were to be thoroughly described in terms of such elements as participants, channel, code, message form, topic, and setting. Later, Hymes revised his model of the speech event. The new framework defined the key elements of speech events in the acronym SPEAKING: "Setting, or Scene; Participants or Personnel; Ends (both goals/purposes and outcomes); Act Characteristics (both the form and the content of what is said); Key (tone, manner, or spirit in which an act is done); Instrumentalities (channel and code); Norms of Interaction and of Interpretation; Genres (categories or types of speech act and speech event)" (Bauman & Sherzer, 1975, p. 100). This framework was used to assess such problems as speaker competence and cultural attitude toward speaking.

INFLUENCE IN COMMUNICATION RESEARCH

The 1960s and 1970s saw the development of a field of communication ethnography, with several anthologies and field studies and programmatic statements marking its progress (see Bauman & Sherzer, 1975; Leeds-Hurwitz, 1984; Stewart & Philipsen, 1984). A journal, *Language in Society*, was established with the study of speech in social life as its purview. Several others, *Language, Research in Language and Social Interaction*, and *Text and Performance Quarterly* among them, publish many articles on ethnography of communication. Among the important ideas emerging from this period are those of *speech economy*, or the differential allocation of communicative resources in a community, and *communicative competence*, which considers the ways in which a speaker's knowledge is indexed in his or her expressive ability, as evaluated by the speech community. Although communication ethnography shares many of its aims and methods with conversation analysis, the former's interest in explaining role structure and role enactment by analyzing speech performance marks its distinctive purpose. For example, fieldwork has been conducted that describes role-based communicative styles as they function in particular subcultures or social situations (Katriel, 1987; Philipsen, 1975). Through these studies, we learn how communities "enforce" speech norms, and what happens when they are breached. The speech community is viewed as a constantly performed accomplishment, with a basis in consensual rules.

Unlike ethnomethodology and symbolic interactionism, both of which are based in sociology, the ethnography of communication has thrived in an interdisciplinary spirit. Certainly much of the work produced by communication scholars is not very different from that of ethnographers of communication in other disciplines. Within what is known institutionally as the field of communication, the ethnography of communication has been identified with the Annenberg School for Communication at the University of Pennsylvania (where Birdwhistell and Hymes were on the faculty), although its graduates brought the approach to other universities during the 1980s.

Two distinctively "social communicational" themes can be briefly mentioned. One concerns the construction of moral or cultural conceptions of self through spoken discourse (Katriel & Philipsen, 1981). For example, Carbaugh (1988b) examined many of the *Donahue* television programs, and consulted program transcripts, viewers, and program guests, in order to evaluate the cultural rules for presenting the self and granting or respecting others' rights to personal expression. *Donahue* discourse, he argues, reveals opinion stating as a distinctly American mode of claiming a personal self and recognizing the selves of others.

A second theme concerns the productive activity of people making personal art, as in Musello's (1980) study of the use and aesthetics of family snapshots, Schwartz and Griffin's (1987) study of an amateur photography club, and Katriel and Farrell's (1991) study of personal scrapbooks. The authors' success in eliciting members' talk about how they were socialized to their art forms, and the structural and aesthetic properties of the works themselves, yield fascinating insights into often overlooked worlds of visual communication. Their work reveals the folkloristic strain of the ethnography of communication while incorporating newer influences, such as the sociology of culture.

Cultural Studies

A POLYGLOT TRADITION

As Raymond Williams documents generously in his book *Keywords* (1976), "Culture is one of the two or three most complicated words in the English language" (p. 87). From its early meaning of the "cultivating" of resources and knowledge, the word took on its current usages: (a) "a general process of intellectual, spiritual, and aesthetic development"; (b) "a particular way of life, whether of a people, a period, a group, or humanity in general"; and (c) "the works and practices of intellectual and especially artistic activity" (p. 90).

All three usages, Williams notes, are closely related, but in the social sciences the second meaning has predominated. In cultural anthropology, where the concept is crucial, culture is the system of meanings through which social practices make sense to a people, and by which those practices carry on across generations in an enduring form (Geertz, 1973; Schneider, 1976). Culture also distinguishes the range of behaviors and statuses permitted to members of a group. Artifacts such as totems metaphorically clarify the identities of tribes and ethnic groups. Considered as a system, culture makes it possible to think of all the material and organizing efforts of a people—their agriculture, economics, arts, crafts, marriage and family relations, and spiritual practices—as an organic whole. The ethnography of communication, as we learned in the previous section, largely adopted this anthropological version of culture.

More recently, a lively field called *cultural studies* has developed in which culture-situated communication is a central focus. (Given the centrality of communication in cultural studies, I do not include an "Influence in Communication Research" subsection in this section.) Cultural studies embodies diverse approaches that all have an interest in *signification*: semiotics, sociology, cultural anthropology, ethnography, literary criticism, feminism, poststructuralism, psychoanalysis, Marxism, and other theories of ideology and society. Actually, calling cultural studies a field at all is a problem, because its practitioners try to resist all essentialist labels. Perhaps a better way to characterize it is as transdisciplinary: a zone where kindred concepts and interests travel, meet, and sometimes recombine.

Despite this ambiguity about what cultural studies is, it is clearer what cultural studies has done. Probably its major contribution has been to demonstrate the political meanings at work in all cultural practices and texts in industrial societies. Previously, the kinds of culture described by Williams were studied separately; each seemed to possess its own integrity. For example, critics analyzed a work of art, usually elite Western art, in terms of a legitimate canon of artworks; this is the conception of culture as a "civilizing" sensibility. Anthropologists studied a culture's total way of life without reference to issues of power and imperialism, or to their own disciplinary prejudices. Cultural historians understood history as a procession of large figures and events, without attending to the everyday practices of workers, families, and subcultures, and without recognizing the effects of the narratives they naively imposed on "historical data."

The insight of cultural studies was to abandon these insular ways of inquiry, and to redraw the connections among them. The old distinctions of culture were already giving way in the post-World War II period, especially in Great Britain, as educational opportunities expanded, class divisions blurred, and the mass media penetrated all communities with their consumptive and nationalizing agendas. Cultural studies was an entrepreneurial response to these changes. For communication scholars, cultural studies is nearly synonymous with *British cultural studies,* which itself is mostly identified with the "Birmingham school" of media and culture study (G. Turner, 1990). Particularly during the late 1960s and the 1970s, the University of Birmingham Centre for Contemporary Cultural Studies creatively applied semiotic, psychoanalytic, anthropological (ethnographic), and neo-Marxist perspectives to the study of everyday cultural and social practices. Researchers affiliated with the Centre began to study the meanings in music, soap opera viewing, news, dance, and other forms. The high culture/low culture distinction was leveled. It was recognized that the object itself is *not* what distinguishes a scholarly field such as literary theory. Instead, different cultural objects can be politically "effective" in different ways. It is the discourse in which an object is encoded, and the social discourses surrounding the object, that are important for explicating the myths and political consciousness of an epoch. *The Brady Bunch* and Bruce Lee movies are just as viable texts for study as are the works of Shakespeare and Faulkner. And family television viewing is just as vital a site of meaning production, if not more so, than any high-culture venue. It all depends on what one wants to do.

In some ways like the Chicago school symbolic interactionists, British cultural studies analysts also began to examine in close detail the marginal and struggling elements in society, including working-class male students (Willis, 1977), punk subculture (Hebdige, 1979), and teenage girls (McRobbie, 1982). In their accounts, cultural action is an artful and self-conscious attempt to secure spaces and moments of identity in a society obsessed with instrumental control. Culture was seen in a new light: "Culture is understood *both* as a way of life—encompassing ideas, attitudes, languages, practices, institutions, and structures of power— and a whole range of cultural practices: artistic forms, texts, canons, architecture, mass-produced commodities, and so forth" (Nelson, Treichler, & Grossberg, 1992, p. 5).

TEXT AND METHOD

Often in cultural studies, the object of study, some artifact that has been interpreted holistically as a form, style, or genre, is called a *text.* A television program (or any part thereof), a pop music song, and a Balinese dance ritual are all different kinds of texts. In semiotic terms, a text represents a coherent cluster of signifiers. A text signifies something when it becomes situated in a context for interpretation. A social researcher and a cultural critic may arrive at different meanings of the "same text" because their methods differ and the things they consider to be relevant to interpreting the text also differ.

The concept of *intertextuality*, or "the social organization of the relations between texts within specific conditions of reading" (Bennett & Woollacott, 1988, p. 45), describes a principal method by which meaning is attributed to a text. In other words, the production and use of a text depends on a creative combination of parts of other texts. For example, the figure of James Bond seems to have been constituted and read differently over the years as the relations among Bond novels, movies, publicity, and political events have changed (Bennett & Woollacott, 1988). In a postmodern culture, the intertextuality of a cultural artifact tends to draw attention reflexively to its own stylistic conventions, historical antecedents, and ways of "reading" it (Fiske, 1987, 1991a).

Because just about anything can be a text, and any text's significance ultimately derives from its relationship to other signs, the analyst's purpose in selecting and consulting a particular artifact for study assumes great importance in a cultural studies project. Clifford Geertz's (1973) well-known "thick description," for example, is a shorthand term for the web of meanings that sustain a culture. One way to do a cultural analysis, following Geertz's precept, is to immerse oneself in the sites of a culture's routine textual engagements (such as its storytelling events) and document the process of the immersion. In communication, Neumann and Eason's (1990) study of the casino gambler's world is one such example, as are Simpson's (in press) travels through the performances of rap music and Goodall's (1991) immersions in both a high-tech organizational culture and a rock 'n' roll band.

In some of its forms, feminist research has followed a cultural studies path in attempting to understand how women interpret male and female signs in mainstream texts such as television. Feminist theory holds that everyday communication practices tend to exclude, marginalize, or distort the true interests of women, because these practices serve the interests of a patriarchal social system. Feminist research seeks to document these practices, their effects in gender relationships, and how creative resistance to them can occur. Other feminist studies focus on women's uses of specialized media to explore their own aspirations and identities (M. E. Brown, 1990; Grodin, 1991). In accord with their beliefs about women's culture and interpersonal styles, feminist researchers often use a collaborative approach that involves close relationships with participants in defining and exploring the research problem (Stanley & Wise, 1983).

POLITICAL CRITIQUE

Of crucial importance to most cultural studies projects is their commitment to political critique. Not only do cultural studies analysts understand signs as social phenomena, they also try to understand the ways in which the practices of making meanings are controlled. From a classical Marxist framework, the primary function of ideology is to *naturalize* the conditions of societal inequity and economic class dominance existing in capitalist societies. These conditions are perceived as natural and right by the subordinate, or working, class when they are embedded in popular narratives and themes. For instance, the 1990 film *Ghost* arguably used a "women's film" frame to naturalize the problematic status of black folk culture and sexuality as suggested by the character played by Whoopi Goldberg (McRobbie, 1992). On its face, *Ghost* seems to be a pleasant-enough entertainment. By bringing a critical frame to bear, however, we find a different text from the one casually constructed by the typical moviegoer. Ultimately, qualitative inquiries informed by political critique aim to generate *emancipatory knowledge*: "awareness of the contradictions hidden or distorted by everyday understandings, [which] directs attention to the possibilities for social transformation inherent in the present configuration of social processes" (Lather, 1986, p. 261). Questions of value, power, and authenticity of experience are brought to the very center of the research effort.

Recently, the concept of *cultural hegemony* has been used widely in cultural studies to characterize the political struggle for domination (Gitlin, 1979; S. Hall, 1982). As formulated by the Italian social philosopher Antonio Gramsci (see Bates, 1975), the dominant ideology in a capitalist society cannot simply be imposed on the subordinate classes. Rather, popular consent to an ideology must be won through persuasive appeals (in which the threat of force is implied, but seldom overt). The success of these efforts at securing ideological dominance may be overwhelming at times, but never final. Sometimes the disparity between the ideological strategy and actual historical conditions may widen so far that people question the legitimacy of the reality-framing messages to which they had been accustomed. Consent may even be withdrawn, and ways of "resisting" or "subverting" such messages will be devised. Cultural criticism is aimed at understanding the process of hegemony in popular art and other forms of communication, and sometimes encouraging resistant readings of them.

The nature of subjectivity, or the self, is key to many problems of ideological effect in communication. For example, film and television narratives are rich with signifiers that encourage viewers to identify their interests in certain ways. In films and television programs, the viewer-subject is often spoken to in direct-address fashion, visually inserted in point-of-view and other kinds of shots, and ideologically "hailed" by certain narrative structures and signifying techniques. These can be strong textual means of shaping a viewer's field of awareness.

Moreover, by encouraging a false sense of individual agency in people (especially a consumer-self), the media may try to prevent any recognition of oppressive conditions. In the view of many analysts, the power of choice that consumers in capitalist systems think they possess is illusory. The very concept of choice is seen as a destructive rhetoric because it diverts people from looking very closely at how power arrangements of the corporate state actually close off opportunities of individual expression and collective action.

Many analysts now argue that most reader-viewers are capable of negotiating, or even resisting, a powerfully preferred meaning in a text (see, e.g., Fiske, 1987). This is possible because popular texts exhibit an "excess" of meaning, much of it incidental and unintended. That is, the signifiers of a text will always suggest many other meanings than just the ones intended by its producers. People can sometimes recognize contradictory signs in texts because these signs recall the contradictory realities of their everyday lives. Their local cultural contexts provide other resources for understanding than what is meant by the text's producers. By identifying and critiquing the persuasive efforts of the media, ordinary members of a culture are able to achieve their own tactical interests. Thus cultural studies has moved away from totalizing concepts of the way media function ideologically. The current alternative view is that specific texts and usages are "sites" for contesting the political order, and that these sites shift over time. Ethnography in its different forms has played a large role in examining how dominance, consent, and resistance actually occur in contexts of media use (e.g., Fiske, 1987; Morley, 1992; Press, 1989a; Radway, 1984).

Some proponents of *postmodernism* claim that the media have become so pervasive and diverse, and people have become such skilled readers of mediated culture (and producers of culture, through personal, interactive media), that notions of either ideological dominance by the media or the autonomy of self are passé (Gergen, 1991). Postmodern life is seen as situational, fragmented, fluid, style centered, participatory, and reflexive. The textual form of communication studies exhibits some of these same characteristics, especially in the sense of breaking down the author-imposed master narrative of traditional social science (e.g., Browning &

Hawes, 1991; Trujillo, 1993). In style and content, these studies celebrate the creativity of their subject. When critique does appear in postmodernist studies, it is usually manifested in a tone of irony about the displacement of "authentic" feeling and being in a commodity culture into such modes as nostalgia.

To sum up, cultural studies has no stable object of inquiry. It is up to the theoretical perspective, and often the purpose and style of the individual analyst, to drive work in cultural studies. I close this section with a look at one example of cultural studies work: reception study.

RECEPTION STUDY

Traditionally, the study of media audience response has assumed an a priori meaningful content in the text. This assumption has provided a basis for studying the behavioral effects of exposure to a certain type of content. (In other words, if one is studying the effects of pornography, one needs pornographic material to test; hence the usefulness of an a priori definition of what constitutes pornography.) The assumption also means that the researcher does not have to deal with the audience as made up of people with their own habitats and styles of using media. If a text possesses its own meaning—regardless of how it is used in actual social practice—all that remains to be studied is how people attend to the text, scan it, remember it, and reproduce it in their behaviors.

As argued elsewhere, this assumption faces competition from portrayals of the audience as creators of meanings (see, e.g., Anderson & Meyer, 1988; Jensen, 1991; Lindlof, 1988). In this view, the only meaning in the text is that which someone, or some cultural entity, attributes to it. Reception study developed as a way to understand *polysemy* as a problem of text interpretation (M. H. Brown, 1990; Jensen, 1987). As Anderson and Meyer (1988) put it, "The text becomes a site of contested interpretation with different audience communities producing different sense-making achievements. . . . Regardless of how interpretation is explained, it is the individual as an interpreting actor that is of interest" (p. 314).

The basic procedure in reception study consists of questioning people who have seen or read a media text about their thoughts, perceptions, inferences, and feelings. Patterns of interpretation are then compared against certain characteristics of the text. Demonstration of diverse readings (which invariably happens in these studies) is just one analytic step. The analyst might also propose how the readers accepted, reconstructed, or resisted the strategies that might have been intended by the text's author(s). Often, the scope of the explanation goes beyond the text-audience encounter. Such explanatory frames might involve the audience's identity (e.g., gender) or place in the social structure (e.g., economic class), especially in the context of a critical theory.

A frequently cited reception study is Janice Radway's *Reading the Romance* (1984). This study of romance novel readers is distinguished by a careful analysis of the women's interpretations of different kinds of romance novels. Radway moves from the descriptive (what the women judge as "good" or "poor" examples of romance) to the ideological (how the "good" romance informs women of female aspiration and identity). She achieves this move by applying a theoretical argument based in feminist critique of patriarchal society. Thus reception study offers evidence for variation in the text-audience interaction. It also grants considerable room to interpret participants' meaning-making practices for particular analytic purposes.

The Science of Qualitative Research

Now that we have toured the major sources of the interpretive paradigm, we can move to an overview of the practice of empirical qualitative research. This brand of science claims to be disciplined in its relations with native participants, open in its interpretations, and thoroughly interested in its engagement with ideology.

The kinds of explanations we seek in qualitative research are almost exclusively ones of understanding, not prediction or control. As discussed in Chapter 1, ethnography began when researchers sought to describe cultures that operate on different social, linguistic, and metaphysical principles than their own. Prolonged engagement was considered necessary to carry out such activities as learning the culture's language, describing the features and uses of kin group terms, and collecting and cataloging artifacts. Such involvement also permits one to learn the meanings of rituals and other symbolic forms that cannot be known in advance, but emerge as a result of the investigator's own attempts at learning.

These characteristics—prolonged engagement and gradual acquisition of knowledge—favor an *inductive* mode of inquiry. Through induction, data slowly resolve into concepts and specific research propositions through the investigator's own increasing skill at understanding. It is only near the end of the project that one learns what it is all about. However, just as objectivist science cannot be exclusively deductive, qualitative analysis is not wholly inductive in its inferential processes. The researcher begins to organize a study by reading certain literatures, and later engages in the testing of concepts and propositions suggested by the field experience.

Qualitative interpretations result from the intensive analysis of a single case, or perhaps a few cases. The intimate knowledge gained of individual families, subcultures, organizations, communities, or individuals is written up in a way that discloses the author's insight. The scope of this analysis is called *idiographic* (contrasted with nomothetic). One does generalize in qualitative research, but not in a way that tries to attain the scope of a universal law. Instead, the richness of the particular elements that are documented and the patterns or themes they exhibit allow the researcher to generalize to other cases of the same problem in the larger culture (see Porpora, 1983). By expanding the meanings of the case to historical and other frames of reference, one can compare interpretations of meaning and action from one culture to another. But this is not the same thing as sampling randomly from a population, applying measures, and extrapolating the estimated values to the population. The type of explanation sought is rarely nomothetic in scope; it is not intended to explain a universal, ahistorical mechanism for behavior (Hammersley, 1992).

Theory in qualitative inquiry usually consists of ways to understand and depict rationality in the foreign, obscure, banal, confused, and moral or immoral appearances of human conduct.[4] Here, *rationality* means a sense of reasonableness that members of a culture attribute to their own actions. It has little to do with "being rational"—that is, with classical rules of logic and evidence. That is, most actions arise out of ideas about the world that can be neither confirmed nor falsified[5] (Shweder, 1984). American punks' struggles in the mid-1980s over whether real political change is possible may be seen as one example (Lull, 1987, p. 247). Their expressions of alienation derived from certain beliefs about what politics is for and whose interests it serves.

In turning our attention to a people's rationality, then, we are interested in *their* logic and the kind of evidence *they* consider worthwhile or relevant. We suspend our own notions of what is appropriate or right or logically defensible. It may be that the people we study consider some of their own customs to be "illogical" or "deviant." But that circumstance simply requires us to probe further, to understand the rationality that produces these expressions. Such inquiry requires someone who is willing to understand the truths held by the people studied. This person, the ethnographer, pursues "an opportunistic research program which takes advantage of what comes available while working to make things available" (J. A. Anderson, personal communication, 1993).

Qualitative inquiry tries to understand a people's rationality, but the purposes of research are not exhausted there. To expand the implications of the case(s) under study, we bring other frames of reference to bear, such as the conceptual resources of the communication discipline. One uses the case to inform theoretical and practical arguments about morality, ideology, policy, social interaction, or symbolic representation. A useful representation of the case results from our ability to translate the practices of the other into a language and a set of problems with which *we* in the communication discipline are familiar.

Finally, the qualitative researcher's penetration of others' lives breaches the normal defense of science as a no-fault inquiry. Because he or she is not native to the culture being studied, the researcher is free from having to take up a certain perspective. Such a researcher is a "professional stranger," in Agar's (1980) memorable phrase. Yet the researcher *is* inevitably drawn into the scene, and cannot avoid being part of situations in which moral and political decisions have to be made. The dilemmas can be many: Try to be all things to all people in the scene, or develop close relationships with certain individuals? Remain oblivious to an inequitable or harmful situation to preserve one's research role, or intervene? Withhold meanings not meant to be disclosed, or report everything that the culture does, including the most sacred or sensitive? Rather than try to dispel them, the analyst engages these uncertainties of personal involvement.

Conclusion

This chapter has presented the idea of the paradigm and has reviewed four sources of the interpretive paradigm that have informed qualitative study in communication. The traditions of ethnomethodology, symbolic interactionism, ethnography of communication, and cultural studies have all made distinctive contributions to work in the communication discipline. Certainly, I have taken liberties in calling what so many researchers do *a* paradigm. Undoubtedly some would feel uncomfortable at being put in one tradition and not another, or not in both; others might rather not be categorized at all. However, the human situation of self-consciousness and the implication of meaning in signifying practices are common grounds for this community of interests.

Other variants of the interpretive paradigm have not been treated here. Some, such as action research and the therapeutic approach, represent interventionist approaches to policy or to other problems of praxis. Such research tends to be conducted on an applied basis and does not often appear in scholarly outlets. Nevertheless, these are important kinds of qualitative inquiry. Other approaches, such as the community study in urban anthropology, have not seen very much use in the communication field, either because scholars are not well informed about them or because their strengths do not effectively fit the nature of communication phenomena. There are also variants of the interpretive paradigm that draw on more than one of the four sources mentioned here in combinatory fashion. Anderson and Meyer's (1988; Anderson, 1991) *social action* theory, for example, owes significant and nearly equal debts to ethnomethodology, symbolic interactionism, and cultural studies.

Certainly any theory or concept is itself a cultural phenomenon, contingent on historical needs and opportunities. In truth, the interpretive paradigm is constantly remaking itself. For example, American pragmatism, and its successor in symbolic interactionism, developed a rich tradition for studying the self in social interaction. Yet even symbolic interactionists are seeking contacts of mutual interest and dialogue with such other kinds of inquiry as cultural studies and postmodernism (Becker & McCall, 1990). Cultural studies' engagement with issues of power, text, and reflexive analysis has had an impact on nearly all those who have interests in the socially situated and semiotic character of communication. As Rabinow and Sullivan (1987) remark, we are beginning to realize that "all human inquiry is necessarily engaged in understanding the human world from within a specific situation. This situation is always and at once historical, moral, and political. It provides not just the starting point of inquiry but the point and purpose for the task of understanding itself" (p. 20). Later chapters will explore what this statement implies for the practice of qualitative inquiry.

Notes

1. Another important philosopher of phenomenology bears mention: Martin Heidegger, who was a student of Husserl. Especially as expressed in his *Being and Time* (1927/1962), Heidegger's was a phenomenology that used hermeneutics to articulate how our being-in-the-world is constituted in language as practical action (see Hawes, 1977, for a discussion in relation to communication concerns). This is an important scheme to relate to the conduct of research, especially interpretive research (Packer, 1985).

2. Applying the adjectives *mundane* and *everyday* to *world* may be puzzling to some readers. In the context of phenomenological thought, *the mundane* or *everyday* refers to the collective objects in our surroundings that are seldom problematic in the course of practical action, and therefore do not require any special notice. The mundane world forms the materiality of our most basic presuppositions. For example: Buses are for transportation; buses run on schedules; buses accept all paying passengers; passengers choose seats on a first-come, first-served basis—these are some presuppositions that make up the everyday world of buses. Within that world we accept certain accidents, exceptions, and situational rules without much surprise: Buses are also for socializing; sometimes buses do not run on time; a bus driver may refuse to let certain people board, such as people who are "disorderly." Other practices, such as the segregation of passengers by race, may have been part of the mundane fabric of the past, but would be extraordinarily problematic today.

3. Symbolic interactionism may be one of the few cultural forms, along with jazz, that can truly be said to have originated in the United States. It emerged in the early twentieth century, determined to apply its own brand of *Verstehen* among the communities and subcultures of a rapidly urbanizing, assimilating America. This may explain why it has not traveled well in other cultures, particularly those marked by much more rigid divisions of class, power, and mobility.

4. I say "appearances" because the researcher often confronts his or her own prejudices, personal and professional, in starting such studies. Although *all* scientists try not to allow their own personal reactions to people and events to affect the design and execution of their research, such problems are much more subtle in fieldwork. In fact, personal reactions are useful in certain circumstances, but only if the researcher can manage to keep them under some control.

5. Abraham Kaplan's (1964, pp. 3-11) ideas about the distinction between logic-in-use and reconstructed logic in science suggest some close parallels between what ethnographers and culture members themselves do during the course of a study. *Logic-in-use* refers to the reasoning that scientists engage in while they are doing science. Reconstructed logic consists of those canons of scientific procedure that are used for pedagogy and for presenting science publicly. As Kaplan puts it, the reconstructed logic "idealizes the logic of science only in showing us what it *would* be if it were extracted and refined to utmost purity" (p. 11). It is evident that this is what ethnographers do as well, and this book is intended to be an effective reconstructed logic for communication. What is less evident is that those we study learn how to reconstruct their own activities while they are being studied. They learn a great deal about their own rationality through the lens of their interaction with the investigator. We need to know more about how people learn about themselves (does it produce a different culture member?) and how such learning feeds back into the ethnographer's own logic-in-use (does it even get noticed?).

3

Design I: Planning

Beginnings

At first, all I had was an idea that exercised my imagination: the paradox of personal mass-media use in a profoundly restricted environment. The setting I had in mind was a prison.[1] Perhaps, under other circumstances, other settings might have served my purpose just as well: nursing homes, mental institutions, military bases, isolated science laboratories, prep schools.

I remembered something Doug Foley said in the ethnography seminar I took at the University of Texas: "Fieldwork is like courtship." I wasn't sure what this meant to Foley, but what it meant to me was that the researcher romances a subject of inquiry with authentic interest and respect for its integrity—and with eyes wide open.

My choice of this idea—studying prison media use—was mixed from three parts assessment of my own research priorities, two parts need for some fieldwork experience, one part opportunity, and one part taste for adventure. Maybe it is unseemly to admit to so many self-centered reasons, but that's how it was for me. Admitting it somehow made it all right.

Next I turned to the agenda of audience research. It would have been easy enough to round up one of the usual suspects from mass communication theory to establish a direction for the study. With its emphasis on needs, gratifications, and functional dependencies, uses and gratifications seemed to be a natural. However, I wanted to know what media use in prison *means*, and what forms it takes. Erving Goffman's *Asylums* (1961), with its brilliant depiction of how total institutions work over inmates' lives and how inmates invent strategies for enduring their predicaments, was an inspirational source; I consulted it often. I began to turn my attention to issues of access to media as well as issues of use. I wondered why a prison would allow inmates to have televisions, newspapers, and magazines at all. It seemed plausible that media access is viewed differently by the different actors in a prison, owing to their different placements in the institution. How do prison officials, staff members, guards, new inmates, veteran inmates, and so forth, define media—now, in the past, in the future? An interactionist approach, stressing actors' socially constructed definitions of their own situations, seemed the best way to study divergent perspectives on access and use. But would I have the time to do it, the permission to do it, or the ability to observe and listen? What exactly is the topography of prison social life, and how should I go about taking in parts of it?

This confessional tale (Van Maanen, 1988) recalls in capsule form (and in the manner of looking over my own shoulder) how I began to pull one project together. It does not tell the whole story of that project's start, and it couldn't anyway, even if I wanted to tell it all. Too many obscure and unknown events affect the crystallization of any research. However, a lot of what was important to me at the time is told there: the career calculations, the excitement of being enamored of a new idea, the sober work of splicing a problem approach onto a study setting.

This chapter is about the first choices and moves of research design: the elements that are important in the formulation of problems and the planning of strategies. According to most accounts, a research project originates in "a clean, well-lighted place," to borrow a Hemingway short-story title. We begin with explicit, well-justified, and honorable intentions. Hoped-for contributions to theory, or to disciplinary problems, are often mentioned. A long line of research literature citations documents the worthiness and pedigree of the idea. These are surely important for demonstrating a timely, nontrivial contribution to communication scholarship.

Yet, actual problem formulation represents a rather more tangled mix of motives, many of which stem from the identity and desires of the inquirer. Such motives, and the opportunities they exploit, are essential to the scaffolding that surrounds the construction of a research project. Like real scaffolding, these motives and the other "site-preparation" work are finally pulled away from the view of readers. What usually remains is the clean, well-lighted theoretical argument. This chapter describes the way most projects actually begin. My goal is not to displace the role of theory, but to do justice to the diverse and worldly environments from which ideas spring.

Considerations for Qualitative Design

In many ways, design in qualitative inquiry differs radically from quantitative design. Because popular concepts of research design have been received largely from hypothetico-deductive practice, these differences need to be noted carefully.

First and foremost, design in qualitative research is largely a matter of *articulating compelling and researchable questions that are salient to one or more audiences.* The most important of these audiences—and, ideally, the sternest critic—is the researcher him- or herself, who must marshal the resources, skills, and stamina to see a project through to completion. Hawes (1975) explains that the sensitive management of scientific attitude requires "an ever-present curiosity on the one hand and an ever-present suspicion on the other. The curiosity is manifested in the asking of questions and the suspicion is manifested in the uneasiness with existing answers. This uneasiness generates new questions" (p. 23).

This intensive querying works at many levels. In the early stages of a study, the researcher asks questions about a problem that grow increasingly subtle, pertinent, and penetrating. In the field, the researcher uses questions as cultural-navigational tools: asking naive ones, wise ones, or purposely contradictory ones; asking the same one of many people; crafting permutations of questions for persons in different social strata or different political standings; trying to find the question that everyone can answer or the one that only a few can answer. Many other questions are silent and fugitive, jotted beside field notes or in a journal. The questions that grip the researcher in the middle of a passage may scarcely resemble the ones that enticed him or her at the start.

In most quantitative work, on the other hand, research designs are used to verify or refute a set of questions about the empirical world. The questions asked are rarely about the ontological status of objects and activities. They are questions whose key terms have been defined well in advance of data gathering (Miller & Nicholson, 1976, pp. 11-25), as they derive straightforwardly from a body of theory and empirical findings. Some hypothetico-deductive questions are often not even phrased as questions. They can be declarative sentences that posit a predictive or control relationship among variables. Significantly, hypothetico-deductive researchers take great pains to conceal their questions from those they study. The more human subjects know about the questions motivating the project, the more they can infer of the entire design structure, and the more they tend to assign their own meanings to their participation in it—a situation such researchers wish to avoid. Qualitative inquirers, on the other hand, tend to regard human subjects' notions of their participation as vital data in their own right; this is because these researchers stand inside, not outside, the research event.

A second important difference is that *qualitative researchers develop unique design solutions for every project*. Their interest in understanding impels them to spend time with culture memberships before deciding what is important to know. If the culture is very different from the researcher's, he or she must overcome the opaque or confusing qualities of the everyday social practices of the members. If the researcher shares much the same culture as they, he or she must try hard to become estranged from familiar social practices while still using the member knowledge he or she has (Burgess, 1984, pp. 21-28; Chock, 1986). Either way, researchers must adapt their strategies to the particular nature and historical context of the action.

In contrast, hypothetico-deductive explanations are meant to achieve high generality. The designs of these studies place a high premium on instruments and human samples that meet the same high level of generality. Accordingly, the quantitative researcher enjoys the ability to select "off-the-shelf" survey, experimental, or quasi-experimental designs. A few hypothetico-deductive models can be applied to a wide array of problems and settings. The generic procedure of comparing one or more treatment groups with a control group often takes only minor fine-tuning to fit empirical conditions.

A third important difference, related to the one just discussed, concerns *the uncertain control the qualitative researcher can expect to exercise in the field*. The researcher must be able to fit in with events, or people, that operate by their own rules of conduct. He or she must learn when to watch, when to listen, when to go with the action, when to reflect on pieces of information, and when to intervene tactically (and tactfully). These are judgments that are foreign to most hypothetico-deductive researchers, whose need to build conceptual definitions directly into a design conspires with the tendency to maximize control.[2] The testing of causal statements about behavior would be futile if one could not randomize or control some factors while allowing others to vary along a range of values.

Coming full circle in our discussion, the release of control opens us to unexpected paths of questioning and discovery. Curiosity and suspicion are continually turned on both the design and our own process of converting experience to knowledge. An insistence on control would prevent us from being fully skeptical about how we can know another cultural reality.

To sum up, three considerations distinguish the design process of qualitative researchers:

1. Question formulation in myriad forms is the core feature of designing and starting a study.
2. Every scene and situation presents a unique, never-before-encountered configuration of features, requiring strategic flexibility on the part of the investigator.
3. The researcher willingly shares control in the research scene in the interest of learning the rules and meanings of social life from the inside.

Qualitative design, then, is invented anew each time. This kind of inquiry recognizes that the phenomena being studied are *sentient*. Our own activities are inevitably affected by the feelings and meaning making that naturally go on among the people we study. Our interest in communicative performances and practices—behavior characterized by intentions and informed by orders of relational, cultural, and ideological significance—requires inquiry that registers the fluid, fully participatory nature of social life.

A highly prestructured design is ill suited to these conditions. As Lincoln and Guba (1985) advise, "Design in the naturalistic sense . . . means planning for certain broad contingencies without, however, indicating exactly what will be done in relation to each" (p. 226). In other words, we not only anticipate ambiguity along the way, but plan for it. The best preparation consists of a sense of purpose, some researchable questions, an understanding of our own resources, and some idea of the overall features and dynamics of the setting to be entered.

The Form of Inquiry

Although it is true that every qualitative study must improvise to fit the properties of its subject, most share a general form of inquiry. Interestingly, methodologists describe this form in a number of ways, each of which says something useful about the research process. Four of these descriptions are reviewed here: the form of inquiry as linearity, as funnel, as cycle, and as expanding frame.

LINEARITY

Hypothetico-deductive research is well known for its orderly, linear direction of activities. Qualitative research is equally well known for being inductive, emergent, unstructured, and, well, unruly. However, even qualitative inquirers can and do take a disciplined approach to problems. It is a fact that we have to do ethnography one step at a time and in some sort of sequence. Certainly each of these steps, whether it be a decision about sampling or a decision to validate an interview remark, comes at a self-evidently logical point in the project and builds on what came before.

But there is more to linearity in qualitative research than this. Philipsen (1977) argues that an ethnography that aims to make a theoretical contribution should begin with "a descriptive model which guides inquiry into various [speech] communities, and which integrates the results of such inquiries in a descriptive-theoretical framework" (p. 44). Here, linearity means formulating a descriptive framework as explicitly as possible. By specifying such a framework, a researcher can make comparisons across studies in a given domain of interest and thereby build theory. Later in the project, the framework itself can become an object of inquiry, permitting a critique from perspectives other than the ethnographer's own.

FUNNEL

The metaphor of the funnel (or spiral, as others call it) conveys a sense of research moving in several ways at once. It moves forward, it turns circularly as it goes forward, and it spirals in a gradually tighter pattern. Here is how Bogdan and Biklen (1982) describe the funnel:

> The start of the study is at the wide end: the researchers scout for possible places and people that might be the subject or the source of data, find the

location they think they want to study, and then cast a net widely trying to judge the feasibility of the site or data sources for their purposes. . . . They begin to collect data, reviewing and exploring it, and making decisions about where to go with the study. They decide how to distribute their time, who to interview and what to explore in depth. They may throw aside old ideas and plans and develop new ones. . . . Their work develops a focus. The data collection and research activities narrow to sites, subjects, materials, topics, and themes. From broad exploratory beginnings they move to more directed data collection and analysis. (p. 59)

We get a picture here of a process in which researchers must search, sort, and discard plans and data sources before they learn what it is that is important. Lincoln and Guba (1985) have spoken of the human investigator as an intelligent "homing device," an image that fits well with the funnel metaphor. In other words, like a smart bomb, the researcher begins with a tableau and a rough idea of possible targets, moves into the scene, collects real-time data, and decides which of the data relate to the gradually sharpening picture. The funnel is a good model for the kinds of analysis, such as the constant comparative method and negative case analysis (see Chapter 7), that help the investigator make decisions during long spans of fieldwork.

CYCLE

The funnel and the cycle share the image of circularity, but for the cycle it is dominant. The basic idea is that the researcher formulates a research problem, engages in such activities as participant observation and informant interviewing, and develops tentative explanations. Then he or she goes back to collect new data, possibly consult the literature again, revise and test new explanations, and so on (Carbaugh & Hastings, 1992; Spradley, 1980). The process continues until the researcher "gets it right"—that is, until the task of interpreting problematic data is resolved.

A similar approach has been proposed by Agar (1982), who sees the central ethnographic problem as one of resolving interpretive difficulties. The researcher's failure to make sense of an event he or she observes causes such difficulties, or "breakdowns." Some happen serendipitously during the course of fieldwork, and are called "occasioned" breakdowns. Others, called "mandated" breakdowns, are intended by the ethnographer, usually to test the coherence of an explanation, or "schema," as Agar calls it. Each schema may have to go through many breakdowns, and many revisions, before its coherence is finally resolved. Each of those iterations takes in new data in order to develop and test schemas. The ultimate objective is a schema that the native speaker recognizes as a correct meaning for an event.

Agar's model is based on cultural hermeneutics. Its problems are ones of discerning and resolving meaning. The research task involves configuring new and old data in different ways until the culture member's sense of an act or a piece of discourse becomes understood—thus the circularity of the form.

EXPANDING FRAME

A qualitative study can also interpret the researcher's and participants' recorded experiences through multiple frames of meaning. By *frame* is meant a segment of social action that has been articulated further by means of an analytic device. Its purpose is not only to preserve, but to expand the many meanings of a field episode or other material. If we were to visualize the expanding-frame model, it might look like a turned-around funnel: a single significant event leads to considerations of other events and constructs, which leads to an expanded account of what is known of and implied by the event.

The image of inquiry as an expanding frame refers mostly to the act of creating written accounts—of textualizing the fieldwork. Anderson's (1987, pp. 250-251) characterization of textual meaning as "prolific" and "promiscuous" expresses this well. One day of observation may result in several pages of field notes. Their expansion may take many more hours than went into the original experience, and several times more pages than the original notes. The meanings of the analysis spread still further as it is encountered by other readers.

SUMMARY

The four metaphors just described can be viewed together as complementary aspects of a general form. First, many, if not most, projects originate in a nexus of theory and prior findings, which suggest a set of problems and practices that could be encountered in the scene. This *linearity* has heuristic value for the inquirer at the outset of a project. Second, most qualitative projects do exhibit *funnel-ness* as they proceed through time toward more specific observations. Certain phenomena acquire more importance than others as the researcher concludes his or her fieldwork. Therefore, the funnel metaphor applies best to the changes in emphasis and focus that occur as field activities proceed. Third, most researchers experience situations when they must *cycle* through a number of alternative explanations before coherent meanings emerge. In fact, it is the accomplishment of such instances of meaning resolution that moves a project forward. Finally, most qualitative texts *expand* particularly interesting incidents beyond their original contexts, as the researcher relates them to other incidents and to theoretical, critical, and practical frames of reference. Such expansions usually occur at the same time that field activities tighten their focus, and culminate in postfieldwork text writing.

Preview: Planning and Getting In

Qualitative design can be divided into two broad components: *planning*, which is the process of research problem development, and *getting in*, which involves negotiating access, establishing entry and operational parameters, becoming known to the participants, and sampling empirical units. In this chapter and the next, I tend to portray design as a phase that is over before the researcher fully engages in "data collection." However, it is inevitable that plans will change subtly, and sometimes dramatically, as contact with a cultural scene commences. Decision making about the boundaries, tools, and emphases of the research problem continues right up to the point when one leaves the study setting.

An overview of the design process is illustrated in Figure 3.1. The rest of this chapter takes us through *planning*, which consists of (a) sources of research ideas, (b) foreshadowed problems, (c) resonance tests, (d) consolidating activities, and (e) the drafting of a research proposal. *Getting in*, covered in Chapter 4, picks up design with (f) institutional review and continues through processes of (g) contacting the scene and (h) sampling. In actual practice, one or more of these steps may be combined or skipped, and others may be cycled through more than once before the research goes on. In the interest of clarity, the steps are portrayed here as discrete and sequential.

Sources of Research Ideas

Considerable space is devoted in the following pages to the evolution of the research problem. Although qualitative researchers seldom justify what they do as logical deductions from theory, they are responsible for

Planning

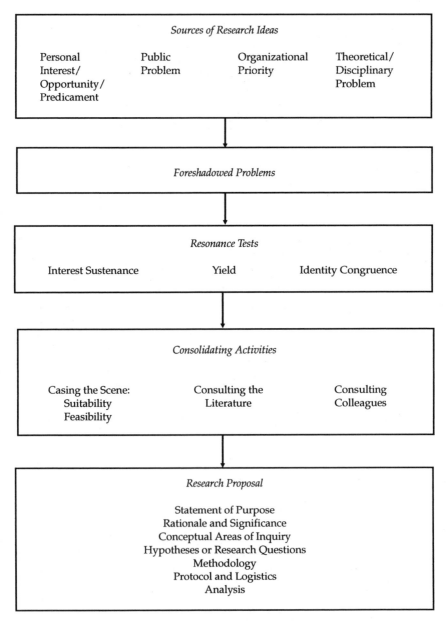

Figure 3.1. The Design Process: Planning and Getting In

Getting In

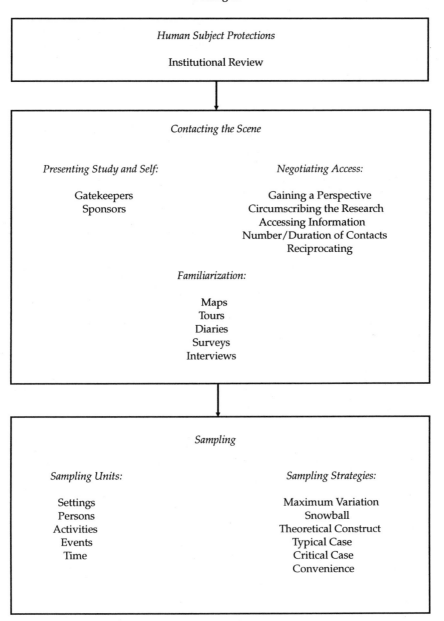

Figure 3.1. (Continued)

clearly stating the sources of their research problems. Researchers should become aware of their personal and disciplinary interests and—in the way of phenomenology—"bracket" them for special consideration. This is a key exercise in which all qualitative inquirers must engage. Our preexisting interests and biases lose the power to deaden our sensitivity to events in the field if we can recognize, record, and periodically consult them. At the same time, our preexisting interests and biases lose the power to enhance our sensitivity to field events if we fail to acknowledge them.

THEORETICAL AND DISCIPLINARY PROBLEMS

Most studies using qualitative methods intend to make a contribution to disciplinary knowledge. It is essential for researchers to draw on the domain of theory when designing and executing projects.

Carbaugh and Hastings (1992) have detailed a four-phase cycle of theorizing communication within ethnography. In the first phase, one explicates a *basic orientation to communication*. This theoretical starting point consists of the assumptions that ground one's understanding of communication, such as might be derived from ethnomethodology or symbolic interactionism. In the second phase, one identifies *specific communication activities or phenomena* (such as the relation of self to interpersonal communication strategy, or generational change in media use practices). Here, one develops a substantive "activity theory," which orients one to look at certain kinds of performances and practices. A theory of *context-bound communicative action*, which is the result of the field experience, represents the third phase. Here, one puts forward a "situated theory" that accounts systematically for the actual performances and practices observed at field sites. The final phase, *evaluation of theory*, returns one to the general theory (especially the second phase) for revision or elaboration.

The first two phases are important for our present purposes. These prefieldwork phases enable the researcher to develop a logically consistent and coherent grasp on a phenomenon of interest and to lay the groundwork for the theorizing that follows. How does one engage these tasks as a practical matter? Lincoln and Guba (1985) declare that "a major distinction must be made between types of studies in which the investigator '*knows* what he or she doesn't know,' and therefore can project means of finding it out, and situations in which the investigator '*does not know* what he or she doesn't know,' in which case a much more open-ended approach is required" (p. 209). Although the distinction may not be as dichotomous as these authors suggest, it does reflect two basic stances for starting a study. The former stance, knowing that you do not know something, relates to being aware of problems that need to be addressed in a body of theoretical or disciplinary knowledge.

To a great extent, the knowledge boundaries given in institutional settings circumscribe our identities as inquirers. For example, I am a scholar, teacher, and student of media studies by virtue of pursuing graduate studies in a department of radio-television-film, studying under scholars of mediated communication, operating as a professor of telecommunications, and presenting research in venues that share those descriptors. At times I find it useful to widen my declared interests to simply "communication." However, the core of my identity and work is "media audience studies," and it is there that I am most aware of what my colleagues and I consider to be unresolved intellectual problems. As I have matured (or, in a less flattering light, grown older), my interests have become more finely discriminated, mining such niches as "family uses of media" and "social construction of mediated communication." So, transposing myself into Lincoln and Guba's formula, I know what I don't know about the media audience (as defined in the academy). Within the niches of my special interests, I *really* know what I don't know.

Each disciplinary area, and subarea specialty, then, contains at any point in time an agenda of unresolved problems. A list of such problems, with examples from media audience studies, might include the following:

- *Inconsistencies or contradictions in the elements of existing theory.* Theoretical explanations are often confronted with contrary evidence, or are vulnerable to challenge for other reasons. For example, Morley's (1980) study of television news viewers' interpretations was based in part on a critique of both uses and gratifications research and Marxist-derived concepts of cultural determination. Because refutation of a theory is so rare in communication, a few discrepant findings are enough to evoke a reevaluation.

- *Lacunae in an existing theory or body of knowledge.* We often come across parts of theories that are underdeveloped, usually because they lack empirical support. For example, Alexander, Ryan, and Munoz (1984) begin their article by noting a lack of attention to the way siblings interact with respect to television use. Similarly, one of the more frequently cited reasons for conducting qualitative research is the "discovery" of a neglected problem or content area. Lull's (1988) volume of ethnographies centering on families' engagement with television in multicultural settings, for instance, was intended to redress the lack of such a focus.

- *The need to apply a new theoretical outlook.* Occasionally, an area seems to suffer from unproductive or ossified thinking and constructs. New ideas, perhaps imported from another field, can offer fresh illumination. For example, in her study of women's romance reading practices, Radway (1984) was one of the first to introduce the "interpretive community" concept to audience research as a way to think about and study the process of interpretation.

- *Unexplored range of how a phenomenon appears or functions.* Qualitative inquiry broadens and enriches our understanding of a communication phenomenon by examining its diverse performances and practices. For example, Alperstein (1991) sought to document the many ways viewers describe and relate to celebrities in television commercials. Fieldwork often uncovers forms of communicative action not suggested by even the most diligent prefieldwork reading. Usually, a researcher cannot anticipate very well the range and content of the "new" subject matter, although he or she *can* plan to expect the unexpected.

- *The need to apply an existing concept or explanation to a critical case.* Arguably, one can learn more about a problematic case by investigating it through an existing concept or explanation than one can learn about a concept or explanation using a test case (Hammersley, 1992). The case requires description in terms of the relevancies stated by the investigator. Those relevancies may also suggest a conceptual approach to use in constructing a research design. My study of media access and use in prison is an example: I began with the problematic case; the relevancies of my interest led me to interactionist concepts for application to the case.

- *The need to account for the historical specificity of a phenomenon.* As historical conditions change, so too does our awareness of change in key areas of social and communicative life. Strover (1991) interviewed teenagers about how music listening and music video use relate to their social and sexual selves; the dynamism of cultural practices in postindustrial society occasionally calls for fresh assessment.

- *The need for methodological experimentation.* Innovative uses of method can contribute to conceptual advancement, or at least invigorate one's sense of what is possible to accomplish. For example, in studying children's understanding of advertising, Wolf (1987) encouraged some children to stage and videotape their own shows and to engage in other performances. Even ethnography itself, a century-old "innovation" when media audience scholars began to notice and apply it, has given vitality to the field, regardless of what it has added to the knowledge base.

Typically, projects are justified by more than one theoretical or substantive reason. For example, Sigman (1986) begins his article on nursing home residents' social adjustments this way:

This [previous] literature has taken a variable analytic approach to studying institutional adjustment by patients, and has not documented the communication processes associated with adjustment. . . . rather than simply
document the staff members' labelling of patients and the resulting "self-
fulfilling" . . . interactions, this study attempts to explore the multiple institutional "tracks" open to patients and the patterned interactional con-
comitants of each track. (pp. 37-38)

Even in this brief excerpt, we see Sigman appealing for both an alternative direction in method and the need to correct a conceptual bias in the
literature.

Obviously, the more conversant one is with a field's literature of
journal articles and monographs, the more one will know what has been
done and what needs to be done. In addition to its knowledge-archiving
function, then, the literature orients readers to the incompleteness of the
field's knowledge and to inadequacies of the paradigmatic frame in
which it was constructed.

Despite many authors' calls for "further research," the literature as a
whole does not declare which problems are the most urgent ones to
address, nor does it recommend a unified agenda of how to engage those
problems. Deciding what needs to be done always involves a subjective
assessment. The judgment of such needs is a matter of how individual
readers read and interpret the literature. Determining what needs to be
done draws on powers of inference, creativity, and articulation that go
beyond simple familiarity with the field's literature. These are not latent
aptitudes, but concrete skills that are developed in practice and, to a
limited extent, in formal learning. Certainly, cues about what is important to study can be gained from influential writers, colleagues, and
teachers, but a degree of independence from dominant currents of
academic opinion (which often harbor inbred attitudes and preferences)
can be valuable for the researcher who wants to formulate questions that
lead to interesting research subjects. One can cultivate such independence by reading widely in communication and other fields, interrogat-
ing one's own and others' deeply held beliefs, and keeping curiosity and
suspicion in the kind of productive tension Hawes (1975) advocates.

Ultimately, it is the field—through its paper reviewers, conference
officers, journal editors, editorial boards, and so on—that passes judgment on the importance of a theoretical contribution. In this very pragmatic realm, a researcher's idea must answer to the way that some
agenda of the communication discipline is configured. As one commen-

tator put it, "An unread ethnography . . . is, in truth, no ethnography" (Van Maanen, 1990, p. 6).

PUBLIC PROBLEMS

Research ideas may also be suggested by what groups, institutions, or agents in the public world consider to be important. This is the arena of *praxis*, in which values and knowledge claims are engaged through practical action and argument. Considerations of what is important are often framed as "problems": circumstances that involve an unsatisfactory or ambiguous state of affairs for some person or group. Social scenes in which the members acknowledge no problems are exceedingly few. (Many ethnographies are justly famous for "finding" problems where none was thought to exist.) Because a scene is usually occupied by more than one group or coalition, one will find conflicts over such things as goals, status, resources, and activity rights. How a group or faction uses communicative strategies not only affects how widely a problem is known, it can also constitute the problem itself.

Public problems can be located in policy debates, social movements, legal action, political campaigns, organizational crises, and resistance to change. Apart from the substantive issues, discourses attending these problems can be the subject of research. For example, the topics of abortion rights (Press, 1991) and the role and use of advanced technology in middle school classrooms (Eastman, 1986), as different as they are, can both be framed and studied as problems of communication performance and practice. How women talk about abortion reveals nuances of moral reasoning. How students and teachers work with a videotex system reveals the problems attending new methods of instruction. Research grounded in praxis can contribute to such goals as the redress of grievances, the revelation of suppressed or unpublicized perspectives, and the advancement of a public good.

Examples abound in the mass media and in one's own locality of public problems that can be studied. For instance, the impact of affirmative action policies for hiring women and minorities is an ongoing national problem. What happens locally when a major employer in a multiracial community enacts its own affirmative action policy? How is middle management consulted, and how does it conform to the new directives? How do the newly hired minority workers understand the company's ethos, culture, and employee expectations? What coping strategies do they adopt as they interact with other veteran workers?

Public problems seem to reassure investigators of the *relevance* of some ideas. In this tautological thinking, if something is enough of a problem to move or trouble people, then it must be important enough to study. Actually, the very prominence of an issue may blind a researcher to what is really problematic about it. Does one study an affirmative action problem because someone is "under the gun" to diversify the workplace, or because it reflects deeper issues about communicative response to a conflicted public policy? *Prima facie* evidence of importance does not relieve the researcher of the need to examine his or her own premises for doing the study and the constitutive framework of knowledge underlying the problem. If anything, it increases that need.

ORGANIZATIONAL PRIORITIES

In most academic settings, one is free to study any subject and use any means of inquiry. Academics are empowered to define their own fields of inquiry. They are seldom compelled by the organizations that employ them to study certain subjects or to shun others.

Priorities that do matter, in terms of the genesis of ideas, come from organizations that fund research. Policy-driven government agencies, such as the National Institutes of Health, respond to legislative and executive mandates in deciding what project areas to fund. Other government agencies, such as the National Endowment for the Humanities, may be more open to the self-defined initiatives of the proposer. Private foundations, such as the John and Mary Markle Foundation (which funds media-related studies), use their endowments to support studies that address the interests stated in their charters. A few professional associations (e.g., the National Association of Broadcasters) and corporations (e.g., television networks) fund academic projects under their own guidelines. These organizations usually issue "requests for proposals" (RFPs) that articulate the areas in which they wish to receive research proposals. RFPs state the forms and deadlines for research proposals, which are then competitively evaluated by review panels.

Qualitative projects in all of the social sciences are often believed to suffer a disadvantage in getting external support. This is especially true of government sources, which are more oriented to short-range problem solving. For many of the reasons cited earlier in this chapter, qualitative designers cannot always assure grantors of conclusive answers to highly focused questions, of timely delivery of reports, or even that the subjects they set out to study will be the ones they report on in the end (Agar, 1980; Marshall & Rossman, 1989). Therefore, the researcher who is inspired by an RFP to generate an idea should be ready to compromise to some degree on how it is formulated and executed. Yet, many do manage to get their studies funded by learning as much as possible about proposal writing (e.g., Reif-Lehrer, 1989), cultivating information about promising funding sources, and adapting the strengths of qualitative inquiry to the stipulations of RFPs.

The last point is important in this discussion. Not only can an agency's priorities alert one to a viable area of inquiry, it can also prompt ideas about how to join those priorities to one's personal research interests. The priorities of funding agencies often coincide with public problems, and occasionally with disciplinary problems congenial to the interpretivist. This best-case scenario enables a proposer to concentrate on the idea itself, rather than spend time defending the merits of the qualitative perspective.

PERSONAL INTERESTS, OPPORTUNITIES, AND PREDICAMENTS

The preceding three sources of research ideas involve connecting with larger concerns and constraints outside one's own immediate sphere. However, excellent research ideas often start with who one is, what one does, or what one experiences in everyday life. The stories of Joel and Monica's projects that open Chapter 1 show that ideas can coalesce from one's immediate contexts.

Essential to the ethnographer's work is being able to sense what is significant in the everyday pragmatics of communicating. Probably the best practice for developing that ability is to seek a variety of experiences in one's own life. One could conclude, only half in jest, that interesting research subjects arise in direct proportion to the amount of time researchers spend outside academic settings.

Decisions to use personal interests as a basis for study can be as varied and idiosyncratic as any other decisions humans make. Paradoxical or ambiguous events in our own lives often lead to personal, tacit theories about them (Marshall & Rossman, 1989). We need to account for these events. Sometimes we do this so that we can act with greater efficacy the next time we encounter a similar event. At other times, our desire to make sense may be more intellectual. Of the literally thousands of homespun "theories" we entertain, only a small number will be seriously evaluated for their relevance to the agenda of the communication research community. What is important is that the interests in our own life worlds *can* be evaluated as candidates for systematic inquiry.

An *opportunity* is simply a "found subject," a fortuitous opening for the researcher. There are many examples of how opportunities have led to studies, although typical published research does not often dwell on the actual development of such circumstances. For example, Philipsen (1975) was a social worker in "Teamsterville," a neighborhood on the south side of Chicago, when he began to analyze the performance of speaking by the men there. Brown and Ragan (1987) observed the ritual of blessing before dinner in one of the authors' families in order to understand how it operates as a conversational event. Of his entry to W. L. Gore & Associates to studying an "empowering" organization, Pacanowsky (1988a) writes: "I got in because my brother was a trusted associate of seven years' tenure . . . I also got in because W. L. Gore & Associates had in the previous three years tripled in growth . . . It was easy for them to see that they had, if not outright problems, at least opportunities for improving their communication practices" (p. 358). Certainly the doors of opportunity can swing in both directions between researcher and the potentially researched, for their mutual gain.

Predicaments are personal beliefs that are ideologically conflicted, or embattled with material conditions, and become viable as research subjects. Predicaments are most salient for individuals whose identities have been challenged at ethnic, age, gender, political, sexual orientation, or other borders of identity (Conquergood, 1991).

Predicaments are less thoroughly documented in articles and books than are opportunities. Part of the reason may be that they threaten to disclose the authors' own political sensibilities or personal histories, which might then call their "impartiality" into question. Reluctance to inject politically contentious issues into studies may also account for their muted presence.

Some authors do avow their predicament-derived motives. One example comes from Yount (1991), who studied women coal miners' management of sexual harassment on the job:

> My interest in conducting this study was generated by my commitment to feminism, the pressing need to facilitate the entry of blue-collar women into higher-paying jobs numerically dominated by men, and the relative paucity of data in the literature on these women. I was drawn to coal mining in particular because I was born in a small coal mining town where a number of my male relatives worked in the mines. (p. 398)

It is likely that no one hopes to resolve a predicament by studying it. Rather, it is a way to wed one's own persistent concerns and ideals more closely with one's professional activities. Conceivably, it creates for the researcher a personally gratifying purpose for doing research.

Certainly, the development of a communication discipline is a human enterprise that responds to societal crises, contradictions, and agendas as well as to the experiences of its individual scholars. It might be desirable for there to be more explicit acknowledgment of the personal origins of research ideas in published texts, both qualitative and quantitative.

Foreshadowed Problems

Early in the planning phase, an idea or two begins to materialize from one or more of the sources reviewed above. The idea may be short, elliptical, and keyed off by a line or paraphrase from an article, lecture, RFP, or reverie. It can be as terse as "the paradox of personal mass-media use within a profoundly restricted environment." Or it might be a sprawling set of barely legible notes, meaningful only to the author. Too much editing of the idea at this point is counterproductive. What is important is that a promising path of inquiry has been foreshadowed. In this regard, Malinowski (1922) notes, "Preconceived ideas are pernicious in any scientific work, but foreshadowed problems are the main endowment of a scientific thinker, and these problems are first revealed to the observer by his theoretical studies" (p. 9).

Although I would not agree that theoretical inspiration should always comes first, it is vital for the researcher to expand the network of associations that a problem or idea suggests. Certainly one set of associations the investigator will expand is conceptual. This involves identifying concepts from communication and other fields that might be relevant to the emerging idea. Other associations relate to the needs of the self, and it is to those we now turn.

Resonance Tests

The term *resonance tests* refers to a phase through which all investigators pass as their ideas mature. They are checkpoints that help one to affirm one's commitment to a study or reject the concept in its earliest stages. The threefold question asks: Is this an idea that resonates with my identity, my interest over the long term, and what I can expect to get out of it?

Of the three elements, *identity congruence* has the lowest threshold. Certainly, if one begins from a personal opportunity or predicament, or even a public problem, this test may already be passed. If one begins from a theoretical problem or an organizational priority, the idea's connection to one's own identity, and the ability of the self to find expression in such a project, will need to be interrogated.

Simply put, the researcher must be comfortable with the prospect of dealing intimately with the people and scenes that will be encountered. The major issues of identity congruence can be phrased as questions: Does this idea embody what I want to learn? Can I manage an effective dialectic between what I personally feel as events happen around me in the field and how I present my researcher face to others? Will I be able to live within the participants' own world at some level? Can I set aside any negative images and biases I may have of the subject? Some of these the researcher cannot answer until he or she is closer to entering the scene, and even then the quality of the "evidence" will be strongly intuitive. To pass this checkpoint, the researcher must answer all these questions in the affirmative.

Because qualitative inquirers often endure being among "strangers" under less than optimal conditions, the essence of the *interest sustenance* test comes down to one question: Can my interest in this project rise above the many boring, disagreeable, confusing, threatening, or pointless moments that will surely occur over the long haul? When posed in that way, the question clearly tempts a strong negative response. However, the researcher should pause to consider several things: the fascination the subject holds, the modestly exhilarating work of investigation and writing, the many rewarding personal relationships that will be forged, and the anticipation of new experiences. The first two considerations are the controlling ones; the last two could be found as readily on a Caribbean cruise as in doing ethnography (and possibly at less expense). For committed inquirers, intellectual curiosity and the prospect of practicing their craft will override all but the most severe discomforts.

The third test, *yield*, is the one that is most amenable to a cost-benefit analysis. This test asks whether the time, resources, and effort the project consumes will yield a tangible value. Here, *yield* refers to the products from the project (principally written) that will go to publication outlets, funding agencies, or other clients.

As with the other two tests, the researcher should be able to ask certain questions and make some rough calculations. Am I at a point in my career that a lengthy project is advisable? What journals or book publishers would be interested in work based on this project? Could, or should, the project's data be divided up? Of what other use is the study? Some individuals do begin studies simply because their curiosity has been piqued, or because their ideas resonate with their sense of self. For most, however, projects must also promise payoffs in the kinds of "currency" required by the field and by the institutions in which investigators labor.

Consolidating Activities

Resonance tests pass the project on grounds of personal appropriateness: Is *this* the right project *now, for me*? Following those questions, or at the same time, the investigator begins to examine the research scene, to take inventory of resources, and to solicit guidance from the research literature and from colleagues. What was at first a diffuse idea begins to consolidate into a fully articulated research problem.

CASING THE SCENE

In principle, any performance of communication can be studied. One should be able to operate as a "human research instrument" anywhere, and insinuate oneself into any group's space. Yet, what is possible in principle may not be what can be done in practice. The researcher must know whether or not the subject is in fact researchable. That is, given the questions being formulated and the resources the investigator has to use, can this project be done at an acceptable level of workmanship?

As a first step, the researcher reconnoiters the scene to be studied. In detective parlance, he or she "cases the scene." The main way the researcher does this is by going to the places where the research is contemplated and looking, listening, touching, and smelling—*hanging out.* He or she can do this in some sort of visitor role, or as an acquaintance of someone who is already a member. If it is a public, open-access setting, the researcher can check out the scene simply as someone who has the right to be there. He or she can also be briefed by one or more native members, consult with "experts," or consult scholarly, organizational, or popular literatures. In some situations, a researcher can briefly experience a scene that is *like* the target scene in some key aspects—sampling actions for their goodness of theoretical fit and for the technical problems the target scene might present. For example, one can "shadow" a university administrator in her daily rounds to see if it would be feasible to study another type of university officer.

The advantage of casing a scene is that one gets a sense of what is possible. In a very real sense, doing a reconnaissance of a scene means trying on an "as if" role and seeing how it achieves some of the purposes foreshadowed in the problem. Ideally, casing a scene should (a) tell one essential facts one will need in developing a research proposal, and (b) assure one that a full commitment to a study will be rewarded.

One problem with doing a reconnaissance concerns the *emic* nature of a scene,[3] which is defined as "the actors' understanding of the situation they are in, and not by settings, behaviors, or other objective character-istics" (Anderson, 1987, p. 283). In the emic view, scenes consist of *the sense that actors attribute to their communicative action*—for example, doing teaching, working, being a student, a friend, or a cop. For example, one actor's conception of teaching may overflow into settings other than classrooms, and involve behaviors that do not match the behaviors that other teachers call "teaching." Teaching, for this person, could involve talking with students over coffee at the student center, or reading some research articles as preparation for a class to be taught next term. Given these considerations, how does one identify a scene before actually par-ticipating in it in some way? Unless one is already a member of the scene, surely one cannot do it. This is a fundamental problem for qualitative researchers. But one *can* inspect the most visible and accessible parts of the scene, knowing that they are not the only aspects or the ones that the actors themselves might say are most central to how they perform.

Therefore, scene casing also involves a measure of *etic* perspective, in which externally derived criteria are applied to a scene in order to size up its candidacy as a research subject and to scout possible ways to gain access to it. More specifically, according to Schatzman and Strauss (1973), a researcher cases a site for several reasons:

(1) to determine as precisely as possible whether this site does, in fact, meet his substantive requirements—a question of *suitability*; (2) to "measure" some of its presenting properties (size, population, complexity, spatial scatter, etc.) against his own resources of time, mobility, skills, and whatever else it takes to do the job—a question of *feasibility*; and (3) to gather information about the place and people there in preparation for negotiating entry—a question of *suitable tactics*. (p. 19)

Some expansion of the last two of these elements is in order here; I will leave discussion of suitable tactics for Chapter 4. A *suitable site or person* should meet most if not all of the empirical conditions forecast in the emerging problem. For example, in my study of media access in prisons, I was not interested in sites of temporary internment, such as jails, detention centers, and halfway houses. I looked for a correctional institution of long-term confinement. I also needed a site that had a reasonably liberal media access policy, whatever *that* meant; it was actually an abstract idea until I began to look at possible sites.

Notions of what is suitable precede the actual reconnaissance, but the scene-casing process can also modify those notions. As site specimens are cased, the research problem may acquire new nuances. For example, when I cased the prison that was eventually selected, I discovered, naively, a complex multiethnic environment. Not only were large numbers of white and black inmates incarcerated there, but also many Hispanics and second-generation southern Europeans. I found that people from these various groups were forced together in many situations. Many of the men I talked to were double-celled with inmates of other ethnicities. Of greater interest were the prison's own practices for averting situations of racial hostility. This became part of the research problem. It can be a good thing to allow certain compelling aspects of a scene to reshape the foreshadowed problem.

Feasibility concerns the researcher's resources in relation to what he or she wants to accomplish in a given study. One usually comes to a scene with questions about what is feasible, for example:

- Can one learn and understand the rules of stranger interaction—in such scenes as television viewing in public places (Lemish, 1982)—without breaking out of the stranger role?
- Can research activities adequately encompass a wide array of actions occurring across time and space—such as approximately 150 persons working in five departments of a commercial television station, housed in three buildings at two sites five city blocks apart (Carbaugh, 1988a)?
- Can one locate people whose only activity held in common is one that is usually performed in private settings and is not a highly valued activity in all of society—such as reading self-help books (Grodin, 1990)?
- Can performances of intimate interpersonal behavior—such as occur in the family (Lull, 1985) or in the life of a couple (Wolf et al., 1982)—stand the continual presence of a researcher?
- Can one record and analyze an action that is highly inventive, tightly coordinated among several actors, and requires an expert, formal knowledge—such as the "organizing" of improvisational jazz players (Bastien & Hostager, 1988)?

Few studies are disqualified solely on grounds of feasibility; as those cited in this list demonstrate, many researchers have found ways to deal with challenging study features. As long as culture members do not actively try to impede inquiry, ingenuity and persistence can surmount most practical problems.

Feasibility is the meeting place of two broad concerns: what Schatzman and Strauss (1973) call the "presenting properties" of the scene and the researcher's own resources. Sometimes, a researcher cannot know much about the presenting properties before entering the scene. He or she can usually learn enough when casing a scene, however, to decide whether the available resources are sufficient to the perceived task. *Time* is always a critical resource. If time is in short supply, one may have to pass up studying a complex culture membership or confine the scope of field-work to a smaller unit of the overall scene. Instead of studying the full array of impression management strategies in an entire department store, for example, one may instead limit the study to observing acts of face-saving in the customer service department. A lack of time can prevent one from achieving true insider knowledge of a domain that needs to be studied in detail, and one may have to adjust the aims of participation and observation. For example, the terms of entry at the prison limited me to four weeks for the qualitative part of my study. This was only one reason, but a key one, that I relied heavily on informant interviews.

The ways in which a scene's temporal cycles, rhythms, and intermittent events mesh with the researcher's own time resources are also central to gauging feasibility. Some scenes seem to display a great deal of equilibrium and predictability, although the words *seem to* here should be kept firmly in mind at this stage. Approaching a social setting at its public interface as an outsider, one often sees the smooth discharge of duties by experienced culture members. What happens offstage may be a very different matter. Many other groups and organizations more obviously go through times punctuated by high levels of activity. Certain events may happen too infrequently, or too sporadically, to be easily available during the window of opportunity for study. Such cycles of activity—along with the occasional traumatic event—occur at different rates and in different levels of even moderately complex organizations.

As an example, take an academic department at a university (please!). One might find many things happening on a particular day in October: the anticipated, but still intense, onset of advance registration for next semester's classes (a semiannual event that spans several days); a problem with a graduate student's teaching that the department chair must address (an intermittent event); the first meeting for a faculty member's promotion case (a four-month cycle); the approaching paper submission deadline for a conference, plunging half of the faculty into a sullen frenzy (an annual event). Even this is a partial list, ignoring the daily occurrences of classes, committee meetings, and the like. The observation that tracking all these events presents a challenge is clearly an understatement. For many researchers, personal obligations prevent their following the full range of action very closely. And a demanding scene can steal time from the critical work of writing field notes, studying notes, making analytic memos, and simply thinking about the progress of the project.

Another presenting property of the scene concerns the *culture codes* that one must understand for the study to be feasible. Culture codes are organized packages of knowledge used by the people in a particular scene in their performance of acts or roles. These codes constitute and regulate different sorts of conduct, such as procedural, occupational, interactional (e.g., politeness and gender-based codes), political, aesthetic, and technical conduct. They range widely in the extent to which they are required for entry into a role as opposed to simple expectations for the good order of a situation. Similarly, codes may be tacit (what everyone should know intuitively) or explicit and codified (what particular persons should be prepared to explain and apply in a given moment). Family and other personal relationships tend to observe tacit codes, whereas formal groups and organizations employ a variety of tacit and explicit codes.

Unfortunately, casual scene casing may not disclose very well the length or difficulty of learning trials required for a novice to master the dominant culture codes. In fact, it is not always clear whether one type of culture possesses more complex codes for acting than another. Clearly, a large insurance corporation embodies levels of complexity not found at a shoe repair shop. But this does not mean that an insurance executive's own scope of action is necessarily more complex or skilled than a shop worker's. Nevertheless, the amount of time that can be devoted to learning codes must be estimated.

The researcher must also evaluate whether the effort and the inevitable mistakes in learning codes will complicate relations with social actors. Some scenes will forgive a novice's imperfect efforts more readily than will others. And even though investigators often pride themselves on their quick grasp of cultural procedure, certain codes resist comprehension. I never did completely understand how inmates were able to obtain the materials to unscramble cable television signals (although it may be as well I didn't). Some cultures protect their codes, refusing to divulge them or even acknowledge that they exist. The codes may be in place to keep certain types of information (e.g., the results of performance appraisals in an organization) from outsiders, including a researcher trying to worm his or her way in. In my research on families and media, for example, I have sometimes found family members declining to answer certain questions, or managing to avoid answering them directly. These generally seem to be questions that touch on how the family conducts itself, often concerning children. The researcher may not realize that such codes exist until he or she is well into the study.

If *multiple sites* are involved, or the *personal characteristics of the membership* become an issue, then personnel resources assume importance in the researcher's thinking about feasibility. When a scene involves multiple sites, or when the conceptual scheme involves a comparative analysis of scenes and sites, the scene-casing process must consider the presenting properties of more than one case. The presenting properties of the sites should match on the key attributes that have been identified. If one finds that a scene's action is performed at several settings, then the scheme for sampling events to observe becomes driven by the dynamics of the action itself. One must evaluate how one is going to be able to cover action that is widely dispersed in space and time.

There is also the need in many instances to study more than one case, such as to build a sample of families or individual media audience members. If one is acting alone, it may be possible to stagger periods of observation and analysis across the several sites. Site B can be observed while Site A's data are being processed, then Site C can be observed while Site B's data are being processed and Site A's notes analyzed, and so on. A team can divide up these tasks, so that each researcher specializes in a particular site or activity. More typically, the team members work on each task together. This permits all of them to work on the same phase of the project at the same time, and to coordinate fieldwork and analysis problems as they go. Less ideally, perhaps, one can forgo being there as a participant and instead compile evidence about different sites and time periods through informant interviewing, document analysis, or other means.

Personnel considerations also arise when the nature of the culture membership seems to call for a special repertoire of skills, status, or experience. We hear occasionally of the unsuccessful field encounter that resulted because members rejected the researcher on the basis of "first impressions." As will be discussed in Chapter 5, studying people who share some of the same key cultural characteristics as oneself (e.g., women researching women about women's issues) has its advantages, especially in establishing rapport early. However, ethnographers are often able to interact successfully with people quite unlike themselves, such as an adult studying children (Fine & Sandstrom, 1988) or a white academic studying poor urban blacks (Liebow, 1967). Major cultural differences between researcher and culture members should not in principle deter a study. If handled correctly, differences can redound to the benefit of the researcher's participation by making more vivid the sensibilities and priorities of the group. Also, researcher roles that differ by age, gender, ethnicity, or some other quality can be handled in part through team assignments.

Finally, but not inconsequentially, the *expenses* associated with traveling to many settings or with the costs of becoming a member in a group may affect how feasible a study is seen to be.

CONSULTING THE LITERATURE

Qualitative inquirers are sometimes advised not to dwell in the research literature at the start, because this may dull or may bias their receptivity to the phenomena about to be experienced. It is also thought that, because a cumulative-knowledge approach to theory is not as vital to interpretivist scholarship as it is to traditional science, the need to survey the literature comprehensively may not exist to the same degree. Still, the researcher needs to locate the conceptual and substantive works that figure in the design of a project. And, as alluded to earlier in this chapter, the literature search plays a specialized, helpful role in the planning of a project.

A researcher can use the literature to become familiar with the problem domain. My ignorance of areas key to the prison media study led me to consult works on institutional theory, prison operations, inmate social life, and the behavioral effects of imprisonment. Such an exploration of the literature is a way to reconnoiter possible settings and strategies vicariously. This is a pursuit that may continue through the researcher's stay in the field and beyond.

If one is unfamiliar with qualitative applications generally, one can study examples from communication journals or such outlets as *Qualitative Sociology* and the *Journal of Contemporary Ethnography*. Table 3.1 lists a sampling of journals from several disciplines and fields that publish qualitative articles. They are best studied as exemplars of field strategy, data presentation, and authorial style.

Design planning also spurs more typical search purposes: to stimulate theoretical awareness, to encounter competing philosophies, to learn

TABLE 3.1   Some Scholarly Journals Featuring Qualitative Research

Communication journals that regularly include articles relevant to qualitative research[a]

> Communication Theory
> Critical Studies in Mass Communication
> Cultural Studies
> European Journal of Communication
> Journal of Communication Inquiry
> Media, Culture & Society
> Research on Language and Social Interaction
> Studies in Visual Communication
> Text and Performance Quarterly

Other social science journals that regularly include articles relevant to qualitative research

> Sociology:
> > Journal of Contemporary Ethnography
> > Qualitative Sociology
> > Sociological Quarterly
> > Symbolic Interaction
> Language analysis:
> > Discourse Processes
> > International Journal of the Sociology of Language
> > Language in Society
> Organization analysis:
> > Administrative Science Quarterly
> > Journal of Management Studies
> > Qualitative Health Research
> Education:
> > Anthropology and Education Quarterly
> > International Journal of Qualitative Studies in Education
> Anthropology:
> > American Anthropologist
> > American Ethnologist
> > Anthropological Quarterly
> > Cultural Anthropology
> > Current Anthropology
> > Ethnology
> > Journal of Applied Anthropology
> > Man
> Other:
> > Family Process
> > Human Studies
> > Journal for the Theory of Social Behaviour
> > Public Culture
> > Semiotica
> > Signs

a. Nearly all communication journals occasionally include articles related to qualitative research.

about specific techniques or variables, to frame questions, and to suggest ways of sampling phenomena (see Strauss & Corbin, 1990, pp. 48-56). To get the most out of these sources, one should gain competence in using indexes, abstracts, on-line databases, and other tools (Helmericks, Nelsen, & Unnithan, 1991; Rubin, Rubin, & Piele, 1990). Helmericks et al. (1991) provide an excellent search model for our purposes by comparing it with the logic of fieldwork.

CONSULTING COLLEAGUES

It can be useful to exchange ideas and information about a developing research problem with colleagues. Individuals with particular expertise or experience can lend vital assistance in scene casing. In the prison media study, I consulted two faculty members outside my department about the potential site: One regularly donated his time and services to the institution, and so was able to inform me about both whom to contact and details of inmate life there; the other suggested useful gambits for approaching prison officials to gain permission. I might have spent hours searching through the secondary sources of unfamiliar fields for this kind of advice, if it was available there at all.

Colleagues can also act individually as sounding boards or collectively as support groups (Ely, Anzul, Friedman, Garner, & Steinmetz, 1991). They can critique ideas in progress, sympathetically, and help recast them in alternative forms. Colleagues' comments may be philosophically bracing and informative, or specific and pointed: Why only these sites? Why the lack of attention to other, relevant concepts? In the best spirit of such consultation, colleagues' advice should be freely given and freely taken or not taken.

The Research Proposal

Pragmatically, the drafting of a proposal prepares the researcher to respond to several audiences, such as a university's institutional review board, a thesis committee, grant or fellowship reviewers, gatekeepers and sponsors at the research sites, and individual social actors who just want an explanation of what the researcher is up to. Each audience must be addressed separately and in a different form of discourse, but, by working from a basic "script platform," the researcher can expand, highlight, or downplay specific aspects for each constituency while keeping the overall story straight. A proposal also enables the researcher to face a moment of truth in which the motivations, goals, and modus operandi for the study are laid out all at once. It is a final check on the coherence and commitment of the endeavor.

A written proposal helps the researcher to enunciate again what qualitative inquiry seeks to do in the context of a single study: to understand the meanings that inform communicative action. The project might also critique the politics of communicative action; describe naturalistic, *in situ* behavior; modify a theory in a domain of communication; or examine the impacts of a policy or organizational procedure. However, these other goals are premised on the explication of the nature and processes of meaning. The elements described below are included in writing most research proposals.

STATEMENT OF PURPOSE

In a concise statement, a few sentences long, one presents the nature of the study: what will be studied and how the investigation will be conducted. This is a capsule description of the project.

RATIONALE AND SIGNIFICANCE

A section is usually devoted to the arguments supporting the significance of the project. In writing this part of the proposal, one needs to anticipate a question that nearly any reader could have: Why does this problem need to be studied (and why now)? Elaboration should follow on such points as the following:

1. the need to address weaknesses or ambiguities in a theory or concept
2. the need to validate a construct
3. the need to describe a communication process about which little is known
4. the need to document the cultural variation of a communication process or phenomenon
5. the need to define the boundaries of a theory or concept by examining critical cases
6. the need to provide information that may relate to societal or organizational goals, structures, policies, or processes

This list does not exhaust the rationales that may be cited. Certainly, at this stage, idea sources other than those that prompted the foreshadowed problem may be added. One should bear in mind that although readers may have some familiarity with the subject, they may not share one's own intimate familiarity—or enthusiasm. One should lead readers through the logic supporting the project in clear, unpretentious, but technically correct prose. Convincing skeptical readers that qualitative inquiry is the best way to engage the problem is a separate, but no less fundamental, issue that one may have to address in this section.

CONCEPTUAL AREAS OF INQUIRY

Readers look forward to learning about the content of the ideas impelling the study: how the "terrain" of the research subject appears to the researcher. A tour of the study's principal areas of inquiry reassures readers that there is in fact a road that the proposer intends to travel. Here is part of what I proposed in my prison media study:

> This study will be important for what it could reveal of the role of mass media in the unique situation of incarceration. Most inmates anticipate eventual release, yet their terms are characterized by very limited direct contacts with the external world. Exposure to media sources of information might "prepare" some inmates for what to expect in society upon release. . . . A major part of the study will also focus on how and why inmates use the media available to them through the institution or their own resources.

Although I didn't say precisely where the study would lead me, I did say in what directions I was preparing to move. The reader will try to determine whether the writer's sense of direction is based on familiarity with any known landmarks—in the theoretical discourse of the field, that is. Most interpretive or cultural problems in communication can be traced to the intellectual traditions discussed in Chapter 2. Disregarding their overlaps for a moment, several areas of empirical inquiry emerge out of those traditions:

- *Communication as a substantive act.* This refers to acts that are consensually regarded as communication in a specific culture, such as television viewing or public speaking. A study might investigate how a culture or a social membership arranges and enacts events of communication—such as the halftime pep talk, or the Catholic confessional—and what situational functions are served by them.

- *Communication as an explicit or implicit referent.* This refers to explicit or implicit "communication" references that appear in discourse. A study might examine how people talk about their communication problems, their habits of communicating, their communicative environment, or how metaphors are used to represent communication practices or problems.
- *Communication as a constitutive component of social action.* This refers to the ways in which cultural forms or social action are constructed or accomplished by communication. A study might propose that leadership style is achieved by certain signifying practices, or that adolescent social skills consist partly of styles of conversation and gesture derived from media texts.
- *Communication as a regulatory component of social action.* This refers to the uses of communication to regulate, organize, or evaluate social arrangements. A study might focus on the way speech is used to rank employees' status in an organization, or to separate what people can do on the basis of gender.

These areas briefly indicate the sorts of claims about communication phenomena that qualitative inquirers can propose. They make sense within the purview of an interpretive science of communication: All turn in some way on understanding the significance of communicative action. What this part of a research proposal must do is inventively define where the study's claims will be found. It must say how the study of some problem, situation, or mystery will make a demonstrable difference in our knowledge of communication.

The writer should pay particular attention to how concepts are described. In qualitative inquiry, concepts are used as probes for getting inside a scene and exploring. The writer should strive for a balance of "sensitizing" and "analytic" qualities (Glaser & Strauss, 1967). The analytic qualities of a concept concern its general or normative meanings in scholarly discourse. Sensitizing qualities suggest the more vivid, experiential details of the concept as it will be engaged in the project. "Exposure to mass-media sources of information" is a good example of the analytic; knowledgeable readers will recognize its origins in mass communication theory. By itself, however, the term is far too abstract. And it may mislead readers into thinking that this is a very different kind of study, one that will measure or test something called "exposure." Therefore, the writer should indicate how the concept will engage the historical, cultural, or social-interactional aspects of the specific scene. The concept, as described to readers, must reflect the investigator's open sensitivity to field phenomena.

HYPOTHESES OR RESEARCH QUESTIONS

Defined as statements about relationships between variables that can be tested for their truth value, hypotheses are rare items in qualitative proposals. Because hypothesis statements define the objects of study in advance of field entry, they are not ordinarily hospitable to the discovery orientation of the research styles discussed here. However, they are not unknown. The writer may suggest several competing hypotheses about a phenomenon; this allows him or her to make inductive inferences in the field in order to test and modify the hypotheses (see Platt, 1964).

Far more common in qualitative inquiry are research questions. Such questions translate concepts and terms into queries tied to the problematics of the intended research site, using the leverage given by initial theoretical readings and pragmatic scene casing. They specify *expectations* of what the researcher will write about when he or she comes out at the other end of the field experience. Like hypotheses, they can be phrased in a declarative mode, although a question form is more suited to the open-ended character of an expectation. Questions can stand alone, but they usually profit from some accompanying exposition.

METHODOLOGY

From the study's interests and concepts, the researcher should be able to anticipate what he or she needs to learn about them and how to go about it. The methodology is best explained as a *strategy*, linking study goals to the type, range, and sequence of methods to be used. If a research team is involved in gathering data, it is helpful for the proposal writer to try to describe the members' respective roles. Unless the readers require it (as thesis committees and grant review committees often do), a full specification of methods can wait until the researcher has contacted the scene.

PROTOCOL AND LOGISTICS

The term *protocol* in this context refers to the actual conditions under which the methods will be applied: how entry to the field settings will be accomplished, how people will be approached for information, how observing visits are scheduled, how interview guides are constructed, the social contexts of observing and interviewing, and so on. Much of what is considered protocol is a matter of the research role one adopts (see Chapter 5) and how it will be performed. Pertinent details of field entry and field exit, especially as they affect the range of the researcher's action, deserve special attention in the proposal. Like so many other aspects of the design, the protocol is liable to change as the researcher becomes involved in the study. Still, a general description of the intended protocol grounds a proposal in real-life contingencies and reminds the investigator that humbling experiences lie ahead.

Logistics concerns the acquisition and management of resources in the project, including audiovisual equipment, computers, tapes and disks, photocopying, transcriber costs, fieldworker responsibilities and wages, payment for human subjects, travel, office space, and other items charged to oneself or the sponsoring institution. The investigator's time, which is always a considerable expenditure, should be factored in as well. Many of these items can be absorbed in a less-than-accountable way by the researcher's academic institution, or even by the group or organization being studied. If the research is uncomplicated and constraints are not pressing, a full assessment may not be needed. But if the project is funded by outside sources, rigorous accountability procedures will have to be put in place. The scene-casing process is vital to identifying and weighing the potential logistics involved in carrying out a study.

ANALYSIS

Although the areas of inquiry and methodology chosen for the study strongly suggest how data will be analyzed, readers will sometimes want to know more about the coding and analytic techniques that will be used. The discussion of the form of inquiry offered earlier in this chapter communicates a general idea about the way data are used to construct propositions. More detailed guidelines to analyzing data while in the field are presented in Chapter 7. Chapter 8, on writing qualitative narratives, considers analysis from the view of the final integration of data, arguments, and claims.

Conclusion

Through the prefieldwork activities described in this chapter, an idea begins to define its purpose and ways of engaging its subject. Only when a problem has been characterized in some form do sources begin to draw together in suggestive relationships. In this way, the researcher's experience becomes *theoretically sensitive* (Glaser, 1978; Strauss & Corbin, 1990).

Theoretical sensitivity involves "having insight, the ability to give meaning to data, the capacity of understanding, and capability to separate the pertinent from that which isn't" (Strauss & Corbin, 1990, p. 42). In other words, *by articulating the research problem, one begins to see its specific possibilities.* In terms of the planning phase, this process matures in a written research proposal. As one begins to contact the scene—to negotiate for access, to speak to participants, to find a space to observe, to designate a sampling scheme—the possibilities of a problem are realized as actual strategies of fieldwork. We continue into this next phase of project design in Chapter 4.

Notes

1. Details about the prison where the study was conducted and the procedures that were applied (consisting of survey and qualitative components) can be found in Lindlof (1987a).

2. It is not true that only hypothetico-deductive researchers are guilty of not appreciating the reasons for relaxing control over field phenomena. Many qualitative researchers are equally uninformed about the value of control in quantitative social research. Unfortunately, scholars often misunderstand styles of research that differ from their own. Effective instructional programs in communication should be ecumenical in their teaching of research traditions and procedures, even if one kind is emphasized more than others.

3. *Emic* and *etic* distinctions in anthropological analysis represent different modes of perceiving and categorizing objects. Emic analysis intends to derive categories of meaning from the native's perspective, in the terms and performances that the native enacts. It is best characterized by the injunction that "the native's categorization of behavior is the only correct one" (Pelto & Pelto, 1978). Etic work tries to discern patterns of behavior from the standpoint of the observer. Its analytic purpose is to make general, cross-cultural statements about behaviors and material conditions. It operates by means of standardized operational definitions that are often used to code and quantify. Although the two are frequently seen as opposites, it is better to think of them as analytic modes that can be applied differently to the same phenomena. The strengths of one may correct the weaknesses of the other, such as the use of etic measures to define emic experience more precisely (Erickson, 1977, p. 60).

4

Design II: Getting In

Risking Commitment

The processes of starting a project, or getting in, move the inquirer into an arena of commitment and risk. One becomes more *committed* as research questions begin to connect to the empirical world. *Risks* accompany the inquirer's actions as he or she shifts from contemplative planning to decision making: who to contact? how to present myself and my purposes? what to negotiate? how to safeguard participants' interests? how to detect the important persons, settings, activities, events, or time periods, and how to sample them? Although the researcher continues to make design decisions right up until he or she leaves the field, it is in these initial contacts that much of a project's future is decided.

Picking up where we left off in Chapter 3, the activities of *institutional review* and *contacting the scene* ready the researcher for generating data. Finishing out this chapter is a discussion of sampling strategies, along with some communication exemplars.

Human Subject Protections

Academic institutions require students, faculty, and staff scientists to submit their research plans to institutional review boards (IRBs) for review and approval. Other public and private institutions that conduct human or animal research, such as medical research centers, also have such boards. The IRB articulates and enforces the institution's particular standards of human subject protection, often modeled after guidelines issued by federal agencies. The major purposes of the review are to ensure that the rights of human subjects are properly respected and that subjects will not be endangered by a study's procedures or outcomes.

This is not the place to go deeply into the origins or politics of human subject protections (see Reiser, Dyck, & Curran, 1977; Reynolds, 1972). Suffice it to say that universities have set up such boards in order to meet federal and state guidelines for obtaining research funding, and as protection against legal actions brought by individuals or groups claiming damages from their research participation. The person who decides to conduct research without the imprimatur of the IRB, for whatever reason, may not enjoy the backing of his or her institution if a problem with human subjects arises.

On a higher plane, protections function as a guarantor of a study's scientific responsibility. Most laypersons are not able on their own to evaluate whether a study follows sound procedures for ensuring anonymity and reasonable levels of physical and psychological risk. They are often mystified by science, or, especially in the case of biomedical research, desirous of its beneficial results. Few people appreciate the fact that science is not engineering; that is, the way of science is not proven application, but mistakes, uncertainties, and calculated risks. Human subject protections are designed to try to inform individuals who participate in research of the risks to which they may be exposed and to reduce the incidence of such risks.

Every person or team who does a qualitative study should apply for and receive IRB approval. In my view, this is a given. Among all the exigencies of starting up a study, it is easy to see IRB review as a bureaucratic hassle. Certainly many people forgo review of their proposals (if they even have proposals) for a variety of reasons: They claim there is not enough time, that the IRB is capricious, that the IRB doesn't understand qualitative research, that the IRB would "expedite" it anyway, that "there's nothing harmful about *my* study," and so on. However, these excuses evade the basic questions that an IRB review poses: Is there anything about the treatment of participants outlined in a proposal that could be improved? Is there anything about the way data and reports are proposed to be handled that could be improved? A review of a project's human subject protections acts as a critical reading not of its premises or substance, but of its elemental fairness.

Qualitative social science presents special ethical problems, as well as some that are common to all human science inquiries. The following subsections examine the major issues that should be addressed about a qualitative study.

INFORMED CONSENT

Anyone who participates in a study should (a) do so voluntarily, (b) be able to understand what the study demands of him or her, (c) be able to understand participation's risks and benefits, and (d) have the legal capacity to give consent. Only those who give their *informed consent* can participate. Even if they consent, they can leave the study at any time without negative consequences. Researchers should explain the terms of informed consent both verbally and in writing, and in language the participants can understand.

The preceding paragraph nicely summarizes the ideal, but practical problems with informed consent arise in many ways, partly as a result of researchers' own ambivalence about what to reveal and when to reveal it (Fine, 1993). Projects are often long, arduous, and emergent. Not even the researchers know exactly how they will turn out. This can be told to participants up front, albeit without going into great detail. It is better for participants to decline at the start than to drop out partway through the study.

Researchers should explicate their studies for potential participants carefully, patiently, and informally, but not ponderously. I find that once I explain some basic principles of qualitative inquiry, people understand why I cannot predict exactly what will happen. They may even appreciate the "benefits" of participating (see the discussion about negotiating access, below). Of course, they still may not consent. Figure 4.1 presents an example of an informed consent form used in a study of video, television, and family life that I conducted with Milt Shatzer.

Some claim that going through the informed consent procedure can damage the rapport one hopes to build with an informant, and even hamstring the project (Agar, 1980). Like a prenuptial agreement, the informed consent might remind everyone of what can go wrong and might therefore spoil the "romance." However, one can usually try to build rapport in some early meetings, and soon afterward sit down with the informant to explain his or her rights in the research. The discussion of informed consent itself can be an important element in establishing a good relationship.

When research is conducted in an open, free-access setting, such as in a shopping mall, it may be quite impractical to inform people that their

Study Title: Uses and Perceptions of Television and Videocassette Recorders by Families

I, _____, consent to participate in the research study under the direction of Dr. Thomas R. Lindlof (Associate Professor of Telecommunications at the University of Kentucky), Dr. Milton J. Shatzer (Assistant Professor of Telecommunications at the University of Kentucky), and Dan Wilkinson (graduate student, College of Communications, University of Kentucky).

PURPOSE OF THE RESEARCH: (a) To investigate the role of television and videocassette recorders (VCRs) in family members' activities, communication patterns, time use, and uses of other household media; and (b) to investigate individual family members' uses and perceptions of television and VCRs. The approach of this research is descriptive, utilizing case studies.

EXPECTED DURATION OF SUBJECTS' PARTICIPATION: June through September 1986. With subjects' permission, their participation may extend through November 1986.

RESEARCH PROCEDURES: The primary procedures will be interviews with subjects, questionnaires, user diaries, and observations in subjects' homes. Interviews will be audio-recorded and transcribed.

RISKS AND DISCOMFORTS TO SUBJECTS: Subjects will not be at physical or psychological risk and should experience no discomforts resulting from the research procedures.

EXPECTED BENEFITS OF THE RESEARCH: This research is expected to yield knowledge of the uses and effects of television and VCR technology in family life, particularly as it relates to the social and intellectual development of children. The research is also expected to result in the formation of hypotheses that will be of value in subsequent studies of this subject. Subjects will receive a verbal debriefing as well as a copy of the research report following the conclusion of the research period. As a result, they may obtain increased understanding of the role of those media in their lives. Subjects will also receive a copy of the book in which this study will appear.

CONFIDENTIALITY PROCEDURES: All data generated in the course of this research will be locked in a secure location at either the first author's residence or his office at the University of Kentucky. The identities of the subjects will not be disclosed to any unauthorized persons. Any references to the identities of the subjects that would compromise their anonymity will be removed prior to the preparation of research reports and publications.

COMPENSATION FOR PARTICIPATION IN THE RESEARCH: No compensation will be provided to subjects for their participation.

Figure 4.1. An Informed Consent Form

WHO TO CONTACT FOR ANSWERS TO PERTINENT QUESTIONS ABOUT THE RESEARCH AND THE RESEARCH SUBJECTS' RIGHTS: Institutional Review Board Office, 315 Kinkead Hall, University of Kentucky (257-8295). The subjects will receive a copy of this consent form.

SUBJECTS:
Participation is voluntary. Refusal to participate will involve no penalty or loss of benefits to which I am otherwise entitled. I understand that I may discontinue participation at any time without penalty of loss of benefits to which I am otherwise entitled.

DATE: _____

SUBJECTS' SIGNATURES : _____

_____

(Minor) _____

(Minor) _____

(Minor) _____

(Minor) _____

INVESTIGATOR:
I have explained and defined in detail the research procedure in which the subject has consented to participate.

DATE: _____

INVESTIGATOR: _____

Figure 4.1. (Continued)

behavior is being studied. The subjects are anonymous to the researcher anyway, and they are interacting in public, so the need to obtain anyone's consent under such conditions may seem nebulous. Clearly there are legitimate research questions about public behavior that can be approached only through covert observation. This does not mean, however, that we should reserve total license to decide when and where a person's actions can be recorded for research purposes. Arguments based on practicality and the oblivious character of public behavior should be weighed carefully against the researcher's superiority and power in such situations.

Finally, subject pools in qualitative studies almost always expand unexpectedly. In my work on family television and microcomputing, friends and relatives of the original participant families showed up suddenly and became part of the study. Even if I had had informed consent forms on hand at those moments, it would have been awkward to proffer them. As a rule of thumb, it is not necessary to get the informed consent of all those who wander unexpectedly onto the scene. It is also not necessary to get the informed consent of everyone in an organization or group if a few key individuals have given consent on behalf of all—assuming, of course, that all have accurate knowledge of what the study entails. It is usually not problematic to obtain consent if the participants become key social actors or informants whose actions or words will be reported extensively.

INSTRUMENTS AND THEIR RISKS

The researcher should submit copies of surveys, interview schedules, and other instruments to the IRB (but not necessarily to participants). The techniques of participant observation do not usually place significant demands on participants, because they are only doing "what comes naturally." However, one might add a clause to the informed consent form explaining that the observing will not interfere with the ability of participants to carry out their normal activities.

The use of covert techniques does need to be justified, especially since the participants usually cannot be debriefed when the study is over. At a minimum, one needs to show why covert observation is uniquely necessary for the study of the problem and to offer convincing arguments that no one will be negatively affected. In general, qualitative researchers need to be wary of the exploitative potential of engendering friendships and other close relationships simply in order to obtain information (see Dingwall, 1980, pp. 879-882).

In interviews, it is not uncommon for respondents to reveal information not intended for a third party, or to bring up sensitive subjects that were not anticipated at the start of the interview. When such events happen, the emotional reverberations can be substantial and potentially long-lasting (LaRossa, Bennett, & Gelles, 1981). It is unethical to use tactics that are meant to cause distress; it is simply unfortunate when the researcher is unable to avert or repair unintended distress.

SPECIAL POPULATIONS

Certain classes of people are considered to be especially vulnerable to the entreaties of researchers, for example, children, the homeless, medical patients, prison inmates, and persons with physical or mental disabilities. Such individuals, like any others, should be told that their cooperation is voluntary. Under no circumstances should the researcher act coercively or allow institutional agents to coerce on his or her behalf. And although the researcher may offer material incentives to potential participants in exchange for their cooperation, this should never be done in a demeaning or exploitative way. The IRB usually wants to know why a special population is needed for a particular project.

ANONYMITY OF SUBJECTS

Publication of qualitative studies carries the potential of revealing vital secrets (including "whistle-blowing"), violating privacy, harming reputations, exposing "uncomfortable realities," and depicting behavior in ways that offend the participants. These issues are exacerbated by the fact that researchers and participants rarely reach true consensus about the nature of the research subject, because they respond to very different values and constituencies (Becker, 1964).

Participants should be told that, given the nature of qualitative narratives, their actions and personal characteristics may be described in some detail. But they should also be assured that their actual identities will be known only to the researcher, and that anything that might identify them will be expunged in reports resulting from the project. The researcher should never be careless about protecting participants in either published or spoken formats. Practically speaking, however, textually modifying the identities of people and places is something of an art form (see Chapter 8); it has been done in many different ways, and with varying success in the eyes of participants. The more specific the research site, and the more visible the research problem (either locally or nationally), the harder it will be for the researcher to construct anonymous identities without altering the "substantive" content.

In a related vein, the researcher should indicate to participants in some way that only he or she is responsible for the particular interpretations of what is observed and heard in the scene. Participants should not be misled into thinking that their words and actions will not be subjected to an independent analysis of which they may or may not approve.

DATA ACCESS

Even if they are not told in advance—and they should be—most participants will soon notice that data inscribed in notes, tapes, and transcripts accumulate rapidly in a project. Though only a small portion of it will appear in published form, the entire set of files and tapes may resemble an FBI data bank and may take on similarly sinister connotations. Participants need to be assured of the confidentiality of everything that is collected. This can be explained to them in general terms, but the IRB will want to know specifics about the data: where they will be kept (they should be stored in a secure location, such as a university office), who will have access to them, and how long they will be stored.

SUMMARY

Attention to human subject protections rarely impedes or even slows down a study. Any inconvenience is outweighed by the benefits it yields to participants without whose trust and presence a study could not be done. Preparing for IRB review has other positive effects as well: It can focus the researcher's thoughts on the entire design; it can impress gatekeepers and participants alike of the professional conduct of the project; and, of course, it affords legal protection to the investigator.

Recently, the value of human subject protections in qualitative research has been questioned. Warren and Staples (1989) perceive private health institutions' refusal to share their patient files with researchers, on grounds of confidentiality, to be a smokescreen to cover political reasons for not wanting critical research scrutiny. McCall and Wittner (1990, pp. 73-74) suggest that the convention of anonymity maintains the power of the author to control voices in a text. And although Cassell (1978) believes participants do need the protection of regulatory institutions, she also points out that it is the fieldworker who often depends on his or her participants for physical safety and even subsistence, and that change is more likely to occur in the observer than the observed. So far, however, human subjects protections seem to work to the mutual interests of researchers, institutions, participants, and society as a whole.

Contacting the Scene

The first days or weeks of a project are, in many researchers' estimation, the "most uncomfortable stage of field work" (R. H. Wax, 1971, p. 15). It is probably the most uncomfortable time for the participants, too. What accounts for this discomfort? I suspect it is caused by deep feelings of vulnerability on both sides, but for different reasons. The researcher feels the vulnerability of the possibility of rejection: The approached group or organization may turn him or her down, key individuals may opt not to cooperate, and others may be less than gracious and accommodating. The researcher is also vulnerable to the subtler terror of a new style of living: Routines are disrupted as he or she visits settings that may be miles from familiar territory, blocks of time must be devoted to writing up notes, and some distress may result from shifting between the high intensity of participant immersion and the lower-key realities of everyday life (Wiley, 1987). Underlying these frontal pressures are background doubts about whether the project is viable after all and where it will all lead. The researcher may bravely acknowledge reassurances that these feelings are normal and transitory, but not really believe them.

The participants sense the vulnerability of being objects of scrutiny. Unless they have extended an invitation to "host" the project, or have enthusiastically embraced the wishes of their trusted leader to cooperate (both of which are unusual), many participants will greet the researcher's coming with misgivings, if not outright suspicion. On the surface, their routines continue as before, but complex currents of questions and conclusions about what the researcher wants to know, and why, will run through participants' thoughts and coffee breaks.

This preamble is not the only story that can be told about the first days and weeks in the field. It is an archetypal one, however, and captures the essence of many of my own first contacts in the field (with more fictional license taken in telling the participants' side). Although some feelings of vulnerability may be healthy, in very large doses they can cripple. The researcher already has a demanding ontological position to cope with: He or she has declared it his or her professional business to enter another's life world with the intention of "seeing" as the other sees, and then to inscribe such experiences in professional genres of written work. Anything that makes the transition to the research setting an easier one is all to the good. It is important to keep in mind, however, that the tactics used to enter a setting should not be marginalized from the rest of the study. The barriers and equivocations that people sometimes throw up in the path of an inquiry are themselves interesting data.

What is called *field entry* (or entrée) is a series of overlapping events, complicated by the fact that each scene presents a different mix of challenges. Some general lessons about field entry can be conveyed, however, along with some provisos about how to improvise in the clinches. The first of these events is usually the presentation of one's interests to those who control access to the desired research sites.

PRESENTING THE STUDY AND THE SELF

Gatekeepers

The term *gatekeeper* should be familiar to students of mass-media organizations. It refers to those individuals (e.g., news executives), working groups (e.g., editors), and operations (e.g., the international desk) that select raw materials to be processed as media content, according to organizational and industrial codes of workmanship (Anderson & Meyer, 1988). A gatekeeper surveys the environment for concepts and events that conform to the needs of a medium.

As applied to those who possess the power to grant access to researchers, the meaning of *gatekeeper* differs from its usage in mass communication in two important ways. First, it is not always evident in a group or organization who the gatekeeper is. This is because the role of gatekeeper is usually a temporary or part-time one that is activated only when someone asks for access. For example, in my studies of families, I am not always aware in my first contacts who will eventually prove to be the decisive gatekeeping party—the husband, the wife, or both. I make it my business to treat both as gatekeepers by presenting myself and the study to each of them, separately or together. Spousal consent operates in various modes across families; children can be influential voices, though they never function as true gatekeepers.

Certainly, some organizations, such as public school districts, regularly field requests for entry from academic researchers and may have developed policies that define the kinds of research that are normally permitted and how they should be proposed. However, there is considerable variance in the ways these responsibilities are assigned. In some organizations, executive committees may be charged with making decisions concerning such requests, whereas in others ad hoc committees are formed on a case-by-case basis, and in still others a single individual will bear most of this responsibility. Usually, however, granting such permission involves the knowledge and approval of those at the highest levels of an organization. In my prison media study, I learned fairly soon that the deputy superintendent was responsible for reviewing research proposals, although even he needed to consult first with an officer of the state correctional system as well as gain final approval for the project from his own superior, the superintendent of the prison. After a brief period of dealing with the deputy superintendent, I understood that he was the key person in the permission line.

A second important aspect that distinguishes the office of research scene gatekeeper is its passive character, and it is from this posture that the power of rejection is derived.[1] Simply put, the researcher needs the gatekeeper's attention and approval far more than the gatekeeper needs the researcher. The gatekeeper can ignore or turn down the researcher's request if the organization perceives that it has little to gain from cooperation and potentially much to lose. Obviously, there are nuances to this attitude. The more an organization or group is accountable to the public—usually conceived in terms of a public service mandate—the more likely it is to treat the researcher's inquiry with seriousness, and even welcome it in some cases. Commercial institutions usually keep their guards up very high, perceiving proposed research as an intrusion into the proprietary nature of their activities.

The researcher may have to walk a fine line between ingratiating him- or herself with the gatekeeper and asserting his or her own interests in the project. Throughout it all, the researcher should encourage a positive, open-ended entry outlook. Taking the steps described below may increase the investigator's chances of gaining access.

Determine who the gatekeeper is. As already discussed, it may take some effort to find out who manages the "gate." The researcher should learn about the gatekeeper's position in the organization and about the person occupying that status. (Does this person have advanced education in the field? How long has he or she been with the company? What other positions has he or she held?)

Look closely at the missions, needs, and current interests of the organization, and tailor the rhetoric and interests of the proposal to them as much as possible.

This is not to suggest that the researcher should present the project as ameliorating the organization's problems, or that he or she should adopt a consultant role. In fact, doing so could be disastrous to the integrity of the project. Rather, by showing familiarity with the language, history, and current state of the scene, and offering some sensible yet politically innocuous benefits of the study to the organization, the researcher can achieve several things: demonstrate the practical value of the study, become sensitized in advance to the gatekeeper's perspective (usually a *management* perspective—a critical qualification for the researcher to bear in mind on the way in), and lay a groundwork for good interpersonal relations.

Attend studiously to the way that the self and the proposal are presented. The researcher should give the gatekeeper every reason to think that he or she is a trustworthy, competent, credentialed, organized person who will be respectful of the internal culture of the group or organization. The proposal should be professionally prepared and free of pretentious or opaque jargon. The researcher should make it clear that in order to conduct a fair inquiry, he or she needs some freedom to experience different levels and sectors of the organization. The researcher should defer to the organization's timetable and mechanisms for deciding to grant access, but should also inform the gatekeeper of any deadlines the researcher may have.

Show a willingness to make contacts with others in the organization, perhaps to solicit their permission as well. This move has more utility in scenes where authority is strongly centralized than in those where the prevailing ethos stresses shared responsibility for company goals and individual autonomy in task performance. Underlying this is the notion that a researcher's associations with authority figures are acutely noticed by members; it is in the best interests of the project for the researcher to find ways to buffer such associations. Kahn and Mann (1969), for example, developed a procedure they call "contingent acceptance decisions," in which the permission line moves downward through the hierarchy until all agree to participate. They note, "It is implicit in this method that a higher level within the authority structure will not veto the study if the researcher can gain the acceptance of those at successively lower levels" (pp. 48-49). One downside of the method is that members at any one level can reject the project. Still, the researcher should seek to gain broad support for the project in the organization, without appearing to "sandbag" the gatekeeper.

Do not make promises that cannot be kept. If there is a liberal estimate and a conservative estimate for the amount of time that fieldwork will take, the researcher should emphasize the liberal figure with the gatekeeper. But if the gatekeeper balks, the researcher needs to be prepared to downsize that figure and the project's scope accordingly. A corollary rule is to keep commitments open-ended by discussing the research in terms of broad objectives to be achieved, which may require varying amounts of time to complete.

So far, this discussion has centered on gatekeepers who enable the researcher to enter a scene and start to work under agreed-upon conditions. Such individuals or committees are sometimes empowered to compel the membership to cooperate with the researcher, or at least to advise them strongly to try to accommodate him or her as best they can. However, there are other gatekeepers who simply give the researcher access to members, who in turn decide whether or not to participate. The researcher must then go to the members, as individuals or when they assemble in groups, and appeal to them directly.

For locating families for ethnographic study, for example, Lull (1985) observes that "contact through some agency of importance to the family is usually necessary to gain access . . . [including] religious and educational institutions, places of work, community service groups, and clubs" (p. 175). Following approval by the executive board of a group such as the PTA, the usual scenario involves either using the telephone list to call members or making a spoken appeal at a general meeting. In trying to reach cooperative families who own home computers, I placed items in the newsletter and on the electronic bulletin board of an IBM users' group, gained access to the roll of a summer computer camp, and got permission from a retail computer store to use its list of recent purchasers. The store list was not nearly as important an agent to the families as the other two organizations, and, not surprisingly, generated the fewest families for my sample.

Sponsors

Gatekeepers typically refrain from becoming too identified with the researcher, so as to avoid getting entwined with negative events that may result from the study. A *sponsor*, in contrast, takes an active interest in the project, vouches for its goals, and sometimes helps the researcher locate informants or move into participative roles. Believing that some good for the group or organization will come out of the study, the sponsor stakes his or her reputation on the researcher's efforts.

In the classical fieldwork sense, the sponsor is someone who will introduce the researcher to others in the community and will serve as an ally and informational resource. The researcher recognizes the need for such a person very quickly. As Rosalie Wax (1971) writes, "[The researcher] is trying hardest of all to find some person or persons who will advise, assist, and teach him, introduce him, or . . . 'go around with him'" (p. 17).

In *action research*, for example, a client (sponsor) engages the researcher to study certain organizational procedures or the introduction of new technology. The researcher is invited to diagnose problems, engage in collaborative analysis of data, and engender problem-solving skills that the organization itself can adopt and modify (Argyris & Schön, 1989; Levitt, 1989). The sponsor in such a study often gives the researcher nearly free rein to examine areas of the organization relevant to the study. In the best case, the organizational membership has already agreed to the concept of an outside assessment before the researcher arrives. Clearly, the value of sponsorship is greatly diminished if the sponsor does not enjoy the confidence of most of the members.

NEGOTIATING ACCESS

Simply obtaining permission from a gatekeeper does not guarantee successful entry. The gatekeeper's approval is a necessary but by no means sufficient condition for setting up a research presence. A sound research design also depends upon the researcher's finding out what people can contribute and *are willing* to contribute.

We usually speak of *negotiating* access. The significance of that term should not be missed: The researcher and the researched must reach some mutual agreement about how the research tasks will be conducted in the social scene. Whereas informed consent is based on a "standard contract" of rights and obligations granted to any generalized human subject, actual access must deal with the realities that exist in the practices of a specific scene. How a person contributes to a qualitative study is always his or her individual decision.

As in any negotiation, the parties involved have their own interests to look after and their own goals to pursue. But unlike in other negotiating situations, the researcher's goals and interests are usually the sole reason for the parties to come together at all for such a discussion. People rarely seek out the scrutiny of a research project. Thus the burden shifts to the investigator to make a persuasive case for them—the family members, the friends, the club, the group, the organization, the department—to create space for an activity that is alien to their normal ways of doing things. In this sense, the researcher bargains from a weak position. Little compensation of any value to the membership can be promised in return. The researcher must agree to accommodate to *their* routines, rules, and schedules, and to answer their questions about the credibility and worth of the enterprise. Let us not sympathize too deeply with the investigator's plight: Research *is* intrusive, and should be accountable to those who are asked to get involved.

Given the nature of this bargaining position, the researcher must come to the negotiation with something other than resources or profit potential to offer. As I have mentioned previously in passing, he or she may base an appeal on the "social good" of research: the advancement of systematic knowledge about the nature and effects of communication. Such knowledge may enable people to become more self-aware, skilled, and responsible agents in their own communication practices. This tendentious logic may not gain compliance on its own, but if the researcher can make explicit the connection between research and teaching, or between research and praxis (especially by using a familiar example or two), the social-good appeal can "cut" more effectively. In talking to families, for example, I often refer to the lack of good research on how children learn to watch television or on how families organize their time and activities with respect to the medium. I do not fail to point out how research can help students and others learn more about a phenomenon of such fundamental importance in nearly every American household. It is interesting to note how people, initially amused at the idea of "watching people watch TV," often come to view the proposed project as legitimate after listening to the argument. Their latent perplexities about television seem to surface during the conversation. It is important, however, that the researcher not promise either conclusive or actionable results from the project.

Of perhaps greater interest to prospective participants can be the researcher's desire to understand their individual expertise or the interesting nature of their cultural domain. This appeal calls for clarifying the special attributes of qualitative inquiry; that is, only by understanding a world from the inside can we comprehend and convey its truths. Cultural members often understand and appreciate this motive. Many people do welcome the opportunity to have their lives understood by a sympathetic outsider and to reveal the artfulness of their activities. They see the chance to teach some of what they know, not only to the researcher but eventually to readers of scholarly and popular publications. Others are curious about how a "disinterested" professional researcher will depict them; however, such an attitude may belie either a therapeutic or a narcissistic side. Still other people want to have their stories told as a way of advancing their own political, professional, or interpersonal interests. However, the researcher should be careful not to encourage any particularly divisive or self-serving motives for participating.

Finally, the researcher can simply claim that engaging in field research is part of his or her job duties, which in turn depends on the good graces of willing participants. The ingenuous character of this appeal does strike a chord for many listeners. After all, we all have jobs to do. Some honor this appeal only for students, because they assume that students are literally "required" to carry out this type of research, and with significantly fewer resources than their supervising professors. Grodin (1990), for example, gained demonstrably more volunteers for her study of women self-help book readers by stating that she was conducting research for her doctoral dissertation.

What kinds of access conditions should the researcher attempt to negotiate with participants at the outset? The following areas apply mostly to participant observation work; Chapter 6 focuses more explicitly on ways to establish relationships with interviewees.

Gaining a Perspective

Whether he or she constructs a study around a single individual or a social collectivity numbering in the tens or hundreds of people, the researcher will utilize at least one *perspective* going into the scene (Anderson, 1987). A perspective is not a purely cognitive exercise in role taking, nor is it a neutral vantage elevated above the social fray. Instead, it is a practical way to interpret events. A perspective aligns with the interests, speaking patterns, dress, customs, and culture codes of a group, faction, or individual. As Anderson (1987) puts it, "Adopting a perspective means that the analyst references his or her behavior within that group" (p. 306). A perspective is a partisan view, but it does not denigrate or ignore the other perspectives within a group.

Everyone acts from a perspective, but the researcher's perspective is a reflexive sense-making device. He or she uses it self-consciously as a method for experiencing situated action—similar to but never exactly the same as the culture member naively using the "same" perspective. The perspective is often not of the researcher's own choosing, again reflecting his or her weak negotiating position. Fortunately, the researcher's perspective is usually redefined over time, as Horowitz (1986) relates in her report on a study of Chicano gang members:

> The first dimension of my identity that I discovered they were constructing was as "a lady" which placed me in a respected but somewhat distant position from them. A "lady" implied that a woman was unobtainable sexually. . . .
>
> However, "ladies" do not sit in the park and are not interested in gang members' lives. Social workers might be "ladies" who asked questions, but there were no outsider-social workers in the community, and the Lions discarded that category for me because I was at the park on evenings and weekends and did not try to make them do anything that would threaten their way of life. Finally, about four weeks after I arrived, one of the gang members declared that I was like Lois Lane, the reporter (Superman's girlfriend). It was an identity that transcended gender. . . . This provided them with the necessary identity with which I could ask about their activities and they could readily respond. Often they would seek me out to relay new stories of gang activities and, later on in research, when someone wanted a story retold, to say, "Ask Ruth, she's been writing it all down." (pp. 414-416)

As this excerpt shows, a perspective develops as a researcher works into a role in the field setting. Much more will be said about role adaptation in Chapter 5. However, it is vital to emphasize here that the researcher's adoption of a role—a range of obligations and expectations for performing—often begins as he or she interacts with gatekeepers. More commonly, a role emerges as the researcher gains entry. In the first weeks of my prison media study, I was almost entirely in the company of prison officials and personnel. The only role available was that of the academic researcher, and I adapted my own dress, language, and manner to those expectations. For better or for worse, this appeared to be the only way to attain my goal of interviewing inmates.

Thus a role and its associated perspective constrain what a researcher can experience and explain. Though a role may be ascribed to the researcher on the way in, opportunities to renegotiate it usually come along in time.

Circumscribing the Research Relationship

The researcher's natural inclination is to consider *everything* in a scene as potential data. Casual greetings and small talk before an interview starts, or farewells exchanged at its conclusion, can reveal a host of inci-

dental details about the participant's world. The reasons given for breaking an interview appointment may be worth noting. Even the rituals of
initial contact and informed consent can indicate quite a bit about authority relations and the sensitive aspects of a group's boundaries.

Not being fully acquainted with the nuances of reflexive, relational
modes of scholarship, the unwary participant may believe that the "research" is confined to certain events. The participant may think that only
speech and action pertaining to an area in which the researcher expressly
stated interest will be noted, and that all other events are either out-of-
bounds or too trivial to matter. Obviously, such perceptions carry ethical
implications, the most serious concerning the privacy to which social
actors feel they are entitled.

The most responsible approach is for the researcher simply to tell the
participant when the research activity will be "on." For some projects in
which interviewing predominates, this could be when the tape recorder
is rolling. For other projects, *all* contacts with participants produce usable
research data. It is probably best for the researcher not to suggest overly
complicated ways of defining what should or should not be used as data:
for example, the notion that some comments be used only on an unat-
tributed-source basis ("deep background"). Such special arrangements
can erode the foundations of trust and consistency on which a project
depends. Basic human subject protections—especially the assurance of
anonymity—should answer most of the questions a participant might
have about the idea that everything a researcher sees and hears can result
in "data."

Negotiations may follow if a participant wants to confine the research act more narrowly than the analyst wants. However, the researcher should not compromise too much if the research problem
demands access to the full range of potential events.

Accessing Information

When I began the prison media study, I asked for information about
the inmates to be sampled, such as their ages, ethnicities, offenses for
which they were convicted, their sentences, and the cell blocks in which
they were housed. I asked to see where the inmates lived, ate, studied,
and worked. I asked for copies of documents relevant to the study, such
as the inmate manual, the state directives for treatment of inmates, and
other written policies. None of these requests was turned down; one or
two others were, however.

Preparations of the kind outlined in Chapter 3 enable the researcher to anticipate the kinds of documents, records, artifacts, and site visits that could be helpful. These materials can aid in the researcher's acculturation, assist in sampling, and sketch in some of the historical and ideological background of the scene. It is wise for the researcher to ask for such access in stages, as it is needed, beginning with the most essential materials. Asking for too much too soon may produce overwhelming amounts of documents, or may overwhelm the organization's ability to provide them. It is also advisable for the researcher not to reach too far beyond his or her own role for information. If he or she is a participant observer in a middle-management setting, for example, getting access to confidential upper-management materials may do more damage to field relations than they are worth. In informal memberships, such as in families or peer cultures, artifacts and documents are usually shared more freely.

Number and Duration of Contacts

Among the most pragmatic interests of participants, and rightfully so, is how often they should expect to be contacted. Most prefer to know the overall length of involvement, the number of visits or interviews, and the approximate time required for each. Many participants would like to minimize all of these. The researcher, on the other hand, would like the participant's commitment to be open-ended: not necessarily "on call," but at least available for "callbacks." Somewhere between these two desires are grounds for negotiation.

If the researcher has succeeded in portraying the project in the most compelling *and* realistic light (no small task), the participant will be ready to make an initial commitment. The first meeting or two, then, should result in an agreement about how their mutual needs will be met: work schedules, visits, or interviews arranged; phone numbers exchanged; contingencies discussed. Chapters 5 and 6 go into greater detail about the attitudes and gambits the researcher should employ for observing and interviewing, respectively, at this stage.

In general, the researcher should strive for specificity and commitment for the opening phase of fieldwork, but leave the middle and end points of the participant's involvement as open as possible. He or she can tell the participant, "I'd like for us to talk about Topic A at our first interview, and at the second and third interviews we will discuss Topics B and C. Because we may not finish everything we need to talk about, we may have another meeting after that. But we can discuss it later." The researcher should estimate carefully the parameters for covering topical areas, for the developing rapport may depend on it. An informant frustrated over still discussing Topic A at the third interview may exercise his or her right to bail out of the study.

Long-term cooperation seems to be enhanced as participants perceive greater salience of a study for themselves, and as contacts with the researcher become more personalized (Thornton, Freedman, & Camburn, 1982). If the work goes well for both parties, it is usually not hard to extend the involvement. In fact, as we will see in Chapter 7, ending a field relationship embodies a very different set of issues from beginning one.

Reciprocating

Even after informed consent has been discussed and the form signed, a participant may express an interest in receiving some type of reward for participating. Researchers sometimes suggest how they might help participants; they have been known to give rides to participants, to buy participants meals or drinks, to help out with household chores, and even to pay part of participants' rent or grocery bills. Some of these might be considered acts of courtesy. Others are more clearly favors given in exchange for data or access.

It is natural for any interpersonal relationship to involve exchanges of time, effort, and services. Relationships that begin from a research purpose are not very different in this regard. Personal interests are expressed, knowledge is shared, affections are felt and displayed, and trust gradually develops. Getting along with an informant, or becoming an accepted member of a scene, depends on knowing what to give and what to take, and when to give and take. Otherwise, the researcher may come across as uptight, as "a stiff," and access will dry up.

Giving rewards, or promising future rewards, as a condition for negotiating access constitutes an overt *quid pro quo*. Monetary payment is the most common method. I paid the inmates I interviewed $3.00 each (in 1983 dollars) for a 90-minute session, an amount that represented roughly 10 hours of work at the prison's wage rate. This incentive induced a high level of cooperation among the inmates contacted. It also appeared to induce in them a seriousness about finding out what I wanted to know. The former effect was undoubtedly salutary for the project; the value of the latter effect was more dubious.

Rewards, especially monetary, are effective when would-be participants have little intrinsic interest in the project or when they have a real need for the reward. The size of the payment should be kept to the minimum amount that will achieve the desired cooperation. In addition to keeping expenses down, a minimal payment tends to suppress the existence of a *quid pro quo*. A payment should signify a simple gratuity (expression of thanks) for participating. The researcher should avoid subsequent payments for specific information or access to services; such a situation is rife with possibilities for informants to "play with" the researcher. In general, a payment-for-participation arrangement gets a research relationship off on a peculiar footing, and should be approached with caution.

Summary

Gatekeepers may open an organization to the researcher, but members have their own reasons to cooperate or even pay the slightest attention to what the researcher wants. Although the researcher may need to use different negotiating stances with different persons in the scene, it is critical that he or she play by fair, consistent rules with all concerned. Closed systems do not exist in social life. The researcher cannot expect to form relationships partitioned from one another and survive the project with his or her credibility intact.

By the same token, the researcher may learn of taboos, alliances, repressed histories, animosities, grievances, and hidden agendas. The knowledge he or she has of these phenomena will always be partial, because the researcher necessarily experiences a scene through a particular perspective. Although this perspective widens and becomes more richly informed as the researcher proceeds through a study, the account it produces will never be complete. Knowing that what one knows is always partial is an important analytic precept, as we will see in Chapter 7. It is also a valid way for the researcher to present his or her capacity of understanding to culture members at the outset and to solidify their trust thereafter.

FAMILIARIZATION

The scene-casing activities discussed in Chapter 3 enable the researcher to determine the feasibility and suitability of an emerging project. At this stage, however, more systematic means of "getting in" to the sites of communicative performance and practice are required. The techniques described here are especially recommended if the researcher possesses little firsthand acquaintance with the scene, or if the action to be investigated is too dispersed or sporadic to be witnessed easily except by the participants themselves.

Maps

The kinds of objects that make up a setting, and the relationships among them, usually indicate the social roles and activity patterns found there. To make sense as cultural artifacts, objects and spatial order should reveal something about the shared values, meaning systems, and histories of the scene's inhabitants. For example, the scatter of toys around a family's television set implies something about how children and their activities are regarded in that family (Lindlof, Shatzer, & Wilkinson, 1988).

A preliminary way to frame these relationships is to construct a map of the setting. Denzin (1978) notes that maps

> give the researcher a working picture of the temporal, ritual, and routine features of the persons or social organizations under study. Representational maps are also graphic. They pictorially display the recurrent and stable features of the social worlds under examination. Typically these graphic maps will describe the ecological and physical layout of concrete social settings. (pp. 95-96)

Figure 4.2 is a map of the household of one of the families that participated in the families and television study mentioned above (Lindlof et al., 1988). Clearly it is not the work of an expert draftsman, but it accomplishes the goal of representing the floor plan and principal pieces of furniture with respect to the focal object of interest, the television/VCR. In this case, the map helped orient the field researcher who worked with this family, and enabled all three of us to work with the transcripts and field notes more effectively.

In complex settings, maps can be essential in helping the researcher to understand where and when the members live, work, or engage in their varied activities. For instance, a map can make clear heavy and light traffic patterns and large and small office areas, as indications of organizational hierarchy. The researcher can construct several maps of the same area over a span of time, noting how changes in organizational procedure result in changes of spatial dimensions and, perhaps, of communication patterns as well. Combined with observational and interview data, maps help the analyst understand the social and cultural import of a physical setting.

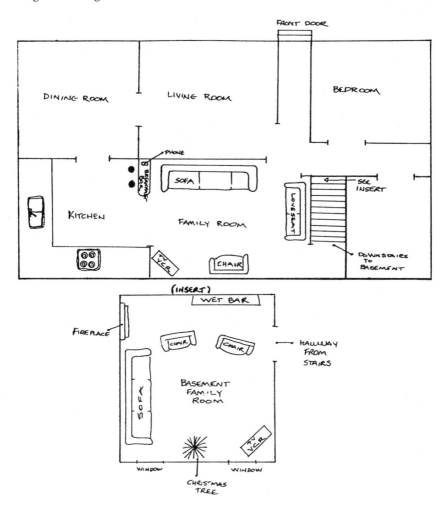

Figure 4.2. A Map of a Family Household

Tours

A thorough walk-through of a setting often leads to the making of a map, but a walk-through, or tour, can also lead to other, more narrative conclusions. The value of this procedure lies in its more experiential grounding in a setting's activities, personae, artifacts, and temporal rhythms.

In organizations or groups, the tour is likely to be "guided," usually by a gatekeeper or some other representative of the membership. In the prison media study, the deputy superintendent (gatekeeper) accompanied me on an hour-long tour of the facility. We visited three different cell blocks, in which I observed where the inmates kept their own televisions, radios, and cassette players, and where group viewing areas were provided by the institution. Our walk also took us through the dining hall (where Sunday-evening movies were shown), the library (where inmates read newspapers and magazines), and the family visiting area. All of these sites were referenced in the inmates' talk later in the interviews. In my family media research, a tour of the household is always one of the earliest activities, even preceding the informed consent ritual.

In open-access places, the researcher can usually tour at a leisurely or studied pace, and usually as frequently as he or she wishes. Before interviewing female readers of self-help books, Grodin (1990) browsed in several bookstores, examining the location and categorization of "self-help" books and noting the genders, ages, and behavior of the patrons who looked at the titles. From these site visits she hypothesized that "self-help" is an ambiguous genre, because many titles could be found in more than one section (e.g., psychology, self-help, sociology, sexuality, health) in the same store. The researcher should record and organize impressions gleaned from tours in field notes, exactly as he or she would in participant observation.

Diaries

Some activities occur only intermittently over long stretches of time, or so spontaneously that direct observation would be inefficient. Still other activities are not easily observable because of the secretive or solitary manner in which they are usually carried out. One procedure designed to document such activities is the diary, or "diary-interview" method (Zimmerman & Wieder, 1977). A diary is a chronological log of events and/or perceptions recorded by a participant. It is normally kept for a standard period, such as a week, with entries made soon after events of interest have happened. As a device for familiarizing the researcher with a scene to be entered, the analysis of diary data may alert him or her to the overall pattern and frequency of an activity. The researcher might then schedule observation at those times when it appears the activity will happen.

Depending on the instructions given to the participant, diaries can also yield detailed information about the content of the activity, and what the participant did before and after the activity in question. The participant can also use the diary to describe his or her own attitudes, usually in a free narrative. Thus the diarist acts as an "informant" of his or her own performances as well as those of others. The participant is then "subjected to a lengthy, detailed and probing interview based on the diary in which he or she [is] asked not only to expand the reportage, but also [is] questioned on the less directly observable features of the events recorded, of their meanings, their propriety, typicality, connection with other events, and so on" (Zimmerman & Wieder, 1977, p. 484).

An entry page from a diary used in a study of family discourse about home computing (Lindlof, 1992) is shown in Figure 4.3. Intended to be filled out after every instance of turning on and off the microcomputer, the diary was kept by each of the 11 families in the study for one week. Some of the problems typical of diary analysis plagued this one, albeit in mild form: uncertainty about how typical the diary week was, uncertainty about how conscientious the diary keepers were, and a noticeable "fatigue" with the task near the end of the week. However, the diaries were useful for learning about each family's computing style, and led to better-constructed interview guides.

Surveys

A significant strength of survey research is its ability to reveal the distribution of behaviors, attitudes, and attributes in a population. Such inferences are possible only if population units are selected according to random-sampling techniques. By making possible statistical analyses of association and difference, surveys afford researchers powerful means of examining how variables relate to each other.

For several reasons, qualitative researchers should consider the strengths of the survey in designing field strategy. First, scene casing, gatekeeper briefings, and other types of contact are not well suited to getting a global perspective on large, complex populations. Surveys can provide such perspectives. Results from panel or other types of tracking designs also indicate movements of opinion or population characteristics over time. The qualitative researcher can use these data to understand an organization or group in its aggregate or modal aspects. Such data can familiarize the researcher with dimensions of the field site that are not available by other means.

SESSION SHEET

Date: **8/24** Day of Week: **WED.** Time Begin: **9:15** (Circle) ⓐ.m/p.m.

USER(S): **Janie**

_____

_____

1. What were you doing before coming to the computer for this session?

   Trip to library

2. How did you use the computer during this session?

Program	Task	Amount of Time
IBM Music Construction :	**Writing music** :	**48 min.**
_____ :	_____ :	_____
_____ :	_____ :	_____
_____ :	_____ :	_____

3. Did you <u>print</u> anything during this session? <u>If yes</u>: **NO**

Type of Printout	Intended Use
_____ :	_____
_____ :	_____
_____ :	_____

4. Did anyone visit this room while you were using the computer?
   <u>If yes</u>:

First Name of Visitor	Relationship	Reason for Visiting
David :	**F** :	**Observing/Helping**
Becky :	**Sis** :	**Helping**
_____ :	_____ :	_____

5. Did anything <u>interesting</u> happen during this session? <u>If yes</u>:

   I discovered there were no repeat signs!

6. What do you plan to do when you leave this session? **Read**

Figure 4.3. A Diary Entry

Another use of the survey is to select both representative and unrepresentative cases for intensive study (Sieber, 1973). For example, my prison media project consisted of survey and qualitative interview phases, in that order. Although the phases were implemented and reported independently, I used certain variables from the survey to select participants for the interviewing: length of time spent at that prison, ethnicity, ownership of media equipment, amount of reported average television and radio use, degree of contact (telephone, letter writing, personal visits) with people outside the institution, and degree to which the inmate felt aligned with institutional ideology. I developed a matrix of these variables in which each potential interviewee could be evaluated. My intent was not necessarily to select a representative sample (see discussion in the next section), but to select interviewees representing some of the major categories of media-using inmates that emerged from the survey study. This use of the survey data increased my confidence that the interviewing tapped into the prison population at theoretically strategic points.

Qualitative researchers often are interested in studying cases that are unrepresentative of a population. An example might be teachers who experience difficulties in communicating effectively in the classroom. Survey analysis is capable of identifying very high- or low-scoring cases on particular variables. Such departures from the norm may then be observed intensively.

Finally, survey questionnaires can provide systematic information about individuals who are later observed or interviewed in field settings. Questionnaires that elicit demographic and other forms of baseline data are especially helpful for the researcher in designing interview guides. They also inform the researcher about the distributions of certain behaviors or attributes in the sample, even though they may not be able to describe the population from which the sample was drawn.

Interviews

Conducting one or more interviews with key informants constitutes another way for the researcher to become familiar with a scene. Such individuals are normally chosen on the basis of their knowledge, long tenure in the social unit, position of authority, wide-ranging access to the activities of the participants, existing good relations with the researcher (such as a gatekeeper or sponsor), or a combination of these. Key informants should be willing to give articulate, detailed responses, and even foresee what the researcher should know but has not thought to ask.

Chapter 6 treats more fully the informant role and the practice of interviewing.

Interviews with key informants at this stage are essentially *briefings*. Their purpose is to bring to the researcher's attention such matters as the group or organization's philosophies, purposes, mythic origins, recent history, current personnel, procedures, immediate challenges, and prospective agenda. More to the point, the core value of these interviews lies in their helping the researcher to raise and resolve any remaining issues about method choice and sampling strategy. They represent a prime opportunity for the researcher to find out how practical it will be to carry out certain field tactics. Key informants are well placed to critique the research design from the standpoint of whether or not it is appropriate to their group or organization. In order to accomplish this, these informants need to ground their briefings in reference to the project's mission. They cannot do this very well if the researcher is not prepared to talk about the project in some depth. Therefore, it is in the researcher's best interest to do interview briefings only after nearly all other prefieldwork activities are completed.

Sampling

No project is rich enough in resources to be able to record every behavior as it unfolds. Even if this feat were possible, the volume of data produced would probably prohibit the researcher from seeing any meaningful outcome in his or her lifetime. Consequently, the researcher must deploy some form of sampling strategy in the field. But there is an even better reason why sampling is key to the qualitative researcher's quest: He or she can analyze the choices made by participants by experiencing what it means to choose within the same constraints.

SAMPLING UNITS

The potential scope of elements to sample is vast. However, the task becomes manageable once the researcher realizes that the overwhelming number of *tactical* sampling decisions occur spontaneously in the field, in real time. Here, however, we are concerned with *strategic* prefieldwork decisions. The researcher must rely on the project's conceptual focus to identify the sampling units of greatest empirical interest: settings, persons, activities, events, and/or time.

Even if he or she studies a single field site, the many *settings* within that site force the analyst to make sampling decisions. Of course, a setting is not just a collection of natural and built objects on a plot of ground. Settings matter because their physical properties have social and cultural meanings for people. Settings are particularly important in the examination of environment-person interactions (their social ecology) and the patterning or recurrence of communicative action. As with all of the sampling units discussed here, settings are selected and analyzed for their cross-comparative and contrastive values.

The salience of *persons* as a sampling unit is most apparent in interview-based studies. The researcher recruits persons for qualitative interviews because he or she is already aware that they know something, or have had some experience, that is important for the project. A researcher may want to sample persons who have some attribute in common, as in focus group or respondent interviewing, or a range of informants whose expertise can help him or her to understand a complex scene. In either case, the person as a producer of discourse—discourse that bears crucially on the study's areas of inquiry—underlies the selection procedure. Chapter 6 develops this theme in more detail.

Activities and events can be discussed together because they are related. *Activities*, such as classroom teaching or selling cars, are ongoing communicative performances that occur in specific settings and time periods. Activities are functionally intrinsic to the enacted purposes of group, organization, or person, and take place in cycles or other schedules. At the outset, an activity may appear as a behavioral stream into which investigative work can dip at will. Closer scrutiny usually reveals that the activity can be broken down into many discrete events, such as afternoon soap opera viewing or evening movie viewing. *Events* are situational, time-bound enactments within activities. Schatzman and Strauss (1973) distinguish three types of events: routine events, which recur with some predictability; special events, which may be fortuitous, though not surprising, to the participants; and untoward events, which represent emergency situations. Within the activity of home video usage, for example, we might sample the routine event of negotiating which tape to rent, the special event of being disappointed with a tape that a friend touted as excellent, and the untoward event of a VCR malfunction. The ease with which these events can be anticipated, and therefore sampled strategically, varies widely.

By itself, *time* is not a very useful sampling unit. Applied to the contexts of settings, persons, activities, and events, however, the time dimension becomes a valuable means for organizing and calibrating fieldwork. In Chapter 3, we learned how important it is for the researcher to evaluate the rhythm and pace of a research site's routines. Such information should not go unused. Observation must be geared somehow into the ways participants temporally divide and unitize their joint acts. In some cases, the manners in which individuals use time differ widely across an organization, or even clash with organizational expectations. The researcher may need to apply different sampling schedules to capture this complexity. The researcher can also sample time retrospectively in interviews by having interviewees recall, describe, interpret, and evaluate critical events or eras from their pasts.

SAMPLING STRATEGIES

Most sampling techniques in qualitative inquiry depend not on principles of random probability, where every population element has an equal and independent chance of being selected, but on *purposeful* selection (Miles & Huberman, 1984; Patton, 1990). That is, sample selection is intentionally biased toward those "information-rich cases" (Patton, 1990, p. 169) likely to reveal the sense-making processes and structures of interest to the analyst. Qualitative sampling is purposeful because its practitioners strive to locate themselves at the sites of specific communicative performances and practices. Thus a study's analytic purpose—as it engages the properties of the scene and the researcher's own resources—suggests which among several nonprobability sampling strategies is appropriate to use.

Maximum Variation Sampling

Maximum variation sampling (Lincoln & Guba, 1985; Patton, 1990) is a common sampling strategy in qualitative research, used especially when the researcher wants to document a range of qualities across many cases. Cases are usually selected serially, with each adding a different, contrasting element to the overall sample. As Patton (1990) stresses, "Any common patterns that emerge from great variation are of particular interest and value in capturing the core experiences and central, shared aspects" of all the cases (p. 172). If the researcher gathers data from each case before selecting the next one, he or she benefits from the practical knowledge gained from the fieldwork. If the researcher already knows the population's characteristics, then he or she can employ maximizing sample variation from the outset. A variant of this, *statistically nonrepresentative stratified sampling* (Trost, 1986), lists key variables, organizes the variables into a "property space" according to the values within each variable (creating a group of cells), and then "fills" the cells with subjects or cases to construct a sample.

In her study of female readers of self-help literature, Grodin (1991) sought interviewees who roughly matched the known parameters of that readership: middle-class working women with at least some college education. In wanting to study core features of the reading experience among the diverse circumstances that lead women to these books, Grodin tried to expand the diversity of her sample. Her description of the 11 women who were eventually interviewed (for at least five hours each) reveals the outcome of her efforts:

> Participants who were interviewed ranged from 22 to 55 years of age. Ten respondents were white; one was black. . . . Their occupations ranged from secretary to university administrator, from community organizer to computer systems analyst. Four of the women (all in their 20s or early 30s) had never married. Of this group, one was living with her male partner, and another was a lesbian. Three of the women were currently married, one was widowed, and the rest had been divorced and were now single. (p. 408)

Snowball Sampling

Snowball sampling uses a person, usually an informant, as a source for locating other persons from whom a type of data can be generated, who then refer the researcher to other persons, and so on. The name of this technique evokes its accumulative result over time. One strength of snowball sampling is its efficiency in finding sites or persons whose attributes are central to the research problem. It also enables the researcher to build a sample that represents an active social network in an organization or community. (More formal, statistical means of analyzing personal networks to locate interviewees in a social structure can be used; see Van Willigen, 1989.) However, any bias in the ways informants nominate others as informants might be reflected in the structure of the sample (Burgess, 1984, p. 57). The researcher can avoid this problem to some extent by asking informants for lists of further persons to be interviewed and comparing the patterns of nominees. Depending on what the problem demands, he or she can then select either the most frequently nominated persons or those who appear less often on the lists.

Press (1991) was interested in the ways that women of middle- and working-class backgrounds interpret the cultural meanings of prime-time television programs that feature women characters. Her sample also had to accommodate generational difference (women under 29 compared with women 60 and older) because this dimension was critical to her thesis. She used the snowball method, but modified it in the interest of representativeness:

> In order to avoid the bias sometimes inherent in [the snowball] sampling method, in which all of the individuals in the snowball are somehow connected with one another, I used several snowballs to start off each group. . . . the women I interviewed at the start of each snowball came to me in a variety of ways—through waitresses I met, friends who taught working-class students, a working-class church, hairdressers. (p. 179)

Theoretical Construct Sampling

Theoretical construct sampling uses properties of the construct under study to orient case selection (Patton, 1990). Thus the terms in which the theoretical argument defines a phenomenon must be translated somehow into criteria for identifying and selecting its manifestations in the field. This is a more formal sampling technique than most others in qualitative inquiry. It tends to proceed deductively, because the nature of the sampling unit is defined well before the researcher goes into the field.

Rawlins (1983) posited that close friendships involve a dialectical tension between openness and discretion, and he wished to investigate the discursive ways in which this voluntary bond is managed intentionally. His criteria for selecting interview participants represent a mix of requirements based on the theoretical argument and other research considerations:

1. Subjects could not be known personally by the investigator.
2. Subjects had to regard each other as "close friends." Siblings, spouses, coworkers, lovers, or fiances were screened out.
3. Subjects had to have been close friends for a minimum of two years.
4. Subjects had to engage in voluntary interaction outside of settings where they were required to be together, such as work or school. This requirement reflected theoretical conceptions of the voluntary character of friendship.
5. Subjects had to be 20 to 29 years of age, inclusive.

6. Subjects had to appear interested and involved in close friendship.

7. Subjects had to be articulate enough to function well in in-depth interviews.

The constructs of relational communication developed by Rawlins explain why some qualities of friendship count as inclusionary sampling criteria and others do not.

Typical Case Sampling

Typical case sampling, common in communication studies, proceeds through the identification of cases that seem to represent the "essence" of the phenomenon under study. Cases that are too deviant or extreme on the key dimensions are ruled out. A typical case can be thought of in a number of ways: as the most frequent case, as the average of a distribution range, or as the composite ideal of a phenomenon (albeit not ideal in the sense of "best"). The typical case makes a certain kind of claim: that this case represents what normally occurs in a scene, how people normally interpret this sort of text, and so on. Not surprisingly, the researcher must select typical cases with great care in order to support the argument of typicality. He or she might consult recent quantitative data, other research reports, and his or her own and others' experiences with the phenomenon.

Lemish (1982) conducted a naturalistic study of how the social rules of viewing television in public places are enacted. She contended that a knowledge of social order is employed by actors to carry out their own personal behavior in public. Television viewing is a particularly apt example because it involves "strangers" in a familiar activity whose rules are tacit. Lemish chose the locations where she observed—shopping locations, bars, university settings, and so on—to maximize variation of physical settings, program content, viewer composition, and convenience. However, she selected the times for observing "according to the level of expected activity. For example, bars were studied in the evenings with special care to be present when sporting events were televised; students' lounges were studied during soap opera time; dining areas during lunch time; shopping areas during the weekends, etc." (p. 760). In other words, she made time selections on a typical case basis. It is vital to recognize that the goal of typical case qualitative inquiry is "*not* to make generalized statements about the experiences of all participants. The sample is illustrative, not definitive" (Patton, 1990, p. 173; emphasis added).

Critical Case Sampling

Critical case sampling is used when the researcher wants to examine a case that exemplifies a theoretical or practical problem. As in typical case sampling, the researcher must be careful in selecting a critical case. It should be a person, event, activity, setting, or (less often) time period that displays the credible, dramatic properties of a "test case." A critical case does not carry the burden of being typical or representative. However, a critical case should demonstrate a claim so strikingly that it will have implications for other, less unusual, cases.

Smith and Eisenberg (1987) proposed root metaphor analysis as a method for understanding the symbolic nature of organizational conflict. They argued that people rely on root metaphors as figurative devices that help them to make sense of and respond to organizational change. They chose Disneyland as a critical site, conducting data collection over a three-year period that saw significant labor strife, culminating in a 22-day strike in 1984. Their analyses of interviews with managers, employees, and key figures in the strike reveal a growing disillusionment with the original Disney philosophy and culture. But why Disneyland?

> Disneyland is sometimes singled out by organizational observers as possessing an especially "strong" or "excellent" culture. Most writers making this claim further contend that such a culture, once established, would be highly resistant to change.... Successful organizations find ways of coping with multiple goals, and of managing the stability-change and autonomy-coordination dialectics described earlier in this paper. The Disneyland experience is not atypical of our times: A large, successful company faces serious financial exigencies brought on by a failing economy, and, in turn, cuts labor costs in an attempt to remain solvent.... What makes Disneyland unique is the distance its employees perceive the company to have fallen, from a utopian vision to the cold reality of the bottom line. (pp. 377-378)

The justification for using a critical case is the claim that it embodies exigencies and challenges found in others of its category, but in less dramatic form.

Convenience Sampling

Convenience samples are the most informal of all. In practice, nearly all nonprobability sampling depends on scenes that are available fairly easily to the researcher. But to the extent that convenience sampling seems dictated purely by expediency, and not by conceptual necessity, it is ranked as the least desirable kind. Certainly, this dim view is justified if expediency is the *only* sampling consideration. (This may be reflected in the fact that it is rare for the authors of published research to refer to their samples as "convenience" samples.) Convenience sampling is not a good idea if it shows a lack of discrimination about what cases to select.

Conclusion

To the charge that qualitative research is neither rigorous nor systematic, Borman, LeCompte, and Goetz (1986) reply that the "flexible, evolutionary, and recursive nature of the investigation" (p. 52) should be documented more effectively. The design of a study, as we have seen in Chapters 3 and 4, frames its subject as something to be learned about, through questioning and dialogue. Only to a limited extent can, or should, this process be determined at the outset. Prefieldwork activities get the researcher into a scene with researchable questions, and with tools and strategies for acquiring some knowledge of its dimensions and properties. Ultimately, the looseness of interpretive inquiry design enables the researcher to correct mistakes and refit method to the authentic character of the phenomena.

Rigor, systematicity, and value in qualitative research also depend on how analysts enter into perspectives of the scenes they study. In the words of Bittner (1973), "If anything said about social reality is to make sense, especially if it is to make unambiguous sense, it must be said in ways such that the point of view is either implicitly obvious or explicitly explained" (p. 118). It is in the very nature of qualitative inquiry that the researcher produces a point of view—or multiple points of view. The next two chapters introduce methods—participant observation and interviewing—that can produce multiperspectival accounts of communicative performances and practices.

Note

1. In contrast, the active, seeking posture of the media gatekeeper deals a significant measure of control to those agents in the environment—such as the police, politicians, and businesspeople—who supply the "newsworthy" events upon which a media organization depends. The relations between media gatekeepers and news makers resemble a dance of interdependence.

5

Observing and Learning

A Field of Adventure

The cultural pattern of the approached group is to the stranger not a shelter but a field of adventure, not a matter of course but a questionable topic of investigation, not an instrument for disentangling problematic situations but a problematic situation itself and one hard to master. (Schutz, 1944, p. 506)

The standard technique is to try to subject yourself, hopefully, to their life circumstances, which means that although, in fact, you can leave at any time, you act as if you can't and you try to accept all of the desirable and undesirable things that are a feature of their life. That "tunes your body up" and with your "tuned-up" body and with the ecological right to be close to them (which you've obtained by one sneaky means or another), you are in a position to note their gestural, visual, bodily response to what's going on around them and you're empathetic enough—because you've been taking the same crap they've been taking—to sense what it is that they're responding to. To me, that's the core of observation. (Goffman, 1989, pp. 125-126)

In the first passage above, Alfred Schutz was writing about the situation of the immigrant (the stranger) approaching a new culture—the knowledge that needs to be learned, and how to orient to it. Having recently resettled in New York City from Germany, he must have found that subject salient for him at the time. Erving Goffman's comments were tape-recorded from a talk he gave on a subject (fieldwork) in which he exerted some influence, although he practiced it himself only once (Goffman, 1961).[1]

I bring these two quotes together here as a dialogue on communicative action. For Schutz, the stranger's problem consists of having to accept the new languages, idioms, recipes for action, and systems of relevance that come with joining a new culture. To accomplish this, the stranger must do more than simply acquire new linguistic rules. He or she must learn new expressions of feeling. As Schutz puts it elsewhere in his article, "In order to command a language freely as a scheme of expression, one must have written love letters in it; one has to know how to pray and curse in it and how to say things with every shade appropriate to the addressee and to the situation" (p. 505). Behind and within every language, then, are social usages that can be learned only *in vivo*, in situations that carry real consequences for the newcomer.

As we segue to Goffman's remarks, contrast the "you" he describes with Schutz's stranger.[2] The observer chooses to accept the condition of the stranger. Goffman advises, "You can leave at any time," but it is precisely the choice *not* to leave on which the research purpose of observing hinges. Leaving a scene too soon or too often, as well as lingering longer than desirable, all pose problems for traversing the passage from stranger to culture member. Further on, he tells us that "you" earn the right to be close enough to people to observe the details of their lives. This is achieved by "sneaky" means such as the stranger might use. However, the person Goffman had in mind probably resorts as well to methods of the professional research trade to get close in a more efficient and motivated fashion. Finally, empathy enables "you" to grasp what is observed because actions with others are geared together in work, play, affection, and other structures of life. What Goffman leaves unsaid, however, is just what Schutz stresses about the experience of the stranger: In constructing a new system of relevance, one must suffer, explicate, and overcome moments and periods of disorientation. The observer goes through this, too, but not just to overcome it. The observer tries to learn, respect, and report something of the disorienting experience itself.

This chapter offers guidance on how to use observing techniques in qualitative communication studies. We have already learned from Schutz and Goffman several important things about the work of observing: It is best conducted in relationships with those we study; it is characterized by a difficult and often ambiguous course of study; it requires discipline on the part of the analyst; it requires attention to detail; and it is not unlike other modes of being in society, such as the situation of the immigrant. Observing is indispensable to the research styles of ethnography, naturalistic inquiry, and the case study. Only the human investigator situated in a scene is able to register the subtle, processual actions of other human beings.

The approach presented here is best captured by Weick's (1985) notion of a "soft technology of systematic observation" (p. 568). *Soft technology* refers to the total sensory and conceptual equipment of the human investigator. By "soft," Weick means that observing is carried out through complex, adaptable, loosely structured rules or schemes. The observer tacks between the unique, phenomenal, situated character of an object and its comparative and contrastive relationships to other objects. He or she begins by noting the ostensible identity of an object—such as an organizational member's job title and duties—so that the phenomenon can be observable and reportable in the first instance. Such framing permits the observer to attend to qualities of the object functioning in its natural contexts—styles of talking to peers and subordinates, uses of authority, and so on.

By "systematic observation," Weick means "sustained, explicit, methodical observing and paraphrasing of social situations in relation to their naturally occurring contexts" (p. 569). As Weick did, we will unpack this definition term by term. The observer does the following:

1. engages the phenomenon for a prolonged period of time (*sustained*)
2. makes self-conscious and full, clearly expressed notations of how the observing is done (*explicit*)
3. goes about the observing activity in an alert manner that allows for tactical improvisation (*methodical*)
4. imparts attention to objects in ways that are in some sense standardized, yet individually trained (*observing*)
5. textually constructs and edits the observing (*paraphrasing*)
6. embeds the observing in the interdependencies of place, actors, and activities (*social situations*)
7. differentiates the background elements of social situations that inform the object on which observing is focused (*in relation to their naturally occurring contexts*)

Weick's definition promotes an understanding of what is required in systematic observing, as contrasted with the casual looking that everyone does. Systematic observing serves purposes ranging from reports of dreams to observational systems that rely on preset rules for sampling, categorizing, and coding streams of events (see McCall, 1984). But the interpretive precept that the observer's own emotional, cognitive, and cultural frameworks are open to change during the course of study is not compatible with the use of highly structured observing schemes. For our purposes, the success of observing depends on what the observer *learns* through participation.

Participant observation is the preferred means of experiencing and recording events in social settings. It entails being in the presence of others on an ongoing basis and having some status for them as someone who is part of their lives. Becker (1970) explains the process this way:

> The participant observer gathers data by participating in the daily life of the group or organization he studies. He watches the people he is studying to see what situations they ordinarily meet and how they behave in them. He enters into conversation with some or all of the participants in these situations and discovers their interpretations of the events he has observed. (p. 398)

By getting involved in the life of a scene, the researcher performs in ways that make sense to the social actors. The researcher notes what is going on and takes part as a responsible agent in the actions of the participants. Their motives are imagined and tested in the researcher's emerging participant self. What the researcher ends up with as data are descriptions of the participants' actions and the researcher's actions individually, and also of how each accounts for the other's presence.

A major part of this action is talk, distinguished from interviewing by the fact that it is embedded in some action other than interview events. Participant observation also includes analysis of other kinds of evidence, such as documents and artifacts. Of central interest in this chapter, however, are the ways in which communication can be experienced directly.

Effective Participant Observation

The validity of participant observation derives from *being there*. Observing and participating work in concert, if not always seamlessly, and competence develops in two parallel directions: (a) The researcher becomes skilled in the standards of performance honored by the group or individual; and (b) the researcher becomes increasingly skilled at creating sharp, detailed, and theoretically informed descriptions. This is a difficult mandate, even though we do not often see evidence of failure. (Narrative reconstruction often repairs flaws trailing from the field.) However, certain attributes and skills can be identified that relate to the tasks involved in observing.

TOLERANCE FOR MARGINALITY

The participant observer often occupies a "marginal" position, in both literal and existential terms. He or she is in a liminal situation, between worlds. Taking a place on the periphery of the social setting, and leaving frequently to return home or to a job, the researcher usually operates as a minor player. He or she is almost always looking in at a scene from an angle different from that of the native participants. Even when the researcher achieves a more central role, the duration of the stay there— and therefore the degree of commitment to the group's goals—may be comparatively short-lived.

Another sense of marginality is felt internally. The researcher's own sense of identity may experience some slippage over the course of a project as he or she increasingly accepts the obligations and emotional investments of other participants. This may happen when the researcher tries to honor the fine points of being impartial while the membership being studied insists on total commitment to its own worldview (e.g., Robbins, Anthony, & Curtis, 1973). It can also happen, in a less distressing way, if the researcher perceives that he or she has more in common with a group than he or she first thought. It can happen in as many different ways as there are individual studies.

Of course, the degree to which these become problems depends on the role commitment itself, as we will see later in this chapter. In nearly any qualitative project, the researcher tries to negotiate between one world that is considered home and another that is adopted and temporary. It is the adopted and temporary world—the research setting—that draws selfishly on the investigator's psychic reserves. As a place where he or she regularly confronts technical or social challenges, the research scene tends to prey on the researcher's thoughts even when he or she is away from it. An ability to tolerate marginal status and turn it into a method of interpretation seems essential for effectiveness in the field.

REQUISITE VARIETY

Imported from cybernetics, the concept of *requisite variety* holds that a system should have a variety of elements at least equal to the variety in the environment that it seeks to measure or regulate. According to Weick (1985):

> The specific link between requisite variety and observing occurs through a twist on epistemology. Rather than assume that seeing is believing, we assume that believing is seeing. This inversion suggests that beliefs are the medium through which the world is examined. Therefore we want to know the size, connectedness, and external orientation of an observer's belief system. An observer who knows many theories, metaphors, images, and beliefs and who has had varied experiences has more elements than an individual who has less content. (p. 581)

We had a hint of this in Chapter 3, in the discussion of the personal origins of research ideas. Suppose a researcher wants to study how the clergy of a particular church formulate the "advisories" they disseminate concerning the kinds of television content that are appropriate viewing for the church membership. The church hierarchy and the laity both probably embody a variety of beliefs and experiences that are relevant to this issue. However, if the investigator identifies strongly with the church hierarchy's perspective, he or she may not recognize the full range of nuances of belief and experience that exist—particularly in the general membership.

A person who is aware of a great variety of beliefs and who has broad knowledge will pick up more from an environment than will someone with lower levels of knowledge and exposure to different beliefs. Further, as Weick (1985) suggests, the more competing beliefs a person is able to entertain, the more open that person will be to what occurs in the world. Requisite variety is another way to express what others have called "tolerance for ambiguity."

MULTISENSORY SENSITIVITY

A visual bias pervades both ethnography and methodological writing on the observing process. Of course, the very terms we use—participant observation, observing, "watching" (Schatzman & Strauss, 1973)—imply that what is done in the field is exclusively looking, gazing, glancing, and fixating. It has even been said that the participant observer should try to mimic the behavior of a camera, as though the researcher's proper mission is to emulate mechanical gear. The primary problem with this (mostly unintentional) way of talking about observation is that it neglects a whole range of sensory modes that can be useful to the research task.

The visual bias also tends to convince us that the act of gazing itself embodies the organizing principle by which the environment is set up. In other words, we may embrace the conceit that it is our expert visualizing that selects the things that are central to "their" world. Clearly researchers have little choice but to experience other data besides the visual, but they have a great deal of choice about whether or not to ignore them in writing field notes.

In the remarks quoted above Goffman has it right: In observing, our *bodies* are (or should be) "tuned up." It is not too much of a stretch to compare participant observation to athletic performance. One works hard to train mind and body for the field. One tries to exploit every sensory clue to gain an edge in making interpretations. As Stoller (1989) points out, we should open up our sensing to the tastes, smells, tempers, touches, colors, light, shapes, and textures of the cultures we study. The effective observer should become a connoisseur of the particular sensory combinations that the culture values.

ON-LINE INFERENCING

The observer should develop a talent not only for noticing things (in visual and other modes), but for noticing things as *evidence.* Considering something to be evidence is the result of an inferential decision process, and as any trial lawyer knows, evidence is introduced only if it relates meaningfully to other evidence, testimony, and argument. Unlike the adversarial context of trial evidence, however, social science is concerned with organizing all evidence toward the best possible explanation—even if it ends up weakening the researcher's own assumptions.

The first line of analysis occurs as the observer experiences and sifts events in real time. What is intriguing about qualitative observing is that the decision to notice an event as potential evidence occurs in an immediate, dynamic context. The researcher never gets another chance to notice that event again. To be effective, the observer must be able to decide what is and what is not important according to criteria that are themselves only gradually being understood. Later in this chapter, we will look more closely at how this works.

BEING A GOOD PERSON

The inquirer's disposition is important at all times. He or she continues to function in a scene only at the pleasure of the culture membership. Although the relationships that researchers form with those being studied can vary widely, there is seldom any strategic reason for researchers to behave disagreeably.

Thus the effective observer should be a good person. (The literature often refers to this as the "good guy approach." *Good guy* connotes a person who is easygoing and unpretentious: a "regular" person. Given that *good guy* might now be considered a sexist figure of speech, I reference the concept here as the *good person*.) The researcher's being a good and humane person enhances confidence among others in the scene (Adler & Adler, 1987, p. 12). It is an all-purpose presentation for engendering goodwill, which may in turn lead to the researcher being included in member activities. As Guba puts it, "Good guys get better data" (quoted in Weick, 1985, p. 585).

Being a good person means giving people the benefit of the doubt, getting along by going along, and not being overly querulous or contentious (Fine, 1993). This can also extend to what is a bit more of a conscious role: that of the naive visitor, the "boob," or the inexperienced academic (Weick, 1985, p. 585). Such an appearance (which may not have to be faked) can be useful when the researcher wants to be taught things by culture members, especially at the start of a study. However, as Weick points out, too much of this naive behavior may convince members not to trust the researcher with important information or tasks. The researcher will want to become more useful as time goes on, in order to be included in increasingly complex or interesting areas of social life.

Most essential to good-person comportment is general social competence—knowing when to be passive and when to be gregarious, when to share information and when to keep it under wraps. The real utility of being a good person lies in the scope of social situations and relationships it opens for the researcher.

CULTURAL DIFFERENCES

A fair amount has been written on the impact of the researcher's cultural identities—age, gender, race, and so on—on success in field research (see Burgess, 1984, pp. 88-92; Warren, 1988). The fact that one is a certain age, gender, or ethnicity matters in such problems as entering a scene. For example, it might have been much harder for a woman to have gained access to the men's prison I studied. Of course, given the control often exerted by white male gatekeepers over research access, hypothetical field relations problems may simply constitute handy excuses for restricting persons of color or females from field sites.

What is more important about the researcher's cultural attributes is that they give him or her a common experiential grounding with those who have the same attributes. Often following from this is the advice that women should study women's problems, African American researchers should study scenes populated by African Americans, and so on. Such pairings smooth the way initially, promote empathy, and lead to better field relations and quality of data. Researchers who study groups who share their own cultures also benefit from having advance detailed knowledge of at least some elements of the scene.

On the other hand, what may seem to be a special endowment of a class of people may instead be a set of styles, codes, social skills, and understandings that others outside the category could learn if they had the opportunity. For example, interviewing tactics developed by women who study women's interests could generalize to other problems and be adopted by the other sex. And it is conceivable that there are advantages that accrue from dissimilar pairings in fieldwork (e.g., a young person studying a senior citizens' center), with greater insight resulting from the interaction of *differences*. A fascination with the border separating "us" and "them" is sometimes the impetus for inquiry.

One would be badly mistaken to think that the societally conflicted domains of gender, age, and race are not also conflicted in research settings. However, blanket prescriptions cannot readily be given. Researchers must case themselves as they case the scenes of potential study. They should carefully consider the possible effects of their culturally ascribed identities on the politics of conducting research.

Adapting Roles

The novice researcher often expresses an interest in being the proverbial fly on the wall: seeing and hearing without being seen or heard. He or she may try to do this by "blending in," by practicing civil inattention in public places, or by being astoundingly passive in the midst of a busy scene. But even a fly on a wall has a role, and so does the novice who bumps into someone while trying to blend in.

Every role has a generic character: a range of actions, obligations, and rights that go with being in a certain relation to others in a social system. A role also has a situated character: adjustments of the self to specific people in specific situations. The participant observer often starts by taking on a role already available in the setting or modifying one for his or her own purposes (Olesen & Whittaker, 1967). Sometimes a role can be created solely for the observer to inhabit, with the assent and help of the scene's actors. In either case, role adapting should not be construed as operating under false pretenses. Rather, it is *through the role*—living it and working through its particular problems—that certain kinds of observing become possible. Two broad ways of considering research roles are presented in this section: roles based on degree of participation and roles based on social function.

ROLES BASED ON DEGREE OF PARTICIPATION

Conceptions of research roles often come to us as typologies. The best known of these are based on the degree to which the researcher participates. For example, Schwartz and Schwartz (1955) distinguish between the "passive" participant observer, who tries to operate as anonymously as a scene permits, and the "active" participant observer, who tries to mix it up with some group of people as much as possible. The two types involve different assumptions about the researcher's presence: the passive observer believes that high levels of participation provoke "unnatural reactions"; the active observer believes that by lessening the status and activity differences between him- or herself and others, he or she can gain a better understanding of the scene. A more refined typology has been developed by Gold (1958), who proposes four "master roles": complete participant, participant-as-observer, observer-as-participant, and complete observer.

Complete Participant

For the complete participant, role pretense is the dominant motif: The researcher is a fully functioning member of the scene, but is not known by others to be acting as a researcher. He or she is known only through a real self that has no other revealed purpose than the one that is understood in the scene itself. Two examples will illustrate how this is done and justified.

In studying the organizational culture of Al-Anon, a self-help group for friends and family members of alcoholics, Stephanie Zimmerman (1987) decided that revealing her research interests would hinder her ability to observe group meetings effectively in the time she had available. And because Al-Anon depends on the anonymity of participants (no last names are used), it may not have been possible for her to gain access overtly as a researcher. As Zimmerman notes:

Simply being present at a meeting could . . . be considered a task routine, for Al-Anon members assumed that those who sought out Al-Anon meetings did so out of a need for help with alcoholism. . . . I was never questioned as to why I was at a meeting, or asked to establish my legitimacy as a group member. Attendance was a sufficient performance for membership. (p. 8)

At the invitation of a former student, Thomas W. Benson (1981) decided to join a film crew for a few days to shoot some political commercials. When he arrived in "Sunbelt City," the principal scene of his research narrative, Benson began meeting the people with whom he would be working. Soon enough he was asked to explain himself:

The drink ordered, Clark turns to me with a smile. "And who are you in real life?"

This is exactly the right question, and defines the situation. But I am not prepared for this directness, and the anonymity that Gary [Benson's friend] offered me so vaguely seems out of place, not really an option, since Gary is not here, and my host has asked a friendly and direct question. The situation settles my doubts about how to represent myself.

"I'm a professor of Speech Communication at Penn State University." (p. 358)

As far as Zimmerman was concerned, revealing her research identity was not a good option, given the expectations of the group and the impracticality of doing so. In Benson's case, complete participant status was more ambivalent. He joined the film crew to get close to the action of a campaign. His research interest was only hinted at, and the anonymity he worked out in advance with Gary was fleeting and inconclusive. Benson found that he must improvise his identity at the site. But revealing who he is in real life did not elicit much more than small talk, and soon the press of events shunted the issue aside.

A complete participant role allows a researcher to use the self to understand behavior in a natural setting. In that sense, it holds real promise for getting inside the subjectivity of communicative action. Certainly there is no better path to knowing the feelings, predicaments, and contradictions of the "other" than to be with the other in an authentic relationship. And for scenes characterized by guarded access, or by belief systems that do not easily admit critical elements, acting in the complete participation mode may be the only viable way to get in.

Once inside, the researcher will often become involved in situations not usually available to outsiders. Private information is revealed because only a private relationship is assumed. It is important to point out that the complete participant's presence does influence what goes on in the scene. The other social actors respond to the researcher as a fellow actor, rather than as someone with a research agenda.

For several reasons, qualitative communication analysts do not embrace the role of complete participant as often as its benefits might suggest. For one thing, the researcher's freedom of movement and ability to tailor specific relations with other members are severely curtailed. The scope of the researcher's own movements is limited to what he or she can experience in the member role, which necessarily spans only a part of the total activity of the group. A covert role does not usually permit the use of such directive techniques as interviewing to refine and test hypotheses. For this reason, complete participation seems to be best suited for studying cohesive memberships.

Second, sequestering of the researcher identity can be difficult to achieve, and worries over having one's cover blown often attend fieldwork of this style. The complete participant occasionally needs to retreat and regroup, to "cool out" psychologically. Yet it may not be possible for him or her to do so to the extent desired, because of the self's involvement in the scene.

Third, the researcher may lose analytic detachment as a result of overidentifying with the perspectives of the people studied. This phenomenon, "going native," raises the specter of the researcher not being able even to conclude a project, but few go that far. In a mild form, Benson's description of his jaundiced reentry to the lifeways of academe after his adventure in Sunbelt City expresses this sense of having acquired new eyes to see with. But it is one thing to go back to one's own community with a new sensibility, and another not to go back at all.

Finally, the complete participant's pretense raises questions about the ethics of role concealment. It may be seen as a violation of the faith that people place in others' motives in everyday situations. It may signal a breakdown of the code of human subject protections, described in Chapter 4. With regard to our two examples, on some counts Zimmerman's ethical position was more tenuous than Benson's. She avoided speaking as much as possible in the meetings to avert risk to the self (and, in a sense, tried to approximate the "complete observer" role, described below). Possibly, Zimmerman did need to act like a member to penetrate the Al-Anon scene, although nowhere is it stated that every setting *must* be studied. The fact that Al-Anon is fundamentally based on anonymity to encourage disclosure about sensitive issues among members casts Zimmerman as an exploiter of the group's basic trust. Benson did admit who he was, but in terms of occupation only; he did not mention the research thrust of his participation. One could argue, after reading his entire account, that the political campaign scene is one in which candor is neither expected nor especially valorized. In this regard, Douglas (1976) argues that a successful inquiry may depend on covert tactics when evasion, "fronting," and outright lying are regularly practiced by the members.

On the other hand, it is not easy to see what Benson gained by hiding his research goals, except that he avoided raising alarms about his trustworthiness in the competitive context of a political race—a fear that was only anticipated, not tested. In her report, Zimmerman did apply appropriate measures to mask the identities of the participants. In a sense, she honored the Al-Anon ethos by using not only no last names, but no names at all. The veil of pseudonyms Benson employed for the people and places of Sunbelt City would probably yield rather easily to the reader motivated enough to unmask them.

If one believes that ethical correctness can be situational, then one may view one kind of complete participation as less problematic than another. However, some practitioners believe that all covert study is exploitative and thus never justifiable (Anderson, 1987; Dingwall, 1980). Suffice it to say that any researcher considering the role of complete participant needs to think through his or her motives thoroughly, and may want to consult others about the ethics and effects of the concealment.

Participant-as-Observer

In the role of participant-as-observer, the researcher enters a field setting with an openly acknowledged investigative purpose, but is able to study from the vantage point of one or more positions within the membership. As the name of this role implies, observing pivots from the perspective of participating. The researcher goes through the prefield-work activities outlined in Chapter 4 to check out the sorts of relationships that give the best view of the culture. Whereas the complete participant is less a role at all than a real immersion, the participant-as-observer enacts a role that is, in a very real sense, rewarded with involvement. Everybody who interacts with this researcher knows in some way that a transaction of interests is at the bottom of the participation. In media studies, for example, such involvements have ranged from the intimacy of in-home boarders or leasees with the families under study (Bryce, 1987; Wolf et al., 1982), to a frequent visitor with female viewers of a particular British television serial (Hobson, 1982), to a friend of an

Indian family living in London (Gillespie, 1990). The relationship with members that makes this possible can be an enduring one, lasting for weeks or months.

Unlike the complete participant, the participant-as-observer does not operate as a member fully integrated into the routines and subjective realities of the group. Participation is part of a "deal" negotiated with gatekeepers (or sponsors), and usually involves a special status—a part-time, temporary, voluntary, and/or "play" role. As a result, the responsibilities that go with *real* participation in the group are not full and binding. As Gold (1958) puts it, "The role [of participant-as-observer] carries with it numerous opportunities for compartmental-izing mistakes and dilemmas which typically bedevil the complete participant" (p. 221).

Thus engagement in the scene proceeds on a basis of being lightly supervised or even protected to some degree by the more accountable members. Under normal conditions, these people might not suffer fools gladly. But for the participant-as-observer, normal rules do not apply. The researcher can enjoy cooling-out periods when he or she needs to, taking time to write field notes or to return to real-life responsibilities for a while. The field role can also be terminated rather easily. Of course, the researcher's role might involve activities in the group or organization that are of a nontrivial nature; if this is the case, the researcher can give notice before leaving and offer to help in a process of transition.

Trujillo and Dionisopoulos (1987) wanted to know how the drama of routine police work is communicatively performed. According to these authors, the public's mythic notions of "police work" obscure the true organizational and interpersonal dramas enacted in the daily grind. By being present during police work, they were able to witness and describe the situated language use that is part of these performances. Trujillo and Dionisopoulos were members of a research team that accompanied police officers during "ride-alongs" on their shifts—" 'cruising' the streets, responding to dispatched calls, joking at the station house, and drinking at 7-11. Informal interviews were conducted with the officers, but we mostly watched, listened, and made written notes of their activ-ity" (p. 200). Among their interpretations of police work were the cops' uses of labeling ("scrotes," "dirtbags," and so on) to demarcate them-selves from perceived negative elements of the public and a "talking tough" ritual for upholding cultural norms of the cop membership.

Trujillo and Dionisopoulos's protocol placed them at the locations (in the front seats of patrol cars) and in the attitude (that of receptive listener) that enabled them to hear the stories of the cop world. In their report, they do not offer many details about the status of their participation, or much else about the times of day they rode along or how their involvement was greeted and interpreted by the officers. Yet one senses that they must have made innumerable decisions about such matters: with whom and when they should ride along, what to do in case of emergencies, and so on.

For this role, achieving an insider's insight may require a more complicated procedure than is needed in the role of complete participant, whose use of the self enables a tighter coupling of participating and observing. The participant-as-observer's involvement in the members' world demands ongoing adjustments of the terms of participating. Members must be brought up to date and reassured about what the participant observer's role is supposed to be. Contacts with informants enable the researcher to gain the trust of key sectors of the group, and to sample among the factions or the various points of view. Interviewing bears a greater burden for getting through to members' inner realities quickly and comprehensively. None of this may be very onerous for the typical member, but for the researcher it makes the building and maintaining of trust a key issue over the entire course of a project.

To sum up, a greater degree of reciprocity distinguishes the participant-as-observer role from that of the complete participant. The participants and the researcher must negotiate a space to cohabit. They often do this expecting little or no reward. Ultimately, the demands of the researcher's role dictate how the game of reciprocity is played.

Observer-as-Participant

In the observer-as-participant role, participating pivots from a central position of observing. In other words, an agenda of observing is primary. Gold's (1958) lack of enthusiasm for this role type is evident: "Because the observer-as-participant's contact with an informant is so brief, and perhaps superficial, he is more likely than the other two to misunderstand the informant, and to be misunderstood by him" (p. 221). Undoubtedly this is true, but only up to a point. The observer-as-participant may value *Verstehen*, but mainly as a way to enter the scene, to foster good member relations for the duration of a study, or to validate propositions at the very end.

The observer-as-participant negotiates with gatekeepers in a manner different from that used by the participant-as-observer. He or she can show what kind of information is needed and the amount of time and other resources needed to obtain it. Gatekeepers can grant access with more confidence that their lives will not be disrupted, and that the study will not stray into unforeseen areas. There is much less uncertainty about what counts as data.

Interviewing is a common method for doing an observer-as-participant study. A schedule of questions with well-defined aims can be administered easily, and misunderstandings of a superficial kind, such as about the intent of a question, can be resolved on the spot. Researchers in this role can sample a relatively large number of incidents, time periods, persons, or groups with efficiency.

When observing is the chief "instrument," the observer-as-participant tries to record and understand the behaviors that fit the categories of interest. For example, Lemish (1987) was interested in how infants respond to television in their households. The background for her study derived from the cognitive developmental theory of Jean Piaget, which posits stages of knowledge and ability through which all children pass. Within this scheme, television's rich stimuli are believed to be noticed and comprehended differently by children depending on their levels of cognitive ability as well as the social character of the viewing environment.

Lemish visited 16 families in their homes four to five times each over a period of several months. In addition to interviewing parents, who also kept viewing logs, Lemish observed the babies' behavior for one- to two-hour sessions. She achieved good relations with the family members, but she makes little mention of how she was perceived other than in some concluding remarks about the normality of family behavior in her presence. She describes specific episodes and general patterns of behavior in a detailed, detached fashion, revealing that she was there only to examine infant-television interactions. Lemish's study allowed her to learn much of what she set out to learn: that very young children's involvements with television—orienting to it, vocalizing with it, imitating it, manipulating the set—do change at roughly regular intervals as they grow up. The use of a psychological model, however, constrained her field role and what she could explain in the way of meanings at the level of the cultural or social collective.

Because of its fleeting contact with real participants, it is tempting to say that the observer-as-participant role falls short of the criteria for interpretive social science. Clearly it does not engage the researcher in an intimate, prolonged study of a culture. However, the role does allow conclusions about communicative action to emerge over time. The analysis that results from its use does integrate regularities of behavior or discourse with theoretical problems concerning the attribution of meaning.

Nevertheless, researchers who observe with minimal participation run the constant risk of reading too much of their own conceptions into what they see. Such ethnocentrism, or blindness to the perspective of the other, is antithetical to good qualitative work—or to good scientific work of any kind, for that matter.

Complete Observer

"You can observe a lot just by watching," Yogi Berra is supposed to have said. This kernel of wisdom from the former New York Yankee great is indeed taken seriously in the last role of the typology, the complete observer.

The complete observer takes the role of observer-as-participant to what might be its logical conclusion: observing without being "present" to the participants. Not only do participants not recognize the complete observer as a researcher, they often do not recognize him or her in the scene at all. This is the least palatable style for many, because the absence of the analyst's "presence" runs counter to the idea of the human-as-research-instrument. It is also the rarest role in the literature, for technical as well as ontological reasons.

The complete observer role can be usefully compared with its opposite, the complete participant role. Both are hidden roles; no one in the scene reacts to a research project. However, there are striking differences in the life worlds inhabited by the complete observer and the complete participant. The complete participant enacts a research agenda through a self that is naively accepted by others in social relationships. The complete observer's role, in contrast, is nearly a solipsistic one, because the absence of meaningful contact with human subjects denies those subjects the capacity to influence the researcher's interpretations. So, whereas the danger of "going native" supposedly lurks within the complete participant's project, the threat of "going ethnocentric" relentlessly stalks the complete observer.

As alluded to earlier, Zimmerman's role in her study of Al-Anon resembled the complete observer approach. Yet, as she concluded, mere attendance at an Al-Anon meeting is tantamount to membership, and even silent witnessing counted as participation to those around her. Naturally, a complete observer operates best in free-access settings. Crowd scenes offer excellent opportunities to observe without the risks of revealing or having to account for the self (e.g., Lang & Lang, 1953). Generally, the more remote from the action one can get, the more complete an observer one can be. The technologies of video, photography, audio, and computers, among others, enable such remote sensing to be done with a low probability of detection. Knuf (1989-1990), for example, used a camcorder to tape the ritual boundary maintenance activities of a sorority rush; he had no face-to-face contact with the members.

The ethical situation of the complete observer differs somewhat from that of the complete participant. The complete participant acts in ways that are sensible and correct within the expectations of the group being studied. This closeness usually brings the investigator to an understanding of, and respect for, the rationality of the members' moral order. Knowing what is valued by them, the complete participant can avoid doing things that might harm their interests. But the complete observer has no identity that is explicitly recognized by the social actors under study; consequently, he or she may have little conscience about how he or she interprets their actions, or about how those interpretations are circulated.

ROLES BASED ON SOCIAL FUNCTION

Gold's typology has influenced the thinking of many qualitative practitioners, mostly because of its simplicity. However, the adequacy of this typology, and others similar to it, has been questioned. Adler and Adler (1987) believe that the covert/overt distinction is not useful as it is drawn. It splits the researcher into a participant role that interacts with members and an observer role that gathers data. Adler and Adler urge us to think of researcher involvements in terms of *committed membership*. Essentially, they recast the complete participant and participant-as-observer into three roles—complete member, active member, and peripheral member—according to their centrality to and integration into a social scene. These roles entail different obligations, liabilities, and chances for experiencing social life:

> Peripheral-member-researchers participate as insiders in the activities of the group they are studying, but they refrain from engaging in the most central activities. . . . [Active-member-]researchers participate in the core activities in much the same way as members, yet they hold back from committing themselves to the goals and values of members. . . . Complete-member-researchers study their topics from the perspective of full members by either selecting groups to study in which they have prior membership or by converting to membership in these groups. (Adler & Adler, 1987, p. 35)

It is important to note that these role types relate to each other through an overarching concept of member positioning. It is easier to see how one kind of member positioning can evolve into another across the span of a project. In rejecting the duality of participation and observation, Adler and Adler argue that going native is not a serious possibility as long as the researcher continues to treat the experience of being with participants as an experience in theorizing.

Adler and Adler's scheme moves the idea of roles to another plane, that of the *social functions* they have. Thinking of research roles simply in terms of degree of participation in the abstract does not take us far in applying them to specific situations. Making this criticism more directly, Snow, Benford, and Anderson (1986) explain:

> The utility of these classical typological distinctions is limited . . . because they sketch only the broad contours of one or more ideal-typical roles, thereby leaving each role relatively empty, nondescript, and uncodified. . . . they provide prospective field researchers with little direction on how to proceed once they enter a field setting. (p. 378)

Functional roles are designed for specific problems. In many ways, it is both more meaningful and more practical to conceive of the role of the researcher (whether a natural member or not) as an experiential mode of being. For example, Anderson (1987, pp. 315-317) describes several generic strategies for learning member activities: the apprentice and the mentor, playing, take a course, and using past experience or present involvement. The first three involve the researcher in learning situations, with differences in the depth of material to be learned and the seriousness and formality of the endeavor. The fourth strategy—using past experience or present involvement—requires the researcher to take a more analytic perspective on something he or she has already learned, in order to reflect critically on the structure of that knowledge.

Functional roles can be defined more concretely to fit a specific field site. Snow et al. (1986) identify four roles derived from the social movements (e.g., a peace group) and marginal groups (e.g., an American Buddhist sect) they studied over several years: controlled skeptic, ardent activist, buddy-researcher, and credentialed expert. Two of these can be briefly discussed here. Acting as a convert to a religious group, the *controlled skeptic* is able to solicit members' points of view in a naive, curious, yet skeptical manner. An *ardent activist* role—which entailed embracing the means, ends, and ideology of a peace movement—was adopted to understand the full potency of the group's beliefs and to explore the backstage regions in which decisions were made. By treating research roles as having real functions, one can better anticipate the kinds of information that specific sorts of experience produce.

Finding a Role to Study Children

Some populations confront the investigator with major challenges for creating a role. What one usually tries to do is note deviations from an expected model of communicative practice ("The Xs here do not behave like the Ys in the literature") or from personal habits of thought and feeling ("They're not behaving like me"). Either path *estranges* the investigator from familiar knowledge and interpretive practice (see Gurevitch, 1988).

In the case of studying children, the researcher may have to work very hard at becoming estranged. Even though children live in nearly every community and all adults interact with them in some manner, concepts of "the child" do not always take account of children's own ways of making sense. Tales and symbols involving children appear regularly in the popular media, inducing a sense of easy familiarity among adults concerning how children perceive and what they are interested in. The notion that every adult was once a child and thus has an intrinsic understanding of children's needs, concerns, fears, and joys is also widespread. Children's cognitive, emotional, and moral lives are often viewed as simply primitive versions of adult capacities.

The qualitative inquirer faces other obstacles in describing the child's world. Children normally live in closely supervised circumstances, which can make it difficult for the researcher to get close to them for data-gathering purposes. On the other hand, adults possess a mandate (which is certainly not reciprocal) to involve themselves in the affairs of the children under their charge, which can impede the development of a less asymmetric research relationship. Children's lack of adultlike speaking, writing, and memory skills also poses problems for those who try to understand what they mean by what they say.[3] More fundamentally, children truly live in a range of cultures of their own, constructed in their own games, lore, language forms, and rules of conduct (Denzin, 1977; Speier, 1973). The fact that young children have interests very different from those of adults, attend differently to their environments, and experience more intense ranges of emotion than do adults bespeaks their otherness.

Qualitative researchers have made efforts to enter the world of children by forging relationships that "make sense" (see Fine & Sandstrom,

1988). Fine and Glassner (1979) suggest a fourfold typology of research roles constructed from two relational dimensions: the degree of positive contact between adult and child and the degree of authority exercised by adult over child. The *friend* role operates in the absence of direct adult authority and in the presence of positive contact; it is egalitarian, trusting, intimate, and (because it departs so far from normal adult-child relations) infrequent in use. The role of *observer* assumes the absence of both direct authority and positive contact; here, the researcher purposely distances him- or herself in order to reduce the obtrusiveness of the adult presence. As Fine and Glassner note, this role is inconsistent with the participation called for in most fieldwork, in which the subjective states of members are a focal interest. With its lack of positive or sympathetic affect, the *supervisor* role is not likely to lead to insight into children's lives. The role of *leader*—which invests the researcher with an oversight responsibility, albeit in the context of positive intent—is the one that most closely aligns with a normal adult role vis-à-vis child groups. However, children will still withhold certain behaviors from the scrutiny of this researcher because of the authority role positioning.

Fine and Glassner believe that the adult participant observer's effort to align values becomes more tenuous as the adult tries to become a peer. In their view, knowledge of children's social meanings may not be fully attainable, not only because children will not accept an adult acting as a child, but because rituals of privacy underpin parts of children's culture.

Other analysts dispute the idea that a researcher cannot approach children on their own terms (Silvers, 1983; Speier, 1973). Mandell (1988) advocates a position she calls the *least-adult role*. Arguing that "even physical differences can be so minimized when participating with children as to be inconsequential in interaction" (p. 435), she studied children's action in adult-structured, semistructured, and free-play times at day-care centers. Her description of how she proceeded is revealing:

> Over time I became an active participant, not merely a peripheral, passive, or reactive observer. This means I closely followed children's ways, initially observing and imitating their words, actions, and responses, and gradually fitting my line of action into theirs. As an active participant I committed many mistakes by acting in nonchildlike ways that the children either did not comprehend or mistook for adult responses. . . . in the process of actively role-taking with the children, I came to grasp their meaningful social objects. Since many young children cannot articulate clearly and many others cannot act with adults in an adult perspective on objects, it is pointless to ask young children what it is like to be a child and what is important to them. It is only by engaging them in action that these questions are answered. (p. 439)

Interestingly, Mandell encountered many of the same field relation problems endemic to working with other populations: encountering "Who are you?" queries from the members, bargaining with gatekeepers (teachers) to preserve the integrity of the research role, and trying to keep pace with her subjects' movements. She eventually became accepted within the preschoolers' scenes, and thus was able to describe their "access rituals"—the techniques that open interactions.

Simply letting go, and keeping faith with one's desire to learn, may be the most functional of all strategies—no matter how different the other. One tries to learn to be useful on a personal level, and in being useful in that way, one then participates in a world of meanings-in-action.

SUMMARY

The idea of roles guards us against thinking of participant observation as mere surveillance, but we should also guard against its "evil twin": treating a role as if it really exists. This is a problem of *reification*. Any role strategy, like the apprentice and mentor, simply helps us normalize certain kinds of interpersonal relations (Van Maanen, 1981). If I want to be *like* an apprentice at the beginning of a study, I will try to find someone who will act *like* a mentor for me, simulating the sort of intimate learning-by-modeling relationship that mentoring conjures up. If I find such a person, what we do together will fail to match the ideal image of apprentice and mentor. Rather, the researcher accommodates to the distinctive qualities afforded by the actual relationship. After all, what we really want to study is the rationality of some situated action, not an ideal type.

Tactical Observing

Soon the investigator is ready to commence observing. Beginning to observe is less like sprinting from a standing start than like running one leg of a relay. The groundwork of planning and role preparation already has the researcher moving close to the social scene. In starting to observe, he or she simply uses this momentum and knowledge to move *into* the scene via the opening afforded by a role. Role strategy begets particular modes of participating, which beget tactical observing of certain kinds.

Initial observing involves understanding where and when the field is. The "field" is best thought of as the physical settings and social activity arenas of the research problem. As we learned previously, the "scene" encompasses the self-defined meanings of actors engaged in a form of social life. *Scene* and *field* reference the differences in how participants and researcher act on their own interests. The researcher begins with a heightened sensitivity to the field—who is doing what, when, and where *with respect to the research problem*. But the researcher has a very under-developed sense of what scenes are enacted therein, at least at the project's start. The social actors, on the other hand, have a sure grasp of their own scenes (their performed life worlds), but "the field" is not familiar to them. It is a construction of the outsider.[4]

This is a perplexity familiar to qualitative inquirers, yet it is central to the process of participant observation. The first task of observing is simply for the researcher to notice as many personae, things, and events in the field as possible within his or her own scope of action. As Patton (1990) writes, "It is helpful to treat units of activity as *self-contained events* for the purpose of observation. The process of looking for patterns across units of activity is the process of analysis" (p. 224; emphasis added). Observation should be done nonjudgmentally, without trying to force closure or to fit what is observed into a theory of how or why it occurs. At this early stage of the work, the researcher should just live the novice experience:

> Novices in research worry too soon about developing salient categories for final analysis, about developing brilliant concepts, and about establishing "patterns of interaction"; in short, they want quickly to prove to themselves and others that they are social scientists. Not so our model researcher; he is quite content, for a considerable time, to experience the ambience of the scene. He has great patience, as well as a tolerance for ambiguity and for his own immediate ignorance. Far from acting like a scientist and telling himself he is one, he is genuinely busy being a learner—indeed, a novice—and perhaps a participant. (Schatzman & Strauss, 1973, p. 54)

Whereas it is in fact good to remind oneself of the project's scientific purpose, the above advice underlines the disciplined character of being watchful. To try to assert themes of communicative action after only a session or two of observing is to overreach one's own competence.

The observer spends most of those first days or weeks accomplishing two objectives: learning to develop a perspective on the field from his or her role positioning, and making careful observations of the full range of behaviors and objects in the field. With respect to the first, the re-searcher should take direction easily, learning where it is appropriate to sit, stand, and move, and when it is appropriate to talk, listen, and act. This, of course, is consonant with the good-person stance discussed earlier. By reducing personal resistance to the role as much as possible, the researcher more quickly enters a perspective for inspecting the action. True, the perspective is usually one that has been tailored at least in part for a person who does not yet know all the ropes. Yet it is a perspective that expresses *their* (the members') priorities within a scene they inhabit. A role negotiated for the inquirer is the work of a culture's own organizational logic. As such, it represents a sensible decision of the members, and can be utilized by the researcher in interacting with them. Patience in faithfully performing a negotiated role is often rewarded later with more varied or natural roles to play.

The researcher achieves the second objective—making careful observations of the full range of behaviors and objects—by sensing the field, by beginning to adopt member perspectives on what is sensed. The sampling strategies reviewed in Chapter 4 enable the observer to identify the arenas of action in which consequential observations might occur.[5] The all-purpose question for the researcher is, What is going on here? Because the scene is new to the observer, and probably puzzling in many ways, this question tends to emerge on its own. To be most useful in a research context, however, the question needs to be asked in various ways, so as to produce descriptive observations (Spradley, 1980). The questions discussed below are typical ones for orienting observational activity in the beginning and middle phases of a study.

WHO ARE THE ACTORS?

The researcher should first learn the nominal statuses of the actors in the scene being studied (e.g., father, mother, son, daughter; manager, assistant manager, crew chief, line worker). Certain responsibilities and obligations of a formal, legal, or "natural" kind go with those statuses. For example, what are these workers' jobs, and how do these job descriptions relate to the way they spend their time here? What does a man or woman need to do to qualify for or fulfill the status of student or teacher? What are the understandings that underlie family roles and how these family members relate to each other? These are status positions to which people are recruited, hired, assigned, or born.

Taken as a whole, the formal statuses of the actors reveal the structure of a scene in a prescriptive sense. Such knowledge lets us answer the question—as a first approximation anyway—What is this person here to do? How are these people *supposed* to function together in this group or organization? The statuses of social actors tell a great deal about how they associate with each other. Even if these distinctions are part of a briefing given by the gatekeeper prior to entry, the researcher should strive to evaluate them independently.

The researcher should remember that nominal status does not predict how the role is actually performed or how the role incumbent is perceived by other actors. Closer observation will reveal that certain norms, expectations, rules, and taboos come into play in certain situations. For example, how does on-the-job status get negotiated in other contexts, such as at Christmas parties or on the company softball team? The researcher may find that the deference employees normally display to their superiors in the work setting is not a factor on the softball field, where a team spirit thrives.

In other words, the researcher now looks at the negotiated, contextualized statuses of the actors as they communicate, which of course are much more dynamic and emergent than their nominal statuses. Often, there are tensions or conflicts between actors' statuses and how they actually perform. These can become key themes as the researcher begins to analyze data.

HOW IS THE SCENE SET UP?

The choice and organization of artifacts in a scene signifies what is important to the members' group or personal identities, as well as the images they intend to project to external groups or persons. Decor, furnishings, and objects of play or work can be examined in the context of social action. There may be times when certain props are needed for certain acts to occur at all. The analyst may learn later that certain elements characterize or divide up territory in ways that are meaningful to the membership. The researcher can also check a scene for "physical traces" of human activity—unobtrusive measures of the ways that people use objects and interact in their physical environments (Webb et al., 1966).

Here is Goodall's (1991) description of the office environment of a computer software company he studied:

> One significant aspect of the B-BCSC culture is nonverbally clear: There is a strong tradition of individualizing one's office area or workspace. So clear is this tradition that certain motifs become apparent. The motifs include some ordinary and expected symbols: symbols of family and families with

pets, symbols of academic and professional achievement, symbols of recognition and reward. . . .

A second motif concerns symbols that are inner pathways to a mindscape
of petty fears, rages, senses of humor, and bellicose warnings that coalesce
into a collage of general and specific corporate psyches and that oddly
enough correspond to the individual positive symbols of home, and learning, and achievement.

For example, "Shit Happens" is an emblem, a sort of badge really, that is
laced through the building next to degrees and family snapshots, a common
source of strategically ambiguous identification with an anonymous but
ever-present enemy. (pp. 91-92)

There is more to his reading of this organization's symbolic faces to the
world, including the architecture and landscaping of the site and the
cultural implications of the cars and trucks parked in the company lot.
Goodall also notes some differences in "persons and things" that occur
when the company moves to a new building. Such interpretations develop after many lengthy periods of observing. At the outset, however,
a careful descriptive assessment of the material culture can help the researcher to understand how actors understand their scene and the parts
they play in it.

HOW DO INITIAL INTERACTIONS OCCUR?

The ways in which persons interact for the first time can reveal much
about the socialization procedures of a group, how it polices its boundaries, and the communicative styles of individual actors. In public
settings, such as health care organizations or bars, there are many opportunities to observe these critical moments. In assessing how initial interactions contribute to relationship development, for example, Donald G.
Ellis (1980) advocates an analysis of such elements as the people, physical environment, objects, and time dimensions (sequencing of information disclosure) and such processes as greeting, asking, establishing an
identity, and judging.

In the first phase of a study, the researcher will meet many people for
the first time, thrusting him- or herself into these initial interaction
dramas. These are key moments in the making of a normalized role in
the scene. The researcher's experiences in initial interactions, if carefully
noted, can be recalled later and inform an interpretation.

Such situations also represent openings for eliciting background information about actors. In my study of family video use, I met the grand-

mother of the children in one family about a third of the way through my period of observation. She was initially wary of what I was doing in her daughter's home, especially because I played freely with her grand-daughter. But after she was assured of my good intentions, she and I had a conversation that led to an account of the family history from her side, as well as helpful perspectives on how the youngest children had developed as television viewers.

WHEN AND HOW DO ACTORS CLAIM ATTENTION?

Veteran members of a group—having long ago survived the uncertainties of initial interactions—are apt to be experts on each other's preferences, habits, and manners. As such, they normally have little need to exchange explicit information on what is already known to be part of the group's stock of knowledge. The information they do exchange and debate is often highly goal oriented, nuanced, or surprising (from the standpoint of the experienced). It may also be notable because it *is* so routine.

Acculturated members have usually internalized a scheme of how lines of responsibility operate within their group. This means that information that does not concern the group as a whole might circulate only within certain subgroups of the membership. There may also be tacit rules for when a piece of information carries such significance that it needs to be conveyed to the entire group.

These are only a few of the features of ordinary behavior that present problems for the inquirer, who must somehow penetrate the surface of normality. In fact, one of the daunting tasks of entering a scene is simply that of understanding when and how the social actors claim each other's attention. Why do some items incite talk and action and others do not? What are the routes by which messages travel? How are these messages recognized? How do the actors know what needs to be the object of joint attention and what does not?

At first, the participant observer should pay close attention to those things that are somewhat confusing to him or her but clear to the others. These may be terminologies, procedures, or nonverbal behaviors. The researcher should ask, whenever appropriate, to be briefed on the meaning of an item, perhaps leaving for later the task of fully comprehending the full range of goals it serves. Less intrusively, the researcher should track the flow of information, along with the routine or unexpected responses it attracts. Certainly, any event that provokes comment or mobilizes action among the membership is one that invokes members' basic interests, and thus is one that merits close study.

WHERE AND WHEN DO PRINCIPAL ACTORS ORDINARILY CONGREGATE AND INTERACT?

On the way to understanding the nature of the actors' activities, the observer notes who associates with whom, and under what conditions. The ways in which actors *congregate*—that is, come together or disperse—should become readily apparent to the observer. This can be distinguished from "interaction" in the sense that people can do things together in a space (e.g., walk on a sidewalk, watch television, work side by side on separate tasks) without intentionally trying to coordinate behavior within the scope of a specific act. The observer also considers the human traffic patterns, the proxemics (spatial relationships) of the actors, and how they orient bodies, gestures, and faces to each other (Meyer, Traudt, & Anderson, 1980).

It may take longer for the researcher to notice and begin to generalize about members' *interactions*—the coordination of joint action. It is very important to note where and when certain kinds of interactions occur among certain individuals. We can safely assume that most interactions do not happen randomly. The location and timing of interactional episodes provide key evidence for beginning to understand their communicative functions. As will be discussed in Chapter 7, detailed field notes provide a basis for reasoning about the rules, codes, and meanings of behavior, and about whether and how the researcher should engage in further rounds of observing.

A formidable challenge I faced in my family video study was that of noticing the times and places of family members' congregations and interactions. Not only did the husband and wife have their own careers, they worked unusual shifts, and so were often not home together in the evening. Theirs was a blended family consisting of one child from the wife's first marriage, two children from the husband's first marriage, and two children from the current marriage. With ages ranging from 2 to 14, the children had different friendships and interacted with one another in vastly different ways. They entered and exited the house on very complicated schedules, and did chores and homework and used media (audio, video, print) together and alone, often away from their parents. Although I was mainly interested in behavior around the television sets, the task of grasping the contexts of all media use in the family occupied much of my attention throughout the study.

Observable aspects of interactions can tell us a great deal about the relationships among the interactants. Two important concepts for identifying relational public behavior have been called "markers" and "tie signs" (Petronio & Bourhis, 1987). They are especially useful when we try to define or describe particular social collectivities in open-access places. *Markers* are those behavioral signs of proximity and bodily engagement that distinguish a relationship. For example, some of the publicly tolerated markers of a familial relationship include hand-holding, interlocked arms, waist-holding, hugging, kissing, immediacy, and verbal interaction exclusivity. A heterosexual romantic relationship might be inferred from slightly different inflections of the same behaviors between opposite-sex persons of roughly the same age. *Tie signs* are symbols or social artifacts that indicate a type of relationship. Among the tie signs that usually signify family are wedding or engagement rings, contiguity of children (particularly when they solicit adults' attention regularly), parental accouterments (strollers, diaper bags, toys), and familial addresses. Of course, these concepts assume that relationships are performable in a culturally consistent way that permits the inferences noted above. One needs close familiarity with the normative performing of social roles to be able to apply markers or tie signs to instances of interaction; even with such familiarity, errors will be made.

Gleaning information from informants about unobserved interactions is one alternative to being there. The behaviors we witness often become the standard by which we interpret the ones we cannot see. As the analyst learns how the more available types of interaction occur, he or she can evaluate reports of private interaction partly by how plausible they seem. However, it is useful for the researcher to keep several simple points in mind: (a) The interactions we do see are *always* affected in part by our own presence, (b) the interactions we are not able to see will *always* be different from what we know because we are not there, and (c) the reports we get of unobserved interactions *always* reflect the purposes and position of the speaker.

WHAT COMMUNICATIVE EVENTS ARE SIGNIFICANT?

Similar to the question of identifying how people interact is the question of how to define the scene's communicative events. Soon after I started to observe the family mentioned above, I began to understand how units of activity cohered as events, some of which displayed the character of ritual: the 4-year-old's viewing of certain videos over and over with her neighborhood friends; the wife's daily taping and play-back (sometimes with her mother, sometimes not) of a soap opera; the family gathering to watch *The Cosby Show*, the only show they watched together; the older children's late-night viewing in the upstairs alcove, sequestered from the parents' view.

Recognizing the event *as an event* is a matter of unitizing experience at a higher level than congregations and interactions. Perceiving communicative events in a stream of behavior is an outcome of data analysis. The researcher consults field notes for records of actors' motives, accounts, feelings, and actions in order to define the major events and their properties. Among these properties are openings and closings for interaction, references to membership, sequences for taking turns, and conversational devices for keeping a topic on track (Speier, 1973). Analysis is a means of reconstructing the form, content, and sense of communication in social life.

We learn to recognize events by performing in them, by taking lines of action that make sense to the participants.[6] We also learn to recognize how events express the various realities of a scene, such as interpersonal conflicts and dilemmas, economic and political power, and cultural beliefs of various kinds. In other words, the act of analyzing field data consists largely of learning to *narrate* consciously and coherently what we did much less consciously and coherently before, in the field.

Conclusion

At this point, there is little more to be said about observing without invoking the processes of making texts: field notes, transcripts, documents, and visual media. Encoding our experiences in the field through these media allows us to *tell the stories* of those experiences. As we will learn in Chapter 7, the written records of observing yield a visible, consultable, and permanent (yet revisable) way of using our experience long after it is over. Such records perform many other functions in tandem with fieldwork, especially giving guidance on what to observe next and when to leave the field.

The next chapter takes us into the process of eliciting discursive experiences from people. Interviewing offers the researcher another mode of participation, one that encourages people to reveal things of importance through directed talk. As we will see, interviews can serve either as a self-sufficient research approach or as a companion to observing in ethnographic work.

Notes

1. Lyn H. Lofland, who transcribed and edited Goffman's talk, notes that even though Goffman explicitly asked not to be recorded on that occasion, someone in the audience recorded his remarks anyway. Because of that "unethical" action, his talk survived. In their own modest way, the circumstances of the article's publication are a fitting coda to Goffman's lifework, which focused so often on everyday acts of duplicity.

2. In his essay, Schutz (1944) sets clear limits on the range of situations to which the problem of the immigrant-stranger does and does not apply. Pertinent to this discussion is his exclusion of the case of "the visitor or guest who intends to establish a merely transitory contact with the group" (p. 499). On the face of it, this implies that the qualitative inquirer's experience is very different from that of Schutz's stranger. However, I believe that the problems faced by both are similar. Because the researcher must behave "as if" he or she cannot leave, as Goffman suggests, and because the researcher's communicative tasks involve the same imperatives for coordinating meaning as those of the immigrant-stranger's, their problems run parallel for some distance. Their respective prospects for permanent residence in the approached group's world typically mark the point of divergence in their existential predicaments.

3. If researchers employ appropriate techniques, however, children seem able to function adequately as informants (Amato & Ochiltree, 1987; Tammivaara & Enright, 1986).

4. For example, in my own academic department I have a native's knowledge of the normal activity patterns of my colleagues, teaching assistants, and staff. Yet at times I am surprised that I don't know certain locational or temporal items in this "familiar" terrain, such as office numbers or phone numbers, who uses what software, who is around at certain times of the week (when I am not present), and so on. In a few other situations I may not retrieve certain information about the department even when someone has a need to know, not because I'm being perverse, but because the question is not phrased explicitly enough.

5. As Weick (1985) sees it, "Investigators use expectancy as a control. Expectancies are the controls of both common sense and science; surprise is an indicator of the abuse of expectancies" (p. 573). At the outset, the observer's "controls" (expectancies) are rather global scenarios populated by broadly drawn character types, informed almost exclusively by what the researcher has learned from secondary sources. As the researcher becomes situated in a scene and begins sensing, his or her expectancies change. His or her controls become reconstructed regularly and with finer articulation. Moreover, the expectancies the researcher takes into the field gradually become the property of both the observer and the observed; increasingly, what surprises the investigator is also what surprises the social actors.

6. I should point out that we try to perform in ways that honor the history, ethos, and purposes of a group, but *not* in ways that are blameless. An influential part of a researcher's learning process lies in accepting even the bad consequences of his or her actions, as these are defined by the locals.

6

Eliciting Experience: Interviews

Conversation With a Purpose

For students of communication, speech performances are the primary means by which social life is enacted, organized, and understood. In Chapter 5, we learned that a participant observer attends to the conversations and other forms of speech that occur naturally in a scene. The researcher's growing competence at interpretation depends partly on whether participants accept him or her in their verbal routines. Yet, in many situations, the researcher needs to intervene more directly to learn what people mean when they act, to hear multiple perspectives on an event or issue, and to test emerging ideas about communicative action. Observing speech may also be impractical in certain instances.

The principal alternative to observation is interviewing—especially those styles known as in-depth, informal, unstructured, and semistructured interviewing. The practice of interviewing leads one to "quite literally . . . develop a *view* of something between (*inter*) people" (Brenner, 1985, p. 148). At its best, the qualitative interview creates an event in which one person (the interviewer) encourages another person to articulate interests or experiences freely. The interview's ability to access experiential or subjective realities has made it a preeminent method in

163

communication and the other social sciences. Indeed, some sort of interviewing is used in nearly all qualitative projects—a fact that underscores the importance of the study of its forms, practices, and limitations.

A qualitative approach to interviewing contrasts sharply with the use of surveys. Surveys rely on standardized sequences and forms of questions and, usually, sets of closed-ended responses. Strengths of surveys include their usefulness in systematic coding and analyzing of responses among the members of a sample and in the inference of population values. Survey methodology also aspires to high levels of validity and reliability through the minimization of the impact of the research experience itself on individual responses. But, from the stance of interpretive inquiry, the weaknesses of surveys are the exact opposites of these strengths. Surveys treat responses as though they are independent of the contexts that produce them (Mishler, 1986), ignore the expressive richness of respondents' own language, and do not allow the interviewer and respondent to explore and negotiate mutually the meaning of the objects of inquiry. Although the survey and the qualitative interview may usefully complement each other in a study, only rarely can one substitute for the other.

The styles of interviewing discussed in this chapter can be called, collectively, "conversation with a purpose" (Bingham & Moore, 1959). Interviewing takes on the form and feel of talk between peers: loose, informal, coequal, interactive, committed, open-ended, and empathic. Similarly, qualitative interviewing can emulate the kind of talk that passes between researcher and social actor further into a participant observation project, after they have come to know and trust each other.

Interviewing, however, is not just conversation. The distinctiveness of the interview as a performance is informed by its purposes, and to some degree by its structure (see Jorgenson, 1992). The *purposes* of an interview are usually conceived by one person, the researcher. Interview talk "covers a wide range of topics, which are not selected by one of the talkers—the respondent. It is talk that is organized so as to give one person (the interviewer) greater control over the other (the respondent). It is talk that is (typically) furnished for someone else's benefit" (Denzin, 1978, p. 113).

The *structure* of a qualitative interview also differs from that of ordinary conversation. It emphasizes turns of questions and answers, with the interviewer moving the discussion in a desired direction by asking most of the questions. Even long narratives produced by participants are usually impelled and punctuated by queries deemed relevant by an interviewer.

However, the interviewee does have some control in an interview, and can negotiate the interview's topics, processes, and outcomes. Collaborative styles have been developed that reduce power differences in the interview situation and grant considerable voice to the interests of the interviewee. Concerning this dynamic process, Paget (1983) writes:

> What distinguishes in-depth interviewing is that the answers given continually inform the evolving conversation. Knowledge thus accumulates with many turns at talk. It collects in stories, asides, hesitations, expressions of feeling, and spontaneous associations. . . . The specific person interviewing, the "I" that I am, personally contributes to the creation of the interview's content because I follow my own perplexities as they arise in our discourse. (p. 78)

Thus the conversational medium of interviewing invites ongoing revisions. The nature of the researcher's relationship with a participant precludes certain turns or topics in the conversation and encourages others. As we will see, variations in purpose and structure intertwine with the social situation to yield different genres of qualitative interviewing.

Stated simply, the researcher defines a purpose for such conversations to occur, and selects certain social actors to advance the conversational purpose. The researcher then elicits talk about their experiences. Through this method the communication researcher tries to gain a critical vantage point on the sense making in communicative performances and practices. A review of common objectives underlying the use of interviews reveals what they have to offer communication inquiry.

Objectives of the Qualitative Interview

In this chapter I take the view that interview talk is the rhetoric of socially situated speakers, *not* an objective report of thoughts, feelings, or things out in the world. Certainly, interview remarks do have a "referential" function (Briggs, 1986). They refer to events, processes, or objects that can be verified by other sources.[1] Interviews would be of dubious value if the material they produced did not refer to something outside the immediate dialogue. Yet interview talk cannot transparently reproduce an event, process, concept, or object. A specimen of talk exhibits contextual (or "indexical") features of semantic and syntactic choice, vocal inflection, timing, turn taking, and nonverbal (such as gestural) behaviors that derive from the cultural and ideological identities of the speaker. In talking about the same event, then, any two persons will use different words and speech styles. In so doing, they construct the truth value of the event in distinctive ways.

Therefore, no interview response, even one from an expert or a seemingly unimpeachable witness, can result in a complete meaning of the matter at hand. The response must be interpreted within the entire matrix of information about the interview event and the research problem. This premise—of the interview response as a subject's rhetoric about his or her experience—is key to understanding the seven basic objectives of qualitative interviewing reviewed here:

- learning about things that cannot be observed directly by other means
- understanding a social actor's perspective
- inferring the communicative properties and processes of interpersonal relationships
- verifying, validating, or commenting on data obtained from other sources
- testing hypotheses the researcher has developed
- eliciting the distinctive language—vocabularies, idioms, jargon, forms of speech—used by social actors in their natural settings
- achieving efficiency in collecting data

Even though interviews cannot lead a researcher directly to an event, or at least a completely accurate record of an event, they do enable him or her to *learn about things that cannot be observed directly by other means* (Patton, 1990, p. 278). In other words, informant interviewees can perform a needed surveillance-and-report function. Well-conducted interviews with an articulate participant who acts almost as a surrogate colleague can uncover details that the researcher cannot personally witness. For example, it is sometimes difficult to be at scenes where certain media, such as books, are used. These situations are hard to observe because there is no place for an observer, because the activity itself is dispersed across space and time, or because stigmas or other sanctions associated with the activity make observing problematic (Lindlof & Grodin, 1990). Thus interviewing can compensate for some deficits of observing.

Again, however, the researcher must remember that he or she can never be sure that what the informant says represents the full story. This uncertainty is greatest for events that occur so regularly and routinely in the life of the person or group that they elude awareness (Becker & Geer, 1957). Moreover, informants sometimes lay claim to more knowledge than they really possess. To deal with these problems, and the faulty inferences that could result, the analyst needs to have a good grasp of the participant's world going into the interview. Triangulation of interviews with other data sources (see Chapter 7) can ease, but not eliminate, these uncertainties.

Interviews are especially well suited to helping the researcher *understand a social actor's own perspective*. Often, a researcher will interview persons only if their experience is central to the research problem in some way. They may be recruited for their expert insight, because they represent a certain status or category, or because of critical events in which they have participated. The researcher expects the special nature of what they have experienced to result in a special articulation: words that can be expressed only by someone who has "been there."

Sometimes this entails developing a line of inquiry concerning actors' *accounts* of their behavior, which Scott and Lyman (1968) define as excuses or justifications of questionable conduct. For example, during an 18-month field study of a police agency, Hunt and Manning (1991) interviewed police officers about the social contexts in which they would lie. Police lying to colleagues and in court cases was found to serve a variety of pragmatic purposes: saving face, retaliating against disrespectful suspects, compensating for an ineffective justice system, avoiding unnecessary paperwork, and protecting fellow officers. In fact, according to Hunt and Manning, "learning to lie is a key to membership" (p. 54). What these researchers sought was the insiders' perspectives on this morally ambiguous activity, especially their notions of "normal" or "acceptable" lies. The interviews helped Hunt and Manning to analyze tensions between the needs of the police officers' self and the demands of the organization and community in which they work.

Of course, actors also produce *explanations* of their behaviors. Interviews may reveal how they apply their expertise in certain areas of their lives, how they negotiate sensitive issues or impasses, how they have made transitions to different stations in life, what specific media texts or styles of media use mean, and so on. The interviewer's goal is to draw out the cultural logics that people employ in their everyday experiences of communicating.

The researcher may also take advantage of the performance qualities of the interview event itself to *infer the communicative properties and processes of interpersonal relationships*. The qualities of disclosure and tact that characterize most relationships can be cultivated within the frame of the interview. The effect of this is to simulate the features of a relationship. Illustrative of this purpose are Rawlins's (1983) work on the communicative accomplishment of friendship and Grodin's (1991) study of how women use self-help books to inform their relational and personal identity concerns.

Researchers often use interviews to *verify, validate, or comment on data obtained from other sources.* An observed event can occur so quickly, or with such vague implications, that only the aid of a good informant can rescue its meaning. This help can come in several ways: from someone who was a central actor in the scene, from someone who witnessed the action, or from one who is so familiar with similar performances that he or she can comment knowledgeably without having been present at the specific performance. Documents also may require such interpretation by an informant. In my study of media use in prison, interviews with various staff members were critical to my understanding of the official policy on inmates' media use privileges and how it was actually implemented.

The researcher should be cautious about using actors' comments in this way, however, because unassisted retrospection can be superficial or a reaction to perceived demands of the interview situation (Merton, Fiske, & Kendall, 1956/1990). Also, the explanation offered may have been influenced by later events in ways unique to a particular informant.

Similarly, the researcher may use interviews to *test hypotheses he or she has developed.* "Exit interviews" or "member checks" (Lincoln & Guba, 1985) with key persons are often used near the end of a study. Chapter 7 considers in more detail the role played by informants in helping to refine and test propositions that emerge in analysis of field data.

Another purpose of interviewing in communication studies is to *elicit the distinctive language—vocabularies, idioms, jargon, forms of speech—used by social actors in their natural settings.* Acculturation in any realm of social life involves learning and practicing a native language. "The ethnographer seeks to encourage informants to speak in the same way they would talk to others in their cultural scene," notes Spradley (1979, p. 59). In studying academic life in a communication department, for instance, one might hear faculty members speak of a colleague as "a young turk," "a star," "deadwood," or "a politician." Factions in the department might be described as "green eyeshades," "production types," or "number crunchers." [2] An understanding of the language is usually essential to anyone hoping to interpret the political culture of a scene.

However, we must recognize the limits of interviewing for helping us to understand the situated use of language, as well as the reluctance (or eagerness) of informants to talk about and analyze their own language.

The researcher is usually on firmer ground simply recording language as it plays out in natural settings.

Finally, the interview is often used to *achieve efficiency in collecting data*. This is especially true when it is compared with prolonged participant observation. Even a project involving lengthy interviews with a sample of moderate size usually consumes fewer "contact hours" than an observational study.

But roughly the same dictum about the questionnaire-interview comparison applies here, too: Observing and interviewing can usefully complement each other, but the researcher should regard one as a substitute for the other warily and only after carefully studying their respective merits for addressing a problem. Moreover, the efficiency factor applies only to time in the field. Preparing interview transcripts takes as much time and effort (if not more) than field note taking in observational work.

In a given study, then, interviewing may serve from one to all seven of the above-discussed objectives.[3] Together they add up to a compelling set of reasons for researchers to include the interview in their research repertoires. Next, we examine some genres of interviewing that are prominent in communication studies.

Interview Genres in Communication

The interview is a remarkably adaptable tool. It can be conducted in a university research laboratory, during a walk along a beach, or in a teenager's bedroom. It can be a one-shot meeting as brief as 20 minutes, or it can extend in many sessions over weeks, months, or years. It may involve a gradual revelation of the most intimate thoughts, or it may elicit top-of-the-head responses.

Although interviewing styles are improvised to fit specific needs, several widely used formats have evolved. These formats, or genres, can be compared and contrasted along several dimensions: *content comparability* of topics covered across persons interviewed in a study—with "high comparability" meaning that one can analyze frequencies and distributions of responses in topic categories, and "low comparability" meaning that responses and topics vary greatly across interviews; *depth and range* of topics to be covered; *kind of discourse* expected of the interviewer and interviewee; *length and number* of interview sessions for each participant; and *sample characteristics*. These dimensions, elucidated below, provide some guidance to the researcher in selecting the type of interview needed for a given investigation.

ETHNOGRAPHIC INTERVIEWS

The ethnographic interview—also known as an "informal conversational interview" (Patton, 1990, pp. 281-282) or a "situational conversation" (Schatzman & Strauss, 1973, p. 71)—occurs in the course of a participant observer study. It is the most informal, conversational, and spontaneous form of interview. The ethnographic interview often does not even seem like an interview to the actor. Typically, a casual exchange of remarks leads to questions related to the researcher's interest.

Such interviewing appears effortless. Certainly the questioning is rather seamlessly geared into the work and talk already at hand. It does not require a special site or special preparations, and can be picked up again at a later point. The questions are usually, but not always, related to a current situation or to the individual experience of the person. However, this informality belies the skill involved in exploiting these moments:

> People often like to talk about themselves, what they do, and their worlds in general. The fieldworker's presence then offers to those in the setting a rare and perhaps gratifying opportunity to speak with some authority on subjects they know best. These are comfortable grounds, and creating situations in which such talk can occur is the essence of competent fieldwork. (Van Maanen, 1981, p. 478)

The researcher must be able to identify quickly something of interest in what is said or done and develop a line of questioning on the spot. This shift to the researcher's interest must not be abrupt or intrusive; it should make sense to the other person and should sustain the flow of conversation. Sensitive to the needs and nuances of the moment, an ethnographic interview is the most flexible way of eliciting talk. However, it yields data that are not always directly comparable to those from other interviews.

INFORMANT INTERVIEWS

In the course of fieldwork, the researcher will see certain people as more valuable than others for achieving the research objectives. These people may have more mobility in an organization than most others, or more experience in certain settings; they may command respect from their peers, superiors, and/or subordinates. They almost always display a facility with the local language, and are more willing than others to assist with the project goals. Occasionally, a person might be a good source because of his or her marginal status; a singular or deviant view can help the researcher reconstruct the rationality of what is considered normal in the scene. Some combination of these qualities can make a good informant.

The would-be informant's role and perspective must be functional for the purposes of the project. Different informants can offer a variety of insights because they have had unique experiences in the scene. For example, in studying how underage patrons use "fake IDs" to negotiate access to a club, Scheibel (1992) "befriended the club's doormen and was subsequently allowed to stand next to them as they interacted with the customers. Near the end of some evenings, doormen would show me fake IDs they had confiscated from customers earlier in the evening and explain why the IDs were 'bad' " (p. 161). Other informant interviews with students, customers, and past employees helped Scheibel understand the cultural and historical contexts of fake-ID use, and the experiences of those who proffer and examine fake IDs at nightclubs.

Many aspects of the informant genre—such as the development of a personal relationship with the interviewee and the often improvisational nature of the interview itself—are reminiscent of the ethnographic interview. However, an informant is normally consulted many times by the researcher about specific domains of information, usually with prepared questions and set times and places for interview encounters. Whereas ethnographic interviews are generally brief, informant interviews take place in longer meetings (up to two or more hours). Whereas ethnographic interviews are tied to concrete situations, informant interviews range more widely and go more deeply into the person's experiences. When using several informants, the researcher usually organizes questions so that the separate discourses can be compared and cross-referenced for the research report.

RESPONDENT INTERVIEWS

As its name implies, the respondent interview elicits open-ended responses to a series of directive questions. In contrast to the kinds of interviews discussed above, the respondent interview resembles the traditional survey in its standardized protocol, high content comparability, and relatively large samples of interviewees. "Respondents" are rarely encouraged to expound their own notions of what is important for the researcher to know. Instead, a strong conceptual framework drives the question design and sample selection concerns of such interviews.

Moreover, the respondent interview is frequently used as a stand-alone procedure rather than integrated with other data-gathering techniques in a field study. The respondent's contact with the interviewer is limited to one or two sessions. By asking the same questions of all respondents in roughly the same order, the researcher minimizes interviewer effects and achieves greater efficiency of information gathering.

The aims of this genre have changed little since Lazarsfeld (1944) described them 50 years ago: (a) to clarify the meanings of common concepts and opinions, (b) to distinguish the decisive elements of an expressed opinion, (c) to determine what influenced a person to form an opinion or to act in a certain way, (d) to classify complex attitude patterns, and (e) to understand the interpretations that people attribute to their motivations to act.

In audience research, reception study has largely adopted the aims and methodology of the respondent interview to study how individuals "read" the codes of ideology, class, gender, and race in popular texts (see Hoijer, 1990; Lindlof, 1991). An example of its use in interpersonal communication is Rawlins and Holl's (1987) study of adolescents' notions of friendship, especially the ways in which communication strategies engage the tensions, ambiguities, and boundaries of close relationships. The interviewer "used a standardized protocol containing 35 open-ended questions. . . . address[ing] several issues relating to adolescent friendship, e.g., respondents' views on the nature and benefits of friendship, their use of time, the relationship between friends and family, cross-sex friendship, and significant others" (p. 347). As in most respondent interviews, Rawlins and Holl treated each participant as an authoritative speaker on behalf of his or her own behavior. The interview schedule promoted comparability among responses, which furthered the researchers' aims in the analysis phases of generating and refining interpretive categories.

NARRATIVE INTERVIEWS

Stories are a very useful construct for analyzing processes of reality construction, especially in personal relationships and organizational cultures. Narrative interviewing is based on the premise that the events of our lives, and the events of groups and organizations, are communicated through storytelling (Brown, 1990; Bruner, 1987; Graham, 1984; Langellier, 1989). Storytelling operates as a device for sense making in nearly all social worlds by drawing upon a shared fund of myth, story grammar, plots, character types, and performance competencies. Some argue that the urge to narrate is a universal trait of humanity (e.g., Bruner, 1987; Fisher, 1985; White, 1981). More than a means of amusement, stories encode the information needed by members of society to carry on the most critical activities of social intercourse, economy, politics, art, spirituality, birth, and death.

The narrative genre utilizes storytelling as an empirical technique, and also examines storytelling performances, practices, and functions as an analytic goal. For example, the *life history*, an ethnographic form popularized by Thomas and Znaniecki, Clifford Shaw, and others of the Chicago school in the first half of this century, seeks to interpret the significant experiences and perceptions of an actor (Becker, 1966; Plummer, 1983). A life history may (a) embrace all of the significant streams of an actor's life, (b) identify one aspect of the actor's life and present that aspect fully, or (c) intersperse a primary text with the analytic comments and annotations of the researcher (Denzin, 1978). The life history documents "a subjectivity told by a subject," and is often employed as a way to understand the history of a culture. Other modes of the narrative, such as interpretive biography, autobiography, self-stories, organizational stories, and oral history (Denzin, 1989), rely on basically the same principles of method and interpretation. However, the last two of these focus more on narrations of external events and processes than on narrations of the self.

Collecting stories may be one part of a field project and may involve differently situated storytellers, as in Feldman's (1990) study of top leadership change in an electronics company. Feldman found that the departure of the company's founder created a climate of instability that company managers rationalized by "scapegoating" the new president—a motif that emerged from stories. Sense can also be made of interpersonal relationships through telling stories about them. For example, Bochner and Ellis (1992) describe how a man and a woman reconstructed their decision to abort a pregnancy by collaborating on a narrative derived from self-interviews, field notes, and consultations with friends and colleagues.

Narrative interviewing usually depends on a long-term, trusting relationship between researcher and social actor. Given that the goal is a detail-rich account of perceptions and affect, the researcher tries to establish the most comfortable conditions for letting a person talk. This may entail simply allowing the person free rein to tell his or her story, or it may mean fostering a dialogue between researcher and actor. Either way, the researcher's role is to facilitate, not to direct or manage.

FOCUS GROUP INTERVIEWS

The genres reviewed so far are based on dyadic encounters. The interviewee is assumed to "possess" information waiting to be released by an astute interviewer. However, the act of being interviewed is more like a struggle to produce and repair meaning than a delivery of cognitions complete unto themselves. Moreover, the individual interview cannot capture very well the dynamic processes of natural group interaction or collective interpretation.

Focus group interviews offer a methodological response to these problems of individual interviewing. Focus groups create settings in which diverse perceptions, judgments, and experiences concerning particular topics can surface. Persons in focus groups are stimulated by the experiences of other members of the group to articulate their own perspectives. The ways they support, debate, or resolve issues with each other can resemble the dynamics of everyday social discourse. In short, the strength of this genre is "the explicit use of the group interaction to produce data and insights that would be less accessible without the interaction found in a group" (Morgan, 1988, p. 12).

The operation of focus groups is deceptively simple. A sample of 6 to 12 persons who are demographically homogeneous, or who have certain experiences in common, is selected to meet at a neutral site to discuss subjects of interest to the researcher. Often the members of the group do not know each other, but in some cases they share social histories of some sort. The interviewer (or "facilitator") makes introductions, discusses the purposes and interactional rules of the group interview, possibly displays a stimulus (e.g., a media text) to orient the group to the research subject, and begins with a question. Thereafter, the interviewer manages the group with a light hand, particularly if a relatively unstructured discussion is desired. The interviewer usually consults an interview guide of questions, and may interject with probes. Ensuring that all persons speak, and that all topics are addressed, constitute the major challenges in focus group interviewing.

Merton et al.'s (1956/1990) classic work on the "group interview" in the early 1940s stemmed from research on war propaganda effects, and recent qualitative studies of mass communication audiences have revived Merton et al.'s methods. These studies expose viewer groups to samples of popular television programming to investigate how their interpretations are affected by gender, class, or ethnic identity (e.g., Liebes, 1984, 1988; Morley, 1980; Press, 1989a; Schaeffer & Avery, 1993).

For all of its intriguing features, the focus group interview suffers from burdens and ambiguities that limit more widespread use. It continues to be perceived more as a marketing research tool, or as an exploratory technique, than as a fully legitimate academic research method. More critically, the relative merits of different formats for conducting focus groups and different ways of presenting findings are not well understood. Merton et al.'s (1956/1990) prescriptions remain useful, but it is only recently that methodologists have begun to scrutinize such issues as how many groups and what size groups should be run, how to evaluate the information from group interviews against that gathered using other methods, and how to analyze the interactional episodes such interviews produce (see, e.g., Fern, 1983; Krueger, 1988; Morgan, 1988).

Interview Practice

If interviewing is partly conversation, then the interviewer must be a skilled conversationalist. If interviewing is partly cross-cultural encounter, then the interviewer must be a translator of cultural norms. If interviewing is partly the "digging tool" of social science, then the interviewer must be an effective, nonthreatening interrogator. If interviewing is partly a learning situation, then the interviewer must be a willing student.

Most interviews are all these things, and more. Interviews are made up of many overlapping tasks that require ongoing decisions. The researcher may not perform each task brilliantly, but if he or she responds flexibly and sensibly, a successful interview becomes more likely. Some key interviewing procedures, and their communicative presuppositions, are outlined below.

THE INTERVIEW AS PLAY

My own interviewing experience has endured its share of misunderstandings: the prison inmate who responded to my questions with suspicion and hedged, unrevealing remarks; the woman who didn't think she would be a good subject for my study because it was her husband, not she, who used the family's computer; the time I arrived at a high school for focus group interviews only to find that our contact did not yet have a room for us, and then when an empty classroom was found, the teacher there busied herself as the students talked "confidentially."

These incidents point to the fragile nature of the interview as a ritual event. Undoubtedly, as Benney and Hughes (1970) assert, "there is an enormous amount of preparatory socialization in the respondent role—in schools and jobs, through the mass media" (p. 193). However, the researcher and the interviewee do bring to the event separate definitions of what it means to interview and be interviewed. They have different notions of the purposes and rules of the interview, role incumbencies for each party that describe their "rights" and positioning in the interview, and rhetorical tactics for communicating. In fact, *interviews are speech events informed by norms and rules, in which every utterance and nonverbal sign contributes to the social reality created in the interview.*

Researchers who conduct surveys and highly structured interviews usually have a certain purpose in mind for the participants. Subjects are encouraged to be "good respondents": to be cooperative and provide the information the researcher seeks (Mishler, 1986, p. 54; Sudman & Bradburn, 1983, pp. 4-7). The good respondent should ignore all signs of the interview's context, and instead focus on the referential, standardized discourse favored by the survey researcher. A survey's design attempts to gear into this "opinionatedness"—a generalized stance people use to describe how they relate to their own opinions and attitudes (Manning, 1967). According to textbook lore, the "good respondent" attitude helps a study achieve general validity across cultures and across time (Mishler, 1986).

The social power relations between interviewer and respondent also affect how the event is perceived. A typical survey interview transpires between two people who are strangers to each other. One of them is a credentialed expert in communication science. As in many stranger encounters, signs of social, economic, and cultural power weigh heavily in setting the tone of this interaction. The researcher initiates the relationship and defines its ground rules. The interviewee agrees to give good-faith consideration to each of the questions and to provide adequate responses. It is not the survey respondent's place to challenge, contradict, or "talk over" the researcher. The respondent should not go beyond what is wanted from the questions, or respond in ways that are "irrelevant" (Mishler, 1986). Thus the researcher's interests usually preside over the setting in which they meet. This asymmetric relationship carries over into the research texts that result from their meetings.

Such hegemony runs counter to good qualitative interviewing. The challenge facing the qualitative researcher is how to encourage self-expression and a sense of empowerment in the participant yet also achieve the aims of the study. The researcher must somehow persuade the participant to "enlarge on the definition of the situation as interview by reading the interview also as an interesting and satisfying encounter, as a chance to express his dislikes, disappointments, and ideas" (Brenner, 1978, p. 130). The interview must be framed as a consensual project.

This goal is more likely to be met if the interview is treated as a form of play (Bateson, 1972): both parties acting as if they are equal partners. A significant element of this play lies in expanding the interview roles themselves. The informant takes on some of the perspective of the researcher in telling his or her stories. At the same time, the researcher begins to understand important properties of the informant's world, from that person's own situation.[4] Gradually, the informant begins to perceive that he or she has a stake in the project. Not only does the conversational play frame induce a more committed relationship with the researcher, but by adopting some of the researcher's analytic interests, the informant develops a desire to "get it right." The validity of the account, story, or explanation becomes a real concern for the informant, just as it is for the researcher.

Thus a sort of "contract" between the researcher and the interviewee emerges:

> By offering a program of discussion, and an assurance that information offered will not be challenged or resisted, self-expression is facilitated to an unusual degree [that] is inherently satisfying. In this sense, then, the interview is an understanding between the two parties that, in return for allowing the interviewer to direct their communication, the informant is assured that he will not meet with denial, contradiction, competition, or other harassment. As with all contractual relations, *the fiction or convention of equality must govern the situation.* (Benney & Hughes, 1970, pp. 194-195; emphasis added)

It is important to note, as emphasized in this passage, the fictional aspect of equality in qualitative interviews. In many ways, power still resides with the researcher: Real research objectives are operative, real questions are asked, and the researcher edits the final product. Yet the essence of any play frame is that the play is taken seriously by its participants. Within the qualitative interview frame, the interviewee can raise issues unforeseen by the interviewer, resist responding to certain questions, ask the interviewer to clarify a point, suggest the relevance of one thing over another, and so on.

To sum up, the equality framing of qualitative interviews is no less authentic than any other play frame in which special norms and rules apply. The research professional becomes someone who wants to learn what the culture member has to teach. When power differences are reduced to some degree, participants can think more clearly, calmly, and creatively about the nature of their communication practices. It is to the interviewing performance that we now turn.

ASSESSING INTERVIEWEES

Because qualitative interviewing rarely uses probability principles in selecting human subjects, the search for suitable interviewees becomes a major concern. Among fieldworkers, certain benchmarks of the good informant (respondent) are considered essential. First and foremost, the prospect should have *appropriate experience in the cultural scene.* Obviously, the researcher is not interested in talking with someone who has no experience at all in the scene, so the decision to interview someone turns on what is meant by *appropriate.* In most cases, appropriate experience is "thorough enculturation" (Spradley, 1979) in a group, organization, or relationship. Those with such experience have participated in the critical events, decisions, routines, and career paths that ensure a rich lode of information and stories.

In some cases, however, the research objective calls for a lesser degree of enculturation. The Rawlins and Holl (1987) study discussed earlier was based partly on the idea that adolescence is a time when close friendships are first experienced and tested. In my study of families' home computing (Lindlof, 1992), it was important for me to talk with nonusers (mostly women) because they were also involved in the construction of the computer's family meanings and its consequences for family identity and relationships. More than quantity of information, or seniority in a group, the key consideration is, Who has the relevant information (Gorden, 1969)? Or, Who can tell the most valuable stories?

Another major benchmark concerns *the ability and willingness of the prospective interviewee to articulate his or her experience in the interview context.* Willingness has much to do with whether people think the interview poses threats to their ego, social standing, or political or economic well-being. To dispel these fears, the researcher can emphasize the human protections by which the study abides. The researcher can also appeal to the actors' senses of altruism, pride (*they* are the experts), curiosity, and collaboration in a common enterprise. The more they feel a part of the research, the more likely it is they will want to cooperate.

It may take some effort for the researcher to recognize whether or not a person can articulate effectively in the interview setting. A basic requirement of an interviewee is the ability to produce a desirable amount of talk. Just as important, the prospect should be able to speak clearly and reflectively about his or her experiences. Certainly many researchers, especially novices, favor informants who can "code switch"; that is, people who can switch easily from one form of discourse (their own culture's) to another (e.g., the researcher's middle-class professional culture), and even "translate" between language styles. The researcher may consider such people great informants because he or she can interact so effectively with them, and because they may even seem to do some of the researcher's work. On the other hand, researchers are sometimes confounded by people whose communication norms and social etiquette differ crucially from their own, creating very real problems in the interpretation of remarks, silences, and body behavior (Briggs, 1986). A researcher may consider such interviewees to be inarticulate, especially if he or she has not taken care to evaluate the scene's cultural norms in advance. This is actually a problem of cultural misunderstanding, not interviewee deficiency, and should be treated as part of the research problem itself (Briggs, 1986; Patton, 1990, pp. 337-340). Still other persons may not verbalize very well as interviewees because of shyness, or because they cannot recall very much or reflect very deeply about what they see and hear. As respondents they might function reasonably well, but as informants they might provide too little of use to be worth the effort.

Finally, potential interviewees should be assessed for *the time they can devote to being interviewed*. Interviews vary in the amount and flexibility of time required of participants. For informant and narrative interviewing in particular, the researcher strives for an open-ended commitment. Persons leading very busy lives or who have unpredictable schedules will be least able to make good on their commitments. Unexpected time demands will occur in anyone's life, and the researcher should accommodate them with equanimity.

Where and when to interview constitute another issue. Unless special technologies or group seating arrangements are required, qualitative interviews can be conducted almost anywhere. The major considerations are low ambient noise (to ensure a clear audio-recording), avoidance of interruptions or undesirable supervision by others, and a level of comfort that the participant finds agreeable.

Researchers sometimes hold interviews at sites at their own institutions for the sake of controllable, consistent interviewing conditions. In most cases, the researcher should defer to the actors about what makes for comfortable surroundings. Most will choose settings that combine convenience (theirs, not the researcher's) and privacy. Often, these will be on their turf, such as in their homes or offices. Some prefer public locations, such as parks, for their anonymity.

When interviews should be conducted is a matter of wide variability. Best results are usually obtained when the participant is relaxed, feeling neither highly energized nor fatigued, and when competing demands on his or her attention are unlikely.

RAPPORT

Because the parties meet each other as strangers, the interviewer must do whatever is needed to put the participant at ease. The interviewer must try to anticipate the images and questions the participant brings to the meeting. Reasonable people may privately ask skeptical, even suspicious, questions of a research project, even after they have consented to be interviewed: What does this person want to know about me? Am I allowed to say what I really think? Will I be ripped off by someone who doesn't really care about me? Of what value is this research anyway? Researchers would be wise to recall their own hard-edged feelings when market researchers or pollsters implore them to answer questions. The interviewer needs to respond to the qualms participants may have about the study, the rules of the interview, and what kind of professional—and person—he or she is.

What the interviewer wants to achieve is *rapport* with the interviewee, or the ability of both parties to empathize with each other's perspective. Each party may not agree with the content of the other's perspective, but nonetheless recognizes and respects its validity. The existence of rapport also means that the interviewer and interviewee are in basic accord on communication style and the subject matter that can and cannot be talked about. In this sense, rapport is "simply the sharing of a common language" (M. H. Kuhn, 1962, p. 201). It clears away the burden of having to translate what one wants to say into a formal or foreign style. It clears away the fear of being misunderstood. It means that, for *this* occasion, conditions are right for disclosing thoughts and feelings more readily.

The existence of rapport does not imply a deep or intimate bond between people. Rapport is a quality of a communication event, not of a relationship. As Spradley (1979) notes, "Just as respect can develop between two people who do not particularly like one another, rapport can exist in the absence of fondness and affection" (p. 78). Also, rapport should not be confused with neutrality on the part of the researcher. Patton (1990) makes the distinction this way:

> *Rapport is a stance vis-à-vis the person being interviewed. Neutrality is a stance vis-à-vis the content of what that person says.* Rapport means that I respect the people being interviewed, so that what they say is important because of who is saying it. . . . Yet, I will not judge them for the content of what they say to me. (p. 317)

With friends, we have rapport without being neutral. In other relationships, we can be neutral about someone without having rapport with that person. It is the inquirer's job to seek rapport *and* neutrality, assuming of course that it is possible to be neutral, or morally nonevaluative, to some degree.

Because the researcher initiates the contact and has limited time to complete the interview, a high priority is placed on tactics for starting and maintaining rapport. Arguably, this encourages a distorted view of rapport as originating with the researcher and serving only the researcher's needs (Jorgenson, 1992). Certainly, no one party can "possess" rapport; by definition, rapport is a social accomplishment. But it remains the researcher's responsibility to lay the groundwork for a mutually gratifying conversation.

Rapport begins with *clarity of purpose.* Participants should be given clear, succinct, and honest reasons why they have been contacted, the aims and value of the project, and how the interview will be conducted. This general advice was introduced in Chapter 4 in the context of ethical responsibilities. But the personal, intensive nature of interviewing calls for special handling. Each participant should be advised that there are "no right or wrong responses," that the interest is in "how you and others like you (others in this organization)" communicate in the setting, and that it is important to hear this "in your own words." The participant should understand that, unlike other, more formal styles of interviewing, this experience will be more like a conversation. The interviewer can invite the participant to raise his or her own topics and expand into areas not anticipated by the interviewer's questions and comments. If interview schedules or guides are used, the interviewer should make it clear that he or she needs to cover a set of topics in the allotted time. Usually, participants appreciate knowing what they are expected to do to help the interviewer get the job done.

Interviewer self-disclosures can also engage the participant's interest and pave the way for him or her to talk freely. For example, when I interviewed families about their home computing usage, I typically began with an anecdote or two about my own first experiences with my Apple II-e. As I related these pleasures and confusions of bygone days, I noticed that the participants loosened up quite a bit. In fact, the first few minutes often found them "interviewing" *me*, asking questions about my computer, how I purchased it, and how much my daughter used it. Through such self-disclosure, the researcher gives the interviewee some idea of the kind of event the interview will be and the level of detail the researcher is looking for. This relieves the interviewee of having to start answering questions cold. The interviewee may also learn enough about the researcher to form an opinion about the person he or she is dealing with. If the researcher continues to use personal stories judiciously throughout the interview, a sense of reciprocity (and rapport) will often unfold.

Alternatively, the interviewer can take the tack of asking participants to describe their own family histories, what their jobs consist of, and other aspects of their lives. Aside from eliciting background data, the main purpose of these *participant self-disclosures* is to break the ice, to help the participant feel comfortable talking about personal issues. The participant will find that it is not difficult to talk in this context, and that other disclosures will be assured a receptive audience. The participant will discover that being an interviewee is a constructive role to play.

For the researcher's part, this gambit is neither frivolous nor a throwaway. During this part of the interaction, the researcher can note discreetly the participant's speech patterns, recall, and storytelling ability. He or she can take into account the participant's performance in these opening minutes and adjust the order and wording of questions. It is important to note that this type of opening question should key in on a positive experience of the participant, or at the very least an innocuous experience. When I first started interviewing inmates, I began by asking them to recount how they came to be incarcerated. It soon became abundantly clear that these were *not* pleasant memories. By the time I interviewed my third inmate, I had a new opening question, focusing further back in time on where he grew up. Later, after gaining the interviewee's confidence, I would work toward the incarceration question. Obviously, the effort to establish rapport suffers badly if negative emotions are brought to the surface at the outset.

The effects of *demeanor and personal appearance* should not be underestimated in rapport building either. The good-person stance discussed in Chapter 5 applies as well to the interviewer's introductory moves: A skillful self-presentation involves a positive, nonjudgmental, nonargumentative, eager-to-learn demeanor. And whatever people's notions of the "dress code" of academics may be, a formal style of dress will probably not help to diminish most participants' anxiety about being interviewed. Within reasonable limits, the researcher should be attired in much the same way as those being interviewed. One scholar in his late 30s who was studying the punk subculture claimed that he cut and dyed his hair so that he would fit in better with the people he was studying. Although this approach may have enhanced rapport in his case, it might be totally wrong for someone else (me, for example). Unless the researcher can act the part convincingly, a radical style intended to conform to a group's norms might be seen by its members as patronizing or crudely inauthentic. No matter what their own norms may be, group members usually respect a researcher whose dress and demeanor reflect a sensible reading of the situation.

Finally, *listening* represents a crucial—maybe the most crucial—way to demonstrate an empathic attitude. At one level, listening means "paying attention" to what is said. Showing that one is listening carefully tells the participant that what he or she says is credible and interesting on its own terms. Perhaps because words can seem insincere, the mere act of paying attention may come across as a purer sign of engagement, of wanting to hear more.

More substantively, *active* listening means trying to hear the *significance* of the interviewee's remarks. Here, the convenience of tape-recording releases the researcher from the role of stenographer, and enables him or her to process what the interviewee says at deeper, more complex levels. The interviewer can attend to the emotive accents of what is said, the figures of speech, the inconsistencies, the buried connections, the obscure references, the startling insights, the repetitions. The interviewer must be able to take in a lot of discourse in real time, mentally tag items of interest, and compare and contrast them with what is said later. He or she should listen to possible meanings in what the interviewee says, what the person might have meant, and what the person's remark might mean outside its immediate context (DeVault, 1990). In active listening, one is actually keeping "a watch on oneself, a self-consciousness" (Cottle, 1973, p. 351).

Evidence of listening is displayed in head orientation, nods, smiles, looks of concern, and the "yes," "uh-huh," and "I see" that sustain talk and affirm the grounds of understanding between the researcher and participant. The researcher can also indicate listening by asking follow-up questions or by asking the participant to amplify his or her thoughts on something just said. Even the noticing of contradictory statements can be done in a way that does not cause embarrassment to the participant (Lindlof & Grodin, 1990). By asking the participant what two statements mean, even if they seem to conflict, the researcher reinforces the sense of two people working together on a common problem. Rapport between interview parties leads to involved listening, and involved listening promotes rapport. Listening becomes the vital connective tissue of the interview.

QUESTION DESIGN AND USE

Questions are the best-known tools of the interviewer's craft. We could easily (and misleadingly) coin a maxim: To interview is to ask. Although interviewers' questions do not always appear in research publications, they are an object of concern and scrutiny at nearly every stage in a study. Questions are also the most forceful tools available. Questions have the capacity to guide discourse along certain tracks and not others, and to affect the pace and tone of the talk. Used appropriately, they can aid in eliciting truly essential accounts; used inappropriately, they can lead the participant into confusing terrain, or even stall the conversation completely. This section considers the design, ordering, and uses of interview questions. It concludes with some cautions about participant truth shading and the role of the audiotape recorder as a third party in the interview process.

Interview Schedules and Guides

All forms of interviewing entail preparatory work. Even the relatively spontaneous style of ethnographic interviewing is driven by an agenda of puzzling findings and emergent conclusions that the researcher continually updates in and out of the field. This changing agenda usually emerges in journal entries and the "observer's comments" of field notes (see Chapter 7). The manner in which such questions are used depends on the opportunities created by the researcher.

A formal preparation of questions is required when interviews are the chief method of gathering material, or when longer, more focused sessions with participants are needed. One of these instruments, the *interview schedule*, is used when a project requires uniformity of question wording, order, use of probes, and the contexts in which interviews are conducted (Gorden, 1969, p. 264; Patton, 1990, pp. 284-287). This emphasis on standardization resembles the use of questionnaires, except that interview schedules elicit open-ended responses in the participants' own language and encourage interviewers to clarify ambiguous, opaque, or mistaken responses. Variations on a master interview schedule may be adapted for different subsamples, but typically questions are asked of all respondents in the same order, in the hope of maximizing the reliability and credibility of the findings and the ability to generalize to a population. Interview schedules are also preferred when many trained interviewers are involved. They reduce the risk that differences in interviewers' skills or tactics will cause severe unevenness in the information collected. Respondent interview studies are most apt to work from interview schedules. For other qualitative work in communication, interview schedules' inflexibility is seen as a hindrance to capturing fully the social actors' experiences and insights.

The instrument of choice for most qualitative interviewers is the *interview guide*. As might be guessed from the term, an interview guide simply organizes a menu of topics to be covered and leaves the task of determining their exact order and articulation to the interviewer in the field. To be sure, it is often expected that certain topics or questions will be asked of *all* participants in roughly the same way. But freedom exists for the interviewer to employ optional questions, pass on others, and depart briefly to go down an unexpected conversational path. Especially when it comes to interviewing informants, whose experiences can vary widely, the interviewer may reshuffle topics to pursue new ideas. An interview guide also lets its user adjust to the verbal style of the participant. To sum up, "the interview schedule . . . emphasizes the means of obtaining information, [whereas] the interview guide emphasizes the *goals* of the interview in terms of the topics to be explored and the criteria of a relevant and adequate response" (Gorden, 1969, pp. 264-265). Part of an interview guide from my family microcomputer study is shown in Figure 6.1.[5]

Questions and Probes

Qualitative interview questions are meant to elicit an interviewee's experience in the words that are natural to that person. The last thing the researcher wants is to have his or her own categories and assumptions

A. BACKGROUND ON COMPUTER

Why did you buy your computer?

Probe: Any other reasons?

How did you go about buying this computer?

. . . previous experience . . . friends' advice . . . etc.

What did you think of personal computers before you bought this one?

Did the introduction of this computer in your home change your family's leisure-time activities?

Probe for when and why of changes

Change any other activities in the home?

How did it change your wife/husband's . . . _____'s?

B. CHILDREN'S USES OF COMPUTER/COMPUTING

What are _____'s primary interests at school?

(subjects)? Special talents, abilities?

. . . at home? (hobbies, play, work)

Overall, how would you characterize _____'s interest in the computer?

How has _____'s *interest in/enjoyment of* the computer *changed* since it's been here?

Probe for problems using/understanding it . . .

Games or programs . . .

Engagement with friends, siblings . . .

Figure 6.1. Excerpt of an Interview Guide

simply reflected back. The purpose is to help the interviewee introspect effectively about his or her communication practices. For this reason, general, nondirective questions work best at the beginning of an interview.

Grand-tour questions unravel the participant's familiar knowledge of a routine, ritual, procedure, cycle of group activity, round of duties, career path, or event.[6] The interviewee becomes the tour guide describing what it is like to experience something with which the researcher has only formal or secondhand acquaintance.[7] This approach accesses the how-to, procedural knowledge a participant has acquired by dint of socialization, trial and error, and folklore. Grand tours are also good rapport builders, because they give the interviewee a chance to display his or her expertise and experience. By asking many people the same grand-tour question, the researcher may notice the inflections that mark social-structural or cultural status differences.

The researcher may ask for either an ideal-typical grand tour ("So, tell me how a sci-fi convention usually goes, starting with when you get to the hotel") or a memorable tour story ("How did your first sci-fi convention go, from start to finish—with any and all surprises, highlights, expectations confirmed, expectations denied, and so forth. Tell me all about it."). The first grand-tour example simply sketches the thrust of the question, giving the interviewee an open field to run. If the story gets told too quickly or too vaguely, the researcher can ratchet down the pace by probing for more detail—with the quick "eyebrow flash," by softly repeating key phrases, or by asking, "Tell me how *that* happens." In the second example above—eliciting a story tied to a memorable circumstance—cues in the question tell the participant about the kind and depth of detail desired. At a possible cost of constraining the story too much, this tactic may cause fewer interruptions or changes of pace.

Rather than engage in a string of probes, the researcher can wait for the story's end and then ask *example* questions or *experience* questions (Spradley, 1980, p. 88). The nature of an example question is self-explanatory. Experience questions ask participants about specific experiences they have had in particular roles or settings or situations. The idea underlying both is to elicit deeper profiles of certain experiential sites, like a geologist taking core samples. If the kind of experience sought is exceptional in some way (e.g., the most distressing, the most enjoyable, the most surprising) instead of typical, the participant may need more time to retrieve the memory. To make this "search time" less awkward, the interviewer can simply build a longer question, incorporating a personal anecdote or more explanation of the thrust of the question. The question may also be submitted to the participant in advance (this is one of the few instances when this might be desirable).

After the interviewee has described an example or experience, the interviewer might probe for the *motives* of the person or other actors in the story (e.g., "What were you trying to accomplish?" "Why do you think she said that?"). However, this needs to be done prudently. The fact that an individual or group motivation has not been brought up could be critical to the story's telling. Maybe the issue of motive will resolve itself as the interview goes on, or as the researcher collects and compares other accounts. At all times, the researcher must stay sensitive to what matters to the interviewee, what he or she is capable of telling, and the emotional tones of the interview event.

Grand-tour responses usually involve a time dimension. A more focused version is the *time-line* approach (Shields & Dervin, 1993). The interviewer aids the participant in articulating events and experiences that happened on a time line moving from past to present. This kind of questioning is well suited to studies of self formation or of collective history. Grodin (1990) used a time-line approach to learn how women read self-help books in some correlation to their personal crises and life-span transitions. Foreman (1994) used it to understand how employees of different tenures and organizational subcultures interpreted some key events at their company.

A spatial/visual analogue of the time line, the *auto-driving* approach (McCracken, 1988), uses a picture, video, some other graphic material, or a text to aid the participant in providing an account. Clearly, there is more specificity in this question-framing process, and so it is more obtrusive. However, it "helps to both foreground and objectify aspects of the respondents' experience that are otherwise difficult to bring into the interview" (McCracken, 1988, p. 37).

Another follow-up to the grand tour is what Schatzman and Strauss (1973) call *posing the ideal*. The participant is asked to speculate about an ideal state of affairs, or ideal goals, for the group or organization. Alternatively, the researcher may take the lead in proposing an ideal ("which pushes an observed process or role to its logical and desired extreme"; p. 81) and then have the participant react to this construct. This strategy is used to get some sense of an ideology or myth held by the membership of a group or organization. *Hypothetical-interaction* questions (Spradley, 1980, p. 90) also call on the interviewee to imagine a situation, but one that is based in actual or plausible relationships (e.g., "What would you say if Kendra told you she watched an R-rated movie at a friend's house?"). The choices of words and concepts for constructing an answer are of interest here.

Actors in virtually all cultural worlds learn and use specialized terms in their normal routines (see the earlier discussion of "distinctive language"). *Native-language* questions (Spradley, 1980, pp. 89-90) try to elicit not only those terms and their exact phrasing, but also when they were learned, who knows them and who does not, and in what contexts they are typically found.

The types of questions just reviewed elicit the participant's imaginative and concrete experiences. The researcher is an ally in this effort of generating stories, incidents, and native terms, and of wanting to know what they mean. As the interview proceeds, the researcher may shift to more directive styles of questioning.

Structural and contrast questions (Spradley, 1980) enable the interviewee to define what he or she means more exactly by a term or concept, especially in relation to other terms. A *structural* question is used to discover "*how* informants have organized their knowledge" in a domain (Spradley, 1980, p. 60). For example, by asking a manager, "What are all the different ways to deliver 'bad news' to a worker?" [8] we specify the domain ("bad news"), the one doing the discriminating (the interviewee-as-manager), and how he or she is supposed to discriminate (telling about the different ways bad news is given to workers). By asking several informants this same question, the researcher can start to develop a taxonomy of meanings of the act. We might also ask, "What are the different stages involved in preparing your workers for 'bad news' and then giving them the news?" The domain has not changed, but now we want the interviewee to discriminate a sequence of events.

In both cases, the objective is the same: The participant is to explain as exhaustively as possible the range of elements of a domain, in terms of a given task (e.g., sorting, ordering, ranking). Because the participant may have to recall quite a bit of information, the interviewer should be prepared to assist. Ways of prompting the participant include restating the question, repeating the entire list or the last one or two statements, asking if there is anything else the participant wants to say, and returning to the question later. Of course, these prompts should be done in an easy, unhurried, and nonprejudicial way. *Leading questions,* which front-load a clearly biased premise (e.g., "Given that most employees hate hearing 'bad news' from managers they consider weak, how do you personally do it?"), should be avoided unless the researcher is trying to penetrate a front (Hammersley & Atkinson, 1983, p. 115).

A *contrast* question develops the meaning of a term or concept by setting it against other terms or concepts. For example, the question, "What's the difference between giving 'bad news' to a new employee you don't know well and giving 'bad news' to an employee you've known for years and personally like?" turns on the concepts of knowing and liking employees. What is held constant in the contrast set is the act of delivering bad news, which presumably the interviewee has done before. In designing such a question, the researcher can vary the conceptual "distance" between the contrastive terms according to the researcher's intent and the participant's own realm of experience. Compared with descriptive questions, structural and contrast questions set limits on what is relevant for the participant to say.

Another directive technique involves *posing emergent ideas* about the phenomenon, then asking the interviewee for his or her thoughts about them—including the validity of the ideas themselves. Here is an example: "It appears, in many cases I've heard about, a manager begins a 'bad news' talk by saying that the company has no choice but to follow a course of action that's in the best interests of the company. How does that square with your own experience? Do 'bad news' talks start with justifications of that kind?" Idea-posing questions give the interviewee a perspective (*not* the researcher's own opinion, or a named person's opinion) to push off against. It is to be hoped that the interviewee will voice a position on the matter and cite experiences that confirm, refute, or qualify the researcher's argument. The researcher can learn much about what is right or wrong—from a culture member's perspective—with an analytic claim that is in the making. However, it is crucial that the researcher regard the participant's reaction as partly contingent on the participant's own structural or political location in the scene. (For example, an interviewee who has been a receiver of bad news him- or herself might consider the above to be a cynical ploy.)

The researcher could also frame the question as an opinion expressed by a specific, but anonymous, informant (e.g., "You know, one manager told me that he always begins a 'bad news' talk by saying . . . "), which may have greater concreteness for the interviewee. But this tactic should be handled carefully. It risks a potentially explosive breach of confidence of the person being quoted, and it might also lead the participant to think that no one's opinion is safe with this researcher.

A well-known variant of the idea-posing approach is the *devil's advocate* question, in which the researcher raises an argument that is unpopular, untrue, or counterintuitive. There is an element of confrontation in such questions; for example, "Why should management care how 'bad news' is given to employees?" The tactic is designed to get the interviewee to talk about basic assumptions and arguments underlying his or her beliefs. However, unless the question is asked in a climate of good rapport, the interviewee might respond defensively, or even angrily. Accordingly, such questions should be asked only after rapport has been well established. Devil's advocate questions should come late in an interview because they often "test" the researcher's emerging understanding of an individual or the research problem as a whole.

As a rule, *highly sensitive* questions of a personal or political nature are left for the end of an interview. Not only does the researcher want to cement rapport well in advance, but he or she may need to ask many other questions to establish the relevance of asking such questions. This rule may be broken, however, if a close relationship between the researcher and participant preexists the study, or if participants thoroughly understand the sensitive character of the study going into it. The communicative compatibility of researcher and informant, as in the case of women interviewing women (Finch, 1984), can also lead to more intimate discussions.

Near the conclusion of the interview, before the researcher thanks the participant and inquires about another interview meeting (if needed), time should be reserved for what might be called *loose-ends* questions. These consist mainly of questions that occur to the interviewer during the session but are not asked immediately so as not to disrupt the flow of talk or the prearranged order of questions. Such questions are often prompted by surprising or otherwise intriguing remarks. The interviewer should clearly tell the participant about this transition: "Now, I'd like to ask you about a few things you told me earlier . . . ." The very last questions should be devoted to the participants' own interests: "Is there anything further you'd like to say? Is there anything we've missed that would be important for me to know?" Thus the researcher returns the agenda to the interviewee. This is an opportunity for the interviewee to fill in or clarify an answer, to "set the record straight," or to suggest entirely new issues of relevance. If the interviewee is unable to finish answering, the interviewer may make arrangements to continue in another interview, or by phone, mail, or electronic mail.

Lies, Evasions, and Audiotape

For the most part, the above discussion has assumed an ideal interviewee, whose good-faith outlook only needs to be hailed by a sincere researcher. But is sincerity always repaid with truthful responses? Clearly, in research interviews as in the rest of life, it is not. Researchers should not view lies and evasions only in moral terms, for "false and misleading information is exceedingly valuable to the fieldworker when it is recognized as false" (Van Maanen, 1979, p. 544).

Lies are deliberate distortions of what a person believes or knows about the "facts" of an event.[9] *Evasions* are deliberate efforts to conceal information or to sidestep the implications of a question. Lies and evasions do not occur in the absence of a quest to know by someone. Thus it is important to bear in mind that people tend to lie or evade when they perceive a vital interest in doing so *and* when they believe that their interlocutors do not possess other information that might incriminate them. Only the so-called pathological liar would lie when those conditions are not present. It is also important to separate lies and evasions, which are *intended* to deceive others, from situations in which people mislead themselves (and consequently others) because of ignorance of key information, a psychological dependency that inhibits their normal powers of judgment, or an obliviousness to taken-for-granted features of their lives. The unintentional deception is no less a problem for the researcher; it may be less actively defended by the participant, but it will be defended nonetheless.

The fabric of discourse encountered in fieldwork sometimes makes it hard for a researcher to tell a lie from an evasion, or to tell intentional from unintentional deception. Two examples from my family microcomputer study illustrate this problem. One husband said that his two sons had free access to the family's computer, which was located in a spare bedroom/office; in talking to one of the sons, however, I learned that Dad did not hesitate to move the boys off the computer when he was ready to use it. In another family, the husband claimed that the neighborhood children who visited his son, often to play at the computer in the son's bedroom, could come and go as they pleased, and that theirs was a house "open" to anyone; however, in talking to his wife, I learned that she was frequently disturbed when kids came through the house, and sometimes barred them from coming in. Several possibilities arise with these cases: The husbands could be lying; they may be withholding discrepant information (evading); they may not be aware of their false characterizations; or the other informants (the son in the first case, the wife in the other) may be lying. Given the knowledge I acquired of the family situations and the informants' own interests in being interviewed, the fourth possibility was deemed highly unlikely. But, without breaching confidences, it was not easy to decide among the other possibilities.

Why do interviewees deceive, and how can deception be detected? The incidence of fronting (Douglas, 1976)—lies, evasions, half-truths, facades, and so on—seems greatest in settings that are either publicly visible or publicly stigmatized, and with people who either have or desire power. When actors perceive the stakes to be high in what they say or do, their threshold for succumbing to the temptation to deceive may drop. Alternatively, Graham (1984) argues that the "opportunity for fabrication" can be a way for the interviewee to control the kind of information he or she wishes to present. Thus, "in a situation of inequality, both honest stories and fabricated tales are resources by which informants can redress the balance of power" (p. 120).

Informants' lies and evasions may also result from either ulterior motives, usually directed at a person or group other than the researcher, or a desire to please the researcher (Whyte, 1982). In desiring to please, an interviewee usually operates with a model of behavior in mind (e.g., "the caring, benevolent father"). In such cases the researcher should try to distinguish between statements about things in general, statements about specific events, and actual behavior. The researcher can evaluate deceptions provoked by ulterior motives by discreetly checking the statements with those who are named in or affected by them. The researcher can also check on the reputation of the interviewee and his or her capacity to have reported the events in question.

Van Maanen (1979, p. 545) notes that conscious deception may indicate the existence of information that, if disclosed, would *discredit* individuals or groups. The researcher may stumble across the "hidden failings" of a person: shameful events or stigmatized behaviors that have been carefully covered over. "Rotten apple" disclosures are flagrant violations or taboo-breaking activities associated with someone else; these are rarely mentioned and, in fact, are usually protected to uphold the moral code of the group. Finally, "collective secrets" are widely known but suppressed aspects of group life that would be controversial if revealed outside the group. Close involvement, especially through researcher participation, seems to be the only way to penetrate these kinds of fronts. Certainly, an understanding of how and why lies and evasions occur offers the researcher highly useful data for understanding the domain.

What of the role of audiotape recording in such problems? An audiotape recorder enables the researcher to obtain a verbatim record of the verbal features of the interview. It also frees up the researcher to participate more fully in the conversation than if he or she were trying to write it all down.[10] The researcher can minimize the impact of the recorder's obtrusiveness—it must be placed at the center of the interaction to capture all voices clearly—by using a compact cassette machine and taking care of its functions (starting, stopping, changing cassettes, checking batteries) before or after the interview, but not during. Still, as Whyte (1982) points out, "informants are likely to talk more 'for the record' with the machine than without, even when they have been told that the interviewer is going to write up the interview later" (p. 118). Arguably, then, tape recorders may result in a certain formality in their talk, at least until some rapport is achieved.

This for-the-record schema might work in favor of more accurate responses, because a recording represents indisputable evidence of a statement and its source (but not motivation or context). Being self-conscious of their articulations and meanings, which they know will be compared with other data, interviewees may be less inclined to lie. In such circumstances, there may be a slightly greater incentive to evade a question. There are, after all, few penalties for something *not* being recorded. Ultimately, the effects of recording on what is said are not easy to assess, unless the participant comes out and talks about them.

Conclusion

To return to a central theme of this chapter, interviewing is a social accomplishment of all its participants. Recognizing this denies to interview questions the status of "instruments" for creating data. Questions are merely one element of communicative engagement, set apart by their conceptual origins and the fact that they are purposely inserted in a conversational stream. The main event of the interview is *dialogue*. Chance, surprise, and persistence contribute at least as much to the happy results of an interview as advance planning.

The practice of interviewing also calls on the researcher to reflect on the identity that others perceive. The ways researchers talk, look, introduce themselves, and intervene in people's lives leak signs of cultural capital. Some of these signs may be of personal power and authority, and indicate the values and responsibilities of academic work. It is not uncommon for the communication researcher to talk about the need to study the skillfulness or the special meanings of communication acts. For many people, this "professional" interest, in itself, is unusual. It is comprehended and acted upon in a variety of ways, including a refusal by some informants to align their interests with the researcher's (e.g., Seiter, 1990). Elite interviewees, for example, may believe they know the worldviews and trade secrets of researchers at least as well as the researchers do, and therefore feel free to evade, dismiss, or critique questions (Manning, 1967; Radway, 1989). But other "important people" gauge their participation by how the researcher tries to gain access and whether he or she has adequately prepared for the interview (Ostrander, 1993; R. J. Thomas, 1993).

In the end, it is hard to escape the notion that an interviewer is also a participant observer. As a participant, the researcher engages in language games, some of which are specific to the interview and others of which derive from identities in life worlds beyond the interview. It is through the participant self that the interviewer can be in something of an authentic relationship with another person. In the observer mode, the researcher allows interests of the "project" to inform decisions about what to ask and how to respond. These interests are indicated to the participant in measured tactical moves—not to manipulate, but to frame, inform, encourage, and enjoin.

Notes

1. Of course, this statement assumes that the interviewee chooses to provide an honest, high-fidelity reference to a correspondent reality. In actual situations, interviewees may not honor the research "contract," and this can result in erroneous, incomplete, duplicitous, evasive, or idealized accounts. Such answers are in fact common, and will be discussed later in the chapter. However, no interviewee—regardless of his or her specific attitudes about the interview task—can avoid employing a host of interactional, cultural, and ideological codes to embed the "information" he or she conveys.

2. A translation of this folk terminology, derived from my personal immersion in that world, goes like this: A *young turk* is one who is young by the standards of academia, has achieved some scholarly recognition, and seems poised to achieve more in the near future; a *star* is a mature academic of major scholarly accomplishment and "visibility," who is usually the beneficiary of many material and status perquisites; *deadwood* refers to an academic, invariably tenured, whose long-term motivation to be a productive contributor to the discipline and institution has flagged considerably; and a *politician* is an academic who works rather self-consciously at becoming an important "player" in disciplinary or institutional governance. The other terms describe categories of communication academics. *Green eyeshades* refers to journalism faculty members whose interests lie almost exclusively in teaching professional skills, and who usually disdain the emphasis on research. *Production types* refers to the telecommunications counterparts of the green eyeshades ilk. *Number crunchers* are faculty who produce quantitative research (usually a lot of it), and for whom theory is not a great concern. To my knowledge, a similar term has not developed for qualitative researchers, although "soft scientists" comes close (see Chapter 1).

3. Open-ended, unstructured interviewing is often used as a formative way station for generating survey questionnaire items, particularly in "exploratory" quantitative research.

Qualitative interviews are also used in pilot tests to reveal flaws in question wording and response options, as understood by members of the intended population. These uses are not mentioned among the primary objectives in this chapter because they serve an intermediate role in studies whose purposes do *not* include cultural or interpretive analysis.

4. However, we should pause to consider Van Maanen's (1981) admonition that "the fieldworker can never fully apprehend the world of his informants in its 'natural' form. Even though he may sense the situated meanings his informants attach to the objects of their world, such meanings will remain largely exhibits of what his informants think rather than the 'true' meanings of such objects. Involvement and identification can be at best only transitory, simply because the research situation is not the actual life situation of the researcher" (p. 483). In other words, the qualitative researcher risks displacing the actor's highly practical, action-oriented attitude toward objects with a metaphorical, subjectivist meaning of those objects. The person acting in his or her real world is rarely so contemplative about having "a perspective" as the researcher's constructs would have it.

5. I was interested in how parental discourse about computers reveals problematic aspects of the technology's presence in the family. I studied 10 computer-owning families for approximately one month each. As the key element among several field techniques, lengthy semistructured interviews with parents covered such topics as family decision making, computing styles, how the computer was acquired and integrated into family life, types of and changes in use of the computer over time, children's concepts and uses of computers, and family orientation to other household media. More details about the protocol can be found in Lindlof (1992).

6. A variant of this question strategy, called the "mini-tour" by Spradley (1980, p. 88), concerns smaller units of experience, such as individual tasks or events.

7. If the researcher knows the subject intimately, he or she may feign ignorance and still use this approach in order to hear how the participant makes the presentation.

8. I want to thank Ruth Waggoner for the idea for this example and the ones that follow.

9. I have put *facts* in quotes here to indicate that although the facts of any event may be open to dispute and variant interpretations, a person may still make deceptive statements about what he or she truly believes the facts to be.

10. Note taking can prove helpful even when an interview is being tape-recorded. The researcher can periodically note "loose-ends" questions to use later, the interviewee's paralinguistic behaviors, and particularly arresting comments that should be checked out before the tapes are transcribed. The researcher should be very careful, however, that the participant is not made uncomfortable by the note taking.

7

Creating and Analyzing Texts in the Field

Stepping Aside

A few minutes late for our 8:00 a.m. meeting, I walked into the conference room. Milt sat sideways to the door—sleep-filled eyes, right hand on a steaming cup of coffee, a dormancy in his posture as though he had been there all night. Dan, facing me, called out a greeting. I took a place at the table, put my own cup down, and proceeded to pass around several paper-clipped sets of paper. Milt and I traded our usual complaints about the snarled parking situation, about our faculty permits being just "hunting licenses." Then Milt looked down at the material. It was my cue.

"Here it is," I said. "Copies for everybody. Just so you know where we are, these are the notes up through a week ago today. Let's take a few minutes to see what we have."

Less than completely awake myself, I swallowed black coffee and tried to focus on what I had in front of me. We were collaborating on a study of six families' television and VCR use practices. The end of the fieldwork was near, and now, somewhat belatedly, we were getting to the analysis. The idea was for each of us to code "our" families (we worked with different families in the field), using as categories some concepts we brought into the study and the kinds of actions we had observed in the homes and typed up in field notes. Because we had been talking regularly about the project, I felt it wouldn't take much time to bring our separate coding schemes into line.

As I scanned Milt's material, I saw some codes that were like my own. But I also saw categories and subcategories that didn't fit, and a few that I did not have at all. Turning to Dan's, I saw a smaller set of codes than mine, with each code seeming to characterize actions in bigger chunks than either mine or Milt's. I was definitely waking up now. Milt and I lifted our heads almost simultaneously, eyes meeting.

"You know, Tom . . . "

He didn't have to finish. "Right, right," I said, rubbing my temple. "This is going to be interesting."

Our dilemma worked itself out over the next two weeks as the three of us reconciled the coding schemes. Following Glaser and Strauss's (1967) constant comparative method, we first coded incidents in as many categories as possible and characterized their properties, and then began integrating the categories as the theoretical arguments took shape. Eventually, we were able to identify commonalities of action, talk, and concept across all six families. Our system also included codes for incidents that seemed unique to the individual families.

Compared with the statistical algorithms used in quantitative inquiry, most forms of qualitative analysis seem impossibly intuitive and inexact. Some researchers say that they simply continue to read their data until themes "emerge." Others act as impresarios of their own data-analytic enterprise. They cultivate an individualistic I-did-it-my-way method that seems to work because their studies get published, and (continuing this circular logic) their studies get published because the inscrutable method works.

There are grains of truth in these images, which should be no cause for embarrassment. In a sense, data-texts do speak to the researcher, because of the coherent discursive form in which they were produced and recorded, and because the researcher was close to the originating events. And researchers do work best with methods of handling data that are suited to their temperaments, skills, and senses of what looks and feels right—not unlike a woodworker who uses antique tools and odd joinery techniques to create furniture pieces for customers who are none the wiser. Many researchers gladly subscribe to this code of pragmatism: that the only imperatives that should stand in the way of a trenchant analysis are moral and ethical ones.

Yet all inquirers must answer for how their claims are constructed. As we will see in Chapter 8, a text gains authority in part from a "covering legitimation": a description of method and mode of argument that supports the page-by-page description of a scene. Readers expect that a disciplined intelligence was brought to bear on data in order to produce a final text that is comprehensible and valuable in its own right.

Proof that these are serious matters can be found in cases of ethnographic disagreement, when one ethnographer charges that another got the facts or the interpretation wrong. Heider (1988) calls this the "Rashomon effect," after the famous Akira Kurosawa film in which an encounter involving a bandit and a samurai and his wife in twelfth-century Japan is interpreted differently, and apparently truthfully, by four different witnesses. Heider suggests why these disagreements occur: (a) Someone actually is wrong (requiring an independent verification source), (b) each is looking at a different culture or subculture, (c) all are referring to the same culture at different times, or (d) all are looking differently at the same culture—because of differences in personalities, value systems, traits, theoretical orientations and research plans, length of time in the field, rapport, language knowledge, and effects of previous fieldwork (pp. 75-78). It is the fourth category, "looking differently" at a culture, where choices in data-analytic strategy assume the greatest importance. In communication, public differences between ethnographers over how to explain particular cultures or events have been rare (but see Carbaugh, 1991; Dillon et al., 1989; Fiske, 1991b). For any example of interpretive research, however, a Rashomon effect is possible, and data-analytic practices are always contestable.

The creation of data-texts is the first arena in which analytic decisions are made. These texts—field notes, documents, transcripts, and visual media—convert field experiences into running records that can be consulted, broken down, and reorganized. In the next arena of decision making, the researcher develops a system for coding data-texts in order to retrieve incidents efficiently. The coding experience also gives the researcher an opportunity to think through the data, to infer what the performances and practices mean. The construction of exemplars is an enabling move in this process. Finally, analysis prepares the researcher for quitting the field and starting the write-up. In all of this, the analysis of data and the continuing investigation of sites and informants go on simultaneously.

Stepping aside, then, is a felicitous metaphor for the creation and analysis of texts. One does not step completely outside the field situation or leave it behind. Rather, one steps aside, writes for a while, tries to make sense of what one has learned, and rejoins research settings in order to test and retest the ideas one is developing. The field is kept in view, obliquely. Increasingly, it becomes a resource to which the project can go for data pertinent to analytic problems. If the concepts and propositions are corroborated in key aspects, then confidence in one's ability to model a scene's actions and meanings is enhanced, and the end of fieldwork cannot be far off.

Creating Data-Texts

The familiar term *data* describes evidence that has been made suitable (i.e., converted into certain formats) for analytic purposes. The grafting of the word *text* onto it introduces the notion that some kinds of evidence are meant to be *read* and *interpreted* as discourse.

FIELD NOTES

Scratch Notes and Headnotes

First come scratch notes and headnotes. Scratch notes (Sanjek, 1990b, pp. 95-99)—also called "observational notes" (Anderson, 1987) and "condensed accounts" (Spradley, 1980)—are written by the researcher within the field situation, or soon after leaving it. They are simply notations about actions, statements, bits of dialogue, objects, or thoughts (the researcher's) that will be expanded later in field notes. The researcher inscribes scratch notes as a step linking a field experience with its lengthier, more reflexive elaboration in field notes.

The forms and activities of scratch note taking range widely. Some researchers carry small notepads on which they write in shorthand. Local customs permitting, this note taking can be done openly among the people being observed.[1] For even more tolerant populations, there are technologies such as the Stenomask, a sound-shielded microphone attached to a tape recorder on a shoulder strap, which lets the fieldworker talk continuously about an activity without the participants being able to hear (Patton, 1990, pp. 248-249). Many other researchers excuse themselves periodically from the public areas of a setting to scribble on whatever material is available. A mnemonic code, consisting of key words or abbreviated phrases, can be used to re-create whole passages later in field notes. Countless others before me have found the restroom a satisfactory retreat for this activity—doing our part to maintain ethnographers' reputation for having weak bladders. Still another option is to wait until a stretch of fieldwork is over and write scratch notes at the first available moment.

When scratch note taking is not feasible or desirable, headnotes may span the interval until field notes are recorded. Headnotes are memories of specific events as well as impressions and evaluations of the project as a whole. Some researchers have impressive memories and do not need to engage in much scratch note taking at all. Others, like myself, rely on a combination of scratch notes and headnotes; but even scratch notes do little more than anchor a large mass of material existing in memory. For both, it is crucial that the researcher cognitively retrace and rehearse experiences in order to stabilize their features and facilitate recall. One should not expect to "download" headnotes all at once. The first pass should occur as soon after a field session as possible, but it may take days for all residual headnotes to surface. Even so, there may be furtive images, remembrances of dialogue, and other enduring notions about a project that never find their way into written form.

Field Notes

Field notes represent the evidential foundation of studies using participant observation. Even in studies that rely mostly on interviews, we write field notes about social and physical contexts and the skein of analytic reflection inhabiting our periods of rest. What are field notes? They are "gnomic, shorthand reconstructions of events, observations, and conversations that took place in the field" (Van Maanen, 1988, p. 123); "this body of description, acquired and recorded in chronological sequence" (Sanjek, 1990b, p. 99); "the product of observation and participation at the research site and considered reflection in the office. . . . They are written so the analyst can reenter the scene of the action and of the research at a later date" (Anderson, 1987, p. 341). Jean E. Jackson (1990) interviewed an assortment of anthropologists about their opinions of and experiences with field notes:

> Most interviewees include in their definition the notion of a running log written at the end of each day. Some speak of fieldnotes as representing the process of the transformation of observed interaction to written, public communication: "raw" data, ideas that are marinating, and fairly done-to-a-turn diagrams and genealogical charts in appendixes to a thesis or book.

Some see their notes as scientific and rigorous because they are a record, one that helps prevent bias and provides data other researchers can use for other ends. Others *contrast* fieldnotes with data, speaking of fieldnotes as a record of one's reactions, a cryptic list of items to concentrate on, a preliminary stab at analysis, and so forth. (pp. 6-7)

Despite some faint agreement that field notes are supposed to describe the field experience, it is less clear what the contents and functions of notes are supposed to be. The mystique that shrouds fieldwork, the absence of any tradition or mechanism for sharing field notes, and the personal feelings that researchers attach to their notes (J. E. Jackson, 1990) all tend to occlude an understanding of this vital part of qualitative inquiry. Recently, however, some authors have attempted to outline procedures for producing and organizing field notes (e.g., Anderson, 1987; Ellen, 1984; Sanjek, 1990a; Spradley, 1980).

Field notes make up the permanent record signifying—and verifying—that field events did in fact occur in particular ways. They objectify events that were once fluid and contextual and open to a wide range of meanings. Researchers can write notes at any time and in as many versions as they please, but they cannot rewind events and play them again. Inevitably, the field note *becomes* the event. Moreover, raw notes are generally not available to anyone but the researcher because of the privacy promised to participants. As a result, their quality will seldom be critiqued. This privileged status of field notes places a burden on the researcher to undertake their writing with great care.

Several principles can inform the craft of writing field notes. As mentioned before, field notes should be written immediately after each field experience. The more time that elapses after observing, the more likely a rapidly deteriorating memory will dilute the fidelity and detail of the account. Even scratch notes lose their significance if they are not used soon. Fieldworkers should plan on reserving some time immediately after field visits to write. They should also consider *not* discussing the site visit with anyone until after field notes have been written, to protect against compromising their own firsthand understandings. Comparing notes against others' accounts of what happened can always be done later.

Field notes should be written and organized *chronologically.* Nothing of any importance should be left out, including negotiations with gatekeepers and other participants. How they responded to the researcher's entreaties, presentations of the project's aims and methods, and so on, are all matters for the researcher to think about as the study progresses.

Adhering to a chronology ensures that the record will reflect historical changes in the participants' individual and group lives, the project's twists and turns of decision making, and the researcher's own self-consciousness.

Entering a scene in the first days and weeks, the researcher may have already articulated a number of conceptual interests. In some cases, a researcher may have developed checklists or inventories of specific behaviors, activities, events, and forms of language use, with the intent of applying them to what he or she observes *in vivo*. However, the researcher should resist this approach. As recommended in Chapter 5, the first order of business is to get a working grasp of the scene: how it is organized spatially and temporally, its artifacts, who the actors are, how their roles are performed, what their predominant activity patterns are, the informal interpersonal relations and cultural knowledge, and so on. Unless the researcher is already a member of the culture, he or she must also learn how to be a member in some sense. This opportunity happens only once in the life of a study.

Field note taking should set out to replicate this learning curve. The researcher should describe all significant details of the scene with massive concreteness and completeness. The researcher silently asks, What is going on here? (Of course, the question can be asked aloud of the participants, but only after the researcher has observed the act carefully and considered alternative hypotheses.) This question generates others: Who are these people? What are their roles (duties/responsibilities/ranks)? What is this activity? How, when, and where does the activity seem to take place? Is this event part of the activity? What other events make up the activity, and in what order? Are these artifacts usually involved in the activity? Who uses the artifacts, and who else has access to them outside this activity?

Extensive (if not exhaustive) description is called for. In the beginning, the researcher should not try to write beyond the experience of being a novice or apprentice or tourist in a new terrain. "Why" interpretations can wait. At this stage, the researcher concentrates on "who," "when," "where," and "how" expositions of the scene. The researcher does not settle for describing the action in glossed-over terms; rather, he or she breaks every action down into its smallest observable bits. Nothing is too trivial or too obvious to be noticed and documented. Special attention should be given to the dimensions, sensory qualities, and purposes of an artifact or segment of action. The researcher should try to quote actors' remarks and conversations verbatim—especially when what is said or how it is said is notable. In characterizing the nuances of unfolding action and the way actors look, move, and talk, the researcher should choose adjectives and adverbs carefully. It is typically preferable for the researcher to write in the active voice rather than to use passive constructions, but he or she should not hesitate to use any mode of language that can reveal and expand the entire action.

There may be times when a field note statement seems to sum up an observed event, but summing up is dangerous in descriptive note writing. On closer inspection, the researcher may find that the note conceals more than it reveals, and key details of how the event actually happened will be gone forever. The researcher's interest in making the familiar strange and the strange familiar is advanced by meticulousness in these descriptions.

It may help to think of this kind of writing as an effort to convey to someone who is culturally ignorant of a situation (like the author of the notes?) how to understand or decode its surface features. Accordingly, these first accounts should be set down in clear, uncomplicated language. The communicative action in a new scene is built gradually, from the details up. The strict, unforgiving practice of describing in this way, day after day, will result in the researcher's developing more discriminating abilities of observing and improved capacity for remembering. The researcher will be rewarded with a dense, fact-filled archive that he or she can use later to interpret changes in the scene and in his or her own cultural competence.

The writing should also capture the researcher's personal reactions to learning how and where to fit in. Although these can be recorded methodically in another medium (such as in journals and diaries), occasional insertions of the researcher's first-person presence—especially in the form of insights, conjectures, misunderstandings, or baffled responses—can help document what it was about a certain action that either blocked or aided sense making. More generally, field notes must be written from the perspective of one who is socially engaged with others.

Figure 7.1 displays a field note excerpt from the study of family television and VCR use mentioned at the start of this chapter and earlier in the book. Three actors are present: the spouses Kay and Phil, and the researcher (who knew them slightly before the project began). This was the researcher's second observational visit to the home in fall 1986; some interviewing with Phil and Kay had already taken place. The actions described center on the viewing of two television programs. Out of all the material and social-interactional details that he could have cited (which are theoretically infinite), the author focuses his notes on two

B.1
B.2

M*A*S*H was on. We watched the entire program through with only some occasional conversation, much of it about the program itself. The stories weaved into one show, in typical M*A*S*H style, were about Hot Lips' encounter with a brave but unruly enlisted man named Scully, who cared nothing about rank, and about Honeycutt and Winchester arguing over who deserved first authorship on a paper they wrote about a breakthrough medical procedure. Early in the program Phil told me to watch and see if Winchester didn't remind us of Daryl, a mutual acquaintance. Even before Winchester came back onscreen, I agreed -- "even though I had never thought of that before," I said. Phil followed up my agreement with, "Even the way he moves," and laughed. I agreed with that also. When Winchester did come on, Phil said, "There's Daryl!" and we all chuckled.

J.1

B.1
D.2
D.3

The next show on was Starman, a season premiere, and Kay wanted to watch it, but Phil didn't. She pleaded in a playful way to see the show for a minute or so, and Phil asserted there might be a ball game on another channel, so I wasn't sure if we would watch it or not. Kay said, "Phil doesn't like space shows," half smiling. She went into the kitchen to make some coffee, and while she did, Phil used the remote to flip through the channels. He didn't stop long for any one channel, and by the time Kay walked back in it was back on the channel we had been watching. (OC: Phil had control of the remote all night).

J.1

J.1
B.1

Kay commented a lot of the way through Starman on the plot and the story from the movie it was based on. Phil remained uninterested and Kay continued to say how things related back to the original movie. When it was over they speculated some about whether or not the show would make it this season. Harry seemed to think it wouldn't, and Kay agreed, on the grounds that "you had to see the movie or read the book." Kay has done both, and Phil has done neither. I asked Phil if it wasn't a good show and he said, joking, "It's a good show to sleep by." (OC: It seems plausible that Phil almost surely knew Kay had seen the movie and read the book, and he realized this was a show where Kay would be able to dominate the conversation.)

Figure 7.1. A Field Note Example

conversational themes that incorporated elements of the respective programs. A metatheme of the conversations might be the social negotiation of the personal relevance of media content.

In the first conversation, the author mainly depicts Phil's bid to associate a TV character to someone they both know. Here, it is important to relate something of the *M*A*S*H* episode to understand the "point" of the conversation, and this the author does. The author conveys some of the turns taken in the conversational event, most of which depended on the researcher's acquiescence to Phil's assertions. However, the description provides relatively little of how the utterances were expressed, what gestural and facial expressions accompanied them, and what meanings may have been intended by either Phil or the researcher. The action as described is too condensed.

In the second part of the field note, the program itself is not as much at issue among the participants as questions about whether to watch *Starman*, the show's chances for "making it," and the kind of background knowledge needed to appreciate it. Wisely, the author does not attempt to describe the program's content. Rather, he concentrates on the on-again, off-again sparring between Kay and Phil throughout the program. The researcher's perspective is less active here than in the prior conversation, and essentially constitutes an (arguably nonpartisan) spectator. Bodily expression ("half smiling"), paralinguistics ("pleaded in a playful way"), and other details of behavior are evident, but references to what the participants felt or did ("Phil remained uninterested") could have been described more concretely. As in the first conversation, verbatim quotes lend some characterization to the participants and enhance the reader's sense of being there. But, contrasted to the first, we get a more satisfying sense of storytelling, so that when Phil answers the researcher's question at the end with, "It's a good show to sleep by," we might surmise that he was also commenting on his wife's viewing tastes or even her efforts to affect the agenda of what to watch. A kind of closure on at least two levels has occurred.

Finally, the author inserts two "observer's comments," marked OC, the first one adding information gleaned from the whole site visit, and the other advancing an hypothesis about one possible meaning of the action. These are analytic side notes that the researcher intends to think about for later visits. It is best to demarcate these from the scene descriptions.

As the fieldwork proceeds, fewer events take the researcher by surprise. Attention turns to those situations that remain unexplained by the growing analytic framework. This change is reflected in field note writing. If the researcher is interested in the repetition of events, often a sure clue to cultural patterning (Spradley, 1980, p. 70), he or she will still need to notice these faithfully as they come up. But the level of fine-grained, painstaking detail that went into the first sets of field notes will not be needed as much. The descriptive focus becomes more *selective* and *intensive.* "How" and "why" questions can be treated more often. Field note writing goes into greater depth about the complexities of the actors' skills and experiences.

If the researcher moves into a different role, or enters a new scene, his or her note taking may again widen out descriptively. But before long, the process repeats: patterns of communicative action and themes of significance once more become familiar, and the notes adjust selectively to foci of interest.

Field note writing should follow a regimen of bookkeeping and safety procedures. Some researchers type up notes; fewer still write in longhand. By far most researchers today utilize word-processing programs, storing their text files on hard drives and backup diskettes.[2] Each set of notes should be dated (and perhaps marked for the field site and participants), and the researcher should create an index for notes that lists them according to date, site, and subject or theme. Because computing equipment sometimes fails, with disastrous results for data files, it is good practice to print out *at least* four hard copies of field notes: one to be kept as a chronological record and placed in a three-ring binder, two to be used for coding, and one to be sent to a secure location (the last-resort emergency copy). Wide left and right margins on field note pages allow room for annotations and coding marks.

Journals and Diaries

Fieldworkers often need companions in the field even when there are no colleagues around in whom to confide. Journals and diaries fill this need. As Sanjek (1990b) states, "Chronologically constructed journals provide a key to the information in field notes and records; diaries record the ethnographer's personal reactions, frustrations, and assessments of life and work in the field" (p. 108). A journal keeps up with the rising tide of data by serving as a place to record field site visits, names of persons met and persons interviewed, and so on. It might also include thoughts about procedural problems and options.

Diaries are an outlet for turbulent emotions, doubts, private prejudices, and other meditations. Being alone is not the only reason to keep a diary. It is also a place (outside one's own head) to vent feelings about interpersonal situations in the field, where a tight lid usually has to be kept on strong personal reactions. Diaries and journals are the hidden subtexts of qualitative research, and their occasional publication can be celebrated events—for example, Malinowski's *A Diary in the Strict Sense of the Term* (1967) and Claude Lévi-Strauss's *Triste Tropiques* (1955/1974)—in which the person behind the master ethnographer is unmasked.

DOCUMENTS

Even as we swiftly enter an age of electronic messaging, written documents remain critical to the functioning of organizations, groups, and individuals. To the analyst, documents are very important because they are the "paper trail" left by events and processes. Documents indicate, among other things, what an organization *produces* and how it *certifies* certain kinds of activities (e.g., a license or a deed), *categorizes* events or people (e.g., a membership list), *codifies* procedures or policies (e.g., rules for using equipment), *instructs* a readership (e.g., an operating manual), *explains* past or future actions (e.g., memoranda), and *tracks* its own activities (e.g., minutes of meetings). More reflexively, an organization or group will sometimes put out documents that *memorialize* its own history or achievements (e.g., yearbooks, stockholders' reports, press releases).

By themselves, documents are of limited significance. When related to other evidence, however, they have much to offer the analyst. First, documents may be part of the talk and other action the researcher is observing. They become items of analytic interest when they are seen as resources in the participants' speech performances (e.g., Hawes, 1976). Second, documents can help the researcher to reconstruct past events or ongoing processes that are not available for direct observation. Social scientists can learn much about how to do this from resourceful investigative reporters. For example, in the *Washington Post*'s Watergate investigation, Woodward and Bernstein's "reconstruction of the organizational structure of the Committee to Re-elect the President (CRP) from its telephone roster was one of the most ingenious uses of a public document. The reconstruction . . . enabled the reporters to ascertain who had responsibility for decisions" (Levine, 1980, pp. 627-628). Although documents are often accurate (because people depend on it for their own good functioning), it is still vital for the researcher to know how reliable and valid a given document's contents are for the task at hand. In using documents as accounts of long-ago events or periods, he or she must also evaluate the subtle prejudices that may have affected the construction of the "facts" therein (Blee & Billings, 1986). Third, documents reflect certain kinds of organizational rationality at work, such as news media procedures for defining who is or is not a legitimate spokesperson for a public group. They often present the decision rules (but not necessarily the reasoning behind the rules) for how members of a social unit *should* behave. How members actually behave is not as much at issue when the researcher is interested in the document as a regulatory, ideological, or philosophical artifact.

When working with documents, the researcher should obtain originals whenever possible. Such aspects as size, paper quality, binding, and photographic color tones are evidence of how the document is valued and used by participants. Next in order of preference is a photocopy of the document. Clearly, it is undesirable for the researcher to be barred from copying a document at all, although this does happen, usually for legal or proprietary reasons. In such cases, the fieldworker should try to make scratch notes of the document's relevant aspects for later field note writing.

The formats and content features of documents should be characterized with the same devotion to detail as that found in any other field notes. The researcher should try to describe each document's origins and history, who uses it, who issues it, when and how often it is circulated, and how it is referenced in ordinary communicative action. A separate file and index of document exhibits should be set up, especially if the researcher anticipates collecting many of them.

INTERVIEW TRANSCRIPTS

If an audiotape recorder is not used, then reconstructing an interview follows virtually the same process as field note writing. However, as mentioned in Chapter 6, tape recorders free the researcher to attend more fully to the conversation, the nonverbal actions, and other elements of the situation. More important, audiotaping of interviews yields the closest thing to a verbatim record. Tapes do need to be transcribed, which entails a different set of skills and challenges from those related to field notes.

Beginning with the mechanics, audiotapes must be labeled for tape number, date, interviewee name, interviewer name (if more than one person is doing interviews), and, optionally, for subject or theme of the interview. *This should be done immediately before or after an interview,* to avoid confusion in identifying an unlabeled tape. An index compiles this information for all tapes in the project. The researcher would be well advised to give each newly recorded interview a once-through listen, to check for damage to the tape or parts of the interview that were not recorded. It is easier to notice these problems and do something about them if they are caught very soon after the event.

Transcription of audiotapes can be accomplished efficiently, and with a minimum of frustration, with the use of a tape transcriber machine (available for both standard-size cassettes and microcassettes). The big advantage of transcriber machines is that the tape transport functions (play, stop, rewind) are handled smoothly by foot-pedal movements, which releases the hands to enter text at a keyboard. The advice given above regarding creating and storing computer files for field notes also applies to interviews.

Unlike field notes, there would not seem to be a dire necessity to transcribe an interview immediately. After all, hasn't the tape "captured" the event, without an unreliable memory to contend with? Can't we label and store the tapes until it is time to transcribe them? However, this approach ignores the researcher's contextual memory, the participant's mood and demeanor, the events preceding and following the interview proper, and other factors that affect interpretation of the voices. Unless the text of an interview is converted soon to field notes, these memories can be volatile. Transcribing while still in the field can also alert the researcher to other sources that should be pursued, or to hypotheses that seem promising. It is not unusual to hear a researcher speak of an interview that now (weeks or months later) seems different from what he or she thought originally—for instance, it is now a much more interesting interview, or it is not as good in quality. These evaluations can save a project if the researcher is still in the field when the transcribing starts.

Despite the convenience of transcriber machines, the work of transcription is undeniably tedious, and it is made more difficult by the fact that full concentration on the task is required. A clear utterance of moderate length can take two or more passes to transcribe correctly. And utterances are often less than clear. A remark spoken off-mike may suddenly drop in volume. Or noise in the background may suddenly engulf the voice that is speaking. The person transcribing must stop, turn up the gain on playback, and try to figure out what was said. Even when the voice comes through clearly, some quirk of pronunciation or pitch change may render a critical part of a sentence incomprehensible. With focus group interviewing, it is common for two or more people to speak at once, sometimes at length. This can sometimes be interesting: Interpersonal rules of discourse and conversational repairs for saving face can be studied in the instance of one person coming in on another's speaking turn. But it can be maddening for trying to get an accurate transcription of what each voice said.

Most people who transcribe have their own rules of thumb concerning the number of times they will play a section of tape back before giving up on an unintelligible word or passage; for me, it is usually six. Unintelligible parts are shown in transcripts with ellipses (. . .) or underscores (blanks). How long it takes to transcribe an interview fully depends on the quality of the recording, the number of speakers, the pace of the talk, and the transcriber's skills. It takes me four to five hours to transcribe a one-hour interview involving two voices. The researcher should let some time elapse after the transcription and then listen again to the tape. He or she may find that parts of the transcript are in error and need editing.

Full transcriptions, including the interviewer's questions and remarks and all small talk, are preferred in most cases. A complete record enables the researcher to take in the full scope of the event and to engage in several kinds and levels of analysis. If resources do not allow this, the researcher can fully transcribe selected sections and employ a log to indicate the content of the untranscribed material. Notes taken during the interviews can orient the researcher to the most relevant parts of the tapes. Numbering lines of interview text in increments of five allows effective access to parts of a transcript.

The extent to which a researcher uses notations in the text to indicate speech patterns and speech forms is a matter of varying practice. Among analysts of conversation structure or speech performance, for example, numerous notations are used to show timing, intonations, sound lengths, emphases, speech overlaps, and other aspects. Figure 7.2 shows the ones used most often, but there is no one set of speech-text conventions that all analysts follow. For interpretive studies of communicative action—such as those that make up nearly all of the examples in this book—notations are used minimally, because the sociolinguistic patterns and technical organization of speech are not often a focal interest. Interpretivists study samples of talk for the relevance of their topical content, or for their expressive and rhetorical qualities. I suspect also that most interpretivists believe that the heavy use of notations is not an aesthetically pleasing way to portray speech in research texts, and limits the amount of speech they can study.

Still, interpretive researchers must decide how to edit recorded talk for the transcript page. Editing may mean, for example, correcting the

} {	bounds speech spoken softly
}} {{	bounds speech spoken very softly
:	extended sound
| |	bounds utterances that are produced simultaneously by two speakers
(.x)	indicates a pause of .x seconds
(.)	indicates a noticeable pause too short to be accurately timed (.2-.4 seconds)
(( ))	bounds transcriber's comments
( )	bounds uncertain transcription
'h, 'H	soft and loud inbreath
CAPS	loud volume
underlining	words spoken with emphasis
dec	speech slowing
(ha)	laughter
# #	bounds quickly spoken speech
?	rising intonation
,	falling intonation
=	short transition time between two words
-	preceding sound is cut off

EXAMPLE:

Jean: OH YE:S I think that (1.1) just in gen:eral (.8) u:m (2.3) as I grow: and become a Christ ((slowly)) AS I be (.5) come more and more wull I-I *am*.a Christian #I can't say I become *more* a Christian# 'h (.5) as I *grow:* (1.8) ah in the Christian life (.7) I feel (.5) more (1.9) I-I understand who I am (.4) and what I'm all about and I bec-I feel like I become more human.

Figure 7.2. Common Speech-Text Notations
SOURCE: Peter G. Stromberg, "Ideological Language in the Transformation of Identity." Reproduced by permission of the American Anthropological Association from *American Anthropologist* 92:1, pp. 53, 55, March 1990. Not for further reproduction.

"ungrammatical" street talk of urban youth, removing the mannerisms of middle-class preadolescents (e.g., "like, you know"), or eliding an informant's mid-sentence topic change. As DeVault (1990) notes:

> The purpose of editing is to cast talk into a form which is easier to read—and more compelling—than raw interview documents, which are often lengthy, rambling, repetitive, and/or confusing. Another rationale emphasizes the redundancy of talk: the researcher should include only as much detail as needed to illustrate the analytic points to be made. (p. 107)

The researcher can certainly create a more fluent interviewee. Talk that does not look like Standard English on the transcript page can be edited. Stutters, repetitions, self-corrections, malapropisms, cultural inflections, long pauses, outbreaths, inbreaths, laughs, groans, and the like may be either not reported or only selectively reported. What really is lost in such editing? On the side of preserving actual speech, one may argue that the individual stylistics of informants' talk reveal much about their identities and the situated character (indexicality) of their speech. On the side of editing, one could say that representing the "messiness" of everyday talk distracts readers from its content, and may make the speaker appear unfocused or ignorant. It is the researcher's judgment call, but one that requires principled criteria. As Mishler (1986) says, more expansively: "The mode of transcription adopted should reflect and be sensitive to an investigator's general theoretical model of relations between meaning and speech, selectively focus on aspects of speech that bear directly on the specific aims of the study, and take into consideration the limitations of the basic data and of resources available for analysis" (p. 49).

VISUAL MEDIA

In communication research, the use of video, film, and still photography has been rare. As mentioned in Chapter 5, researchers could employ video cameras to observe covertly in public places. In focus group interviewing, it is not uncommon to videotape the proceedings from behind a one-way mirror. But communication ethnographers seldom shoot film or video with the intent of editing it for public presentation. And when photographs are used at all in qualitative communication studies, it is to show readers how a cultural scene appears (e.g., Lull, 1988), not to analyze the photos for conceptual reasons.

Film and video records are well suited to "microethnographic" concerns, such as behaviors that play out so quickly or in such detail that some elements escape the notice of even the most acute human observers (Erickson & Wilson, 1982). Humans are constrained by their own self-consciousness and by having to focus on one thing at a time. Cameras, on the other hand, can take in the whole action of a scene, either from a stationary, locked-down position or by one or more mobile units. By varying the focal length of the lens, among other techniques, the camera operator can isolate and follow particular parts of a scene. The filmed or taped result allows repeated viewings at a variety of speeds (including frame by frame), enabling the researcher to try different interpretive strategies—or to have other observers view it and construct their own meanings (Albrecht, 1985).

Filming or videotaping can also be done in a more narrative mode. After getting established in the culture under study and understanding the major arenas of action, the researcher may gradually introduce camera and sound equipment. It might even be feasible for the participants themselves to do some of the camera work, to express their personal perspectives of what is important. The processes of editing and postproduction—combining shots, synchronous and "wild" sound, narration, and graphics, in coherent form—constitute an analysis of data.

Compared with film, video is winning favor for its small, lightweight cameras, ease of use, automatic functions, low cost, ability to be viewed immediately after shooting, and compatibility with computer-driven editing stations. Video is even approaching film in image resolution.

Like film and video, still photography yields a visual imprint of some action that can be viewed repeatedly in different ways. Although its imagery is static, still photography is not inferior to moving-image media for every purpose. With photography, we compose images more carefully and are more attuned to "the moment" in a stream of action. Photography forces the researcher to be selective. Some combination of photographic sophistication and sensitivity to what is important theoretically is more likely to produce insightful pictures (Becker, 1986a; Collier & Collier, 1986). As widely used, low-tech devices, 35-mm cameras can be part of the researcher's presence from the first days in the field. Pictures can be taken to "map" scenes and generate rapport. Later, "the photographer will be alert for visual embodiments of his ideas, for images that contain and communicate the understanding he is developing. . . . his theories will inform his vision and influence what he finds interesting and worth making pictures of" (Becker, 1986a, p. 249).

Pictures contribute to a project by allowing the researcher to (a) survey an environment (with high or wide-angle shots), (b) depict the artifacts found in a setting and the ways they are arranged, (c) show groupings and interactions of people in order to infer the meanings of their relationships, and (d) pick out sequences of action with great clarity, especially with the use of a motor drive. Photography is also the medium of choice for capturing the unforeseen—the serendipity of human life.

Besides the safety and working conditions of the equipment, there are three concerns with visual media in the field. First, their use can fragment or distort the attention of those being studied. Participants often experience a heightened sense of being watched when cameras are present, and may even feel that their privacy has been invaded when particularly vulnerable moments are shown later (see Gilbert, 1982). These reactions usually subside over time, especially if the researcher intrudes the camera only as the situation allows. At any rate, many behavioral routines must go on, with or without cameras around. The second concern is the obverse of the first: The researcher should not begin to think that audiovisual records are any more objective, precise, or pristine than data obtained by other means. He or she should stay cognizant of their limits: the setup, framing, and focusing of shots; the quality of film stock or videotape; and how participants adjust to this mode of data collection. Audiovisual material is typically most effective as complementary data. Finally, like any other data-text, the accumulating tapes, negatives, and prints must be indexed and related meaningfully to the other materials.

Analyzing Data-Texts

OVERVIEW

There are far too many issues involved in the field analysis of data for me to be able to do them justice in a brief introduction. The areas touched upon here represent only some of the most salient concerns. They are organized around four interrelated domains: process, reduction, explanation, and theory.[3]

Process

Analyzing qualitative data is best thought of as a process that is continuous throughout an entire study. Although qualitative texts may sometimes be written up in the linear style of "hypothesis → method → analysis → conclusion," this should be considered only an arrangement of convenience. At best, it is a forced presentation; at worst, it is misleading. The process is far more cyclical (see Chapter 3), with fieldwork, data-text translation, coding, and conceptualizing all going ahead at the same time, albeit at different rates of progress.

As we have seen, it is nearly impossible to avoid some preliminary analysis as one writes field notes or transcribes tapes. When something unforeseen but important turns up, the researcher can quickly move into that area and probe more intensively. Such flexibility enabled Sigman (1987a), for example, to expand upon his discovery of the significance of television viewing among nursing home residents, even though his original design did not take media use into account as a domain of interest. This aspect also makes qualitative analysis ideal in situations where not much is previously known about the topic under consideration, or when rapid changes in the subject necessitate flexibility in the design, as in the case of communication technologies (Williams, Rice, & Rogers, 1988).

Just as it would be an error to ignore analytic work in the field, it is also a mistake to attempt to reach closure prematurely. Validity is always at issue in qualitative research because of the danger that the researcher may impose his or her own unwarranted personal definitions on what is observed. This is especially true if he or she infers too much before the bulk of the data have been collected. One certainly cannot go into a scene as a blank slate simply waiting to be written on, but neither should one approach it with all prejudices left unexamined and intact. Striking an optimal balance is a difficult and probably endless task.

Reduction

Any kind of analysis involves the reduction of data. In quantitative research, this takes the form of numerical coding and the use of statistical procedures. With qualitative data, the reduction comes in two forms: The first is primarily at the physical level, and the second is at the conceptual level.

Physical reduction of data occurs because most qualitative research projects quickly generate such huge volumes of material that dealing with all of it on equal terms would be almost impossible. *Reduction* in this sense means being able to sort, categorize, prioritize, and interrelate data according to emerging schemes of interpretation. Several options are available. Coding data-texts, as we will see in the next section, allows the researcher to locate concepts brought into the study as well as to generate and refine concepts discovered in the field. Some kind of text coding represents the most popular option for physical data reduction. Miles and Huberman (1984) advocate configuring data in visual displays, such as data matrices and flowcharts, so that the patterns of social action can be grasped readily. Other analysts who have something of a quantitative inclination even when working with data-texts would transform qualitative data into a quantifiable form in order to examine such things as repetitive or patterned behaviors (see, e.g., Halfpenny, 1979). The researcher who would follow such a course should do so cautiously, to avoid violating the assumptions under which the project was conducted.

The other, more problematic aspect of reduction takes place at the conceptual level. For the field experience to make sense retrospectively, and to be shared with others in a communicable form, the qualitative analyst must devise a conceptual structure. This is never easy, because the analyst must be careful not to impose an external system on the data. Ideally, the concepts used in an analysis grow naturally out of an interaction between the kinds of action noted in the field and the theoretical ideas with which the analyst began the study. It is a process of creativity (not just verification), in which the analyst is "running things up provisionally, taking a look at them in the light of standards deriving from experience and knowledge, and modifying, rejecting or accepting parts or the whole before moving on to develop other ideas" (Fineman & Mangham, 1983, p. 299).

Explanation

Although making detailed descriptions of settings, events, persons, or discourses is a goal of any qualitative project, most analysts also enter into research with the aim of *explaining*: understanding the coherence of meaning and action in the case(s) under study. "How" questions stand out as primary, but "why" questions are also asked and answered in qualitative explanations. It is important to point out that the kind of coherence referred to here is an achievement of the analyst, not of the social actors in the scene. In other words, the analyst makes sense of the way that social actors make sense of their own actions, goals, and motives.

Social actors' own methods of making sense are what Van Maanen (1979) calls *first-order concepts*: "the situationally, historically, and biographically mediated interpretations used by members of the organization to account for a given descriptive property" (p. 540). First-order concepts are the indigenous ways of explaining that are characteristic of a culture or an interpersonal relationship. *Second-order concepts*, on the other hand, are "notions used by the fieldworker to explain the patterning of the first-order data" (p. 541). Second-order concepts depend on first-order descriptions as evidence, but do not always converge with them as interpretations. The analyst seeks coherence even in the "irrational" act. As Charles Taylor (1977) points out: "The meaning of a situation for an agent may be full of confusion and contradiction; but the adequate depiction of this contradiction makes sense of it" (p. 109). It is in fact these instances of *not* converging that confront analysts with their greatest challenges—and often result in the most significant contributions.

Theory

When analysis of qualitative data offers explanations about social situations *with respect to generic social (communicative) processes*, then it must be considered in the context of theory. Many researchers concede a role to qualitative studies in the initial formulation of theory and hypotheses, but then suggest that these be tested further with more "rigorous" methods (e.g., Williams et al., 1988). Indeed, qualitative research does excel at finding points of entry into new areas of inquiry. But there are those who answer the criticism that qualitative research is unable to test or build theory, and thus to have significance beyond the immediate case. Eckstein (1975) and Mitchell (1983), for example, contend that cases can be treated in different ways in order to advance both theory formation and hypothesis/theory testing. For the latter purpose, Eckstein proposes crucial case studies that function like experiments. He states that case studies "are . . . most valuable at that stage of theory building where least value is generally attached to them: the stage at which candidate theories are 'tested' " (p. 80).

Science has been lauded for proceeding in a logical, progressive manner through a series of inductive steps (Platt, 1964). These steps include the devising of alternative hypotheses and the use of an "experiment" that determines which of the hypotheses to exclude. Once the researcher has eliminated some hypotheses (or set them aside temporarily), he or she can continue to test others in a branching manner until a satisfactory conclusion is reached. Although qualitative studies proceed at a different pace and style from quantitative studies, they are not essentially different in their adherence to the model just described.

However, it is probably true that the canons of survey and experimental research are more compatible with the demands of theory building, as it is typically understood. By its nature, a theory is an ever-evolving construction that depends on the comparison of cases. The intensive examination of a single case can certainly test how and where a theory can be applied. It may also aid in the discovery of theoretical possibilities (Glaser & Strauss, 1967). But such studies incorporate the contingencies of the time and culture in which they are situated. These site-specific features do not always permit the kind of careful cross-comparison of cases that builds and modifies theory.

However, Prus (1987) has argued that generic principles of group life can be abstracted from "a plurality of ethnographic contexts" (p. 262). In other words, one can examine diverse substantive studies for what each reveals of the generic elements of group life: perspectival, reflective, negotiable, relational, and processual. The need for moving to the theoretical level, Prus argues, is recognized in the areas of teaching, reporting findings, editing, conferencing, and networking. In each of these areas, there exists the potential for contributing to the awareness of and testing of generic social concepts. Similar efforts could prove valuable in the development of theories of communicative performances and practices.

ANALYTIC CODING

Without some method of categorizing, tagging, and sorting data, the transition out of fieldwork would be about as inviting as trying to enter a trackless desert without a map or guide (or any other metaphor one prefers for a forbidding prospect). Coding tools give the analyst fairly efficient access to the content of data-texts and artifacts, but codes function as more than a retrieval system. Coding is also integral to the task of interpreting communication phenomena. It demands that the analyst decide what is worth saving, how to divide up the material, and how a given incident of talk or behavior relates to other coded items.

Preliminary Readings

As mentioned earlier, at least one copy of all materials (field notes, transcripts, and other data-texts)—an *archive file*—should be printed, organized by type, and kept in the original, chronological order. Other copies will be dedicated to analytic uses in which they may be marked up or cut up.

Preliminary to serious analytic work, the researcher should read through the archive file several times. These readings will reacquaint the analyst with the events of the case and alert him or her to changes in perspective, social actors, and level of detail over the duration of fieldwork. This immersion will help the researcher to take in all of the fieldwork as a totality, as well as renew his or her contact with individual situations or samples of discourse.

The next readings are more purposeful. The researcher begins to look for indicators of concepts identified as relevant at the start of the study, assuming they are still relevant at this point. He or she can also jot down notes about compelling incidents, sequences of action, repetitive acts, and other critical details that inform his or her understanding of the scene. These readings are essential to the work of coding.

Concomitantly, the researcher pays attention to the completeness of the data, to see whether there are any glaring gaps in the field notes, whether any scratch notes remain unconverted to field notes, whether the interviews are all transcribed, and whether the indexes correctly access the listed items.

Codes and Categories

As Charmaz (1983) puts it, "Codes . . . serve as shorthand devices to *label, separate, compile,* and *organize* data. Codes range from simple, concrete and topical categories to more general, abstract conceptual categories for an emerging theory" (p. 111). Ideally, codes develop out of the readings described above. The first level of coding sorts out the more discernible things in the texts: persons, behaviors, settings, time periods, events, activities. These are the simple, concrete, and topical categories to which Charmaz refers. This coding does not require very complicated decision rules of inference for identifying instances of particular categories.

Other codes are more ideational. They may characterize concepts, beliefs, themes, cultural practices, or relationships. The researcher gains access to them by looking for, among other things, subjects that are dramatized by the participants, or that are glossed by them; puzzling or conflicted situations; elements that are recurring; conditions that evoke actions; key expressions in participants' talk that indicate how they regard themselves, their situations, or their surroundings; and communal acts (rituals) that seem to embody beliefs or processes of the culture. These subjects may be either implied or explicit in the data-text. The researcher must pit the insider knowledge he or she has gained at the site against his or her own analytic detachment to tease these categories out of a complex mass of data.

These initial stabs at making sense require enormous ingenuity on the part of the analyst. He or she often proceeds on an intuitive, looks right/feels right basis, leaving the actual formulation of coding rules until later in the process. If the analyst is unable to go beyond a certain point or simply desires a more systematic way of searching for categories, he or she may consult a list of universal or culture-specific category terms. For example, Spradley (1980, p. 93) advocates using the following semantic relationships as a guide for generating domains (categories) from the field observations of virtually any culture:

- *Strict inclusion:* X is a kind of Y.
- *Spatial:* X is a place in Y, X is a part of Y.
- *Cause-effect:* X is a result of Y.
- *Rationale:* X is a reason for doing Y.
- *Location-for-action:* X is a place for doing Y.
- *Function:* X is used for Y.
- *Means-end:* X is a way to do Y.
- *Sequence:* X is a step (stage) in Y.
- *Attribution:* X is an attribution (characteristic) of Y.

Coding categories may need to be described extensively, so that it is clear how an incident counts as an instance of a category. It can be useful for more than one person to check whether these decisions make sense and are appropriate. However, the notion of calculating intercoder agreement as found in formal content analysis does not apply in qualitative content coding (see Altheide, 1987). The purposes of qualitative coding are to tag segments of interest and to look for ways to categorize action or talk that will lead toward inductive proposition.

The following is an example from the television/VCR study mentioned above. We developed several coding categories, of which Control of Media and VCR Use were two:

D. Control of Media (including, but not limited to, turning on or off, selecting program, changing channels, deciding what to purchase or rent [except for VCR; see G])

  D.1. Someone exercising control of the *VCR*. How this control is demonstrated. 8, 11, 13, 17, 19, 26, 28, 29

  D.2. Someone exercising control of the *television(s)*. 4, 5, 8, 9, 13, 14, 20, 22, 23, 26, 27, 28, 31

  D.3. Someone exercising control of *audio media.*

  D.4. Someone exercising control of (reading or buying) *print media* (including books, magazines, newspapers). 28

  D.5. Someone exercising control of *computer.*

G. VCR Use

  G.1. Recording off-air.

  G.2. Playing back off-air recorded material (time-shifting). 8, 19

  G.3. Saving video material (i.e., video library). 24, 25

  G.4. Buying cassettes, deciding what to do with them. 24

  G.5. Renting cassettes. 3

G.6. Engaging nonfamily persons in VCR viewing. 27, 30
G.7. VCR-in-general (here: missing the VCR) 33

As a category label by itself, Control of Media is somewhat nebulous, so we included in the heading a short list of some key examples that was not meant to be exhaustive, only suggestive. The codes themselves reference subcategories of different kinds of media in which one or more persons exercised some control. It is important to note that the codes could have been organized differently—for example, by subcategories of different kinds of control behavior (irrespective of type of medium). The researcher should be guided by his or her sense of what is most valuable to pull out of the data. The numbers next to each coding subcategory are the page numbers for one family's data-texts (combined observational field notes and interview transcripts) on which at least one instance was found and coded. Two subcategories—audio media control and computer control—are empty for this family. A look at the other subcategories reveals pages of field notes and transcripts in which more than one code was applied, sometimes to the same social action. Codes from within and across categories may not only overlap on the same segment of action (or discourse), but also cross-reference each other.

The second category "family," VCR Use, is more explicit in its referents to social and individual actions than is Control of Media. There is no need for examples; the subcategory labels are fairly obvious. Category G.7—VCR-in-general—was designed as a "leftovers" subcategory in which each case (a family, in this study) would have different incidents. For this family, only one G.7 incident ("missing the VCR") was located.

Going back to Figure 7.1, the codes for this field note text are shown along the left margin. Vertical lines indicate roughly how far the coded incident runs. The one instance of Control of Media—Phil "channel surfing" while Kay is in the kitchen—is coded D.2, for exercising control of the television. No incidents relevant to VCR Use show up in this excerpt. (The B code category noted in Figure 7.1 references conversations about the act of using television; the J code category references conversations about television content, such as characters, plot, themes, and issues.)

Coding Process

One of the most influential descriptions of coding, and still frequently used in one guise or another, is Glaser and Strauss's (1967) *constant comparative method.* Two features of the method are crucial: It specifies the means by which theory grounded in the relationships among data emerges through the management of coding (hence, *grounded theory*), and it shows explicitly how to code and conceptualize as field data keep flowing in. As such, the method blends all four considerations of analysis: process, reduction, explanation, and theory. A brief tour of the constant comparative method illuminates its general advantages. (Interested readers should consult the original Glaser and Strauss, 1967, work as well as Glaser, 1978; or such article-length treatments as Charmaz, 1983; Corbin & Strauss, 1990.)

The first stage, *comparing incidents applicable to each category,* calls for assigning data-text incidents to categories (in the manner already discussed). When considering a new incident, the analyst continually compares it with ones that have already been grouped in the same category in order to determine its goodness of fit. Before long, the analyst "starts thinking in terms of the full range of types or continua of the category, its dimensions, the conditions under which it is pronounced or minimized, its major consequences, its relation to other categories, and its other properties" (Glaser & Strauss, 1967, p. 106). This process marks the overt emergence of a theoretical sensibility. The analyst builds and clarifies categories by going back through the evidence more than once; he or she either reassigns problematic incidents to different categories or splits them off to form new categories.

At some point during this stage—often when uncertainty arises over the core or extensional attributes of the category—the analyst writes a *memo* that elaborates on the coding category as it currently exists. Analytic memo writing fleshes out ideas that may be only implied in the gamelike coding activity; it also acts as an outlet through which the researcher can explore the conceptual possibilities of a coded category. It is not uncommon for the analyst to write a series of memos as the analysis progresses. The final versions may be articulated so well that they can be transferred into the first draft of the report. Like field notes, memos are private materials, and the forms they take reflect the diverse working styles of practitioners.

Here is an excerpt of an early memo produced from one of the coded categories we looked at earlier (D.2, controlling the television):

Control of the TV was evenly distributed throughout the observations, with Phil and Kay being the main ones to express an interest in certain programming and exercise an influence over what was watched. Dan [their son] never made any attempts at controlling the programming, but he does control the volume and change channels. Once the TV was on for the evening, the family engaged in very little if any channel changing or volume control. When Phil did exert control over what was on the TV, Kay and Dan chose other options; Kay left the room, and Dan watched TV in the library. When Kay chose the programs, Phil stayed on the phone and later went to watch baseball. Dan watched the programs Kay likes with her, after he finished his homework. . . . I observed just one instance of Phil trying to change the channel on Dan, and it didn't succeed.

Next in the constant comparative method, the analyst begins to *integrate categories and their properties*. Comparisons among incidents become less intuitive. Explicit decision rules are now developed inductively to account for the category's defining *properties*. It is a dialectical process: As the analyst integrates incidents with like features into properties, he or she uses these properties to verify whether or not incidents should stay in particular categories. The analyst has more confidence in assigning incidents to categories as new data come in. The purpose of seeking new data is to test the viability and value of the integrated categories and their increasingly better-defined properties. The task of integration changes the nature of categories from mere collections of (more or less ambiguously) coded incidents into constructs, which moves the analyst closer to "a particular construction of the situation at hand" (Lincoln & Guba, 1985, p. 343). The development of exemplars, as we will see later in this section, begins during this stage.

By *delimiting the theory*, the third stage of the method, the analyst achieves *parsimony* and *scope* in the range of phenomena to which a grounded theory applies. At a practical level, this means that relatively few new data will be needed. In Glaser and Strauss's view, the category set becomes "theoretically saturated": new incidents add little, if any, new value to its conceptual content. On an explanatory plane, "the theory solidifies. . . . Later modifications are mainly on the order of clarifying the logic, taking out nonrelevant properties, integrating elaborating details of properties into the major outline of interrelated categories and—most importantly—reduction" (Glaser & Strauss, 1967, p. 110). What is reduced are not the data, but the terminology and the categories that are necessary for a focused, selective accounting of the phenomenon.

Coding is a process in which the researcher creatively scans and samples data-texts, looks for commonalities and differences, and begins to formulate categories of interest. Some codes may refer to first-order concepts: the descriptive practices of a cultural membership. Other codes may be second-order concepts of the researcher's own invention or constructs existing in the literature. But their relevance must be founded on meanings learned within the situated action (first-order concepts). If not, they are being imposed illegitimately. The coder's first obligation is to respect the form and the sense of the original action.

Organizing Coded Data-Texts

Possibly the majority of qualitative inquirers still engage analysis as a hands-on craft. The materials they use—paper, index cards, file folders, binders, scissors, tape, paste—are primitive by most scientists' standards, and seem ill suited for the punishing job of analyzing hundreds of pages of data. Yet somehow researchers have managed to get the job done using them.

I usually keep a working copy of my notes in a ring binder and organized in the same system (divided by cases, ordered chronologically) as the archive file. Tabs at the front of the case files separate several sections: (a) coding schemes (all editions), (b) analytic memos, (c) indexes, and (d) any summary information related to each case (e.g., tabulated results of questionnaires or diary logs). Whenever the coding scheme is revised significantly, I print out another copy of the notes to install in the binder (saving all the predecessor copies). Then I mark the new copy, using both the new coding scheme and the copy with the old coding marks as references. (I also use different color pens in coding material, to represent different categories.) When I am ready to begin defining categories or themes, in the later phases of an analysis, I simply pull the pages relevant to each code out of the binder temporarily and store them in the pockets of an expanding file while the analysis is under way. When I have completed the writing, I return the pages to the binder. This procedure entails much exchanging of papers in and out of binders and files, but it satisfies my strong desire to keep the material intact.

There are at least two other procedures for manually organizing code data-texts (Tesch, 1990, pp. 127-130). The *cut up and put in folders approach* involves cutting segments of material out of a copy of the data-texts, pasting or taping them onto clean pages, and filing them under the appropriate codes. Alternatively, the material can be written on index cards in either verbatim or abbreviated form. Either way, it is important to put some contextual information on the card or page—such as participant(s) involved, date, page number. An advantage of this approach is that it allows the researcher to spread out and see the cards or pages all at once. He or she can also sort and shuffle through them to see what comes out of different ways of arranging a category. The *punched-card approach* relies on cards on which data have been typed. Around the edge of each card is a row of punched holes that can be notched individually to correspond to analytic codes. The cards can be stacked in any order, relieving the analyst of worrying about a filing system. When the cards for a certain code are needed, a device similar to a knitting needle passes through the stack at the appropriate hole and lifts up only the cards notched for that code. A major advantage of this system, besides its convenience, is that each card can easily accommodate several codes. However, the approach does demand that category-making decisions happen *before* any holes are punched, making it more suitable for write-up than for processual analysis.

So much for physical handling of data. Microcomputer technology and software are playing an ever larger role in the manipulation of qualitative texts. Of course, word processing has already introduced researchers to some of the strengths of electronic data handling, such as the abilities to move and copy sections of text quickly and accurately, to search for and highlight key words, to develop indexes, and to "hide" comments or leave "bookmarks." Many word-processing programs also enable the user to employ macro commands by which coding terms can be inserted directly and easily into notes. And it is a snap to create different forms of a text by using edit and file commands.

For actual analysis, however, the real power lies in database management programs. Such software can save enormous amounts of time, avoid certain kinds of inaccuracies, identify category relationships systematically, and apply coding techniques to entire data sets (not just the parts that the analyst has time for). Tesch (1990) describes how database managers perform many of the tasks that qualitative researchers usually do manually:

> They invite the researcher to mark segments and code them in preliminary fashion as often as necessary while developing a coding system, or to attach the codes permanently for final analysis. Assigning several codes to one segment is accomplished as easily as attaching to each extracted segment the appropriate source information. The latter happens automatically, so that the researcher does not need to waste time or mental energy on so mundane a task. The programs produce versions of the original data documents with marked and coded segments, and they also print out new documents in which all segments relevant to one category have been brought together—by the computer, not by the researcher. (p. 132)

Many programs also provide for the use of Boolean operators (OR, AND, and NOT search commands) and key-word-in-context concordances for finding and listing chunks of text. A variety of database managers for ethnographers are now available (for descriptions of computerized techniques and some of the programs, see Pfaffenberger, 1988; Tesch, 1990). They are not, however, a panacea for all of the supposed backwardness of qualitative analysis. The programs do not retrieve nonstandard lengths of data very well (the unitizing problem), and do not allow the kind of play with data that is vital to interpretive inquiry. Finally, the programs cannot automate the process by which insights emerge, despite the advent of "expert systems." This is still the unique domain of human beings, and is likely to remain so.

An important new technology worth looking into, *hypermedia* (Hesse-Biber, Dupuis, & Kinder, 1991; Howard, 1988), combines the ability to connect information in multiple sequences and hierarchies with the ability to use multiple media (text documents, video, audio, and pictures). For example, hypermedia makes it possible for a user to access informant descriptions of a ritual, see and hear the ritual being performed in a video sequence, bring up the ritual in graphic or model form (which can be rotated three-dimensionally), and relate all these data sets to other concepts. In many ways, hypermedia could alter the way we "see" and conceive of data in the future, and may facilitate their exchange with colleagues through information networks.

CONCEPTUAL DEVELOPMENT

Exemplars and Inference

In his celebrated essay "Thick Description: Toward an Interpretive Theory of Culture," Clifford Geertz (1973) wonders what anthropological analysis amounts to as a form of knowledge. To explicate the answer—"thick description," borrowed from philosopher Gilbert Ryle—Geertz cites Ryle's example of two boys "rapidly contracting the eyelids of their right eyes" (p. 6). As the boys' eye movements are identical, they could be either involuntary twitches or the winks of two conspirators signaling each other. So when does rapid eye contraction count as winking? Geertz writes: "Contracting your eyelids on purpose when there exists a public code in which so doing counts as a conspiratorial signal *is* winking. That's all there is to it: a speck of behavior, a fleck of culture, and—*voila!*—a gesture." Of course, he goes on to say, one boy's wink could actually be a parody of the other's wink (or twitch?)—adding yet another wrinkle to the cultural performance of rapid eye contraction.

Several pages later in the essay, the arc of Geertz's thinking brings him to the conclusion that ethnographic writings are "fictions," in the sense of an imaginative rendering of other people's interpretations. Given this, he ponders how we can tell a good ethnographic account from a worse one—the long-standing issues of verification and value. "But that is precisely the virtue of it. If ethnography is thick description and ethnographers those who are doing the describing, then the determining question for any example of it, whether a field journal squib or a Malinowski-sized monograph, is whether it sorts winks from twitches and real winks from mimicked ones" (p. 16).

An inference that works is one that sorts the *true* meanings of a performance or practice—the meanings that were operative at a particular time among the participants—from other potential meanings. This truth is tested in our ability to problematize a subject (recognition) and to unpack the cultural logics-in-use of that problem (explication). We see evidence of these inferences at work in our interpersonal relations with the other, in the inscription of data-texts, and in the codings we do. All of these activities are explications of something that is problematic. But explications can only partially represent an original meaning. Interview talk that is not heard or understood, or behavior that eludes our grasp of it as a sensible act, exists beyond the pale of the analyst's explanation. The failure to sort winks from twitches, however, is not a wasted effort. Failures are noteworthy in their own right and inform even successful efforts at reconstructing the other's life world.

Beyond thick description, the analyst tries to develop a conceptual understanding. Attention turns to disciplinary interests, concepts, constructs, and theories. The facts of the case are now viewed as instances of a more general process, relationship, or set of conditions. The descriptions of a scene and the terminology of some branch of the communication discipline begin to interpenetrate.

This move, however, does not mean that indicators are simply found to fit a construct. What it does mean is that the analyst seeks "an interplay between finding indicators and conceptualizing the analytic categories" (Hammersley & Atkinson, 1983, p. 185). Through encounters with thickly described cases, theory becomes a useful device. We learn more about the limits of a theory's interface with the empirical world. Its constructs and propositions may require revision in the face of disconfirming ethnographic evidence. The general theory, in turn, may (or may not) illuminate the significance of the case and its concepts of situated action.

Of great importance in conceptual development and inference are *exemplars* (Atkinson, 1990). Also called incidents (Spradley, 1980), examples (Jacobs, 1986), episodes (Anderson, 1987), strips (Agar, 1982), and case studies (Mitchell, 1983), an exemplar consists of one or more parts of a project's data record that are shaped (or constructed) to advance a conceptual argument. As we will see in the next chapter, exemplars are very important to the crafting of a rhetorically persuasive research text. For the purposes of data analysis, exemplars are *embodiments of an inductive construct*. Without exemplars, the claims of a work of qualitative research would be empty and unpersuasive.

But exemplars are not evidence in the usual sense. Instead of trying to characterize all of a project's data, as a conventional analysis might do, the analyst identifies and uses only those data that lend insight into a social action or discourse. As Atkinson (1990) puts it, "Such 'forceful' examples are provided as rhetorical devices which may help the readers to enter into the author's argument" (p. 91). The analyst's experience in an event, the data-texts of that event, and the conceptual principle(s) underlying them are all employed in the development of an exemplar. The exemplar can then be used to test a claim. The analyst can evaluate how plausibly it explains the descriptive act and how well it explains new data, or he or she can ask native informants to appraise its truth value.

Exemplars are derived from "concrete interactional events, incidents, occurrences, episodes, anecdotes, scenes, and happenings somewhere in the real world" (Lofland, 1974, p. 107). The forms they take can range from excerpts that have had little or no interpretation added (e.g., an interview remark detached from its original context) to a story that has been spun from several sources.[4] In qualitative studies that focus on conversation structure, exemplars are used as "examples" of a certain pattern of discourse (Jacobs, 1986, 1990). The analyst assesses how "intelligible" an example of talk is, as disclosed by the participants' own purposes and strategies. In ethnographies and other interpretive studies, an exemplar tends to be drawn from several data sources, exhibits the form of a narrative, and requires the reader to expend some effort to complete the terms of the argument being advanced. As Blumer (1939) writes, "The judgment of the reasonableness of an interpretation is based upon the background of the reader's own experience and also upon the authority of the person who makes the interpretation" (p. 147).

A potent exemplar brings out the salience and the inherent order (or contradictions) of an event. It functions to show how social actors' first-order constructs are spoken or acted out in time- or place-bound situations. This is the exemplar's descriptive mandate. These features usually come clear to readers only against the background of an entire research argument. That is, "the single case becomes significant only when set against the accumulated experience and knowledge that the analyst brings to it" (Mitchell, 1983, p. 203).

The exemplar should also embody many, if not all, of the indicators specified in an emerging concept. Recall from the discussion of the constant comparative method that incidents from data-texts are used to construct and define the properties of a concept. As these indicators are organized into one or more research exemplars, they acquire a new significance: Formerly first-order constructs only, they now go to work in the analyst's second-order analysis. When writing up the report, however, the analyst should try to distinguish the exemplar from its conceptual elucidation. The analyst-writer owes his or her audience the chance to read and evaluate the exemplar independent of its use in theoretical argument.

A look at some strategies of qualitative analysis—typological, meta-phorical, dramatistic, discursive, and phenomenological—along with examples from communication studies, shows how exemplars are used to advance an argument. A couple of disclaimers must be mentioned: The strategies discussed here are merely illustrative of what can be done in qualitative analysis; they should not be taken to be exhaustive, nor should they be considered definitive uses of these strategies.

Typological Strategy

Often, the analyst notices a rich variation in the phenomenon being studied, occurring along one or two key dimensions. By documenting as much of this variation as possible, the analyst goes some distance toward developing a *typology*, a classification system of some aspect of the world. The analyst has given names to the types, and the interpretive task consists of describing each in terms of its natural contexts and modes of behaving. The analyst might even begin to construct a *taxonomy*, an exhaustive classification of a phenomenon according to certain laws (or strong principles) of variation.

Some typologies are derived more or less indigenously—*emic* typologies. That is, the culture members themselves provide most of the types and even the names for them, especially if the informants' naturalistic talk is a focal interest. For example, among the three role-defining practices of referencing media among some small-town cops, as discovered by Pacanowsky and Anderson (1982), was the use of "media nicknames." The authors state some general properties of this practice, *inter alia,* that media nicknames are usually regarded positively by fellow cops, that they represent something quintessential about the specific cop (or police work), and that the commentary surrounding a nickname has to do with the way the name plays off some aspect of the media world. They then offer several exemplars ("Bogart," "Mr. Bill," "Kojak," "Pete Lacey," and "Mikey") that indicate the extent of the typology of media nicknames; here is one:

> Another nickname which is used by members of Valley View's detective division is Kojak. Unlike the TV Kojak who works on and solves interesting cases, the detectives in Valley View have a frustrating lot. Most of their investigations are of petty theft—from houses or unlocked automobiles.... Most of such crimes go unsolved, attributed to "juveniles," but only after considerable paperwork. The nickname of Kojak for one of the detectives then is a commentary by irony and counterpoint. Not unsurprisingly, the detective so addressed is the one whose hair is the curliest of all the detectives on the force. (p. 747)

We do not need to know how often this nickname is used, how long this individual has had the nickname, or how many other police forces in the country have officers nicknamed Kojak. What is important is that ethnographic study uncovered this functional practice where none was anticipated. The nicknames noted by Pacanowsky and Anderson were evaluated in comparative fashion, and properties emerged inductively by this procedure. Each exemplar exhibits a type of the category "media nicknames." And each exemplar offers sufficient description for readers to assess it on their own.

Other typologies derive from the analyst's own conceptual resources—an *etic* perspective. Such properties and types are reasoned in a deductive manner from prior theory. The participants whose actions are described may have little awareness that the sort of variation claimed by the analyst exists in their life world. There may be logical grounds for classifying, but unless the variation is actually recognized or used by the participants in some way, its utility can be questioned.

Metaphorical Strategy

Metaphors are used frequently as sense-making devices in qualitative analysis. In research, as in ordinary usage, a metaphor can create a new meaning through analogy, especially between two concepts that are not usually thought of together. Of course, the analyst needs to interpret this enlightening juxtaposition further in order to make a research claim. Metaphoric comparisons also afford vivid, concise ways to suggest complex ideas (Crider & Cirillo, 1992).

Like the emic typology, a metaphor drawn from the words of social actors can be an effective tool of analysis. For example, in Rawlins and Holl's (1987) study of adolescents' friendship concerns, mentioned in Chapter 6, degree of trust emerged as one of the most significant themes for evaluating level of friendship. To know whether someone can truly be a friend, apparently one must risk the possibility that secrets will be revealed to others. Not surprisingly, then, Rawlins and Holl's analysis took up violations of trust as a major problematic to be explored.

The most severe breach of trust mentioned by the participants was "backstabbing"; "the violence metaphorically implied by the phrase 'backstabbing' captures the poignancy and revulsion these adolescents attributed to a friend's betrayal through talk" (p. 355). Another participant term, "talking behind my back," was related to backstabbing, albeit at a less severe level. Underlying both acts is malicious intent. How did Rawlins and Holl warrant and develop their claims? Mostly by way of exemplars:

In characterizing what he valued most in a friend, one male stated:

> Um, well definitely someone whom you could talk to, whom you could trust. No one who would, um, stab you in the back or anything like that. Somebody who could, uh talk, you know, you could talk with or you could, you know, someone who you could trust.

Notice his virtual equation in friendship of someone to talk to and trust. In discussing why friendships break up, a female related:

> I used to be friends with her. Pretty much she stabbed me in the back really bad. And I'm, I'm not used to that happening 'cause I choose my friends carefully; but when she pulled that, I said forget it.

This quotation indicates the practice and need for careful selection of friends as well as her conclusive reaction to backstabbing. (p. 355)

Interestingly, nowhere in the quotes do the participants explain what they mean by the metaphor. The meaning is inferred from the context of their talk, and from the framework developed for us by the authors. The treachery spoken of in the participants' comments about "backstabbing," and "talking behind my back" to a lesser degree, is vivid and concise enough (e.g., the sign of the "back" as a vulnerable, unwary site of injury) to adopt whole from these quotes, and to apply to similarly stated complaints that do not mention "backstabbing" explicitly.

Generally, researchers use metaphors, whether they come from participants' own words or not, to thematize areas of interest, including behavioral routines. Metaphors can be more than just nifty tropes, and metaphor making can be a creative act of analyzing data.

Dramatistic Strategy

The concept of communication as performance is well suited for engaging in an analysis framed as *drama*. Attention is paid to the enactment of roles, the qualities of those who perform the roles, the settings and artifacts that serve as performing contexts, the scripts that are evoked, and the audiences who receive, evaluate, and act upon the performance (Anderson, 1987, pp. 278-281).

By seeing a local scene through these constructs, a researcher can develop a close-in description that can be elevated to archetypal status. That is, when a person is perceived as "performing" a role of some kind, the particulars of the case often attain a larger-than-life aspect. The case material can be mundane, but more often the researcher will select an exemplary or problematic drama. For example, a social drama, as Victor Turner (1957) characterizes it, represents an account of societal rupture, crisis, and resolution: "The social drama is a limited area of transparency on the otherwise opaque surface of regular, uneventful social life. Through it we are enabled to observe the crucial principles of social structure in their operation and their relative dominance at successive points in time" (p. 93).

In Trujillo's (1993) "Interpreting November 22: A Critical Ethnography of an Assassination Site," a single site—Dealy Plaza in Dallas on the twenty-fifth anniversary of the Kennedy assassination—becomes the performative context for exploring "the multiple meanings which define [the event's] meaning in American culture" (p. 449). Some of the themes informing the author's study include the postmodern commodification of experience, the ideological struggle over the assassination's meaning, and the fragmenting of community that followed in its wake.

Trujillo reconstructed and edited "performances" of different kinds in a complex arrangement. In a section titled "The President Is Shot, the Community Is Shattered," for example, Trujillo presents exemplars in the following forms: a flashback episode of the moment of the fatal shot to Kennedy's head, testimonies of visitors to the plaza that day in 1988, and an elegiac commentary on the "annihilation" of the American community of the early 1960s. Here is an exemplar from this narrative:

> A white woman in her fifties expresses her feelings to one reporter: "Our country took another direction after his death, an *evil* one. It's not the same world anymore. All I can say is that with him, it would have been much better." A white male in his forties echoes similar feelings when he tells another reporter that if Kennedy had lived, "we wouldn't have had Vietnam or the situation with drugs on the streets that we have now." (p. 453)

We hear and see people playing their parts as nameless, ordinary citizens who are giving opinions to reporters—a well-known style of performance. The fact that the comments are given to reporters only adds to Trujillo's persistent theme of the media-mirrored nature of the Kennedy assassination. The content of this exemplar, along with quotes from two other citizens and a description of 20 strangers paying solemn respect, implicitly expresses the author's theme of the assassination as a rupture in the surface of history.

Discursive Strategy

Language forms the greater part of all the exemplars examined so far. This should not be surprising, given that language does a great deal more than convey the "content" of our thought. Oral and written languages constitute the primary means by which individual experience becomes a social reality. Or, to put it another way, it is through the practice of language that we define and accomplish goals in relationships. Indeed, if we want to know how something is done and what it means, we have to consider how it is talked about.

Interviewing is the dominant method for carrying out the latter goal. Interviewing, Jensen (1989) observes, "is a very efficient generator of language, so that, ultimately, the qualitative researcher finds himself/herself face to face with a mass of data which requires some form of *textual analysis*" (p. 99). We make sense of an interview text by examining either the commonalities and differences in orientation to speech topics (themes) or what a sample of speech is trying to accomplish as a social act. For either purpose, but especially the latter, it is essential that we have a deep understanding of the culture. Unless the culture is known to us through its social practices, it is hard to make sense of its linguistic forms. Similarly, we should think carefully about what a topic or theme means in local contexts of talk. It is altogether too easy to claim the presence of a topic. But topics do not simply announce themselves. We must look for signs of topical recognition by participants; the beginnings, endings, interruptions, and ebb and flow of topic; the expressive modes of topic; and, of course, the semantics of topic—what is meant (by the participant) by what is said.

Tracy and Baratz's (1993) "Intellectual Discussion in the Academy as Situated Discourse" seeks, at a general level, to expand knowledge of everyday talk practices. Specifically, the authors are concerned with the ways in which the academic institutional context, with all of its status distinctions and avowed commitment to open scholarly discourse, affects the actual conduct of intellectual conversation. They undertook their study because they wanted to find out how people do intellectual talk.

Analyzing interviews about the weekly colloquia in a communication department, Tracy and Baratz "looked for evidence of what participants' face concerns were and how they saw them being expressed" (p. 305). How did this evidence emerge? First, the researchers asked participants straightforwardly what their own and others' concerns were likely to be at these colloquia. This apparently yielded answers that needed no further interpretation. They also asked participants for *evaluations* of others' actions. Their objective was to get at the participants' "reasoning-in-action . . . what is a good and right way to act or what is believed to be bad or inappropriate." Evidence for this mode of reasoning was acknowledged to be "culled more indirectly," as goals had to be inferred from talk about action. For example:

> Participants used talk as a way to assess a discussant's intellectual ability. Faculty member, Edward, comments about fellow participants that "the way they react to issues is a pretty good clue to how they think" (Q14). In particular, participants who asked tough and challenging questions were often seen as smart and competent. This was implicitly oriented to by what participants sought to avoid, namely, the asking of "nice, little supportive questions," as one faculty member labeled them in jest. Consider faculty member, Tom's response to a question about the most active participants (Q7):

> > Among the graduate students, the people I think about are Jess, Tim, uh let's see. Felicia will ask a question but it'll be a nice little supportive question.

Implicit in Tom's description of Felicia's participation is a contrast between the unspoken and desirable type of participation—big, tough, challenging questions—and the spoken one. Tom's characterization not only portrays supportive questions as not desirable, but goes further to suggest that they count questionably at best, as participation in intellectual discussion. This negative assessment of supportive or information questions is reflected in graduate students' comments as well. (pp. 308-309)

For Tracy and Baratz, respondents' topical remarks may be taken either at face value (as in Edward's comment) or as subtle indicators of some other, more evaluative, dimension (Tom's comment). We see that Tom hints broadly at what he "really" means, but it is the analyst who risks naming and unraveling this implicit meaning. The authors' claim about Tom's comment depends on some shared social knowledge of how a certain style of discourse (belittling by giving false praise) works. And Tom probably intended to have it interpreted that way. Thus it is Tom's comment that takes priority in this exemplar, not Edward's, which serves merely to open up the issue. Later in the same section, Tracy and Baratz use other exemplars to corroborate and develop further their claim about the nature of a "good question."

Phenomenological Strategy

As we learned in Chapter 2, transcendental phenomenology was developed as a method for comprehending the essence of lived experience. It can also be used to analyze social data, as in ethnomethodological investigations or the study of personal constructs of communicative practice.

By means of the *epoche*, the first step of the method, the analyst attempts to become cognizant of all the preconceptions (including biases, prejudices, and other prior personal conceptions) he or she holds about the object of study. These are "deconstructions" of the object, and are set aside as a study progresses. Then, the object is *bracketed*; that is, it is confronted without any preconceptions and defined on its own terms. This is the step of "reduction," in which the meanings of an object for the self and for others are located, interpreted, and developed into a tentative statement. In the next steps, the full array of data about the object are examined, grouped into meaningful clusters, explicated, and, finally, synthesized as a structure. In that final step, the meanings of the phenomenological experience are brought to surface, revealing the essence of the object (Patton, 1990, pp. 407-410).

For example, in "Media Consumption and Girls Who Want to Have Fun," Peterson (1987, p. 41) demonstrates a phenomenological method for analyzing audience meanings of Cyndi Lauper's hit song. The analysis consists of these phases:

1. *description:* the discovery of "signification systems in the lived reality of everyday life"
2. *definition:* "the reduction of the description to systematic knowledge"
3. *interpretation:* a reflection on the previous two phases to "specify the logic and value that unite description and definition" in order to locate the "value of social existence"

Application of this method to 34 student essays about the meanings of "Girls Just Want to Have Fun" resulted in the emergence of seven thematic clusters: danceability, fun, freedom, rebellion, performer (the Lauper persona), audience/youth, and critic (meaningfulness). Listening to music was found to serve these purposes of inscribing social meaning and organizing pleasure for audience members. Further analysis of these themes resulted in a development of three interpretive positions: liberal individualist, liberal feminist, and teeny-bopper. Thus Peterson's research sought to explain why and how the song was able to function for different segments of its audience in ways that vary from a dance tune to a feminist anthem.

EVALUATING INTERPRETATIONS

In research based on objectivist assumptions, data are usually evaluated for their reliability and validity. The question of reliability has to do with the stability of observations: whether a research instrument, testing the same thing in the same way, will yield the same results time after time. Most threats to reliability come from flaws of inconsistency in the way a study is carried out.

The question of validity has to do with the truth of observations: whether the research instrument is accurately reporting on the object of interest. Validity is often characterized by its internal and external dimensions. An internally valid inquiry is one in which the variation of an independently controlled variable results in a pattern of variation in a dependent measure. Potential threats to internal validity include factors in the research context (e.g., instrument changes, subject maturation, reactivity, history of testing) that create misleading findings ("artifacts"). An externally valid inquiry is one in which an observed pattern generalizes to other times, settings, and persons. Potential threats to generalizability occur, usually, when random probability sampling procedures are not followed. One can assume reliability if validity can be established; but an instrument that is reliable is not always valid (for more on these concepts, see Cook & Campbell, 1979; Lincoln & Guba, 1985).

For many reasons, these canons of evaluation do not apply very well to qualitative research based on interpretive assumptions. The interpretive paradigm recognizes the constantly changing character of cultures, perceptions, and forms of action. Because what can be observed of a scene is profoundly contingent on time, and on the individual human-as-research-instrument (whose properties change as time in the field increases), little is gained from trying to achieve reliability. Applying the concept of validity to qualitative inquiry is also difficult. A world consisting of multiple, constructed realities does not permit the researcher to identify any single representation as the criterion for accurate measurement. And because the inquirer operates reflexively as a participant, it is doubtful whether the usual way of conceiving internal validity has much relevance. Finally, the qualitative researcher studies social action and cultural sensibility situated in time and place; the move to generalize in the traditional sense is neither warranted nor particularly desirable.

Qualitative inquirers do seek credible, dependable data (Lincoln & Guba, 1985). Basically, we want to inspire confidence in readers (and ourselves) that we have achieved right interpretations. Notice that I do not say *the* right interpretation. There are many possible interpretations of a case. But we stand a better chance of arriving at very plausible interpretations if we can evaluate competing ones incisively. Several techniques have proven useful for doing this: triangulation, negative case analysis, member checks, and quitting the field.

Triangulation

Soon into the family television/VCR study, we became aware during interviews with both husbands and wives of remarks claiming that the males in the families are more adept at using the VCR than the females. Considered only as evidence of beliefs (or ideological constructions?), interview reports were quite adequate to support this finding. But if we were to consider these statements as evidence of family behavior, we needed other sources of evidence as well. At that point, observations were about to start, so we thought it would be worthwhile to pay attention to gender in relation to VCR use. Subsequently, a triangulated analysis of diary, interview, and observational data led us to an understanding of the dependency of belief and situated behavior. (Incidentally, the "belief" that VCR operation was a male domain, circa 1986 in Lexington, Kentucky, was largely confirmed in observations.)

As this example indicates, triangulation involves a comparative assessment of more than one form of evidence about an object of inquiry. Although it is typically a method of verification, triangulation can also be used to develop a concept, construct, or proposition. There are many ways a researcher can triangulate data. *Multiple sources* from one technique can be compared, such as husband and wife interviews on the issue of VCR use in the family. The separate informants should be socially positioned such that each can say something meaningful about the phenomenon in question. Probably the most familiar kind of triangulation, *multiple methods* can be applied to the same problem, as in the use of observational field notes and interview transcripts in the example related above. Depending on the target of inference, somewhat greater credibility can be invested in data from one of the triangulated methods; data from the complementary method can then enrich, or impose qualifications on, explanations arising from the primary one. *Multiple investigators* are also used to compensate for their individual styles, biases, or shortcomings, or to exploit their specific strengths (Douglas, 1976, pp. 189-226). Two or more observers may be deployed in the same setting, or analysts can work as a team on coding and other analytic business.

Triangulation may look suspiciously like pursuing the holy grail of reliability—that is, the convergence of evidence toward a consistent outcome. This could be true in some of its applications, especially when two or more observers go into the field with the intent of confirming what each observes. But usually, multiple sources, methods, or investigators add their own distinctive spins on a common problem. Even in situations when triangulation produces divergent outcomes, which is not uncommon, the "problem" may not be in the method or source itself; rather, we learn that phenomena behave differently through the specific media of our methods (Lever, 1981). Explanations become more credible, not less so, in such instances. A commitment to multiple modes of data generation leads to thickly described cases, which allow users to compare them to the known attributes of other sites of social life—the qualitative analogue of generalizing findings to other populations (Lincoln & Guba, 1985).

Negative Case Analysis

Also known as *analytic induction,* negative case analysis is "a process of revising hypotheses with hindsight" (Lincoln & Guba, 1985, p. 309; citing Kidder, 1981). As the researcher develops a hypothesis or explanation through an inductive process such as the constant comparative method, additional field data are generated and put to the test of the hypothesis. If the new data confirm the hypothesis, it becomes stronger. But if some aspect of the new data disconfirms the hypothesis, or relates to it ambiguously, the analyst must redefine the hypothesis to accommodate the data. The analyst keeps considering new data, and revising the hypothesis, until there are no more negative cases to account for. Ultimately, negative case analysis results in a highly confident statement about a phenomenon, one that even approaches universal coverage.

Clearly this is a stringent procedure, and not every analyst has the time or the patience to follow through on it. Further, negative case analysis does not establish the criteria for coming to a determinate end of the testing process (Hammersley, 1992). Yet, even in slightly less demanding forms (e.g., Agar, 1982), negative case analysis provides a way to develop a right interpretation, and to back it up.

Member Checks

It was the day after Christmas in Oaxaca, Mexico, and my wife and I were taking a morning walk around the *zócalo.* As we passed a sidewalk restaurant, an American in his early 20s suddenly got up and trotted out to us. Motioning to the people at his table, he said, "I have a bet with my friends that I can guess what you do." "Okay, go." "Uh, you're in the academic world. Maybe a writer." "Yeah," I muttered, my smile fading to a grimace. The youth immediately turned to his friends, shook a fist victoriously, and shouted, "Yes!" A smattering of applause was heard from the table. I looked at Joanne and said, "I don't like being *that* easy to figure out." A member check had just occurred.

Member checks are opportunities for the researcher to test hypotheses, concepts, interpretations, or explanations with members of the local culture he or she is studying. Although they are ordinarily based on longer relationships than was the case in Oaxaca, it is not mandatory for the researcher to engage a close confidant. Anyone who can comment knowledgeably, and willingly, on key practices may participate. Member checks can be carried out on an informal, spur-of-moment basis (see the section on the ethnographic interview in Chapter 6), or on a by-appointment basis.

Member checks, which generally come near the end of fieldwork, constitute critiques from individuals who are both "insiders" (to the culture) and "outsiders" (to the project). Member checks can be important situations of interpretative validation. Much of what the researcher wants to accomplish is a depiction of the subjective world of the other, so it is the other whose judgment may matter most. If the researcher and the participant enjoy a good deal of mutual respect, the researcher might present for comment some of the more uncomfortable or controversial conclusions he or she has reached. New information and insights may also be gleaned during member checks that can be added to the database.

It is vital for the researcher to remember, however, that no participant is a dispassionate, fully informed member of his or her culture. A person's alliances and passions about certain things, and disinterest about others, surely affect what he or she can authenticate.

Quitting the Field

Some reasons researchers quit the field are obvious; some are not so obvious. Endings can be caused by events from outside the needs of the project, such as acts of God (personal or physical misfortune), depleted funds, fatigue, interpersonal distress, and job constraints (Kirk & Miller, 1986; Snow, 1980). Such forced exits are all too common, and often leave the researcher with regrets about what was not done. Paradoxically, these are the endings that are usually well understood by the members of the culture. Their exigencies are visible to all.

If the researcher is in the luxurious position of not having to leave the field prematurely, the project's internal needs may control when he or she exits. Snow (1980) cites three tests for what he calls "informational sufficiency": the extent to which enough data have been collected to address the project's questions sufficiently. The first factor, *taken-for-grantedness*, suggests that it is time to disengage from the field when very little the participants do surprises the researchers anymore, or when the scene acquires the aspect of being routine. A concept encountered earlier in this chapter, *theoretical saturation*, defines the second factor of informational sufficiency. Simply put, this occurs when the researcher reaches a point of drastically diminished returns—when new data add very few new or useful features to categories, concepts, or explanations. In practical terms, "saturation is signaled by the continued observation of what is already known, and by repetitive field notes" (Snow, 1980, p. 103). Finally, a *heightened confidence* that "the observations and findings are faithful to the empirical world under study and shed light on preexisting or emergent questions and propositions" (p. 104) can suggest that the time for closure has come.

In actually quitting the field, the researcher should take some of the time remaining to check questionable hunches, evaluate the credibility of informants, and run through a final negative case analysis (Becker, 1958). These are activities that can be done only "on the ground." The researcher should also settle any outstanding moral and material debts to informants and others. It is vital that the fieldworker leave on good terms, if for no other reason than to not damage the site for future investigators.

Sometimes, a kind of separation anxiety sets in. Participants may wonder how the project went, what conclusions the researcher came to, and how they will be portrayed. Depending on the nature of their relationship at that point, the researcher might choose to "debrief" participants in some way. In any case, the fieldworker should do more than simply leave a forwarding address. He or she should reaffirm any plans for staying in touch, which may include the possibility of more fieldwork. Quitting the field does not mean an end to the relationship, only a physical distancing.

Conclusion

I began this chapter by noting the legendary imprecision of qualitative analysis. Although we can state reasonably well how to create and analyze data-texts, there is still more than a hint of mystery about how a rambunctious fieldwork experience is turned into a finished text. The "system" a researcher ends up using has usually come by way of some greasy, under-the-hood work with factory models (i.e., books like this one). The satisfaction one feels at finishing a study can be even greater when one has invented a way of working that, surprisingly, worked.

Yet the development of computer technologies and software, some designed for qualitative data applications, is proceeding apace and seems to be exerting some influence on analytic practice. Many of the latest programs and technologies employ rational action models of behavior that come from cognitive psychological theory and artificial intelligence. Such efforts are aimed at systematizing cogent rules for recognizing or determining patterns in strings of words. They are also meant to counter the effects of the large amounts of manual work, the small amount of procedural clarity, and the scarcity of institutional rewards for the art and craft of qualitative work. This move in the general direction of science offers an outlet for those who would prefer to err on the side of certainty.

Moving in a different direction are ongoing efforts to find out how the terrains of social science, politics, history, symbols, and literary criticism speak to one another. In these explorations, data analysis is not an abstracted procedure. Rather, analysis is oriented both to the ethical concerns of the situated fieldwork and to the demands of writing compelling texts. Analysis becomes a matter of hearing the voices of the other and deciding which voices should be included and how those voices are to be stitched together. Chapter 8 introduces many of these issues, as we look toward the uses of narrative and rhetorical devices to develop qualitative research claims.

Notes

1. Open note taking is much more prevalent among anthropologists studying cultures markedly different from their own. Sociologists and communication researchers must be more circumspect, as they share much the same culture as their subjects and are expected to observe the same codes of politeness and respect. Sometimes, the researcher is able to embed note taking in a field role. For example, student researchers observing family media use have disguised their scratch note taking as "homework" (Lull, 1985)—a situationally appropriate activity that is not likely to be challenged. Of course, the researcher must weigh the benefits of this tactic against the possible consequences if it is challenged and exposed by the participants.

2. A former colleague was fond of telling anyone who would listen, "God protects those who back up their files." Although I seldom bought this person's advice on things metaphysical, I did buy into this particular hip-pocket philosophy.

3. Joel Kailing provided useful ideas and assistance in the conceptualization of these four domains.

4. Gluckman (1961) has described three kinds of case studies that appear to be useful as exemplar types: (a) an "apt illustration," a description of a typical event that illustrates a general principle; (b) a social situation, "some restricted and limited (bounded) set of events . . . in which general principles of social organization manifest themselves in some particular specified context"; and (c) an extended case study, a sequence of events involving the same actors and settings over a long period of time that demonstrates a process in operation (cited in Mitchell, 1983, p. 193).

8

Authoring and Writing

Going Public

Culture is not itself visible, but is made visible only through its representation. (Van Maanen, 1988, p. 3)

Eventually, the time comes when the researcher begins to write a text to be read (or heard) by an audience. The time for undertaking this challenging task may arrive just after the researcher leaves the field or months afterward. The text may be an account of the researcher's total experience in a culture, or it may be the first of many papers that treat the empirical, conceptual, political, or methodological aspects of the project. The audience may be a thesis committee (who will read the work assiduously), attendees of a conference session (who may not read it at all), readers of a communication journal, or readers of popular non-fiction—especially if the work, like Kanter's *Men and Women of the Corporation* (1977) or Liebow's *Tell Them Who I Am* (1993), connects to a contemporary theme. In writing up a study, the researcher conceives as a finished presentation the ideas and stories he or she once shared with subjects and colleagues in fragmentary discourses.[1] The project begins to "go public."

Going public signals a profound change in the researcher's work habits and modes of thought. Before that point, he or she labors in a sociable world and faces the agendas and activities of people trying to deal with their own interests first and the researcher's second. But as the stay in the field winds down, these demands on the researcher's self also fall away. The researcher is now alone with an abundance of material, facing the task of making a text out of it. At first, this prospect can be more terrifying than inspiring, as Shannon Jackson (1993) vividly recounts:

> My field notebook was mangled and bursting with notes, pieces of paper marked key places, and on these pieces of paper more notes were written. Statements to myself could be found in the subject notebooks of my other classes. I attempted to organize. I wrote outlines on paper, hoping that by placing numbers and letters before my bits of phrases, I could write my way into an organizational strategy. I taped pieces of paper over the wall, arranging interview transcriptions, quotes from cultural theorists, and my own insights into a kind of wall-paper collage. I was astounded by the absurdity of my task. The sheer volume of voices in my research was compounded by the fact that much of this research had taken place in embodied interactions and in multiple locations. And yet, somehow, I was called upon to represent this work. (p. 24)

Called upon to represent it? By whom? The duty of all ethnographers is visible in that phrasing. One can always not write. But inevitably one must honor the reasons for doing the study in the first place as well as the collective investment of all those who became involved in it. Not to consummate a project in the act of writing is, in a sense, to disavow one's basic professional commitments. Unless a project breaks down in logistical or financial distress, or in an interpersonal failure of some sort, a written account is legitimately expected by all parties.[2] Research never belongs to the researcher alone.

Of course, much of Jackson's confession exposes a pathos familiar to ethnographers everywhere: how to turn a littered research trail into a confident, authoritative narrative that tells what happened and what it means. Certainly there are many models that can be used for writing, but the complex, always unique trajectory of a project resists the easy application of a model. At the heart of any contribution to what we know, particularly one based on an interpretive or cultural premise, is an *innovative articulation* of claims, evidence, and warrants. The truths learned in qualitative fieldwork cannot be separated from the particular ways they are expressed. These choices become extremely important to the project's persuasive effect.

In this chapter I describe some paths and problems in writing qualitative communication research. As in preceding chapters, the itinerary eventually takes us to pragmatic concerns—in this case, about stylistic conventions and criteria of effective writing. Later in the chapter, I unpack the "writing" of the chapter title: the strategies and tactics of representation. To avoid being too didactic about "how to write," I offer an examination of two exemplars of published communication research. Of special interest are the authors' methods for depicting communicative phenomena and for establishing the credibility of their claims.

But first, I take up the recent debates, mostly in anthropology and sociology, concerning the epistemological status of ethnographic texts and scientific work as a whole. Most of the participants in these debates question the purely objectivist, descriptive thrust of the long tradition of "ethnographic realism." They argue that realist texts are characterized by controlling, yet invisibly, ethnographers' voices, which obscure the actual relationships between the investigators and the experiences of the people studied.

The impact of these critiques has been extensive in all of the human sciences. Probably the most general consequence is a growing understanding that knowledge is socially and culturally constructed through language. Such a view undermines the notion that all of a culture and its practices can be captured in a text. This new self-consciousness presents the qualitative researcher with many more choices of expression than before. With those choices go responsibilities for author-izing interpretations of a people and their practices. Thus the first part of this chapter examines "authoring" as a matter of making decisions about how to represent, "where one assumes authority over the inscription of the word, [requiring] that one take up a fundamental attitude toward experience of the world, toward other authors and texts, and to the way inquiry is formulated within the established conventions of a discipline" (Rose, 1986, p. 319). The question that precedes and influences the writing decisions that follow is, What kind of author do I wish to be?

Within communication, innovative styles of writing have not appeared widely, probably because of the newness of qualitative work in a discipline that has long valued scientistic norms. Book-length ethnographies are still rare, and journal articles often mimic the typical hypothetico-deductive piece. However, communication scholars have stayed close to the experiments and discussions of textual form taking place in other disciplines, and are now contributing to this dialogue (e.g.,

Carbaugh, 1991; Fiske, 1991b; Morley, 1992; Pacanowsky, 1988b, 1989; Strine & Pacanowsky, 1985). With its fundamental interests in rhetorical inquiry, the social construction of meaning, and semiotics, communication is as well situated as any other discipline to exploit new discursive resources. More experiments and critical dialogue are sure to come in the years ahead.

Authoring

SCIENCE AND RHETORIC

Even today, one has to search hard to find "writing" in the curriculum of a college social science program, or in the syllabus of a methods course. It is assumed that students already know how to write by the time they arrive. Of course, the local English department is there for any upgrading that needs to be done, and a brush with literary criticism is duly appreciated. But acculturation to professional science writing seems to occur later, as a by-product of analyzing examples of published science, or through mentoring relationships with senior scholars.

There is, however, a more fundamental reason writing has been ignored: The classical view of science induced what amounts to a "trained incapacity" among many scientists to use, or even recognize, language as a central part of their work. Especially after the arguments of Enlightenment philosophers such as Francis Bacon, René Descartes, and John Locke, rhetoric came to be seen as an obstacle to the achievement of discoveries about nature. Nature was assumed to embody objective truths, quite apart from the values, passions, and actions of human communities. In order to penetrate and reveal these truths through science, it became important to make inquiry an impersonal process. Thus the philosophy that dichotomized mind/body and subject/object also favored the use of Method (idealized in the experimental method) as the way to discover facts and relationships "out there." The ultimate goal was to describe the external, ahistorical reality accurately, so that its component parts could be predicted, controlled, and recast in the form of technologies.

Following this hardy empiricist thinking, writing strategies and formats were viewed as *neutral instruments* for reporting science. Mathematical notation was considered the ideal way to enact this version of science. Not only is mathematics a precise and universal language, it represents quantities, relationships, and transformations in ways that seem to mirror nature itself. The language used in most scientific reports aspires to this ideal. Whatever values, emotional content, or poetic speech appear in such reports should be ostensible properties of the world being described, not inventions of the writer. As much as possible, then, the world described in the scientific report is one that is self-presenting: a world that reveals its nature and mechanisms through the operations of the researcher. This self-presenting character of the world requires an author who is self-effacing. The author must recede from view—become invisible—for the report to be convincing to a reader (who shares the same norms). Gusfield (1976) calls this the "window-pane" theory of scientific language, which "insists on the intrinsic irrelevance of language to the enterprise of Science. . . . language and style must be chosen which will approximate, as closely as possible, a pane of clear glass" (pp. 16-17).

But are there alternative ways to write and read science? Does the language we know and use affect *what* we claim to know? Could science be mostly an enterprise of persuading others to our way of understanding what the "facts" are? These questions become clearer as we consider the rhetorical and narrative bases of science. Nelson, Megill, and McCloskey (1987) argue that a "rhetoric of inquiry" rests on assumptions of both unity and diversity. All academic fields draw on the same rhetorical resources and devices—metaphor, synecdoche, appeals to authority and audience, and so on—as any other human enterprise. No matter how "rigorous" the field of study, its research tries to persuade us to one or another view of reality. The arguments used in a research article are not different in kind from those used in everyday speech. They involve such human goals as informing, accounting, praising, damning, and calling to action. Even in the so-called hard sciences we find appeals to beauty and intuition in the construction of arguments (Hunter, 1990).

At the same time, there is diversity in the use of research rhetoric. Each academic field develops a style of discourse that is consistent with its own conceptions of correct practice. For example, Bazerman (1987) studied the evolution of official writing style prescribed in the *Publication Manual* of the American Psychological Association (APA). From its origin as a six-and-a-half-page style sheet in 1929, the APA manual has grown into a 208-page volume (third edition, 1983) covering nearly every aspect of article format, expressive style, submission to journals, and editorial process. Bazerman documented changes in the guidelines of the manual's first 20 years that parallel American psychology's own journey from a rich diversity of approaches to mental phenomena to the full hegemony of behaviorism.

Bazerman (1987) argues that the behaviorist worldview—stressing the environmental shaping of human response, at the expense of cognitive processes—has affected the way articles are organized. Reasoning about theory has taken a secondary role to "identify[ing] behavior that has been inadequately described and design[ing] an experiment to exhibit it" (p. 138). Thus the opening section of the typical article has become increasingly oriented to the declaration of the research hypotheses. The methods section has been shortened and reduced in importance to simple validation that the experiment was done cleanly and correctly. The results section has become the "center" of the article, with greatest prominence given to statistical displays, evidence, and limitations. Conclusions consist mainly of statements about whether or not the hypotheses were confirmed. Through this organization, "authors began presenting results as ends in themselves, to fill gaps in other results, rather than as potential answers to theoretical questions" (p. 139). The APA manual reflected and aided these changes in its increasingly detailed and rigid prescriptive advice.

Other fields also use conventions in structuring knowledge. Recently these conventions have been "discovered" by analysts of social science rhetoric. Gusfield (1976) examined sociological research of drinking drivers by an analogy to what playwrights do for their audiences when they write plays. For example, drinking drivers are cast metaphorically as "problem drinker" and "social drinker" types in order to conform to certain moral themes useful to the research narrative. Calas and Smircich (1988) evaluated management journal articles to understand how that field constructs its beliefs about "leadership" research. They looked at the codes used to establish legitimacy and importance, such as specialized language, highly valued terms ("sample," "reliability," "instrument"), section headings, citations, and the rhetorics of author acknowledgments and institutional affiliations. They then identified signifiers of leadership and told a "saga" of the prototypical leader (and what it says about the management research community) gleaned from the separate studies. Calas and Smircich assert that this literature tries to produce a governing "science" narrative about its object—a goal that, in their view, is impoverished and ill equipped to speak and listen in multiple languages about leadership.

According to rhetorical analysts of science, "How we are expected to write affects what we can write about" (Richardson, 1990, p. 120). Our practices of inquiry and the truths we attain are thoroughly embedded in the beliefs of a particular community (Rorty, 1979, 1987). Instead of converging on a metanarrative of reality, inquiry generates many alternative theories and textual models. It is the originality and explanatory power of a truth claim, its form of expression, and its relationship with the larger public that produce value in scientific communities and add to the ways members of society imagine themselves. This concept of science may seem threatening to those who want to retain the window-pane perspective, but it is probably liberating to those for whom social theory and empirical studies have poetic purposes.

AUTHORITY IN QUALITATIVE WORK

If we cannot trust science to deliver the unvarnished truth, on what grounds can we believe a research text? What must an author do to persuade readers that a study's assumptions, evidence, arguments, and overall workmanship are "correct"? Such questions center on the *authority* of research texts—especially the authority for mediating between disciplinary interests and the interests and actions of the people written about.

Marcus and Cushman (1982) define *ethnographic authority* as "the combined structure of a covering legitimation and the styles of evidence derived from it for the page-by-page descriptions and claims of a text" (p. 38). To a degree, readers make some decisions about vesting legitimacy in a piece of research as soon as they encounter it. A paper's title (especially its "title: subtitle" allusions) may be a tip-off to its topic and perspective (Atkinson, 1990, pp. 75-81). Where the paper is published, who wrote it, the citation list, and basic elements of the layout—through these signs, readers come to some threshold conclusions about its value. Even the prejudices of a given genre-readership axis may have something to do with how a report is perceived. Qualitative articles that appear in *Human Communication Research* and *Cultural Studies* may be considered "legitimate" in different ways by their respective readerships.

However, a more fundamental sense of legitimacy is at stake. No matter what journals or research ideologies they prefer, readers need to be convinced of a description's authenticity and significance. The researcher must *win* authority by skillfully reconstructing data, contextual features, and his or her own observing-and-experiencing self. The goal is to convince readers that what the study purports to be is in fact what it is. For most qualitative studies, authority takes the form, "You are there, because I was there" (Clifford, 1983, p. 118). By conceding that the author knows certain social facts by having earned their intimate acquaintance, the reader eases off on the skepticism that he or she might otherwise bring to bear.

How do ethnographies and other qualitative texts accomplish this work of convincing? Clearly, the field text creation and analysis processes described in Chapter 7 are important precursors. The ethnographer sorts through data of scenes, acts, and speech, including tales of "experiential savvy" and "fables of rapport" (Clifford, 1983), for materials to build a world. These scenes, acts, and speech should be described with a concreteness and detail that could only come from someone who was there and had the opportunity to reflect on how they occurred. If this world is unfamiliar to most readers, the author's role as an expert mediator (or tour guide) of the cultural unknown looms large. If the world is familiar to readers' everyday experience, the researcher often promises to reveal the underlying sense or "back region" of this well-known territory. Or the writer tries to shock readers into seeing it in a new light by radically juxtaposing surfaces of the object. For such studies, the rhetorical work of convincing may be tougher.

Narrative Presence

Textual authority hinges largely on the style and centrality of the author's narrative presence. The "voice" in which the author writes influences how readers imagine a scene and evaluate the text's research claims. Adapting concepts from literary criticism, Strine and Pacanowsky (1985) propose three dimensions of authorial presence in research texts: *authorial stance,* or the closeness of the researcher to the subjects' world, which can range from full involvement to detachment; *authorial status,* which refers to the researcher's presence within the discourse, from a voice that speaks intimately at the center of the work to a virtual absence from the subjects' world; and *contact,* which refers to the "writer-reader relationship that the researcher's stance and status enables" (pp. 288-289).

In many cases, stance and status are highly related; in other words, the researcher's style of involvement with participants is matched by the prominence of the researcher's textual role. In the genre of *ethnographic realism,* the author is usually a "scientific (invisible or omniscient) narrator who is manifest only as a dispassionate, camera-like observer; the collective and authoritative third-person ('the X do this') replaces the more fallible first-person ('I saw the X do this')" (Marcus & Cushman,

1982, p. 32). The tone is often nonjudgmental, giving all sides their due. By lowering the author's profile as much as possible, the text promotes a style of reporting that seems untainted by the investigator's physical or social habitation in the scene, or by any personal sympathies the researcher might have developed. There is a sense of the text having written itself from a base of indisputable evidence. The use of the omniscient, third-person voice encourages a timeless, holistic description of a culture or social group.

Ethnographers use a variety of strategies to make themselves less intrusive in their own stories. They claim that they "faded into the background" over time; they assert symbolic detachment from the scene (becoming ethnographers who are both nowhere in particular and everywhere at once); they personalize the ethnographer-informant relationship (becoming less like "ethnographers" and more like "just one of them"); and they falsely represent research interests or identity (Stoddart, 1986). These are disclaimers that allow the author to write an "objective" account of what happened. The subtext is, This would have happened even if I hadn't been here.

Even when authors seek to be objective, however, how they write may disclose their feelings and attitudes about the object of inquiry. Especially if the researcher has worked closely with one group of people, the text might implicitly take the point of view of those people's interests and motives. This is often the case when the participants are seen as experiencing oppressed, resistant, or conflictive relationships with others. As an example, in "Thrashing in the Pit: An Ethnography of San Francisco Punk Subculture" (1987), James Lull offers a systematic examination of the customs, dress, speech, music and media use, interpersonal relations, and identity politics of a "punk community" during the mid-1980s. He presents the piece in a plainspoken, documentary style, making liberal use of direct quotes, vivid vignettes, and close-up descriptions of numerous symbolic details. In his only mention of method, Lull says that the study involved "hundreds of hours of participant observation and interviewing in the locations where punks congregate—the places they live, eat, hang out, and attend music shows" (p. 226). But the article's authority derives mostly from its global sweep of seemingly every concern of importance. Lull claims his covering legitimation by showing us, in page after page, the very practical logic by which punks live their lives. Lull shows the subculture's outward exotica, often meant to shock or incite others, to be a "reasonable response" to the stifling conventions of the larger society.

Lull achieves this purpose, of depicting punks as reasonable and creative people, by aligning his stance closely with the participants' point of view while simultaneously objectifying events. An excerpt from the section headed "Enemies of Punk" shows some of this strategy at work:

> There are categories of people that for one reason or another cause problems for the punks. These groups also occupy the streets, where they come in contact with the punks. In many cases, they are other oppressed minorities. Generally, the conflict that takes place between punks and others is a function of multiple occupancy of the street.
>
> The most powerful and feared opponent is the San Francisco Police. Punks say that uniformed police often harass them for their appearance and behavior, particularly loitering. Proprietors of shops and boutiques also sometimes telephone the police if they believe a congregation of punks near their place of business is hurting relations with potential customers. Police are also looking for runaways and they sometimes question punks about the whereabouts of young people reported to be in San Francisco. There have been numerous police busts of punk squats. Further, police and punks sometimes clash at the site of demonstrations. David, a 24-year-old punk, told the *San Francisco Chronicle* that a friend was beaten during a peaceful anti-war demonstration because the jacket he was wearing said "One Million Dead Cops," the name of a San Francisco punk band. Another Mohawked punk said he is routinely bothered by the police on the street because of his appearance. "I told the fucking police, okay, if you want to be macho, go ahead and beat me up."

The first paragraph frames the argument by referencing "categories of people" that "cause problems" for punks. The possibility of punks having problems with individuals is not mentioned. This textual move is underscored by the individual punk voices that testify to police abuse further along in the excerpt. By excluding the individual voices of police, Lull effectively reinforces the claim that the police are a category. Moreover, "enemies" are those who victimize punks. The only qualification to this is that some enemies may be "other oppressed minorities," such as street gangs, "jocks," and "bikers" (p. 235). The statement "The most powerful and feared opponent is the San Francisco Police" is presented as factual. Who fears the police? In this context, the punks do. In particular, they fear an authority that seems to act in a brutally arbitrary manner, as the next several sentences indicate. Readers are pulled toward the interpretation that punks are a harmless and unwary people. It is the police, as "opponents" of punks, who "harass" and "bother" others. The point of this reading is not to impugn the accuracy of the account, or to offer an apologia for the enemies of punks. Rather, it is to show that Lull aligns his narrative with the participants in a way that preserves a documentary tone. Cloaked in normative description and the quoted statements of informants, the realist voice operates as a powerful means for enfranchising a particular way to regard a world.

In the realist ethnography, it is not always clear how the author made the journey from field experience to description (Marcus & Cushman, 1982); the "tracks" are either eliminated before publication or presented as the careful execution of an orderly method. If the personal travails by which knowledge was gained were laid bare, the author would risk exposing the partial nature of that knowledge. Above all, the realist ethnographer wants to achieve the effect of *verisimilitude,* or a plausible correspondence of a text to reality. The internal coherence of a text, and its apparent facticity, are important methods for leading readers to this judgment (Atkinson, 1990, pp. 35-56).

Other styles of narrative presence can be more prominent in the text and suggest different relationships with participants and readers. Even when writing in the third person, an author may break away to share an aside with the reader, or to comment ironically on what he or she is describing. Parts of an ethnography may invite the reader to evaluate a scene through the author's own eyes, to take on the author's response to a pivotal situation, or to imagine the consequences of being in the role of a participant. For example, in *Asylums,* his celebrated ethnography of inmate life in a mental hospital, Goffman (1961) uses the subtly humorous modes of satire, sarcasm, and irony to drive home the absurd or barbaric conditions of being incarcerated (Fine & Martin, 1990). This turn to a more personal view should challenge the reader's presumptions, yet it does this from an epistemic or moral perspective that the reader is enjoined to share with the author.

When the author takes the status of first-person agent, he or she often does so to prove that he or she was there at the scene, that he or she was a member in most respects, and that his or her role not only did not subtract from the analysis, but actually verified and extended it. In a sense, the first-person mode provides at least two authors' voices: the experiencing self, who enables expression of the member's perspective, and the analytic self, who enables the discipline's perspective on "the evidence." In his report on his study of the communicative practices of a South Texas high school student culture, Foley (1990) integrates observations of his own actions and reminiscences of his past with descriptions of the popular culture, status rituals, and identity performances of the youth he hung out with. Foley was a central actor in many of the incidents, so it seemed natural to him to write that way—as the "I" who was personally intrigued, bored, amused, and exhilarated by what he experienced. In this style of *confessional* writing, "there is an intimacy to be established with readers, a personal character to develop, trials to portray, and, as with realist tales, a world to be represented within which the intrepid fieldworker will roam" (Van Maanen, 1988, p. 75).

Pushing the Envelope

The reflexive awareness that characterizes fieldwork is now being applied to the write-up of field texts. This intensive deconstruction of the realist ethnography (and other kinds of texts) has unleashed efforts at writing that are often called "experimental," perhaps because they defy past conventions. The experimentalist impulse also justifies works that ask to be read as incomplete-on-purpose—texts that revel in their own limitations.

Especially in anthropology and feminist studies, ethnographies are being written that include voices other than just the ethnographer's. According to one view, such experiments threaten the myth of the heroic "Lone Ethnographer," who bestows rational meaning on a scene and "colonizes" it in the name of the discipline (Rosaldo, 1989, pp. 25-45). The dialogic (or polyphonic) ethnography, for example, makes room for two or more narrative presences, a strategy that enables multiple, contrastive versions of cultural reality to be voiced (Clifford, 1983; Dwyer, 1979). Besides reporting informants' words, the author tries to share responsibility for the interpretations with them. The point of this kind of text is not just for the author to get out of the way of the informants' tales. More generally, its purpose, and intended effect, is to *disperse authority* beyond the researcher's own. By showing in multiperspectival detail how a project gets defined by others, and how the author's self becomes a method, the author purposely shatters the realist illusion of objective description. The dialogic text does not try to be authoritative in the traditional sense. With participants taking a larger role in their own descriptions, they become historically situated persons, not quaint or exotic items.

Cultural critique can also be advanced by providing people the means to describe their own predicaments, arts, and visions (Marcus & Fischer, 1986). Critical ethnography starts out by assuming that most social scenes are characterized by relationships of power, domination, and subordination. The critical researcher recognizes that it is impossible *not* to take sides in conducting a study. As a privileged member of the culture, he or she feels an obligation to try to bring about better conditions for those who are studied, or at least a greater public consciousness of existing conditions. By providing fully realized representations of the lives and views of the less powerful, the ethnography itself becomes a political act (see Brodkey, 1987a; Simon & Dippo, 1986; J. Thomas, 1993). It challenges the dominant narratives of "the way things are (or should be)" that are widely taken for granted. The critical author claims authority from a combination of close-to-the-ground ethnography and the political argumentation that forms its warrant. Indeed, it is a real achievement of some critical ethnographies, such as Paul Willis's *Learning to Labour* (1977), to be able to wed macro-level political concerns with microdescriptions of local cultures.

Unfortunately, there is not enough space available here for further exploration of these experimental texts and others, such as staged performance (McCall, Becker, & Meshejian, 1990; Paget, 1990) and film/video ethnography (Loizos, 1993), that hold interesting possibilities for representing culture. Suffice it to note that, increasingly, qualitative researchers are regarding the realist genre, with its objectivist standards, as an Edenic state to which it is becoming harder to return.

THE READER-GENRE NEXUS

It is worthwhile to remember that authors also read, and that readers are not a passive, absorbent audience. Authors write as they do because of their socialization to particular disciplines, which includes reading those disciplines' "canonical" works as well as less noble ones. Readers read as they do because they compare, criticize, recommend, and, yes, write about what they read. The two parties are profoundly interdependent; the contract that binds them is *genre*.

Genres can be regarded as conventions for "the proper use of a cultural artifact" (Jameson, 1981, p. 106). Ethnographic genres, in particular, enable authors and readers to place individual works in relation to one another and in relation to the cultures and societies they describe. An ethnographic genre "provides expectations as to what a given social world *should* look like. . . . The genre(s) of ethnography give readers and writers exemplary texts against which they can evaluate such claims [of appropriate representation]" (Atkinson, 1992, p. 29). The task of making genre distinctions is key to establishing legitimacy for a research discipline (Rabinow, 1986).

The professional author knows that he or she must solicit attention, and arouse interest, from a more or less well-defined audience. Thus he or she tries to prefigure the likely audience. To an extent, notions of genre work backward from the eventual reading context to inform the production of text.

Marcus and Cushman (1982) and Van Maanen (1988) distinguish the different audiences for ethnographies in terms that apply fairly well to communication. Among what Van Maanen calls "collegial readers" are *area specialists*, who are most knowledgeable about the subject area, theories, and conventions for reading qualitative material. These readers converse with each other in published outlets by means of a technical discourse (or jargon) that maintains the boundaries of the specialty area. This discourse articulates the standards of quality by which specialists judge new contributions to a research genre. In qualitative audience studies, for example, I identified five traditions that draw on distinct intellectual sources and pursue different goals: social-phenomenological, communication rules, reception study, cultural studies, and feminist research (Lindlof, 1991). Although there is overlap among these, each tradition embodies a normative approach to fieldwork and textual form. Adherents will line up behind certain journals (e.g., *Cultural Studies, Media, Culture & Society,* and *Critical Studies in Mass Communication* for the latter three media audience genres) to engage examples of their preferred genres.

Collegial readers of the *general disciplinary* sort are "most concerned with the overall arrangement of a work and with the way theory is brought to bear upon the facts under consideration" (Marcus & Cushman, 1982, p. 51). Compared with area specialists, general disciplinary readers are not overly interested in the specific knowledge the work purveys. Rather, they attend to the elegance, strength, and scope of its theoretical contribution and the innovative ways in which the narrative is utilized. In communication, for example, readers across interpersonal, organizational, and mass communication have paid common attention to Janice Radway's *Reading the Romance* (1984) and Donal Carbaugh's *Talking American* (1988b) for their textual and conceptual contributions. The contributions of the two works to gendered media practices and cultural identity performance, respectively, are of more interest to area specialist readers.

Social science readers are those outside fieldwork traditions who "wish only to be informed about certain facts the fieldworker has unearthed. . . . Ordinarily social scientists take only the raw empirical material of an ethnography and ignore the arguments that surround and give meaning to the facts" (Van Maanen, 1988, p. 30). These readers are not interested in the epistemological, fieldwork, or text-reading problems of the study, and therefore will not be a primary audience for the author. Increasingly, however, social scientists outside communication are mining its qualitative output for information and perspectives useful to their own topics.

The *action-oriented readership* consists of administrators, government officials, research staffers, and others who seek "information which can be directly translated into practical policies and procedures" (Marcus & Cushman, 1982, p. 52). These qualitative reports downplay theory, emphasizing instead problem-specific or site-specific descriptions and options for action. Except for the health and organizational areas (Herndon & Kreps, 1993), "real-world" practitioners and qualitative communication researchers have not yet found much common ground.

Finally, the *general* (popular) readership "looks to ethnography for its message or truth in a culturally familiar framework and demands readability with only enough jargon to legitimize the expertise of the account" (Marcus & Cushman, 1982, p. 52). For ordinary folks, ethnographies of exotic or deviant worlds can be entertaining and instructive ways of confronting their cherished ethnocentrisms (Van Maanen, 1988, pp. 31-33). These readers want a user-friendly text largely devoid of theory. Often regarded by academics as suspect scholarship, popular ethnography sometimes presents plausible, insightful accounts of topics that are not fit for "serious ethnography." On rare occasions, a work can find audiences in both popular and scholarly realms (e.g., Kanter, 1977; Turkle, 1984).

The genre-reader nexus represents a community of discourse (Hunter, 1990). A text invokes a vocabulary of terms and concepts that connects the writer, reader, and the field setting to other texts in its genre (Atkinson, 1990, pp. 53-56). Journal peer review and the institutional reward system serve to stabilize the standards of legitimacy and quality. At times, however, this stability seems to become a goal in itself, creating inward-looking, self-serving cliques. The vitality of a community's intellectual conversation may suffer as members concern themselves with "correct" usages of concept and method. Fortunately, these communities are not closed systems. There are multiple audiences for any social science text, and enough genuine interest in innovation and clarity of expression to renew these communities' perceptions over time. And the unique contact that qualitative researchers have with their participants always opens inquiry to the unanticipated.

Writing

Twenty years ago, in analyzing sociology reviewers' evaluations of qualitative writing, Lofland (1974) remarked that "qualitative field research seems distinct in the degree to which its practitioners lack a public, shared, and codified conception of how what they do is done, and how what they report should be formulated" (p. 101). Has this state of affairs changed, for communication as well as for sociology? Although the human sciences have become more conscious of texts and writing, they are still not very confident about stating how reports *should* be written. In fact, the years since Lofland's observation have seen a blossoming of experiments in ethnographic writing (Clifford & Marcus, 1986), a blurring of genres (Geertz, 1983), and even greater ambivalence about the prospect of codifying rules for representation (see Hess, 1989).

In this section I present a range of options for writing up a study, as well as ways to implement those choices. I then examine two qualitative communication research texts in terms of their organization and rhetorical strategies. My purpose is to sketch some heuristic ideas for writing effectively in a general sense. The reader can take from the discussion whatever he or she finds useful.

TEXTUAL ORGANIZATION

Narrative, in qualitative writing, is a foundational concept (Brodkey, 1987b; Richardson, 1990). The researcher narrativizes the experiences of the people he or she studies through autobiographies, cultural stories, oral histories, jokes, tall tales, legends, myths, and rituals. Then, at the next level of narrative, he or she retells each story through a medium of analytic discourse (a thesis, journal article, book). This telling usually involves a series of connected events, an underlying sense to their connections, and time as an element within or between the events. The kind of text-organizing strategy the researcher adopts in approaching the writing task becomes a crucial decision.

One of the most common strategies, *thematic (or topical or typological) organization* involves the presentation of a set of topics or themes emerging from data analysis. The basic activity here is classifying: making classes (categories) out of the range of materials and experiences noted in the field. The roots of this mode of organization go back to the British travel and missionary accounts of aboriginal peoples a century or more ago (Pratt, 1986). In mid-twentieth-century anthropology, it became formalized as the "notes and queries" model, where standard topics (kinship, marriage customs, political and religious institutions, medicines, folk beliefs, and so on) are used to guide both data collection and ethnographic write-ups. Such texts tried to display and organize all of a culture's important social and cultural elements as an organic whole. Much the same approach can be found in community and urban studies in sociology of the same period (Atkinson, 1992, pp. 32-35).

The themes or topics an author uses may already be available from previous theory, as in the notes and queries model. Then it is a matter of using incidents to illustrate, elaborate, or recast concepts for the case under study. Katriel (1987), for example, studied the meanings of the highly ritualized communicative exchange of treats among Israeli children. She organized the main body of her text after Hymes's framework for studying face-to-face communicative events: instrumentality, setting and scene, act sequence, participants, key, norms of interaction, and ends. Within each topic, Katriel used observations and open-ended interview material, along with other conceptual sources, to explicate cultural patterns of appropriate and inappropriate sharing behavior as perceived by the children.

The theme/topic strategy brings order to a wide range of phenomena and builds theory by comparing studies using the same framework. But "it does have the potential drawback of leading one towards orthodox or obvious themes" (Hammersley & Atkinson, 1983, p. 224). It may also impose categories that have little relevance for a particular culture or research problem. The researcher can deal with this difficulty by building categories from the ground up, from participants' own folk terms and categories of social action, as Lull did to some extent in his study of punk subculture.

In a strategy that Hammersley and Atkinson (1983, pp. 220-221) call *narrowing and expanding the focus,* the author moves the reader through different levels of analysis by introducing a subject, exploring it contextually, and finally arriving at a general explanation—and repeating this for any number of themes. The author might nest each cycle within others, so that he or she finally reaches a superordinate explanation of the entire phenomenon. This effect can be pictured as a zoom lens, focusing close in on or further away from a subject. The narrowing and expanding may go on consecutively, resulting in a sort of edited "montage" understanding.

In my report on my study of parents' talk about home computing I employ a similar strategy (Lindlof, 1992). I first identify three key subjects of family discourse: family hopes and expectations of computing, household location of computers, and software copying. In each section, I introduce the subject briefly, use excerpts of discourse to reveal its complexity, and present an analysis that comes to a resolution. There are no essential connections among the three subjects, except that they represent problematics of families' negotiation of computing. And therein lies a problem for this strategy: "The *appearance* of such analytic presentation may be conveyed by the arrangement of a text, without actually being achieved by explicit argument" (Hammersley & Atkinson, 1983, p. 221).

The *puzzle-explication* strategy starts with an event or performance that is treated as puzzling, as something that needs to be explicated. The puzzle is fleshed out, usually as a story, and sometimes includes the author as a witnessing actor. The analysis pulls the puzzle apart and puts it back together, using one or more theories to reconfigure it. Often the conclusion is a more satisfying understanding of the event, but occasionally, the inadequacy or ambiguity of the theoretical strategy itself is revealed (Bateson, 1936). Geertz's (1973) essay "Deep Play: Notes on the Balinese Cockfight" is a famous example of this approach in cultural anthropology.

An example of the puzzle-explication strategy in communication is Rosen's "Breakfast at Spiro's: Dramaturgy and Dominance" (1985), which begins by unveiling the setting and initiating actions of an important event for a large Philadelphia advertising agency: its annual business breakfast. Throughout the rest of the article, Rosen presents episodes of speeches and other symbolic forms and interprets their ritual power for maintaining managerial dominance in the agency. In using this strategy, it is vital that the author choose an event that is robust—one that is capable of telling much about a scene.

Similar to puzzle explication, a strategy that *separates narration and analysis* provides the reader with two perspectives: one that experiences through the eyes (and other senses) of the author, and one that tries to critique through the disciplinary knowledge of the author. The objective, according to Hammersley and Atkinson (1983), is to solve the problem noted in other ethnographies of the conflation of description and evaluation. The separation of the ethnographic narrative from the analysis allows the reader to assess theoretic claims apart from descriptive claims. In the "narration," the author writes a full descriptive treatment of a culture; he or she sometimes appears in the first person. This narrative is not burdened with technical language, but it is also not totally free of the author's decisions about what to select and how to show it. The reader receives an accessible and informative account "from the inside" of a culture, before being exposed to the author's higher-level interpretations. Short of making all the data available, this may be the best way for the author to show how he or she moved from description to theory.

Foley's *Learning Capitalist Culture* (1990), mentioned earlier, follows this strategy. Most of the book is taken up with vivid, comprehensive descriptions of the key sites where Mexican American youths' experience intersects with the Anglos who politically dominate "North Town"—including the local civil rights movement, football, and the high school. Two essay appendices then appear that, respectively, interpret the ethnography by means of theories of cultural and political hegemony and discuss its field methods, narrative style, and data-interpretive process. Although a narrative-analysis separation strategy has much to recommend it, it is unclear to what extent a narrative can claim to be preanalytic (Hammersley & Atkinson, 1983, p. 222). Also, in some writings using this style, an analytic frame may seem to be simply "tacked on" to the ethnography; authors need to establish clearly the relationship between the two (Lofland, 1974, p. 109).

Two other strategies, the *chronology* and the *natural history* (Hammersley & Atkinson, 1983, pp. 215-220), are explicitly based in the conventions of narrative. A chronology models the text after the phenomenon itself—its phases, stages, or sequences. It is an effective way to express change as a function of the passage of time, and the constraints, institutional and personal, that go with and influence such change. In sociology, for example, symbolic interactionist studies document the "careers" of such social types as medical students, prison inmates, and marijuana users. Typically, the career trajectory begins with an interest (or diagnosis or incarceration or some other precondition), followed by entry into a setting, socialization to its norms and routines, adaptation of the individual's identity to others, and so on.

Although a normal cycle is usually the focus, some studies, such as Susan Krieger's *Hip Capitalism* (1979a), examine crises or transformations. Krieger conducted a field study of San Francisco radio station KMPX-FM during a period spanning the late 1960s to early 1970s, when its innovative format and organizational ethos were being co-opted by external forces. For Krieger, "the passing of time was integral to the possibility of cooptation and dealt with the problem of reference to it throughout by using a chronological order as the main organizing device of the text. . . . The tense of the narrative as a whole was set in recollection" (Krieger, 1979b, pp. 179-180). In her account, Krieger makes sure not to get too far ahead of the story, as it possesses characteristics of a fateful endgame. She also uses "flashbacks" to fill in the actors' histories and to show earlier events as contrastive or comparative signposts to changes later in time.

The natural history also takes a "career" path, but it is the career of the researcher entering and adapting to the cultural scene that organizes the text. We get an account of the author's discoveries and hardships as he or she experienced the "learning curve." This approach has the interesting potential of showing the reader the very process of doing qualitative research. A communication example of this strategy is Simpson's "Constructions of Self and Other in the Experience of Rap Music" (in press), an autobiographical account of the author's emergent interest in rap music, his readings of multicultural theory, and his desire "to explore my experiences, *my experiences*, of confronting rap music, the ways it moves through me." Simpson takes as his textual metaphor the recording technique of the "mix," and proceeds to structure the body of the paper through several mixes: the origins and development of the rap aesthetic, a textual exploration of rap, and a personal immersion in a rap performer's concert. Rather than deal with the mix-cum-analyses separately, Simpson brings out the cross-cultural ambiguities of his insertion in the rap phenomenon in a cumulative fashion that finally bears down on his own identities as researcher and cultural participant.

Hammersley and Atkinson (1983, pp. 215-216) caution that the natural history is difficult to sustain for very long in a text. More seriously, they claim that the natural history cannot really replicate the fieldwork and analysis experience, because the researcher's view of the entire project changes retrospectively. Past events are interpreted through the more sophisticated sensibility of the present. Hammersley and Atkinson assert that the natural history works best as transitional material within the larger text, such as when methodological or field relations accounts are called for. Although this may be true most of the time, Simpson's unapologetic and largely successful experiment tells us that in qualitative text making, there is no rule that cannot be broken.

CONSTRUCTING ACTORS

Qualitative texts in communication and other disciplines are inevitably populated with actors. Putting them into some purposeful motion helps the author to achieve authority in a qualitative research narrative. In most qualitative communication studies, especially those that rely on aggregate samples of informants or respondents, the social actor is specified at a low level. The author introduces an actor only because he or she needs to display an act or opinion or style of speech *representative of an analytic claim.* As we learned in Chapter 7, the qualitative analyst often detaches the words or acts of participants from the full context of available material, and then sort and categorize them many times over until he or she finds the best fit. Thus the researcher's main order of business as he or she begins to write is to craft adequate support for the argument—especially support that is diverse (examples coming from many different sources) or redundant (several examples of the same type of source saying roughly the same thing).

An excerpt from Smith and Eisenberg's (1987) study of change in the Disneyland corporate culture, described in Chapter 4, illustrates this approach:

> The friendly, family atmosphere [of mid-1960s Disneyland] was so convincing that most employees and many managers came to believe it uncritically, seeming at times to forget that Disneyland was a for-profit business selling a highly calculated fantasy world. Indeed, one long-term manager bemoaned the fact that people often forgot Disney was "a shrewd business man, intolerant of incompetence, who certainly knew how to make a buck." Despite recent hard times, the feeling of the "Disney family" persists. Some typical employee comments:
>
> > These people are like my brothers and sisters. (Ride Operator/Male/3 years tenure)
> >
> > It's family-like as far as the employees go. (Attractions Trainer/Female/ 8.5 years tenure)
> >
> > Real close knit . . . better than marriage. (Ride Operator/Male/6 months tenure)

The section continues with two more employee comments in the same vein. The employees' quotes are redundant for a reason: they convey the "persistence" of feeling that the authors claim exists. And the different sexes, lengths of tenure, and duties (the only personal identifiers shown) back up the claim that this is a "typical" sentiment, not confined to one type of worker.

As for the business manager, only one such informant is necessary, because his is apparently a minority viewpoint. He is known only as a business manager, but the way he spoke ("bemoaned") is an important qualifier for making the authors' point. There is no need to characterize how the other employees spoke because their function in the text is served by their numbers alone. Anonymous actors are not described in any psychological depth, nor do they have any temporal reality, because only their behaviors or views are needed to fill in a set piece (Atkinson, 1990, p. 134). Another example of this construction can be found in Lemish's (1982) work on television viewing in public places, in which actors (e.g., "an older nurse," "the only black student around") play brief, anonymous parts to illustrate television viewing rules. Authors use the anonymous actor to chronicle categories of persons and activity in open settings, or to utilize a stock character who is highly representative (or divergent) of a particular role.

It is not uncommon to see biographical profiles of the actors somewhere in a text, so that a reader can place their scattered appearances into some personal context (e.g., Lindlof et al., 1988). But for studies using aggregate samples this is not necessary, and may not be feasible because of space limitations.

A more vexing problem is that of showing how much or how often a sentiment or social action occurred (e.g., "most employees and many managers" in the first sentence of the above excerpt). Readers often trust that the author knows whereof he or she speaks without needing to see any actual frequencies or measures of central tendency. For some readers, however, this practice is problematic.

When the research problem concerns a cohesive group living in a defined setting, when one or more actors assume great importance in a study, or when the text depends on story forms to advance its arguments, more character detail is needed to make sense of the events being told. Full-bodied constructions of actors are found in such genres as holistic ethnography, the community or urban naturalistic study, the life history, oral performance study, and phenomenological case study. These tales are group or person centered, and usually depict events in which agonistic elements of an internal or external sort are encountered and resolved. This is the stuff of drama, albeit a kind grounded in the faithfulness to actual events that social science demands. Converting the other that one observes in the fluid, complex conditions of the field into a "character" is certainly part of the art of qualitative research. Questions arise. How much of the psychology attributed to the "character" is the result of insights about the other learned and verified in the field, and how much is the result of the needs of the narrative? What balance do we strike between describing someone in terms of a role versus his or her fully constituted self?

Even if this is not the place to explore these questions philosophically (see Fabian, 1983; Krieger, 1991), we can consider some of the practical issues of constructing "characters." Ethnographies that concentrate on specific social worlds, inhabited by limited numbers of social actors, usually endow those actors with memorable qualities. How well rounded these actors become, as characters, depends on the ethnography's purpose as well as the author's own resources. Krieger (1979b), for example, recalls some key decisions she made while writing *Hip Capitalism*:

> My guiding questions had to do with text and the problem of developing characters who would be capable of carrying its narrative. . . . I found myself accepting a sketchiness in the description of characters, and the problem then was how to do each sketch. . . . So I turned to their speech, how they expressed themselves and what they were concerned about, which in each case had an apparent coherence, as the chief means of converting them into characters. . . . I did not notice I had failed to give them bodies until I was beyond the point of thinking that would make a difference. I did think it would make a difference to give them lives, lives with ages, roughly designated pasts and uncertain futures, to give them roles with respect to the radio station, and as time went on to give them histories related to the history of the station. (p. 177)

The characters grew into their final form as the narrative itself took shape. The story of the station was in fact inseparable from a specific set of individuals. The characters Krieger contrived were drawn from biographies, talents, motives, and interpersonal relationships. It was through speech, however, that their experience would be conveyed to the reader. For other studies, authors may display authenticity (and its ambiguities) in other ways—by showing us the actor's physical appearance, personal belongings, and behavior toward others, for example.

An author cannot reproduce from notes and memories everything there is to know about an actor. He or she must trim, textually, the enormous individuality of any person in order to describe a *type* of person. Even the heroes of sociological ethnography—such as "Doc" in William Foote Whyte's *Street Corner Society* (1943)—can be discerned as people of a certain type who have functional roles to play in their social systems. In deciding whom to "cast" as central characters, the author looks for actors who display qualities integral to the constructs or conceptual thinking that drive the study, along with qualities that might claim readers' sympathies. Themes that are important to a study are often encountered as personality traits, or characteristic behaviors, of one or more of the main actors. The author may even design the overall work so that the revelation of character corresponds to and supports the development of a conceptual argument. However, a character is revealed most effectively in his or her actions. Authentic characters establish a "feel" for the scene as well as show the substantive things that happen there.

The main and supporting characters, who carry most of the work's action, are usually given fictitious names—pseudonyms—or nicknames in the text. (Some researchers like to use pseudonyms from the very start, and may even let informants choose their own.) In some studies, codes are used instead of names. In any case, a pseudonym should not resemble the true name, to protect the participant's identity and keep him or her from suffering any incrimination that could result from being identified. As much as possible, the author should remove or alter any identifiable characteristics of place, occupation, and personal relationships. These are useful practices to follow because an author's work is cited, distributed, and used in ways that are out of his or her control. Sometimes, however, reasons can be brought forward to warrant the naming of actors. For example, Krieger (1979b) decided not to use pseudonyms in *Hip Capitalism* because (a) most of the people she interviewed wanted to see their names in print; (b) it was "part of a bargain implicit" in participating (having their history written); (c) it would "keep [her] honest," because she would be attaching statements to real people; and (d) it was consistent with the subject she studied, which involved changes in naming, identity, and publicity (pp. 177-178).

EVENTFULNESS

Readers do not read qualitative works just to admire the pure logic of their propositions, or to assess their evidence in the conventional sense of scientific proof. Rather, the most estimable qualitative texts satisfy their readers' desire for vivid, intensive, fine-grained depictions of events.

Exemplars make a text "eventful." To go briefly back to Chapter 7, qualitative data analysis calls for shaping *exemplars* of meaningful action. The exemplar produces significance at two levels. At one level, it explicates a scene from the inside: the actors' own understandings of a communicative event. At the next level of significance, where the exemplar mediates between the scene and the analytic statements of the author, a more active participation by the reader is involved (Atkinson, 1990, pp. 90-92). The exemplar acts as a semiotic sign (Edmondson, 1984), rhetorically indicating a relationship with which the reader is already familiar. Readers use the exemplar to evaluate how plausible an interpretation is. Thus the argumentative mode of exemplars is more like an *enthymeme*: missing (but implied) parts of an argument force the reader to rely on his or her resources of meaning to complete the interpretation.

Exemplars animate the actors' and the author's own voice. They enable a rich author-reader contact by *showing* what happened, and by *suggesting* the kinds of interpretive codes and processes that may be operating. Certainly a study based on participant observation will produce numerous field texts that can be turned into exemplars, but interviews are also important resources for achieving eventfulness. Verbatim first-person reports provide believable anchors of authenticity. The author's management of time and points of view can enhance a reader's sense of what it must be like for members of a social group to experience events important to them.

There is only so much space in a qualitative text, and choices have to be made. Exemplars are not just "examples" in which one choice is as good as any other. Certainly one reason an author chooses a given specimen of field materials is that it "represents" the phenomenon. This could be thought of in the statistical sense of representativeness, of a single event characterizing an entire range of events. But qualitative researchers do not normally ask questions that require statistical answers. Rather, they ask which specimens are most *relevant* to the phenomenon. The researcher wishes to determine whether *this* place in the text is the most favorable site for advancing an argument with *these* ethnographic materials. The governing coherence of the story being told compels empirical support of a specific and timely kind. Not just any example will do. The researcher seeks evidence that addresses the descriptive and interpretive tasks at hand *and* coheres with the longer-range narrative goal.

Along with relevance, *clarity* is another quality of the eventful text. I refer here mostly to the quality of being incisive, of being an exemplar that gets to the heart of the matter. Is the event one that most clearly shows the relationship, ideology, problem, process, or mystery? Other events might be too obscure: The "point" gets lost or sidetracked in social action that is too complicated. Clarity can also mean succinctness. At times, a quick glance at a bit of social action is all the reader needs to understand how a communicative practice gets done, or what its effects are. Or the author can describe the salient features of a setting economically, as in an establishing shot in a movie, before going deeper to look at what the actors do there.

On the other hand, the author should consider the potential of an event to be *expanded productively*. In the field, the author should describe events in great detail and from many vantage points, so that outside the field he or she has more choices for arranging and rearranging the text's architecture. As Spradley (1980) puts it, "The concern with the general is incidental to an understanding of the particular" (p. 162). Before going to higher levels of meaning—such as those of a cultural domain, an entire cultural scene, or the cross-cultural (Spradley, 1980, pp. 162-168)—the author should thoroughly document the original meanings and actions in all their complexity.

Arguably, the sharpest pleasures come from *evocative* writing. Writing that relives the past moment in the analytic present evokes a vicarious experience in the reader. Evocative writing stays close to the ground, close to the breathing subject of the tale. It is writing that causes us to move when the focus moves. The cadence and authenticity of its dialogue include us as involved listeners; its calculating use of lull and suspense keeps us on the edge. Attention to detail is key to these effects. The author must get it right: the speech patterns of each character, the attitude conveyed by gesture, the smell and look of a place. The author must anticipate what the audience wants and needs to know, and when the audience should know it. The author must also manage the shift between the within-scene view and the view from outside. To put a finer point on this: It is critical that the author *know the difference* between the within view and the outside view of a scene, and that he or she be able to play out these views for the reader. Whether the author should try to bring these shifts of view to the frontal attention of readers depends on the desired style of author-reader contact: to produce insight (recognition) by a textual fragmentation or to induce credibility by the invisible editing of views.

Unfortunately, many qualitative reports suffer from distortions of descriptive effect. As Lofland (1974) notes, there is the "abstracted conceptualism style," where mention of field events is sparse and subordinated to a concern with categories, properties, types, and so on, and then there is the tendency of "general characterization," in which a great many individual actors and much scenic detail gets lost in the goal of creating a general type of actor or activity. Finally, Lofland observes, there is the "hyper-eventful style," in which the author describes incidents, interview excerpts, and the like one after another, without making much effort to organize them or reflect on their significance.

Going beyond awareness of these problems, the qualitative author should experiment with rhetorical devices. Three such tropes are hypotyposis, metaphor, and metonymy. Used to place the reader directly at a scene, *hypotyposis* is "the use of a highly graphic passage of descriptive writing, which portrays a scene or action in a vivid and arresting manner" (Atkinson, 1990, p. 71). It is often used at a key juncture, to signal the start of a passage or the arrival of new actors. For example, at the beginning of Rosen's (1985) article on ad agency symbolism mentioned earlier, we get a smartly described look at the smoothly regimented breakfast dining experience:

> Breakfast, one hundred or so eggs Benedict marched in by suited waiters in synchronization, was served almost exactly at 8:30. Nine down at a table, nine down at the next.
> "Coffee or tea for you?"
> "Yes, thank you."
> "Are you finished, sir? Would you like more coffee?" Code for letting them take your near-empty plate. (p. 32)

In Chapter 7, *metaphor* was discussed as a sense-making device in field analysis. In narratives, it is also a sense-altering rhetorical device. Metaphorical description can jolt a reader's taken-for-granted notions or comment cunningly on a conventional act. Again, from Rosen's article:

> When Walter [the agency president] had finished calling the names of those employed at least five years, over 25% of all members were standing, a physical symbol of valued seniority. When Walter asked everyone to applaud themselves, all were subject to the technique of clapping, the loud noise signifying, "We have all achieved," "we are good," "I am good," "the agency is good," "I belong," and so on.

Metonymy describes one aspect of a phenomenon in order to interpret another part of it, or the phenomenon as a whole. In metonymy, then, meaning is created by the association of one thing with another. Because the event selected may be a particularly critical or vivid case, this can be a powerful method of characterization. For example, in the excerpt from Lull's study of the punk community, the use of "demonstrations" as a site of punk-police clashes functions as a metonymic figure for the police posture toward punks. These three—hypotyposis, metaphor, metonymy—do not exhaust the range of devices available to authors, but they are prominent ways to construct events evocatively.

TWO COMMUNICATION TEXTS

It is now time to examine communication texts, to understand how aspects of authorial presence, genre, textual organization, actor construction, eventfulness, and style come into play. The two articles I have selected exhibit high levels of skill in conceptualization, design, and execution. They are not classics, but it is debatable whether there are any classic qualitative communication studies at present. These examples reveal different approaches to representation. It is not possible to offer the full articles here or even to show very much of their texts. Interested readers should read the articles themselves.

Viewing Dave

The title of Richard J. Schaefer and Robert K. Avery's (1993) article in *Journal of Broadcasting & Electronic Media*, "Audience Conceptualizations of *Late Night With David Letterman*," forewarns us that this is not a study of social action as such, but of interpretive practice. This notion is confirmed in the first paragraph, where the authors clear a space, uncluttered by citations save one, to highlight the claim that a "transitory but shared interpretational framework is what marks members of [interpretive] communities as competent readers" (p. 253).

This opening sets up the ensuing three pages of literature review. The authors trace the theoretical nuances and implications of regarding audiences—not media texts or social structure—as the primary cultural locus of meaning in mediated communication. Academic discourse on this subject is depicted as a battleground. Schaefer and Avery deftly organize positions and counterpositions to suggest basic differences between schools of thought (e.g., interpretive social scientists versus critical theorists, self-report versus social-contextual study). This approach leads them to use particular "point people" (e.g., Condit, Carragee) to enunciate positions and to use quotation marks around controversial terms (e.g., "polysemic"), perhaps to distance themselves from the terms. They justify the study by citing the unique properties of *Late Night* and the scarcity of studies on "audience activity, meta-television aesthetics, and communal patterns of interpretation." The overall impression is that of a study founded primarily on a need perceived in intradisciplinary argumentation, and only secondarily in problems or changes in the phenomenon itself.

A detailed methods section lays out the two-part research plan: a survey of self-selected *Late Night* viewers and focus group interviews. A strong element of operationalism runs through the discussion of content coding procedures, response rates, sample sizes, and so on. There is little reflexive comment on field conditions, subjects' interpretations, or the researchers' own roles.

The study's findings follow a themes-and-topics organization, bifurcated into a section on survey findings and a section on analysis of the focus group discussions. The survey part reflects a long audience research tradition of decomposing the audience into an array of demographic, usage, and attitudinal variables. Thus, for early 1988, the habits and perceptions of 190 *Late Night* audience members in Salt Lake City were systematically extracted and processed into a legitimated data format (e.g., "Only about one in nine [11.1%] said that they did not regularly talk with others about the program"; p. 260). The effect of this, whether intended or not, is to convey a certainty about the anatomy of the beast—the view from Olympus of Salt-Lakers-watching-*Late Night*—before going to the slipperier stuff of interpreting a-few-Salt-Lakers-talking-about-watching-*Late Night*.

Schaefer and Avery's authorial presence is generally a detached one. They disappear into the text. The focus group members themselves are anonymous. Besides being fans of "Dave," they have no identities; no personal history attaches to the quotes that are chosen. This audience exists only as discursive subjects, an approach that is not really at odds with the interpretive community concept. However, the interactive nature of the focus group context does not survive into the article. Although there might have been a reason to use focus groups instead of individual interviews, based on the authors' theorizing of interpretive processes, the text displays samples of talk that could have been produced in any number of ways.

The concepts of interpretive competence and community, and the genre rule breaking of *Late Night*, carry over from the introduction to create the themes of the qualitative text, and to introduce the block quotes of the interviewees. This theoretic sensibility, together with the frequent insertion of findings from the survey, seems to anticipate the respondents' remarks, which function almost exclusively as illustrations.

However, the authors counterbalance their superior position in the text by alluding often to the viewership abilities of the respondents. Thus the *Late Night* viewers reveal "close readings of the show's structural, performance, and production elements" (p. 263). They possess "interpretive competence and [a] sophisticated sense of irony" (p. 266). Moreover, "their critical perspective and sense of alienation matched Dave's" (p. 266). The respondents are not only depicted as critics, they are also peers of Dave and the authors by virtue of being very clever and in the know—despite the fact that the fans' insights are expressed in colloquial, nontechnical language. For example:

> Another dimension of the *Late Night* audience is evident in how the survey sample and focus group participants described the program's viewing audience. More than three-fourths (76.1%) of the survey respondents indicated that the typical Letterman viewer was like them—cynical, ironic, young adults. One focus group member even addressed the issue metagenerically by framing the audience in terms of the old and new late fringe aesthetic sensibilities.
>
> > He's [Carson's] going for an older audience and a more conservative audience. I see Letterman and that's my kind of humor; that's the stuff I find funny. I don't think Johnny Carson is unfunny. He's just targeted to a different audience. And I'll tell you this, I think the two audiences—the Carson audience and the Letterman audience—they do intermix somewhat. But I think for the most part the Letterman audience does not watch Carson and for the most part the Carson audience does not watch Letterman. (pp. 267-268)

In their concluding section, Schaefer and Avery revisit the issues that opened the piece. Now, armed with their findings, they assert themselves more authoritatively in the same scholarly conversation that at first was merely observed. They display a greater sureness about their own positions concerning generic understandings of the audience. Interestingly, the quotes are off such terms as *polyvalent* and *polysemic*, which they now accept as meaningful attributes of viewer-text interaction.

Significantly, in the last three paragraphs, the authors critique their own efforts in a context of past and future recommendations for audience research. The piece ends on a note of self-effacement. It is an example of the "claiming less is more" rhetoric often seen in traditional social science articles. In many other ways, such as the format (i.e., literature review/research questions/method/findings/conclusion) and the reticence of authorial presence, the article conforms to APA manual-influenced expectations of what a social science article should look like. However, it should be said that the authors' focused interests and the nature of their contacts with social actors justify a format that takes few risks.

Ballpark Culture

Like the title of Schaefer and Avery's article, the title of Nick Trujillo's 1992 article in *Western Journal of Communication*, "Interpreting (the Work and the Talk of) Baseball: Perspectives on Ballpark Culture," says much about the author's approach. The stylistic device of using parentheses embedded in the title is not gratuitous. The formal part of the title, "Interpreting . . . Ballpark Culture," expresses the article's purpose in disciplinary lingo. But "(the Work and the Talk of)" are simple words, words that the people he studied would understand and use. The words tell what they *do*. The parentheses indicate that this meaning is enclosed inside another order of meaning. Thus Trujillo implies that there is a practical world of talk and work that he has personally visited, and that he will now revisit with his readers from the communication discipline. This enclosing of direct experience within other "perspectives" is indeed what follows in the text.

The first thing one notices, after the abstract, are quotes from three ballpark workers: a newspaper sports reporter, a clubhouse manager, and an usher. This form is unusual for an empirical report, but not for an essay, which this article closely resembles. Each speaker has something different to say about working at a ballpark: It is a job ("The ballpark pretty much is the press box and it's basically my office"), it is a home ("To me, the ballpark is just like home"), it is a place of the heart ("I like to come here in the morning before anyone gets here and I just sit quietly in center field. The ballpark is a theatre for the soul") (p. 350). These sentiments from within the culture offer a contrasting level of experience to the theoretical discussion that comes next. They also preview the sort of ethnographic materials found later in the article.

Trujillo reviews several ways of understanding the organizational culture of baseball, deriving from functionalist, critical, and romantic traditions. He does not pit these against one another, but brings them forth separately as valid ways to "study many aspects of sport in society, of organizational life in a capitalist system, of American cultural values, and of communication and the mass media" (p. 351).

In the methods section, Trujillo relates the depth, breadth, and multiple participatory modes of his two-year ethnographic venture with a baseball organization. In addition to attending numerous games as a fan and being invited to such events as off-season banquets and autograph appearances and employee orientations, Trujillo also became a "ballpark wanderer." Given an employee pass by management, he could tour any section of the ballpark before, during, and after games. This enabled him to talk with his ballpark subjects in natural situations. He also gives ample description of his entry and acceptance in the scenes he observed, including his open note taking. In all, Trujillo provides in this section a strong covering legitimation for the reader's belief that he was there and that he was self-aware of his positions *there*.

Most of the article is organized in a narrowing-and-expanding-focus mode. However, it is more complex than that. Compared with Schaefer and Avery—who set off their participants' comments clearly from their own analysis—Trujillo achieves a more synthetic effect by creating metaphorical descriptions out of his exemplars of work and talk. Most of the theme sections (e.g., "Baseball as Business: The Ballpark as a Site of Capitalist Labor"; "Ballpark Communitas at Home (Plate)") open with evocations of the theoretic frames. For example, "Baseball as Business" begins with a view of sport as a form of "industrialized labor," in which specialization, standardization, and a reliance on science and technology are all complicit with the need to maximize output. Trujillo then moves into a series of exemplars that contextualize this idea in ballpark sites and acts.

Some of the exemplars are spliced together in a "beads on a string" fashion, which concentrates their impact:

> Much formal communication at the ballpark is used to train workers to complete their tasks in a standardized and mechanized manner. Supervisors at pre-season orientations teach routinized procedures to toll booth operators and ticket takers about handling money, to food service workers about making nachos and pouring beer with a one-half inch head of foam, to security guards about talking in ten-dash codes, and to parking lot attendants about controlling traffic flow. (p. 355)

Another is related as a story told by an informant. Her ironic style tells us that she experiences resignation to her job, but that she also resists it:

> As one teenaged plaza attendant described her routinized greeting: "I don't have to strike up a conversation or anything. I just smile and say, 'Hi, three dollars, enjoy the game.' I do that about a thousand times a night. I guess that means I smile about eight-one-thousand times a season." (p. 355)

Still another exemplar tells of a typical sequence of action:

> The cleanup operation at night is a depressing backstage drama, performed for empty seats. During the game, the ballpark is alive with (relatively) fresh

smells and a brightly lit stage for the graceful performances of (mostly) shapely ballplayers who receive musical accompaniments from the Diamond Vision crew and lively ovations from the audience. After the game, however, the ballpark shrouds a dark and dingy procession of shadowy caricatures who stoop awkwardly in the empty stands to the background wheezing of congested airblowers. (p. 355)

What these individual exemplars do not show is the manner in which they are tied together by a metaphor of alienation—the realization that the most alluring of capitalist illusions is built on a rationalized order and numbing routines carried out at the lowest level by nameless, unseen workers. Because the article is based on the notion of "perspectives" (not the discovery or testing of propositions), it is the *tour* of situated voices and scenes that assumes importance. Each section works through large and small exemplars of different sources and forms. It is a seamless discourse in which many voices are brought into the conversation and are given equivalent places within it. We hear from scholars, the sports literati (e.g., Roger Angell, Bart Giamatti), managers, employees, TV people, the team owner, and Trujillo's own musings and observations. Although the scope of his treatment is in the ethnographic realist tradition, Trujillo's micromanagement of ethnographic detail to create montagelike pictures for the reader is actually closer to "impressionist" writing (Van Maanen, 1988).

It is therefore not surprising that the arguments in each section, and in the article as a whole, do not move forward in a linear way. The beginning and end points of the sections are often similar: The opening paragraph introduces the perspective in a fairly abstract way, and the ending summarizes it. Likewise, the conclusion of the piece returns to the worldviews of romantics, functionalists, and critics. There, at the end, Trujillo meditates on his own identification with each worldview as it intersects with the world of baseball.

Finally, Trujillo's authorial presence is a noteworthy feature. His first-person presence rises to the surface whenever there is a turn of focus in the study. It is there when he announces his purpose ("In this study I focused on the meaning of the ballpark to different workers and I examined how various objects . . . were interpreted"; p. 352) and when he writes about his fieldwork procedures ("I also dictated additional notes into a tape recorder as I drove home after the game and then elaborated those notes in writing when I arrived home, sometimes while watching the rebroadcast of the game [my 'video fieldnotes']"; p. 354). This voice helps align us with the one who did the study. More significantly, its absence during the more conceptual exposition helps us separate the Trujillo view-from-the-field from the Trujillo view-of-the-discipline. Even when his "I" is not narrating, the writing is alive with a fine sense of storytelling. The actors appear anonymously, but Trujillo's constructions of their speech and attitudes make these cameos memorable.

Though "Interpreting (the Work and the Talk of) Baseball" can hardly be called experimental, the article does take a more adventurous path than many other examples of qualitative communication research. Its marriage of the essay and the empirical report permits the author some artistic room to "defamiliarize" a familiar cultural scene.

PROFESSIONAL CRAFT

The charge of this chapter is to establish the importance of strategy, style, and claims for writing qualitative texts. In this zero-sum environment of limited space, issues of the craft of writing have been given short shrift. There are, however, several excellent sources that interested readers can consult. For advice on how to write social science prose and avoid dysfunctional writing habits, Becker's *Writing for Social Scientists* (1986b) has become something of an instant classic. A variety of other articles and books cover the basics of organizing materials, getting mentally ready to write, outlining, writing, editing, and preparing manuscripts for publication (e.g., Bogdan & Biklen, 1992, pp. 184-197; Fine, 1988; Fox, 1985; Wolcott, 1990). For communication, Rubin et al.'s *Communication Research: Strategies and Sources* (1990) is a one-stop shopping guide to social scientific communication research practice, including format conventions for writing journal articles. Knapp and Daly's *Guide to Publishing in Scholarly Communication Journals* (1993) poses and answers common questions about submitting scholarly communication research to journals. *The Iowa Guide* (Garner & Dyer, 1989) offers a comprehensive directory of communication journals, including their editorial policies, acceptance rates, circulation, and so on.

Before leaving this subject, I feel obliged to pass along a few maxims of my own, born of my checkered career as a writer and the best of what I have read and heard. First, you should read many ethnographies, for their depth of understanding and styles of presentation. An acquaintance with different genres will expand your own choices in writing. You should also read other forms of writing—especially fiction, essays, and journalism—often to appreciate the inventive ways in which description and narration can be accomplished. More pointedly, because the play of language is so much at the center of qualitative inquiry, you should *enjoy* reading fiction, essays, and journalism.

Wolcott (1990) believes that the serious writer of ethnography should become predominantly a writer, not a reader, of research. And Fine (1988) advocates the cultivation of an authorial persona (or voice) of one's own. For me, the ideas are connected: The more your authorial "voice" feels right, the more you find and exploit a rich program of inquiry, and the more you actually write, the less appeal "reading" will have as a separate activity—and, probably, the less time you can afford to devote to it. This is not to say that you should write unbothered by what else is being published. Rather, the serious writer reads selectively: to inform his or her own work and, of course, to know what's going on in the field.

Virtuosity of expression should not be expected at every sitting. You should become disciplined enough to write when you are not in the best of moods, and tolerant of yourself when the work does not meet expectations. Writing well is an outcome of doing it regularly; not being too censorious (at the first pass, anyway); thinking in terms of steady gains, not long distances; and accepting the critique of others, including journal reviewers, only when you are ready to hear something new, dissonant, or "out of left field" said about your work.

Editing is an ongoing process, done at regular or natural breaks in the writing schedule. But encountering a text at odd times, like seeing a friend in an unexpected setting, can lead to a different and useful take on it. No word or sentence is sacrosanct. Every word and sentence has to pull its weight for the greater good of the manuscript (Becker, 1986b). Prose can be functional *and* aesthetic.

Writing always takes longer than you think it will. Don't be hard on yourself. If you must set deadlines, try to factor in time for unforeseen contingencies, a computer problem or two, and some time at the movies to clear your head.

You should keep audience at the front of what you write. True, we write for ourselves in some ultimate sense, but our effort is wasted if the actual audience finds it obscure, tedious, or precious. Do not delude yourself into thinking that the use of jargon constitutes the coded handshake of a hip circle of scholars, or that the majesty of your thinking will be recognized no matter how you put it on the page. You owe something to your readers: a commitment to understanding, which is advanced by a willingness to speak across to them, not down or within. And finally, your actions as an author have consequences for you and the discipline. You should not submit a paper for publication if you have any questions about its honesty or about violating the ethical contracts struck with gatekeepers, participants, and coauthors.[3] You are known by what appears under your name.

Conclusion

As "custodians of a discourse" (Eagleton, 1983, p. 201), writers of texts like this one often end on a note of self-congratulation. They proclaim as worthy most of what has been learned on the trip, earnestly (but briefly) point out the limits of their teachings, and positively vibrate with optimism for what are billed as challenges of the future. But any future they recommend will probably not be very inspirational, much less dangerous, because it grows straight out of what has been done before—the examples of correct practice. There is no getting around the fact that the methods text is profoundly conservative. Its charge is prescriptive. It speaks an approved language of advice, caution, and detachment. The reader should be suspicious of last-minute enthusiasm from a source of that kind.

Having said that, I find it difficult not to engage in some of the same rhetoric I just warned about. Ethnography and related forms of inquiry have answered the need to study how communicating is actually done in everyday life, and to understand its social, cultural, and historical significance. Qualitative communication research has shown that it can generate socially valuable knowledge whose processes of inference can be inspected and contested. Like it or not, the heady times of the 1980s, when ethnography in communication was new and notorious, are over. The hard-won achievements of qualitative studies have entered and extended the conversation of the discipline.

These achievements have changed the minds of many as to what effective scholarship can be. The turn to a paradigm centered in meanings permits us to observe and listen more intently to the predicaments of our time. It is less clear, however, how these studies permit us to act. In other fields, sociology and education among them, qualitative studies enable less favorably situated individuals, groups, and communities to speak to elites more directly (if not eloquently) than in almost any other discourse form. This still cannot be said of communication studies, which can be characterized generally as critiques in search of someone to tell their stories to.

Finally, the growing self-consciousness about text construction and use is another sign of its practitioners' sophistication. Rightly, I think, the fallacy of believing in science as a revelatory method has been exposed.

So there seems to be an aura of maturity about this enterprise. Maturity is something most of us strive for, because it brings us the rewards of recognition, but maturity can be deadening if it means we no longer take risks. Risk taking is essential for any important endeavor to be worth doing. If we build a project around safety nets, then the game has been lost already. Failure must always be a real possibility.

In risking failure, one risks losing something very dear: resources, time, the trust and cooperation of the people we study, the approval of our peers, professional rewards, or our own basic beliefs and commitments, which can be the hardest of all to lose.

Of course, we do not meet the possibility of failure head-on every time. If we did, it would lose its ritual power. Reckless risk taking is worse than none at all. Certainly we should behave conservatively most of the time, if only for self-preservation. By risking failure strategically, on selected occasions, we expand our own skills and sensitivities and make it more likely that a real advancement for the communication discipline will occur. As readers, we usually know when a risk has been taken, not necessarily by the largeness of the research claim, but by the ingenuity and obvious difficulty of its construction.

In concluding this book, I want to suggest some of the personal and interpersonal resources a qualitative inquirer can draw upon in taking risks selectively. Many ideas suggest themselves, but three seem especially pertinent at the moment.

ASKING BETTER QUESTIONS

The goal of asking better questions may seem to oppose the highest priority of science, which is to increase our certainty about what can be said of how the world works. Undeniably, a basic reason for research is to test claims, refuting (provisionally) those that do not survive and extending the reach of those that do where it is justified empirically and logically. However, the pursuit of verification must always be subordinate to the formulation of questions that are ever more incisive, probing, well crafted, and relevant to the needs and aspirations of human communities. Knowledge, no matter how apparently conclusive, is always partial. Our trust in method is misplaced if we expect it primarily to lead the way out of problems. Methods that locate the existence and nature of problems, contradictions, or mysteries, or that explicate their significance, are far more worthy of our continuing efforts, and perhaps of our trust.

Surely it can be said that qualitative inquiry already expounds a logic of discovery. And experience confronts us continually with situations that seem to discredit, or at least erode, the authority of what we know. It seems that questions will be asked, no matter what. Yet a task of any science should be to develop methods of asking questions about what we want to do, why we are doing it, and how it should be done. Some of this methodology may involve (a) asking the obvious, out loud, from the layperson's view (the more ridicule one gets, the better?); (b) looking for contradictions in an otherwise tight conceptual scheme, by making its own terms strange, or by trying out all empirical variations of its key constructs; (c) submitting oneself to the conditions inhering in the questions one is asking, without holding anything back; (d) asking who gets hurt, and who gets helped, if there is any truth to what one believes; (e) wondering why the currently discredited theory is so bad; and (f) becoming an archaeologist of one's own interest area, not to turn it into a teleological narrative, but so that it starts to appear as a scheme of imperfect and historically contingent artifacts—including the currently fashionable ones.

MAKING THE AUTHENTICITY
OF EXPERIENCE PROBLEMATIC

Qualitative inquiry strives to reach across to the world of the other—but who is this other? Perhaps an intersection of a self and some experiential realities that are not our own? Inquiry is aimed at elucidating the *authentic* character of these modes of being. A presumption of the stability and knowability of the other goes with the researcher into the field. Our own terminology—the field, a role, a coding system, triangulation, and so on—conspires with this interest to seek fixed spatial and temporal referents.

But it is precisely "authenticity" that is problematic. The other is becoming both easier and harder to locate. As world economies continue to integrate, barriers to movement across borders—both legal borders and those that are culturally imagined—come down. Electronic media have expanded pancultural programming on a global scale at the same time that specialized media are marketed into the intimate precincts of interests and lifestyles. The traditional other rises to meet us now, not just in *National Geographic* or anthropological monographs, but on prime-time television newsmagazines, on the subway, on the university campus, and when we arrive at Cancun or Nairobi or Yellowstone Park.

On the other hand, the other is more elusive than ever to identify, much less keep steady in our sights for systematic study. Not tied to geography, or to reliable socionetworks, this other is now more likely to appear in a transient cultural form—in a self-help group, on the Internet, or just passing through the bureaucracy. Knowledge of what we, as members of a scientific community, do is no longer an elite preserve. Notions of "communication" and "the impact of the media," among many others, traverse the most open of public arenas. Disciplinary language exchanges freely with many other discourses, proliferating meanings that are harder or even impossible to trace to their origins. And the notion that science should be accountable to broad standards of ethical and political performance is a profound, but little-noticed, historical change in the way things used to be.

Not where, but *when* is the self and how do we begin to ascertain its protean authenticity? This is a significant challenge on many levels. Does a person now pass through several stages of selfhood (or states of "otherness," even to him- or herself), as in serial monogamy? Is this, in some fashion, how the research career should be conceived as well? How do we make the scene?

MAKING THE RESEARCH ACT
AN INVITATION TO PARTICIPATE

There has often been a tendency among authors to think of themselves as owners of what they have written about, as though the writing of an ethnography *creates* a group, organization, or phenomenon. Of course, this is not literally true. But as a matter of scholarly capital, in which reputation (if not knowledge) rests partly on the exclusivity of one's interpretations, the ethnography does often displace its living subject. Once we have secured a franchise, so to speak, no one else can sell *our* product.

But qualitative inquiry, as we have seen at many points in this book, is thoroughly collaborative. For example, participant observation draws upon many of the skills and stocks of knowledge that are utilized by any socially competent human being. Quite a few ordinary folk are just as good as I am at some of the "research" tasks I do. Informants also become just as much a part of how a project gets defined, and how it turns out, as its investigators. There are questions of who is responsible for an interpretation, and the distinctions of authoring grow ever more tenuous.

Certainly, the appeal to institutional certification is one way to control who can do a qualitative study, and who can get credit for it. But that sort of holding action only exposes the arbitrariness of authority. In truth, there are no entrance requirements for going out and doing an ethnography, and, as novelists, filmmakers, journalists, travel writers, and others have proven, there is no exclusivity that a work going by the title "ethnography" can claim.

A project invites others to participate in the truth of its description, and in the complexity and openness of its interpretations. It invites participation by recognizing its own limits. By what right can we author a culture into existence? What do we risk by giving up ownership rights?

I am reminded of the kind of fishing called "catch and release." We go along a shore until it looks like there might be some action. We try different lures or different tackle until we get it right, until we catch whatever it is we are after. We admire the prize for a while, all of its dazzling surfaces (some of which reflect us), but there is really no reason to keep it out of the water. It is time to release, and move on.

Notes

1. The expression *writing up*, as Atkinson (1990, p. 61) points out, is a folk term among ethnographers that connotes the constructive character of writing an ethnography. Thus one "writes up" a report or monograph from notes that were "written down" in the field.

2. Also, as Crapanzano (1977) suggests, the act of writing is arguably necessary for the ethnographer to work through the dislocations of self incurred in the field experience, and to affirm his or her identity by writing to the ethnographic "other" as an audience. Thus "the act of writing ethnography is an act of self-constitution—of a willing objectivation of self well worth the price of alienation" (p. 72). In a sense, writing continues the confrontation with the "other" people and practices experienced in the field, but now through a professional disciplinary language (and a professional "self").

3. Authorship credit is both important and problematic. It is important because publication authorship and citations are the "capital" with which the academic world operates, and by which the reputations of individual scholars are made. It is problematic because there are no codified rules governing the dispensation of authorship, and abuses between colleagues and between faculty and students sometimes occur. However, some informal guidelines do exist.

Credit for a research article is usually a matter of precedence in an author list. For example, the first author is assumed to have had the most central role in the project, the second author the next most important role, and so on. Only if the authors explicitly state (usually in a note) that they contributed equally to the project does an alphabetical order of author names under the title denote no precedence. Even so, citations of the article in other people's articles or books will not carry this note, and it will again be assumed by casual readers that the first author has the most authorial "ownership" of the piece—the default interpretation. Another way to share credit equitably (if not equally) is to rotate author order if more than one article is produced from a project. Of course, each article should treat a different aspect of the project.

Author credit is ordinarily given if a person was involved in one or more of the following activities: conceptualization of the project (including grant proposal writing), methodological design (including instrument development), data collection (including working "in the field"), data analysis, and report writing. (It is important to note that data collection is a more significant activity in qualitative research than in most quantitative studies, where administering a survey or conducting an experiment involves few in-the-field strategic decisions.) The greater one's involvement in the full range of these activities, the more author credit one accrues. Activities that, in and of themselves, ordinarily do *not* count toward author credit include literature searches, clerical work, serving as human subjects, coding or indexing field notes, transcribing interview tapes, providing advice, and supervising in the role of thesis adviser.

The last item above is probably controversial. Some faculty supervisors of theses and dissertations believe they merit coauthorship on their graduating students' published work, by virtue of their having worked closely and intensively with the students on the projects. Other faculty view themselves as serving in an advisory role, albeit an important one, in supervising projects conceived and executed by students. They will usually not want any author credit on the resultant publications. Some faculty members might make exceptions to their normally consistent modes of action, depending on such factors as how much effort and conceptual influence they had to commit to making particular students' projects successful.

Clearly, graduate students are in vulnerable career positions. Some may feel pressure to make concessions on the rights to their intellectual work. This is a real predicament that is found occasionally in other relationships of unequal power, such as the senior faculty-junior faculty collaboration.

There are no easy solutions to the dilemmas of coauthorship. Even when two people of equal status are working on a project, it is sometimes hard to tell what kind and amount of work merits a certain author order. It can also be a delicate interpersonal matter. I try to adhere to two procedures. The first is for all of the research team members to "inventory" jointly what we will do, in terms of specific activities, and to continue monitoring the workload throughout the project's life. The second is to try to decide, at the beginning of a project, how the authorship will likely be apportioned—and even the types of articles that will be written for journals or other outlets. Changes in the size of team members' roles in the project may result in alterations of the author order. Other unforeseen changes may occur. No matter what procedure one adopts, one should approach issues of authorship with a commitment to full and open information, a strong sense of fairness, and a sensitivity to the needs and knowledge of all who are involved.

References

Adler, P. A., & Adler, P. (1987). *Membership roles in field research.* Newbury Park, CA: Sage.

Agar, M. H. (1980). *The professional stranger: An informal introduction to ethnography.* New York: Academic Press.

Agar, M. (1982). Toward an ethnographic language. *American Anthropologist, 84,* 779-795.

Albrecht, G. L. (1985). Videotape safaris: Entering the field with a camera. *Qualitative Sociology, 8,* 325-344.

Alexander, A., Ryan, M. S., & Munoz, P. (1984). Creating a learning context: Investigations on the interaction of siblings during television viewing. *Critical Studies in Mass Communication, 1,* 345-364.

Alperstein, N. M. (1991). Imaginary social relationships with celebrities appearing in television commercials. *Journal of Broadcasting & Electronic Media, 35,* 43-58.

Altheide, D. L. (1987). Ethnographic content analysis. *Qualitative Sociology, 10,* 65-77.

Altheide, D. L., & Snow, R. P. (1988). Toward a theory of mediation. In J. A. Anderson (Ed.), *Communication yearbook 11* (pp. 194-223). Newbury Park, CA: Sage.

Alvesson, M. (1991). Organizational symbolism and ideology. *Journal of Management Studies, 28,* 207-225.

Amato, P. R., & Ochiltree, G. (1987). Interviewing children about their families: A note on data quality. *Journal of Marriage and the Family, 49,* 669-675.

Anderson, J. A. (1987). *Communication research: Issues and methods.* New York: McGraw-Hill.

Anderson, J. A. (1991). The social action of organizing: Knowledge, practice, and morality. *Australian Journal of Communication, 18*(3), 1-18.

Anderson, J. A., & Meyer, T. P. (1988). *Mediated communication: A social action perspective.* Newbury Park, CA: Sage.

Argyris, C., & Schön, D. (1989). Participatory action research and action science compared: A commentary. *American Behavioral Scientist, 32,* 612-623.

285

Arneson, P., & Weber, D. (n.d.). *Qualitative research methods in speech communication: A bibliography through 1987.* Annandale, VA: Speech Communication Association.

Atkinson, P. A. (1988). Ethnomethodology: A critical review. *Annual Review of Sociology, 14,* 441-465.

Atkinson, P. A. (1990). *The ethnographic imagination: Textual constructions of reality.* London: Routledge.

Atkinson, P. A. (1992). *Understanding ethnographic texts.* Newbury Park, CA: Sage.

Basso, K. H. (1988). "Speaking with names": Language and landscape among the Western Apache. *Cultural Anthropology, 3*(2), 99-130.

Bastien, D. T., & Hostager, T. J. (1988). Jazz as a process of organizational innovation. *Communication Research, 15,* 582-602.

Bates, T. R. (1975). Gramsci and the theory of hegemony. *Journal of the History of Ideas, 36,* 351-366.

Bateson, G. (1936). *Naven.* Stanford, CA: Stanford University Press.

Bateson, G. (1972). *Steps to an ecology of mind.* New York: Ballantine.

Bauman, R. (1986). *Story, performance, and event.* New York: Cambridge University Press.

Bauman, R., & Sherzer, J. (1975). The ethnography of speaking. *Annual Review of Anthropology, 4,* 95-119.

Bazerman, C. (1987). Codifying the social scientific style: The APA Publication Manual as a behaviorist rhetoric. In J. S. Nelson, A. Megill, & D. N. McCloskey (Eds.), *The rhetoric of the human sciences* (pp. 125-144). Madison: University of Wisconsin Press.

Becker, H. S. (1958). Problems of inference and proof in participant observation. *American Sociological Review, 23,* 652-660.

Becker, H. S. (1964). Problems in the publication of field studies. In A. Vidich, J. Bensman, & M. Stein (Eds.), *Reflections on community studies* (pp. 267-284). New York: John Wiley.

Becker, H. S. (1966). Introduction. In C. Shaw, *The jack-roller* (pp. v-xviii). Chicago: University of Chicago Press.

Becker, H. S. (1967). Whose side are we on? *Social Problems, 14,* 239-247.

Becker, H. S. (1970). Problems of inference and proof in participant observation. In H. S. Becker, *Sociological work: Method and substance* (pp. 25-38). Chicago: Aldine.

Becker, H. S. (1986a). *Doing things together.* Evanston, IL: Northwestern University Press.

Becker, H. S. (1986b). *Writing for social scientists: How to start and finish your thesis, book, or article.* Chicago: University of Chicago Press.

Becker, H. S., & Geer, B. (1957). Participant observation and interviewing: A comparison. *Human Organization, 16*(3), 28-32.

Becker, H. S., & McCall, M. M. (Eds.). (1990). *Symbolic interaction and cultural studies.* Chicago: University of Chicago Press.

Bennett, T., & Woollacott, J. (1988). *Bond and beyond: The political career of a popular hero.* London: Macmillan.

Benney, M., & Hughes, E. C. (1970). Of sociology and the interview. In N. K. Denzin (Ed.), *Sociological methods* (pp. 190-198). Chicago: Aldine.

Benson, T. W. (1981). Another shooting in Cowtown. *Quarterly Journal of Speech, 67,* 347-406.

Benson, T. W. (Ed.). (1985). *Speech communication in the 20th century.* Carbondale: Southern Illinois University Press.

Berger, P. L., & Luckmann, T. (1967). *The social construction of reality.* Garden City, NY: Doubleday.

Bernstein, R. J. (1978). *The restructuring of social and political theory.* Philadelphia: University of Pennsylvania Press.

Bingham, W. V. D., & Moore, B. V. (1959). *How to interview* (4th ed.). New York: Harper & Row.

Birdwhistell, R. L. (1970). *Kinesics and context.* Philadelphia: University of Pennsylvania Press.

Bittner, E. (1973). Objectivity and realism in sociology. In G. Psathas (Ed.), *Phenomenological sociology* (pp. 109-125). New York: John Wiley.

Blee, K. M., & Billings, D. B. (1986). Reconstructing daily life in the past: An hermeneutical approach to ethnographic data. *Sociological Quarterly, 27,* 443-462.

Blumer, H. (1939). *Critiques of research in the social sciences: An appraisal of Thomas and Znaniecki's* The Polish peasant in Europe and America. New York: Social Science Research Council.

Blumer, H. (1969). *Symbolic interactionism: Perspective and method.* Englewood Cliffs, NJ: Prentice Hall.

Bochner, A. P. (1985). Perspectives on inquiry: Representation, conversation, and reflection. In M. L. Knapp & G. R. Miller (Eds.), *Handbook of interpersonal communication.* Beverly Hills, CA: Sage.

Bochner, A. P., & Eisenberg, E. M. (1985). Legitimizing speech communication: An examination of coherence and cohesion in the development of the discipline. In T. W. Benson (Ed.), *Speech communication in the 20th century* (pp. 299-321). Carbondale: Southern Illinois University Press.

Bochner, A. P., & Ellis, C. (1992). Personal narrative as a social approach to interpersonal communication. *Communication Theory, 2,* 165-172.

Bogdan, R. C., & Biklen, S. K. (1982). *Qualitative research for education: An introduction to theory and methods.* Boston: Allyn & Bacon.

Bogdan, R. C., & Biklen, S. K. (1992). *Qualitative research for education* (2nd ed.). Boston: Allyn & Bacon.

Bogdan, R. C., & Taylor, S. J. (1975). *Introduction to qualitative research methods.* New York: John Wiley.

Borman, K. M., LeCompte, M. D., & Goetz, J. P. (1986). Ethnographic and qualitative research design and why it doesn't work. *American Behavioral Scientist, 30,* 42-57.

Bostrom, R., & Donohew, L. (1992). The case for empiricism: Clarifying fundamental issues in communication theory. *Communication Monographs, 59,* 109-129.

Bourgault, L. M. (1992). Talking to people in the oral tradition: Ethnographic research for development communication. *International Communication Bulletin, 27*(3-4), 19-24.

Brenner, M. (1978). Interviewing: The social phenomenology of a research instrument. In M. Brenner, P. Marsh, & M. Brenner (Eds.), *The social contexts of method* (pp. 122-139). New York: St. Martin's.

Brenner, M. (1985). Intensive interviewing. In M. Brenner, J. Brown, & D. Canter (Eds.), *The research interview: Uses and approaches* (pp. 147-162). London: Academic Press.

Briggs, C. L. (1986). *Learning how to ask: A sociolinguistic appraisal of the role of the interview in social science research.* Cambridge: Cambridge University Press.

Brodkey, L. (1987a). Writing critical ethnographic narratives. *Anthropology & Education Quarterly, 18,* 67-76.

Brodkey, L. (1987b). Writing ethnographic narratives. *Written Communication, 4,* 25-50.

Brown, M. E. (Ed.). (1990). *Television and women's culture: The politics of the popular.* Newbury Park, CA: Sage.

Brown, M. H. (1990). Defining stories in organizations: Characteristics and functions. In J. A. Anderson (Ed.), *Communication yearbook 13* (pp. 162-190). Newbury Park, CA: Sage.

Brown, M. H., & Ragan, S. L. (1987). Variations on a theme: An ethnographic case study of family blessings. *Research on Language and Social Interaction, 21,* 115-141.

Browning, L. D., & Hawes, L. C. (1991). Style, process, surface, context: Consulting as postmodern art. *Journal of Applied Communication Research, 19,* 32-54.

Bruner, J. (1987). Life as narrative. *Social Research, 54,* 11-32.

Bryce, J. W. (1987). Family time and television use. In T. R. Lindlof (Ed.), *Natural audiences: Qualitative research of media uses and effects* (pp. 121-138). Norwood, NJ: Ablex.

Burgess, R. G. (1984). *In the field.* London: Allen & Unwin.

Calas, M. B., & Smircich, L. (1988). Reading leadership as a form of cultural analysis. In J. G. Hunt, B. R. Baliga, H. P. Dachler, & C. A. Schriesheim (Eds.), *Emerging leadership vistas* (pp. 201-226). Lexington, MA: Lexington.

Carbaugh, D. (1988a). Cultural terms and tensions in the speech at a television station. *Western Journal of Speech Communication, 52,* 216-237.

Carbaugh, D. (1988b). *Talking American: Cultural discourses on* Donahue. Norwood, NJ: Ablex.

Carbaugh, D. (1991). Communication and cultural interpretation. *Quarterly Journal of Speech, 77,* 336-342.

Carbaugh, D., & Hastings, S. O. (1992). A role for communication theory in ethnography and cultural analysis. *Communication Theory, 2,* 156-164.

Carey, J. W. (1975). Communication and culture. *Communication Research, 2,* 173-191.

Cassell, J. (1978). Risk and benefit to subjects of fieldwork. *American Sociologist, 13*(9), 134-143.

Charmaz, K. (1983). The grounded theory method: An explication and interpretation. In R. M. Emerson (Ed.), *Contemporary field research* (pp. 109-126). Boston: Little, Brown.

Chock, P. P. (1986). Irony and ethnography: On cultural analysis of one's own culture. *Anthropological Quarterly, 59*(2), 87-96.

Cicourel, A. (1974). *Cognitive sociology.* New York: Free Press.

Cicourel, A. (1980). Three models of discourse analysis: The role of social structure. *Discourse Processes, 3,* 101-132.

Clifford, J. (1983). On ethnographic authority. *Representations, 1,* 118-146.

Clifford, J., & Marcus, G. E. (Eds.). (1986). *Writing culture: The poetics and politics of ethnography.* Berkeley: University of California Press.

Collier, J., Jr., & Collier, M. (1986). *Visual anthropology: Photography as a research method.* Albuquerque: University of New Mexico Press.

Conquergood, D. (1991). Rethinking ethnography: Towards a critical cultural politics. *Communication Monographs, 58,* 179-194.

Cook, T. D., & Campbell, D. T. (1979). *Quasi-experimentation: Design and analysis issues for field settings.* Chicago: Rand McNally.

Corbin, J., & Strauss, A. (1990). Grounded theory research: Procedures, canons, and evaluative criteria. *Qualitative Sociology, 13,* 3-21.

Cottle, T. J. (1973). The life study: On mutual recognition and the subjective inquiry. *Urban Life, 2,* 344-360.

Craig, R. T. (1989). Communication as a practical discipline. In B. Dervin, L. Grossberg, B. J. O'Keefe, & E. Wartella (Eds.), *Rethinking communication: Vol. 1. Paradigm issues* (pp. 97-122). Newbury Park, CA: Sage.

Crapanzano, V. (1977). On the writing of ethnography. *Dialectical Anthropology, 2,* 69-73.

Crider, C., & Cirillo, L. (1992). Systems of interpretation and the function of metaphor. *Journal for the Theory of Social Behaviour, 21,* 171-195.

Cushman, D. P. (1977). The rules perspective as a theoretical basis for the study of human communication. *Communication Quarterly, 25*, 30-45.

Cushman, D. P., & Whiting, G. (1972). An approach to communication theory: Toward consensus on rules. *Journal of Communication, 22*, 217-238.

Deetz, S. A. (1982). Critical interpretive research in organizational communication. *Western Journal of Speech Communication, 46*, 131-149.

Deetz, S. A. (1992a). *Communication 2000: The discipline, the challenges, the research, the social contribution.* Unpublished manuscript, Rutgers University, Department of Communication.

Deetz, S. A. (1992b). *Democracy in the age of corporate colonization: Communication and the politics of everyday life.* Albany: State University of New York Press.

Deetz, S., & Mumby, D. K. (1990). Power, discourse, and the workplace: Reclaiming the critical tradition. In J. A. Anderson (Ed.), *Communication yearbook 13* (pp. 18-47). Newbury Park, CA: Sage.

Delia, J. G. (1977). Constructivism and the study of human communication. *Quarterly Journal of Speech, 63*, 66-83.

Delia, J. G. (1987). Communication research: A history. In C. R. Berger & S. H. Chaffee (Eds.), *Handbook of communication science* (pp. 20-97). Newbury Park, CA: Sage.

Delia, J. G., & O'Keefe, B. J. (1979). Constructivism: The development of communication in children. In E. Wartella (Ed.), *Children communicating* (pp. 157-185). Beverly Hills, CA: Sage.

Denzin, N. K. (1969). Symbolic interactionism and ethnomethodology: A proposed synthesis. *American Sociological Review, 34*, 922-934.

Denzin, N. K. (1977). *Childhood socialization.* San Francisco: Jossey-Bass.

Denzin, N. K. (1978). *The research act* (2nd ed.). New York: McGraw-Hill.

Denzin, N. K. (1989). *Interpretive biography.* Newbury Park, CA: Sage.

Dervin, B., Grossberg, L., O'Keefe, B. J., & Wartella, E. (Eds.). (1989). *Rethinking communication: Vol. 1. Paradigm issues.* Newbury Park, CA: Sage.

DeVault, M. L. (1990). Talking and listening from women's standpoint: Feminist strategies for interviewing and analysis. *Social Problems, 37*, 96-116.

Dewey, J. (1954). *The public and its problems.* New York: Henry Holt. (Original work published 1927)

Dewey, J. (1958). *Experience and nature.* New York: Dover. (Original work published 1929)

Dillon, G. L., Doyle, A., Eastman, C., Schiffman, H., Silberstein, S., Toolan, M., Kline, S., & Philipsen, G. (1989). Analyzing a speech event: The Bush-Rather exchange a (not very) dramatic dialogue. *Cultural Anthropology, 4*, 73-94.

Dilthey, W. (1974). On the special character of the human sciences. In M. Truzzi (Ed.), *Verstehen: Subjective understanding in the social sciences* (pp. 8-17). Reading, MA: Addison-Wesley. (Reprinted from H. A. Hodges [1944]. *Wilhelm Dilthey: An introduction* [pp. 110-113, 120-124, 128-131, 133, 141-143]. London: Routledge & Kegan Paul.)

Dingwall, R. (1980). Ethics and ethnography. *Sociological Review, 28*, 871-891.

Dore, J., & McDermott, R. P. (1982). Linguistic indeterminacy and social context in utterance interpretation. *Language, 58*, 374-398.

Douglas, J. D. (1976). *Investigative social research.* Beverly Hills, CA: Sage.

Duncan, H. D. (1962). *Communication and social order.* London: Oxford University Press.

Dwyer, K. (1979). The dialogic of fieldwork. *Dialectical Anthropology, 4*, 205-224.

Eagleton, T. (1983). *Literary theory.* Minneapolis: University of Minnesota Press.

Eastman, S. (1986). A qualitative study of computers and printouts in the classroom. *Educational Communication and Technology Journal, 34*, 207-222.

Eckstein, H. (1975). Case study and theory in political science. In F. I. Greenstein & N. W. Polsky (Eds.), *Handbook of political science: Vol. 7. Strategies of inquiry* (pp. 79-137). Reading, MA: Addison-Wesley.

Edmondson, R. (1984). *Rhetoric in sociology*. London: Macmillan.

Eisenberg, E. M. (1990). Jamming: Transcendence through organizing. *Communication Research, 17,* 139-164.

Ellen, R. F. (1984). *Ethnographic research: A guide to general conduct*. London: Academic Press.

Ellis, C. (1991). Sociological introspection and emotional experience. *Symbolic Interaction, 14,* 23-50.

Ellis, D. G. (1980). Ethnographic considerations in initial interaction. *Western Journal of Speech Communication, 44,* 104-107.

Ely, M., Anzul, M., Friedman, T., Garner, D., & Steinmetz, A. M. (1991). *Doing qualitative research: Circles within circles*. London: Falmer.

Erickson, F. (1977). Some approaches to inquiry in school-community ethnography. *Anthropology & Education Quarterly, 8,* 58-69.

Erickson, F., & Wilson, J. (1982). *Sights and sounds of life in schools: A resource guide to film and videotape for research and education* (Research Series No. 125). East Lansing: Michigan State University, College of Education, Institute for Research on Teaching.

Fabian, J. (1983). *Time and the other: How anthropology makes its object*. New York: Columbia University Press.

Faules, D. F., & Alexander, D. C. (1978). *Communication and social behavior: A symbolic interaction perspective*. Reading, MA: Addison-Wesley.

Feldman, S. P. (1990). Stories as cultural creativity: On the relation between symbolism and politics in organizational change. *Human Relations, 43,* 809-823.

Ferment in the field. (1983). *Journal of Communication, 33*(3).

Fern, E. F. (1983). Focus groups: A review of some contradictory evidence, implications, and suggestions for future research. *Advances in Consumer Research, 10,* 121-126.

Feyerabend, P. K. (1975). *Against method*. London: Verso.

Finch, J. (1984). "It's great to have someone to talk to": The ethics and politics of interviewing women. In C. Bell & H. Roberts (Eds.), *Social researching: Politics, problems, practice* (pp. 70-87). London: Routledge & Kegan Paul.

Fine, G. A. (1987). *With the boys: Little League baseball and preadolescent culture*. Chicago: University of Chicago Press.

Fine, G. A. (1988). The ten commandments of writing. *American Sociologist, 19,* 152-157.

Fine, G. A. (1993). Ten lies of ethnography: Moral dilemmas of field research. *Journal of Contemporary Ethnography, 22,* 267-293.

Fine, G. A., & Glassner, B. (1979). Participant observation with children. *Urban Life, 8,* 153-174.

Fine, G. A., & Martin, D. D. (1990). A partisan view: Sarcasm, satire, and irony as voices in Erving Goffman's *Asylums*. *Journal of Contemporary Ethnography, 19,* 89-115.

Fine, G. A., & Sandstrom, K. L. (1988). *Knowing children: Participant observation with minors*. Newbury Park, CA: Sage.

Fineman, S., & Mangham, I. (1983). Data, meanings and creativity: A preface. *Journal of Management Studies, 20,* 295-300.

Fisher, W. R. (1985). The narrative paradigm: An elaboration. *Journal of Communication, 35,* 74-89.

Fiske, J. (1987). *Television culture*. London: Methuen.

Fiske, J. (1991a). Postmodernism and television. In J. Curran & M. Gurevitch (Eds.), *Mass media and society* (pp. 55-67). London: Edward Arnold.

Fiske, J. (1991b). Writing ethnographies: Contribution to a dialogue. *Quarterly Journal of Speech, 77,* 330-335.

Fitzpatrick, M. A. (1993). Communication and the new world of relationships. *Journal of Communication, 43*(3), 119-126.

Foley, D. E. (1990). *Learning capitalist culture: Deep in the heart of Tejas.* Philadelphia: University of Pennsylvania Press.

Foreman, C. (1994). *A critical-interpretive analysis of organizational subcultures.* Doctoral dissertation in progress, University of Kentucky, Lexington.

Fox, M. F. (Ed.). (1985). *Scholarly writing and publishing: Issues, problems, and solutions.* Boulder, CO: Westview.

Frazer, C. F., & Reid, L. N. (1979). Children's interactions with commercials. *Symbolic Interaction, 2*(2), 79-96.

Gans, H. J. (1982). The participant observer as a human being: Observations on the personal aspects of fieldwork. In R. G. Burgess (Ed.), *Field research: A source book and field manual* (pp. 53-61). London: George Allen & Unwin.

Garfinkel, H. (1967). *Studies in ethnomethodology.* Englewood Cliffs, NJ: Prentice Hall.

Garfinkel, H., Lynch, M., & Livingston, E. (1981). The work of discovering science construed with materials from the optically discovered pulsar. *Philosophy of Social Science, 11,* 131-158.

Garner, A. C., & Dyer, C. S. (1989). *The Iowa guide* (3rd ed.). Iowa City: University of Iowa and Iowa Center for Communication Study.

Geertz, C. (1973). *The interpretation of cultures: Selected essays.* New York: Basic Books.

Geertz, C. (1983). *Local knowledge: Further essays in interpretive anthropology.* New York: Basic Books.

Gergen, K. J. (1991). *The saturated self: Dilemmas of identity in contemporary life.* New York: Basic Books.

Giddens, A. (1986). Action, subjectivity, and the constitution of meaning. *Social Research, 53,* 529-545.

Gilbert, C. (1982). Reflections on *An American Family. Studies in Visual Communication, 8*(1), 24-54.

Gillespie, M. (1990, June). *The Mahabharata: From Sanskrit to sacred soap.* Paper presented at the annual meeting of the International Communication Association, Dublin.

Gitlin, T. (1979). Prime time ideology: The hegemonic process in television entertainment. *Social Problems, 26,* 251-266.

Gitlin, T. (1983). *Inside prime time.* New York: Pantheon.

Glaser, B. G. (1978). *Theoretical sensitivity.* Mill Valley, CA: Sociology Press.

Glaser, B. G., & Strauss, A. L. (1967). *The discovery of grounded theory: Strategies for qualitative research.* Chicago: Aldine.

Gluckman, M. (1961). Ethnographic data in British social anthropology. *Sociological Review, 9,* 5-17.

Goffman, E. (1959). *The presentation of self in everyday life.* Garden City, NY: Doubleday.

Goffman, E. (1961). *Asylums.* Garden City, NY: Doubleday.

Goffman, E. (1967). *Interaction ritual: Essays on face-to-face behavior.* Garden City, NY: Anchor.

Goffman, E. (1989). On fieldwork. *Journal of Contemporary Ethnography, 18,* 123-132.

Gold, R. L. (1958). Roles in sociological field observations. *Social Forces, 36,* 217-223.

Goodall, H. L., Jr. (1991). *Living in the rock n roll mystery: Reading context, self, and others as clues.* Carbondale: Southern Illinois University Press.

Gorden, R. L. (1969). *Interviewing: Strategy, techniques and tactics.* Homewood, IL: Dorsey.

Graham, H. (1984). Surveying through stories. In C. Bell & H. Roberts (Eds.), *Social researching: Politics, problems, practice* (pp. 104-124). London: Routledge & Kegan Paul.

Grodin, D. (1990). *The interpreting audience: The therapeutics of self-help reading.* Unpublished doctoral dissertation, University of Kentucky, Lexington.

Grodin, D. (1991). The interpreting audience: The therapeutics of self-help book reading. *Critical Studies in Mass Communication, 8,* 404-420.

Guba, E. G., & Lincoln, Y. S. (1982). Epistemological and methodological bases of naturalistic inquiry. *Educational Communication & Technology Journal, 30,* 233-252.

Gurevitch, Z. D. (1988). The other side of dialogue: On making the other strange and the experience of otherness. *American Journal of Sociology, 93,* 1179-1199.

Gusfield, J. (1976). The literary rhetoric of science: Comedy and pathos in drinking driver research. *American Sociological Review, 41,* 16-34.

Halfpenny, P. (1979). The analysis of qualitative data. *Sociological Review, 27,* 799-825.

Hall, E. T. (1959). *The silent language.* Garden City, NY: Doubleday.

Hall, S. (1982). The rediscovery of ideology: Return of the repressed in media studies. In M. Gurevitch, T. Bennett, J. Curran, & J. Woollacott (Eds.), *Culture, society and the media* (pp. 56-90). New York: Methuen.

Hammersley, M. (1992). *What's wrong with ethnography? Methodological explorations.* London: Routledge.

Hammersley, M., & Atkinson, P. (1983). *Ethnography: Principles in practice.* London: Tavistock.

Hawes, L. C. (1975). *Pragmatics of analoguing: Theory and model construction in communication.* Reading, MA: Addison-Wesley.

Hawes, L. C. (1976). How writing is used in talk: A study of communicative logic-in-use. *Quarterly Journal of Speech, 62,* 350-360.

Hawes, L. C. (1977). Toward a hermeneutic phenomenology of communication. *Communication Quarterly, 25*(3), 30-41.

Heap, J. L., & Roth, P. A. (1973). On phenomenological sociology. *American Sociological Review, 38,* 354-367.

Hebdige, D. (1979). *Subculture: The meaning of style.* London: Methuen.

Heidegger, M. (1962). *Being and time* (J. Macquarrie & E. Robinson, Trans.). New York: Harper & Row. (Original work published 1927)

Heider, K. G. (1988). The Rashomon effect: When ethnographers disagree. *American Anthropologist, 90,* 73-81.

Helmericks, S. G., Nelsen, R. L., & Unnithan, N. P. (1991). The researcher, the topic, and the literature: A procedure for systematizing literature searches. *Journal of Applied Behavioral Science, 27,* 285-294.

Heritage, J. (1984). *Garfinkel and ethnomethodology.* Cambridge: Polity.

Herndon, S. L., & Kreps, G. L. (Eds.). (1993). *Qualitative research: Applications in organizational communication.* Cresskill, NJ: Hampton.

Hess, D. J. (1989). Teaching ethnographic writing. A review essay. *Anthropology & Education Quarterly, 20,* 163-176.

Hesse-Biber, S., Dupuis, P., & Kinder, T. S. (1991). Hyperesearch: A computer program for the analysis of qualitative data with an emphasis on multimedia analysis. *Social Science Computer Review, 9,* 452-460.

Hobson, D. (1982). *Crossroads: The drama of a soap opera.* London: Methuen.

Hoijer, B. (1990). Studying viewers' reception of television programmes: Theoretical and methodological considerations. *European Journal of Communication, 5,* 29-56.

Hopper, R., Koch, S., & Mandelbaum, J. (1986). Conversation analysis methods. In D. G. Ellis & W. A. Donahue (Eds.), *Contemporary issues in language and discourse processes* (pp. 169-186). Hillsdale, NJ: Lawrence Erlbaum.

Horowitz, R. (1986). Remaining an outsider: Membership as a threat to research support. *Urban Life, 14,* 409-430.

Howard, A. (1988). Hypermedia and the future of ethnography. *Cultural Anthropology, 3,* 304-315.

Hunt, J., & Manning, P. K. (1991). The social context of police lying. *Symbolic Interaction, 14,* 51-70.

Hunter, A. (1990). Rhetoric in research, networks of knowledge. In A. Hunter (Ed.), *The rhetoric of social science: Understood and believed* (pp. 1-22). New Brunswick, NJ: Rutgers University Press.

Husserl, E. (1931). *Ideas: General introduction to pure phenomenology* (W. R. B. Gibson, Trans.). New York: Macmillan.

Hymes, D. (1962). The ethnography of speaking. In T. Gladwin & W. C. Sturtevant (Eds.), *Anthropology and human behavior* (pp. 13-53). Washington, DC: Anthropology Society of Washington.

Jackson, J. E. (1990). "I am a fieldnote": Fieldnotes as a symbol of professional identity. In R. Sanjek (Ed.), *Fieldnotes: The makings of anthropology* (pp. 3-33). Ithaca, NY: Cornell University Press.

Jackson, S. (1993). Ethnography and the audition: Performance as ideological critique. *Text and Performance Quarterly, 13,* 21-43.

Jacobs, S. (1986). How to make an argument from example in discourse analysis. In D. G. Ellis & W. A. Donahue (Eds.), *Contemporary issues in language and discourse processes* (pp. 149-168). Hillsdale, NJ: Lawrence Erlbaum.

Jacobs, S. (1990). On the especially nice fit between qualitative analysis and the known properties of conversation. *Communication Monographs, 57,* 243-249.

James, N. C., & McCain, T. (1982). Television games preschool children play. *Journal of Broadcasting, 26,* 783-800.

Jameson, F. (1981). *The political unconscious: Narrative as a socially symbolic act.* Ithaca, NY: Cornell University Press.

Jenkins, H., Jr. (1988). *Star Trek* rerun, reread, rewritten: Fan writing as textual poaching. *Critical Studies in Mass Communication, 5,* 85-107.

Jensen, K. B. (1987). Qualitative audience research: Toward an integrative approach to reception. *Critical Studies in Mass Communication, 4,* 21-36.

Jensen, K. B. (1989). Discourses of interviewing: Validating qualitative research findings through textual analysis. In S. Kvale (Ed.), *Issues of validity in qualitative research* (pp. 93-108). Lund: Studentlitteratur.

Jensen, K. B. (1991). When is meaning? Communication theory, pragmatism, and mass media reception. In J. A. Anderson (Ed.), *Communication yearbook 14* (pp. 3-32). Newbury Park, CA: Sage.

Jensen, K. B., & Jankowski, K. W. (Eds.). (1991). *A handbook of qualitative methodologies for mass communication research.* London: Routledge.

Johnson, F. G., & Kaplan, C. D. (1980). Talk-in-the-work: Aspects of social organization of work in a computer center. *Journal of Pragmatics, 4,* 351-365.

Jorgenson, J. (1989). Where is the "family" in family communication? Exploring families' self-definitions. *Journal of Applied Communication Research, 17,* 27-41.

Jorgenson, J. (1992). Communication, rapport, and the interview: A social perspective. *Communication Theory, 2,* 148-156.

Kahn, R., & Mann, F. (1969). Developing research partnerships. In G. J. McCall & J. L. Simmons (Eds.), *Issues in participant observation* (pp. 45-51). Reading, MA: Addison-Wesley.

Kant, I. (1929). *The critique of pure reason* (N. K. Smith, Trans.). London: Macmillan.

Kanter, R. M. (1977). *Men and women of the corporation.* New York: Basic Books.

Kaplan, A. (1964). *The conduct of inquiry.* San Francisco: Chandler.

Katriel, T. (1987). "Bexibudim!" Ritualized sharing among Israeli children. *Language in Society, 16,* 305-320.

Katriel, T., & Farrell, T. (1991). Scrapbooks as cultural texts: An American art of memory. *Text and Performance Quarterly, 11,* 1-17.

Katriel, T., & Philipsen, G. (1981). "What we need is communication": "Communication" as a cultural category in some American speech. *Communication Monographs, 48,* 302-317.

Kelly, J. W. (1985). Storytelling in high tech organizations: A medium for sharing culture. *Journal of Applied Communication Research, 13,* 45-58.

Kidder, L. H. (1981). Qualitative research and quasi-experimental frameworks. In M. B. Brewer & B. E. Collins (Eds.), *Scientific inquiry and the social sciences.* San Francisco: Jossey-Bass.

Kirk, J., & Miller, M. L. (1986). *Reliability and validity in qualitative research.* Beverly Hills, CA: Sage.

Knapp, M. L., & Daly, J. A. (1993). *Guide to publishing in scholarly communication journals* (2nd ed.). Austin, TX: International Communication Association.

Knuf, J. (1989-1990). Where cultures meet: Ritual code and organizational boundary management. *Research on Language and Social Interaction, 23,* 109-138.

Kockelmans, J. J. (1967). *Edmund Husserl's phenomenological psychology: A historico-critical study* (B. Jager, Trans.). Pittsburgh: Duquesne University Press.

Krieger, S. (1979a). *Hip capitalism.* Beverly Hills, CA: Sage.

Krieger, S. (1979b). Research and the construction of a text. In N. K. Denzin (Ed.), *Studies in symbolic interaction* (Vol. 2, pp. 167-187). Greenwich, CT: JAI.

Krieger, S. (1991). *Social science and the self.* New Brunswick, NJ: Rutgers University Press.

Krueger, R. A. (1988). *Focus groups: A practical guide for applied research.* Newbury Park, CA: Sage.

Kuhn, M. H. (1962). The interview and the professional relationship. In A. M. Rose (Ed.), *Human behavior and social processes* (pp. 193-206). Boston: Houghton Mifflin.

Kuhn, M. H. (1964). Major trends in symbolic interaction theory in the past twenty-five years. *Sociological Quarterly, 5,* 61-84.

Kuhn, T. S. (1970). *The structure of scientific revolutions* (2nd ed.). Chicago: University of Chicago Press.

Kurtz, L. R. (1984). *Evaluating Chicago sociology.* Chicago: University of Chicago Press.

Lachmann, R. (1988). Graffiti as career and ideology. *American Journal of Sociology, 94,* 229-250.

Lang, K., & Lang, G. (1953). The unique perspective of television and its effect: A pilot study. *American Sociological Review, 18,* 3-12.

Langellier, K. M. (1989). Personal narratives: Perspectives on theory and research. *Text and Performance Quarterly, 9,* 243-276.

LaRossa, R., Bennett, L. A., & Gelles, R. J. (1981). Ethical dilemmas in qualitative family research. *Journal of Marriage and the Family, 43,* 303-313.

Lather, P. (1986). Research as praxis. *Harvard Educational Review, 56,* 259-277.

Latour, B., & Woolgar, S. (1986). *Laboratory life: The construction of scientific facts.* Princeton, NJ: Princeton University Press.

Lazarsfeld, P. F. (1944). The controversy over detailed interviews. *Public Opinion Quarterly, 8,* 38-60.

Leeds-Hurwitz, W. (1984). On the relationship of the "ethnography of speaking" to the "ethnography of communication." *Papers in Linguistics, 17,* 7-32.

Lemish, D. (1982). Television viewing in public places. *Journal of Broadcasting, 26,* 757-782.

Lemish, D. (1987). Viewers in diapers: The early development of television viewing. In T. R. Lindlof (Ed.), *Natural audiences: Qualitative research of media uses and effects* (pp. 33-57). Norwood, NJ: Ablex.

Lemish, P. S., & Lemish, D. (1982). A guide to the literature of qualitative research. *Journal of Broadcasting, 26,* 839-846.

Lester, M. (1980). Generating newsworthiness: The interpretive construction of public events. *American Sociological Review, 45,* 984-994.

Lever, J. (1981). Multiple methods of data collection. *Urban Life, 10,* 199-213.

Levine, M. (1980). Investigative reporting as a research method: An analysis of Bernstein and Woodward's *All the President's Men. American Psychologist, 35,* 626-638.

Lévi-Strauss, C. (1974). *Tristes tropiques.* New York: Atheneum. (Original work published 1955)

Levitt, S. R. (1989, May). *Negotiating the epistemological and ethical terrain in conducting organizational action research.* Paper presented at the annual meeting of the International Communication Association, San Francisco.

Liebes, T. (1984). Ethnocriticism: Israelis of Moroccan ethnicity negotiate the meaning of "Dallas." *Studies in Visual Communication, 10*(3), 46-72.

Liebes, T. (1988). Cultural differences in the retelling of television fiction. *Critical Studies in Mass Communication, 5,* 277-292.

Liebow, E. (1967). *Tally's corner: A study of Negro street corner men.* Boston: Little, Brown.

Liebow, E. (1993). *Tell them who I am: The lives of homeless women.* New York: Free Press.

Lincoln, Y. S., & Guba, E. G. (1985). *Naturalistic inquiry.* Beverly Hills, CA: Sage.

Lindlof, T. R. (1987a). Ideology and pragmatics of media access in prison. In T. R. Lindlof (Ed.), *Natural audiences: Qualitative research of media uses and effects* (pp. 175-197). Norwood, NJ: Ablex.

Lindlof, T. R. (Ed.). (1987b). *Natural audiences: Qualitative research of media uses and effects.* Norwood, NJ: Ablex.

Lindlof, T. R. (1988). Media audiences as interpretive communities. In J. A. Anderson (Ed.), *Communication yearbook 11* (pp. 81-107). Newbury Park, CA: Sage.

Lindlof, T. R. (1991). The qualitative study of media audiences. *Journal of Broadcasting & Electronic Media, 35,* 23-42.

Lindlof, T. R. (1992). Computing tales: Parents' discourse about technology and family. *Social Science Computer Review, 10,* 291-309.

Lindlof, T. R., & Grodin, D. (1990). When media use can't be observed: Some problems and tactics of collaborative audience research. *Journal of Communication, 40*(4), 8-28.

Lindlof, T. R., Shatzer, M. S., & Wilkinson, D. (1988). Accommodation of video and television in the American family. In J. Lull (Ed.), *World families watch television* (pp. 158-192). Newbury Park, CA: Sage.

Lofland, J. (1971). *Analyzing social settings.* Belmont, CA: Wadsworth.

Lofland, J. (1974). Styles of reporting qualitative field research. *American Sociologist, 9,* 101-111.

Loizos, P. (1993). *Innovation in ethnographic film.* Chicago: University of Chicago Press.

Lull, J. (1982). A rules approach to the study of television and society. *Human Communication Research, 9*, 3-16.

Lull, J. (1985). Ethnographic studies of broadcast media audiences: Notes on method. In J. Dominick & J. Fletcher (Eds.), *Broadcasting research methods*. Boston: Allyn & Bacon.

Lull, J. (1987). Thrashing in the pit: An ethnography of San Francisco punk subculture. In T. R. Lindlof (Ed.), *Natural audiences: Qualitative research of media uses and effects* (pp. 225-252). Norwood, NJ: Ablex.

Lull, J. (Ed.). (1988). *World families watch television*. Newbury Park, CA: Sage.

Lull, J. (1990). *Inside family viewing*. London: Routledge.

Lynch, M., Livingston, E., & Garfinkel, H. (1983). Temporal order in laboratory work. In K. Knorr-Cetina & M. Mulkay (Eds.), *Science observed: Perspectives on the social study of science* (pp. 205-238). Beverly Hills, CA: Sage.

Maines, D. R. (1977). Social organization and social structure in symbolic interactionist thought. *Annual Review of Sociology, 3*, 235-259.

Malinowski, B. (1922). *Argonauts of the western Pacific: An account of native enterprise and adventure in the archipelagoes of Melanesian New Guinea*. London: Routledge & Kegan Paul.

Malinowski, B. (1967). *A diary in the strict sense of the term*. New York: Harcourt.

Mandell, N. (1988). The least-adult role in studying children. *Journal of Contemporary Ethnography, 16*, 433-467.

Manning, P. K. (1967). Problems in interpreting interview data. *Sociology and Social Research, 51*, 302-316.

Marcus, G. E., & Cushman, D. (1982). Ethnographies as texts. *Annual Review of Anthropology, 11*, 25-69.

Marcus, G. E., & Fischer, M. M. J. (1986). *Anthropology as cultural critique*. Chicago: University of Chicago Press.

Marshall, C., & Rossman, G. B. (1989). *Designing qualitative research*. Newbury Park, CA: Sage.

Martindale, D. (1968). Verstehen. In *International encyclopedia of the social sciences* (pp. 308-312). New York: Macmillan.

Mast, S. (1983). Working for television: The social organization of TV drama. *Symbolic Interaction, 6*, 71-83.

Mayrl, W. W. (1973). Ethnomethodology: Sociology without society? *Catalyst, 7*, 15-28.

McCall, G. J. (1984). Systematic field observation. *Annual Review of Sociology, 10*, 263-282.

McCall, M. M., Becker, H. S., & Meshejian, P. (1990). Performance science. *Social Problems, 37*, 117-132.

McCall, M. M., & Wittner, J. (1990). The good news about life history. In H. S. Becker & M. M. McCall (Eds.), *Symbolic interaction and culture studies* (pp. 46-89). Chicago: University of Chicago Press.

McCracken, G. (1988). *The long interview*. Newbury Park, CA: Sage.

McRobbie, A. (1982). *Jackie*: An ideology of adolescent femininity. In B. Waites, T. Bennett, & G. Martin (Eds.), *Popular culture: Past and present* (pp. 262-283). London: Croom Helm.

McRobbie, A. (1992). Post-Marxism and cultural studies: A post-script. In L. Grossberg, C. Nelson, & P. A. Treichler (Eds.), *Cultural studies* (pp. 719-730). New York: Routledge.

Mead, G. H. (1934). *Mind, self and society*. Chicago: University of Chicago Press.

Mehan, H. (1979). *Learning lessons*. Cambridge, MA: Harvard University Press.

Merton, R. K., Fiske, M., & Kendall, P. L. (1990). *The focused interview*. New York: Free Press. (Original work published 1956)

Meyer, T. P., Traudt, P. J., & Anderson, J. A. (1980). Non-traditional mass communication research methods: Observational case studies of media use in natural settings. In D. Nimmo (Ed.), *Communication yearbook 4* (pp. 261-275). New Brunswick, NJ: Transaction.

Miles, M. B., & Huberman, A. M. (1984). *Qualitative data analysis: A sourcebook of new methods.* Beverly Hills, CA: Sage.

Miller, G. R., & Nicholson, H. E. (1976). *Communication inquiry.* Reading, MA: Addison-Wesley.

Mishler, E. G. (1986). *Research interviewing: Context and narrative.* Cambridge, MA: Harvard University Press.

Mitchell, J. C. (1983). Case and situation analysis. *Sociological Review, 31,* 187-211.

Morgan, D. L. (1988). *Focus groups as qualitative research.* Newbury Park, CA: Sage.

Morley, D. (1980). *The "Nationwide" audience: Structure and decoding.* London: British Film Institute.

Morley, D. (1986). *Family television.* London: Comedia.

Morley, D. (1992). *Television, audiences, and cultural studies.* New York: Routledge.

Morris, G. H., & Hopper, R. (1987). Symbolic action as alignment: A synthesis of rules approaches. *Research on Language and Social Interaction, 21,* 1-29.

Morris, M. B. (1977). *An excursion into creative sociology.* New York: Columbia University Press.

Mumby, D. K. (1988). *Communication and power in organizations: Discourse, ideology, and domination.* Norwood, NJ: Ablex.

Musello, C. (1980). Studying the home mode: An exploration of family photography and visual communication. *Studies in Visual Communication, 6*(1), 23-42.

Myerhoff, B., & Ruby, J. (1982). Introduction. In B. Myerhoff & J. Ruby (Eds.), *A crack in the mirror* (pp. 1-35). Philadelphia: University of Pennsylvania Press.

Natanson, M. (1968). Alfred Schutz on social reality and social science. *Social Research, 35,* 217-244.

Naughton, J. (1982, August 5). Revolution in science: 20 years on. *New Scientist,* pp. 372-375.

Nelson, C., Treichler, P. A., & Grossberg, L. (1992). Cultural studies: An introduction. In L. Grossberg, C. Nelson, & P. A. Treichler (Eds.), *Cultural studies* (pp. 1-16). New York: Routledge.

Nelson, J. S., Megill, A., & McCloskey, D. N. (1987). Rhetoric of inquiry. In J. S. Nelson, A. Megill, & D. N. McCloskey (Eds.), *The rhetoric of the human sciences* (pp. 3-18). Madison: University of Wisconsin Press.

Neumann, M., & Eason, D. (1990). Casino world: Bringing it all back home. *Cultural Studies, 4,* 45-60.

O'Keefe, D. J. (1975). Logical empiricism and the study of human communication. *Speech Monographs, 42*(3), 169-183.

O'Keefe, D. J. (1980). Ethnomethodology. *Journal for the Theory of Social Behaviour, 9,* 187-219.

Olesen, V. L., & Whittaker, E. W. (1967). Role-making in participant observation: Processes in the researcher-actor relationship. *Human Organization, 26,* 273-281.

Ostrander, S. A. (1993). "Surely you're not in this just to be helpful": Access, rapport, and interviews in three studies of elites. *Journal of Contemporary Ethnography, 22,* 7-27.

Pacanowsky, M. E. (1988a). Communication in the empowering organization. In J. A. Anderson (Ed.), *Communication yearbook 11* (pp. 356-379). Newbury Park, CA: Sage.

Pacanowsky, M. E. (1988b). Slouching towards Chicago. *Quarterly Journal of Speech, 74,* 453-467.

Pacanowsky, M. E. (1989). Creating and narrating organizational realities. In B. Dervin, L. Grossberg, B. J. O'Keefe, & E. Wartella (Eds.), *Rethinking communication: Vol. 2. Paradigm exemplars* (pp. 250-257). Newbury Park, CA: Sage.

Pacanowsky, M. E., & Anderson, J. A. (1982). Cop talk and media use. *Journal of Broadcasting, 26*, 741-756.

Pacanowsky, M. E., & O'Donnell-Trujillo, N. (1982). Communication and organizational cultures. *Western Journal of Speech Communication, 46*, 115-130.

Pacanowsky, M. E., & O'Donnell-Trujillo, N. (1983). Organizational communication as cultural performances. *Communication Monographs, 50*, 126-147.

Packer, M. J. (1985). Hermeneutic inquiry in the study of human conduct. *American Psychologist, 40*, 1081-1093.

Paget, M. A. (1983). Experience and knowledge. *Human Studies, 6*, 67-90.

Paget, M. A. (1990). Performing the text. *Journal of Contemporary Ethnography, 19*, 136-155.

Palmer, R. E. (1969). *Hermeneutics: Interpretation theory in Schleiermacher, Dilthey, Heidegger and Gadamer.* Evanston, IL: Northwestern University Press.

Patton, M. Q. (1990). *Qualitative evaluation and research methods* (2nd ed.). Newbury Park, CA: Sage.

Pauly, J. J. (1991). *A beginner's guide to doing qualitative research in mass communication* (Journalism Monograph No. 125). Columbia, SC: Association for Education in Journalism and Mass Communication.

Pearce, W. B. (1985). Scientific research methods in communication studies and their implications for theory and research. In T. W. Benson (Ed.), *Speech communication in the 20th century* (pp. 255-281). Carbondale: Southern Illinois University Press.

Pearce, W. B., & Cronen, V. E. (1980). *Communication, action and meaning: The creation of social realities.* New York: Praeger.

Pelto, P. J., & Pelto, G. H. (1978). *Anthropological research: The structure of inquiry* (2nd ed.). Cambridge: Cambridge University Press.

Peters, J. D. (1986). Institutional sources of intellectual poverty in communication research. *Communication Research, 13*, 527-559.

Peterson, E. E. (1987). Media consumption and girls who want to have fun. *Critical Studies in Mass Communication, 4*, 37-50.

Petronio, S., & Bourhis, J. (1987). Identifying family collectivities in public places: An instructional exercise. *Communication Education, 36*, 46-51.

Pfaffenberger, B. (1988). *Microcomputer applications in qualitative research.* Newbury Park, CA: Sage.

Philipsen, G. (1975). Speaking "like a man" in Teamsterville: Culture patterns of role enactment in an urban neighborhood. *Quarterly Journal of Speech, 61*, 13-22.

Philipsen, G. (1977). Linearity of research design in ethnographic studies of speaking. *Communication Quarterly, 25*(3), 42-50.

Philipsen, G., & Carbaugh, D. (1986). A bibliography of fieldwork in the ethnography of communication. *Language in Society, 15*, 387-397.

Platt, J. R. (1964, October 16). Strong inference. *Science*, pp. 347-353.

Plummer, K. (1983). *Documents of life.* London: Allen & Unwin.

Porpora, D. V. (1983). On the prospects for a nomothetic theory of social structure. *Journal for the Theory of Social Behaviour, 13*, 243-264.

Pratt, M. L. (1986). Fieldwork in common places. In J. Clifford & G. E. Marcus (Eds.), *Writing culture: The poetics and politics of ethnography* (pp. 27-50). Berkeley: University of California Press.

Press, A. L. (1989a). Class and gender in the hegemonic process: Class differences in women's perceptions of realism and identification with television characters. *Media, Culture & Society, 11,* 229-252.

Press, A. L. (1989b, May). *Toward a qualitative methodology of audience study: Using ethnography to study the popular culture audience.* Paper presented at the annual meeting of the International Communication Association, San Francisco.

Press, A. L. (1991). The impact of television on modes of reasoning about abortion. *Critical Studies in Mass Communication, 8,* 421-441.

Prus, R. (1987). Generic social processes: Maximizing conceptual development in ethnographic research. *Journal of Contemporary Ethnography, 16,* 250-293.

Putnam, L. L., & Pacanowsky, M. E. (Eds.). (1983). *Communication and organizations.* Beverly Hills, CA: Sage.

Rabinow, P. (1986). Representations are social facts: Modernity and post-modernity in anthropology. In J. Clifford & G. E. Marcus (Eds.), *Writing culture: The poetics and politics of ethnography* (pp. 234-261). Berkeley: University of California Press.

Rabinow, P., & Sullivan, W. M. (1987). The interpretive turn: A second look. In P. Rabinow & W. M. Sullivan (Eds.), *Interpretive social science: A second look* (pp. 1-30). Berkeley: University of California Press.

Radway, J. (1984). *Reading the romance: Feminism and the representation of women in popular culture.* Chapel Hill: University of North Carolina Press.

Radway, J. (1989). Ethnography among elites: Comparing discourses of power. *Journal of Communication Inquiry, 13,* 3-11.

Rawlins, W. K. (1983). Openness as problematic in ongoing friendships: Two conversational dilemmas. *Communication Monographs, 50,* 1-13.

Rawlins, W. K. (1989). A dialectical analysis of the tensions, functions, and strategic challenges of communication in young adult friendships. In J. A. Anderson (Ed.), *Communication yearbook 12* (pp. 157-189). Newbury Park, PA: Sage.

Rawlins, W. K., & Holl, M. (1987). The communicative achievement of friendship during adolescence: Predicaments of trust and violation. *Western Journal of Speech Communication, 51,* 345-363.

Ray, G. B. (1987). An ethnography of nonverbal communication in an Appalachian community. *Research on Language and Social Interaction, 21,* 171-188.

Reif-Lehrer, L. (1989). *How to write a successful grant application.* Boston: Jones & Bartlett.

Reiser, S. J., Dyck, A., & Curran, W. (1977). *Ethics in medicine.* Cambridge: MIT Press.

Reynolds, P. D. (1972). On the protection of human subjects and social science. *International Social Science Journal, 24,* 693-719.

Richardson, L. (1990). Narrative and sociology. *Journal of Contemporary Ethnography, 19,* 116-135.

Ricoeur, P. (1977). The model of the text: Meaningful action considered as a text. In F. R. Dallmayr & T. A. McCarthy (Eds.), *Understanding and social inquiry* (pp. 316-334). Notre Dame, IN: University of Notre Dame Press.

Robbins, T., Anthony, D., & Curtis, T. E. (1973). The limits of symbolic realism: Problems of empathic field observation in a sectarian context. *Journal for the Scientific Study of Religion, 12,* 259-271.

Rock, P. (1979). *The making of symbolic interactionism.* Totowa, NJ: Rowman & Littlefield.

Rorty, R. (1979). *Philosophy and the mirror of nature.* Princeton, NJ: Princeton University Press.

Rorty, R. (1987). Science as solidarity. In J. S. Nelson, A. Megill, & D. N. McCloskey (Eds.), *The rhetoric of the human sciences* (pp. 38-52). Madison: University of Wisconsin Press.

Rosaldo, R. (1989). *Culture and truth: The remaking of social analysis.* Boston: Beacon.

Rose, D. (1986). Transformations of disciplines through their texts. *Cultural Anthropology,* *1,* 317-327.

Rosen, M. (1985). Breakfast at Spiro's: Dramaturgy and dominance. *Journal of Management,* *11,* 31-48.

Rosengren, K. E. (1993). From field to frog ponds. *Journal of Communication, 43*(3), 6-17.

Rowland, W. D., Jr. (1983). *The politics of TV violence.* Beverly Hills, CA: Sage.

Rubin, R. B., Rubin, A. M., & Piele, L. J. (1990). *Communication research: Strategies and sources* (2nd ed.). Belmont, CA: Wadsworth.

Sacks, H. (1963). Sociological description. *Berkeley Journal of Sociology, 8,* 1-16.

Sacks, H., Schegloff, E., & Jefferson, G. (1974). A simplest systematics for the organization of turn-taking for conversation. *Language, 50,* 696-735.

Saferstein, B. (1991, August). *Constructing and constraining television violence.* Paper presented at the annual meeting of the American Sociological Association, Cincinnati.

Sanjek, R. (Ed.). (1990a). *Fieldnotes: The makings of anthropology.* Ithaca, NY: Cornell University Press.

Sanjek, R. (1990b). A vocabulary for fieldnotes. In R. Sanjek (Ed.), *Fieldnotes: The makings of anthropology* (pp. 92-121). Ithaca, NY: Cornell University Press.

Schaefer, R. J., & Avery, R. K. (1993). Audience conceptualizations of *Late Night with David Letterman. Journal of Broadcasting & Electronic Media, 37,* 253-274.

Schatzman, L., & Strauss, A. L. (1973). *Field research: Strategies for a natural sociology.* Englewood Cliffs, NJ: Prentice Hall.

Scheflen, A. E. (1973). *Communicational structure: Analysis of a psychotherapy transaction.* Bloomington: Indiana University Press.

Schegloff, E. (1968). Sequencing in conversational openings. *American Anthropologist, 70,* 1075-1095.

Scheibel, D. (1992). Faking identity in clubland: The communicative performance of "fake ID." *Text and Performance Quarterly, 12,* 160-175.

Schiller, H. (1969). *Mass communication and American empire.* Boston: Beacon.

Schneider, D. M. (1976). Notes toward a theory of culture. In K. H. Basso & H. A. Selby (Eds.), *Meaning in anthropology* (pp. 197-220). Albuquerque: University of New Mexico Press.

Schutz, A. (1944). The stranger: An essay in social psychology. *American Journal of Sociology, 49,* 499-507.

Schutz, A. (1962). On multiple realities. In M. Natanson (Ed.), *Collected papers I: The problem of social reality* (pp. 207-259). The Hague: Martinus Nijhoff.

Schutz, A. (1967). *The phenomenology of the social world.* Evanston, IL: Northwestern University Press.

Schwandt, T. A. (1989). Solutions to the paradigm conflict: Coping with uncertainty. *Journal of Contemporary Ethnography, 17,* 379-407.

Schwartz, D. B., & Griffin, M. (1987). Amateur photography: The organizational maintenance of an aesthetic code. In T. R. Lindlof (Ed.), *Natural audiences: Qualitative research of media uses and effects* (pp. 198-224). Norwood, NJ: Ablex.

Schwartz, M. S., & Schwartz, C. G. (1955). Problems in participant observation. *American Journal of Sociology, 60,* 343-354.

Scott, M. B., & Lyman, S. M. (1968). Accounts. *American Sociological Review, 33,* 46-62.

Seiter, E. (1990). Making distinctions in TV audience research: Case study of a troubling interview. *Cultural Studies, 4,* 61-84.

Sequential organization of conversational activities [Special issue]. (1989). *Western Journal of Speech Communication, 53*(2).

Shalin, D. N. (1986). Pragmatism and social interactionism. *American Sociological Review, 51*, 9-29.

Shields, V. R., & Dervin, B. (1993). Sense-making in feminist social science research. *Women's Studies International, 16*, 65-81.

Shimanoff, S. (1980). *Communication rules.* Beverly Hills, CA: Sage.

Shweder, R. A. (1984). Anthropology's romantic rebellion against the enlightenment, or there's more to thinking than reason and evidence. In R. A. Shweder & R. A. LeVine (Eds.), *Culture theory* (pp. 27-66). Cambridge: Cambridge University Press.

Sieber, S. (1973). The integration of fieldwork and survey methods. *American Journal of Sociology, 78*, 1335-1359.

Sigman, S. J. (1980). On communication rules from a social perspective. *Human Communication Research, 7*, 37-51.

Sigman, S. J. (1984). Communication ethnography and communication theory: Some technical notes. *Papers in Linguistics, 17*, 33-42.

Sigman, S. J. (1986). Adjustment to the nursing home as a social interaction accomplishment. *Journal of Applied Communication Research, 14*, 37-58.

Sigman, S. J. (1987a). Application of ethnographic methods to communications research: A case study with discussion. In S. Thomas (Ed.), *Culture and communication: Studies in communication: Vol. 3. Methodology, behavior, artifacts, and institutions* (pp. 50-64). Norwood, NJ: Ablex.

Sigman, S. J. (1987b). *A perspective on social communication.* Lexington, MA: Lexington.

Silverman, D. (1985). *Qualitative methodology and sociology.* London: Gower.

Silvers, R. J. (1983). On the other side of silence. *Human Studies, 6*, 91-108.

Simon, R. I., & Dippo, D. (1986). On critical ethnographic work. *Anthropology & Education Quarterly, 17*, 195-202.

Simpson, T. A. (in press). Constructions of self and other in the experience of rap music. In D. Grodin & T. R. Lindlof (Eds.), *Constructing the self in a mediated world.* Thousand Oaks, CA: Sage.

Smircich, L., & Calas, M. (1987). Organizational culture: A critical assessment. In F. Jablin (Ed.), *Handbook of organizational communication.* Newbury Park, CA: Sage.

Smith, R. C., & Eisenberg, E. M. (1987). Conflict at Disneyland: A root-metaphor analysis. *Communication Monographs, 54*, 367-379.

Snow, D. A. (1980). The disengagement process: A neglected problem in participant-observation research. *Qualitative Sociology, 3*, 100-122.

Snow, D. A., Benford, R. D., & Anderson, L. (1986). Fieldwork roles and informational yield. *Urban Life, 14*, 377-408.

Speier, M. (1973). *How to observe face-to-face communication: A sociological introduction.* Pacific Palisades, CA: Goodyear.

Spradley, J. P. (1979). *The ethnographic interview.* New York: Holt, Rinehart & Winston.

Spradley, J. P. (1980). *Participant observation.* New York: Holt, Rinehart & Winston.

Spradley, J. P., & McCurdy, D. W. (1972). *The cultural experience: Ethnography in complex society.* Chicago: Science Research Associates.

Stanley, L., & Wise, S. (1983). *Breaking out: Feminist consciousness and feminist research.* London: Routledge & Kegan Paul.

Stewart, J. (1991). A postmodern look at traditional communication postulates. *Western Journal of Speech Communication, 55*, 354-379.

Stewart, J., & Philipsen, G. (1984). Communication as situated accomplishment: The cases of hermeneutics and ethnography. In B. Dervin & M. J. Voigt (Eds.), *Progress in communication sciences* (Vol. 5, pp. 179-217). Norwood, NJ: Ablex.

Stoddart, K. (1986). The presentation of everyday life: Some textual strategies for "adequate ethnography." *Urban Life, 15,* 103-121.

Stoller, P. (1989). *The taste of ethnographic things.* Philadelphia: University of Pennsylvania Press.

Strauss, A. L., & Corbin, J. (1990). *Basics of qualitative research: Grounded theory procedures and technique.* Newbury Park, CA: Sage.

Strine, M. S., & Pacanowsky, M. E. (1985). How to read interpretive accounts of organizational life: Narrative bases of textual authority. *Southern Speech Communication Journal, 50,* 283-297.

Stromberg, P. G. (1990). Ideological language in the transformation of identity. *American Anthropologist, 92*(1).

Strover, S. (1991, May). *Popular media and the teenage sexual agenda.* Paper presented at the annual meeting of the International Communication Association, Chicago.

Stryker, S., & Statham, A. (1985). Symbolic interaction and role theory. In G. Lindzey & E. Aronson (Eds.), *Handbook of social psychology: Vol 1. Theory and method* (3rd ed., pp. 311-378). New York: Random House.

Sudman, S., & Bradburn, N. M. (1983). *Asking questions: A practical guide to questionnaire design.* San Francisco: Jossey-Bass.

Tammivaara, J., & Enright, D. S. (1986). On eliciting information: Dialogues with child informants. *Anthropology & Education Quarterly, 17,* 218-238.

Taylor, B. C. (1990). *Reminiscences of Los Alamos:* Narrative, critical theory, and the organizational subject. *Western Journal of Speech Communication, 54,* 395-419.

Taylor, C. (1977). Interpretation and the sciences of man. In F. R. Dallmayr & T. A. McCarthy (Eds.), *Understanding and social inquiry* (pp. 101-131). Notre Dame, IN: University of Notre Dame Press.

Tesch, R. (1990). *Qualitative research: Analysis types and software tools.* New York: Falmer.

Thomas, J. (1993). *Doing critical ethnography.* Newbury Park, CA: Sage.

Thomas, R. J. (1993). Interviewing important people in big companies. *Journal of Contemporary Ethnography, 22,* 80-96.

Thomas, W. I., & Thomas, D. S. (1928). *The child in America.* New York: Knopf.

Thornton, A., Freedman, D. S., & Camburn, D. (1982). Obtaining respondent cooperation in family panel studies. *Sociological Methods & Research, 11,* 33-51.

Tracy, K., & Baratz, S. (1993). Intellectual discussion in the academy as situated discourse. *Communication Monographs, 60,* 300-320.

Trost, J. E. (1986). Statistically nonrepresentative stratified sampling: A sampling technique for qualitative studies. *Qualitative Sociology, 9,* 54-57.

Trujillo, N. (1992). Interpreting (the work and the talk of) baseball: Perspectives on ballpark culture. *Western Journal of Communication, 56,* 350-371.

Trujillo, N. (1993). Interpreting November 22: A critical ethnography of an assassination site. *Quarterly Journal of Speech, 79,* 447-466.

Trujillo, N., & Dionisopoulos, G. (1987). Cop talk, police stories, and the social construction of organizational drama. *Central States Speech Journal, 38,* 196-209.

Tuchman, G. (1991). Qualitative methods in the study of news. In K. B. Jensen & N. W. Jankowski (Eds.), *A handbook of qualitative methodologies for mass communication research* (pp. 79-92). London: Routledge.

Turkle, S. (1984). *The second self: Computers and the human spirit.* New York: Simon & Schuster.

Turner, G. (1990). *British cultural studies.* Boston: Unwin Hyman.

Turner, V. (1957). *Schism and continuity in an African society.* Manchester: Manchester University Press.

Van Maanen, J. (1979). The fact of fiction in organizational ethnography. In J. Van Maanen (Ed.), Qualitative methodology [Special issue]. *Administrative Science Quarterly, 24,* 535-550.

Van Maanen, J. (1981). The informant game: Selected aspects of ethnographic research in police organizations. *Urban Life, 9,* 469-494.

Van Maanen, J. (1988). *Tales of the field: On writing ethnography.* Chicago: University of Chicago Press.

Van Maanen, J. (1990). Great moments in ethnography. *Journal of Contemporary Ethnography, 19,* 3-7.

Van Willigen, J. (1989). *Gettin' some age on me: Social organization of older people in a rural American community.* Lexington: University Press of Kentucky.

Warren, C. A. B. (1988). *Gender issues in field research.* Newbury Park, CA: Sage.

Warren, C. A. B., & Staples, W. G. (1989). Fieldwork in forbidden terrain: The state, privatization and human subjects regulations. *American Sociologist, 20,* 263-277.

Wartella, E. (1987). Commentary on qualitative research and children's mediated communication. In T. R. Lindlof (Ed.), *Natural audiences: Qualitative research of media uses and effects* (pp. 109-118). Norwood, NJ: Ablex.

Wax, M. L. (1972). Tenting with Malinowski. *American Sociological Review, 37,* 1-13.

Wax, R. H. (1971). *Doing fieldwork: Warnings and advice.* Chicago: University of Chicago Press.

Webb, E. J., Campbell, D. T., Schwartz, R. D., & Sechrest, L. (1966). *Unobtrusive measures: Nonreactive research in the social sciences.* Chicago: Rand McNally.

Weber, M. (1968). *Economy and society.* New York: Bedminster.

Weick, K. (1985). Systematic observation methods. In G. Lindzey & E. Aronson (Eds.), *Handbook of social psychology: Vol 1. Theory and method* (3rd ed., pp. 567-634). New York: Random House.

White, H. (1981). The value of narrativity in the representation of reality. In W. J. T. Mitchell (Ed.), *On narrative* (pp. 1-23). Chicago: University of Chicago Press.

Whyte, W. F. (1943). *Street corner society: The social structure of an Italian slum.* Chicago: University of Chicago Press.

Whyte, W. F. (1982). Interviewing in field research. In R. G. Burgess (Ed.), *Field research: A source book and field manual* (pp. 111-122). London: George Allen & Unwin.

Wiley, J. (1987). The "shock of unrecognition" as a problem in participant-observation. *Qualitative Sociology, 10,* 78-83.

Williams, F., Rice, R. E., & Rogers, E. M. (1988). *Research methods and the new media.* New York: Free Press.

Williams, R. (1976). *Keywords.* London: Fontana.

Willis, P. (1977). *Learning to labour: How working class kids get working class jobs.* London: Saxon House.

Wilson, T. P. (1970). Normative and interpretive paradigms in sociology. In J. D. Douglas (Ed.), *Understanding everyday life* (pp. 57-79). Chicago: Aldine.

Winch, P. (1958). *The idea of a social science and its relation to philosophy.* London: Routledge & Kegan Paul.

Wittgenstein, L. (1953). *Philosophical investigations.* London: Basil Blackwell.

Wolcott, H. F. (1990). *Writing up qualitative research.* Newbury Park, CA: Sage.

Wolf, M. A. (1987). How children negotiate television. In T. R. Lindlof (Ed.), *Natural audiences: Qualitative research of media uses and effects* (pp. 58-94). Norwood, NJ: Ablex.

Wolf, M. A., Meyer, T. P., & White, C. (1982). A rules-based study of television's role in the construction of social reality. *Journal of Broadcasting, 26,* 813-829.

Yount, K. R. (1991). Ladies, flirts, and tomboys: Strategies for managing sexual harassment in an underground coal mine. *Journal of Contemporary Ethnography, 19,* 396-422.

Zimmerman, D. H. (1988). On conversation: The conversation analytic perspective. In J. A. Anderson (Ed.), *Communication yearbook 11* (pp. 406-432). Newbury Park, CA: Sage.

Zimmerman, D. H., & Wieder, L. (1977). The diary: Diary-interview method. *Urban Life, 5,* 479-498.

Zimmerman, S. (1987, May). *Al-Anon: Communication and culture.* Paper presented at the annual meeting of the International Communication Association, Montreal.

Author Index

305

Subject Index

Accounts:
    in ethnomethodology, 37-38
    in interviews, 167
Act, 34, 44
Action (*See also* social action), 34
Action research, 59, 110
Actors, in qualitative writing, 263-267
Analytic induction (*see* Negative case
    analysis)
Authority, in qualitative writing, defined,
    250-251

Coding, 219-227
Computer technology and programs, in
    analysis, 226-227, 242-243
Concepts:
    in design, 92-93
    in analysis, 216-217, 220, 224-225, 227-
    230
Constant comparative method, 67, 198,
    222-225, 240
Constructivism, 45
Conversation analysis, 38-39
Critical qualitative research, 12, 17, 53-54,
    56, 255-256

Culture, defined, 49-51
Cultural studies, 11, 31, 49-56

Data analysis (*see also* Theory), 95, 161,
    197-243, 251
    as a cycle process, 67-68, 215
    as a funnel process, 66-67
Deception, in interview responses, 191-194
Dialogical ethnography, 255
Diary:
    as research technique, 120-122
    as data-text, 207-208
Discourse, in data analysis, 234-236
Document analysis, 5, 114-115, 208-209
Drama, in data analysis, 233-234

Emic (*see also* Etic), 83, 96 (n3), 230, 232
Epoche, 32, 236
Ethics in qualitative research (*see also*
    Human subject protections), 58, 97-
    105, 114, 143-144, 149, 278-279, 283-
    284 (n3)
Ethnographic interview, 170, 171, 241
Ethnography, 19-20, 56-57

311

About the Author

Thomas R. Lindlof is Associate Professor of Telecommunications at the University of Kentucky. He received his Ph.D. from the University of Texas at Austin and has taught at the Pennsylvania State University. He is the editor of *Natural Audiences: Qualitative Research of Media Uses and Effects* (1987) and, with Debra Grodin, *Constructing the Self in a Mediated World* (Sage, forthcoming). He has published extensively on mediated communication processes, audience theory, and qualitative research methodology, and has served on the editorial boards of several journals, including *Human Communication Research* and *Journal of Broadcasting & Electronic Media*.